INTEGRATED TEACHING IN EARLY CHILDHOOD

INTEGRATED TEACHING IN EARLY CHILDHOOD

STARTING IN THE MAINSTREAM

Philip L. Safford

Professor of Special Education
Kent State University

Integrated Teaching in Early Childhood:
Starting in the Mainstream

Longman Inc., 95 Church Street, White Plains, N. Y. 10601

Associated companies:
Longman Group Ltd., London
Longman Cheshire Pty., Melbourne
Longman Paul Pty., Auckland
Copp Clark Pitman, Toronto
Pitman Publishing Inc., New York

This book is dedicated to the memory of my parents,
Clarence William Safford and Georgia Ingersoll Safford,
and my friend, William Allen Bricker.

Senior editor: Naomi Silverman
Development editor: Virginia L. Blandford
Production editor: Marie-Josée A. Schorp
Text design: Kevin C. Kall
Cover design: Kevin C. Kall
Cover photo: Maria Kaiser
Production supervisor: Judith Millman

Library of Congress Cataloging-in-Publication Data

Safford, Philip L.
    Integrated teaching in early childhood.

    Bibliography: p.
    Includes index.
    1. Handicapped children—Education (Preschool)—
United States.   2. Early childhood education—United
States.   3. Mainstreaming in education—United States.
I. Title.
LC4019.2.S24   1989   371.9   88-23075

ISBN 0-8013-0050-9

89 90 91 92 93 94 9 8 7 6 5 4 3 2 1

Contents

v

Foreword

Beginning in the mid 1970s, the moral, ethical, and educational treatment of young handicapped children was given increased attention by the passing of new federal legislation. With the passing of these federal regulations, the complexities of education in the early childhood field multiplied. The mandating of free appropriate education in "least restrictive" settings alerted teachers to the increased necessity of studying and understanding the concerns, problems, and needs of young special needs children. In his new book, *Integrated Teaching in Early Childhood: Starting in the Mainstream,* Dr. Safford has not only clearly interpreted these laws as they apply to early childhood, but has shown how to implement these mandates using sound educational guidelines and methods.

As an early childhood educator, it is my judgment that this book outlines approaches that are closely aligned with the philosophies and developmentally appropriate practices advocated by the National Association for the Education of Young Children. As Dr. Safford states in his book, "The fields of early childhood education and special education have a great deal in common because of their stress on children as individuals, and their recognition of every child's right to an education that is appropriate to individual and developmental needs."

It has become evident that the team approach (teachers, parents, administrators, and support personnel working together) is the best way to both identify and educate exceptional children. This volume emphasizes the team approach and serves as an excellent resource for planning the educational program for young special needs children in regular and special classrooms. Detailed descriptions of ways in which children with identified handicaps can be integrated into day care centers, nursery schools, kindergartens, and primary classes with the "least restrictive" environment are provided. The author shows how integration provides innumerable opportunities for young children to know and learn from each other. Individual chapters are devoted to the integration into the regular classroom of children with visual and hearing impairments, motor and other physical disabilities, developmental delays and behavioral problems, as well as young gifted and talented children. It is clearly the best reference book I have been able to procure during this period of transition into mainstreaming. Dr. Safford's handling of early identification, case histories, ways of observing and recording behavior, arrangement of classrooms, and use of specialized equipment provides educators with added "tools" to make integration more feasible. One of the outstanding features of the book is that it helps teachers adapt typical learning activities in the early childhood curriculum for the exceptional child. Readers will find the sections on working with parents as partners and an extensive chapter on the use of supportive and supplemental resources invaluable.

In my thirty years' experience as an educator of young children, it has been my observation that many teachers lack real knowledge and indepth understanding of strategies for working with exceptional children in the regular classroom. It has always been difficult to locate resources that can be used by the teacher on a daily basis. This comprehensive book will be an excellent text for use at the college level as well as by teachers in the field.

Dr. Safford, as an experienced scholar and educator, has produced a book that will be used by all those who are vitally interested in the welfare of the young child. We should recommend him for this well-documented, easy to understand, and readily applicable book. He has increased our awareness of the uniqueness of all young children and implores us to understand and appreciate their individuality. These pioneering efforts demonstrate how early childhood and special education educators can work together as partners, implementing integrated teaching as they strive to enhance the development and rights of the young child.

Kathleen M. Bayless
Professor Emeritus
Early Childhood Education
Kent State University

Preface and Acknowledgments

This book is addressed primarily to teachers and those preparing to teach in any of the various settings encompassed by the term *early childhood education*. The concept of early childhood education has grown both more familiar and more meaningful to the American public during the late 1980s, as societal trends and growing needs have led to significant changes in social policy. Of major importance was the enactment in 1986 of amendments to The Education of All Handicapped Children Act (Public Law 94–142) that extended the provisions of that law to include three- to five-year-old children with handicapping conditions, and, in addition, provided discretionary funds for states to serve even younger handicapped or at-risk children.

The present social context is marked by major changes in the ways that all young children—not just handicapped and at-risk children—are educated and cared for. First, a wave of school reform recommendations has inevitably had impact on practices in kindergarten and the primary grades, not always in positive ways. Second, kindergarten is no longer the first educational experience for increasing numbers of children, particularly those from families whose work situations require outside-the-home child care alternatives.

These and other developments bear directly upon the major theme of this book: the integration of special needs children into regular or *mainstream* settings, including schools, community nursery schools and Head Start programs, and day care programs. The focus of our discussion here is limited to young children from infancy through age eight or nine, although the concept of mainstreaming affects children of all ages as well as adults.

The early childhood period presents us with a unique set of considerations with regard to integration of disabled children into mainstream preschool and school classrooms. First, starting off in the educational mainstream increases the likelihood that benefits for all children will be optimized. Second, the application of *developmental appropriateness* as a criterion for early education programs ensures that these programs will respond to the uniqueness of young children generally and individually. Good early childhood programs—and effective teachers of young children—do not simply recognize and respond to the individuality of each child; they *value* such diversity.

The concept of *integrated teaching* is presented in this book not so much as a specific system for teaching as a philosophy and teaching style that builds on and extends practices that are developmentally appropriate for all children. In Part I, you will find a discussion of the underlying foundations of the concept of mainstreaming. In Part II, chapters are devoted to services and adaptations in the mainstream classroom for children who have been identified as vision-impaired, hearing-impaired, or mobility-impaired. Although these children constitute a minority of the population entering school who actually meet the criteria established for *handicapped,* they are the most likely to be so identified early in life. Chapter 8 addresses the majority—those whose problems are less readily identified and defined in the first years of life, but who manifest delays in one or more areas of development or who seem at-risk for educational handicaps. In Chapter 9 you will find a discussion of those children who appear to demonstrate unusually high potential or special abilities. Finally, Part III of this book provides a discussion of the four major areas of integrated teaching at the preschool and primary levels: methods for individualization; working with the group to enhance the likelihood of successful mainstreaming; accessing and using resource assistance; and working with parents.

Although this book is addressed mainly to teachers and prospective teachers in *regular* early childhood programs, my hope is that at least two other groups of readers will find it valuable: parents of young children and specialists—special educators, therapists, psychologists, and others—who facilitate children's transition to, and support their education within, the least restrictive early childhood settings.

A great many people—students at Kent State University, colleagues also engaged, as I am, with parents, and with young children in the preparation of teachers and in the schools—have influenced me in very important ways and, in some instances, have made specific contributions in the preparation of this book. The former are far too numerous to mention, but among the latter are several persons whose assistance must be acknowledged. I would especially like to acknowledge the help of two student-colleagues who contributed greatly to this book's emphasis on application: Kaye Stanley-Bryson, who contributed many of the "case" examples as well as other material, and Maria Sargent, who provided instructional adaptations for young children with visual, hearing, and motor impairment. The suggestions and, in some instances, illustrative examples provided by Bobbe Miller, Janet Stone, Celeste Bajorek, L. Alison Rosen, Mary Beth Mulhauser, Carol Ellison, and Maria Kaiser, Associate Director of the Achievement Center for Children, were much appreciated, and I am grateful as well to colleagues Richard Ambrose, Penny Griffith, and Beverly Shaklee for their help.

A project supported through a grant from The Cleveland Foundation to The Society for Crippled Children of Cuyahoga County provided opportunities to talk with a number of children, their parents, and their teachers, in collaboration with James Harvey, Jennifer Krutilla, Jane Safford, and Ruth Nash Thompson. I am indebted to all involved for the learning experiences these interviews and visits provided.

I continue to grow and learn through association with The Family Child Learning Center, parents and staff members, and especially FCLC Director, Dr. Philippa Campbell, a model for many of us of professional excellence and commitment to serving children with disabilities and their families. Involvement with the Akron City School District/Head Start Preschool Integration Project has also been most valuable to me in completing the book.

The encouraging support of Naomi Silverman, Senior Education Editor for Longman Inc., has been sincerely appreciated, as were the helpful suggestions of anonymous colleagues who reviewed the manuscript. I would also like to thank Virginia Blanford, Marie-Josée Schorp and Karen Philippidis for their assistance on this manuscript. I am grateful also to Elizabeth Safford for her editorial and referencing assistance, Joyce Hanan for her considerate and skilled help in typing the manuscript, Emily Brna for typing early drafts, and Cynthia Miller for her willing assistance with a variety of tasks.

Special thanks are due to Jane Safford for the suggestions she made and ideas as well as specific examples she contributed. As in all my endeavors, I am most grateful for the encouragement and support that she, Lynne, and Beth have given me.

PART I

Foundations for Least Restrictive Early Education

CHAPTER 1

Early Childhood Education and the Mainstreaming Movement

To someone planning to teach young children, learning about "typical children"—how they think and reason, what motivates them, their fantasies and feelings, how they interact with peers and important adults—probably appears challenging enough. If the teacher's responsibilities also include children who are exceptional, the amount of knowledge and skill required must seem vast indeed.

The complexity of preparing for nearly any career role in today's world makes the need for specialization clear. Logic dictates, then, that persons working with exceptional children should be trained in special teaching methods. Can we expect preschool, kindergarten, and primary grade teachers to work effectively with special needs children in the mainstream classroom?

You probably already know that this question is rhetorical; *all* teachers today can expect to have exceptional children in their classrooms, and all teachers must therefore learn to work with them effectively. That does not mean, however, that every teacher of young children must also be a special educator. Nor does it mean that we no longer need such specialists.

Effectively meeting the unique individual needs of exceptional children does require special planning and teamwork between parents and professionals. Additionally, it may require the direct services of such specialists as special education teachers and physical, occupational, or speech and language therapists. However, law and logic require maximum normality in the educational experiences of our children. We want to provide experiences and intervention appropriate to the needs of each exceptional child, but we want to do that in a manner that best promotes normalization.

3

Normalization does not mean that effective early education can cure or prevent handicapping conditions. It does not mean that teachers, parents, and other adults should pretend that such conditions do not exist. And it certainly does not mean that all children should be treated alike, or that the expectations and goals set for one child can or should be identical to those for every other child. On the contrary, the very uniqueness of each child must be emphasized. But individuality is made up of many different components. Some children's individuality includes characteristics associated with a disability; what we must realize is that these same children possess other, equally important, characteristics as well.

WHO ARE EXCEPTIONAL CHILDREN?

Societies define exceptionality according to their own norms and expectations. A person considered "normal" in one culture may be considered "exceptional" in another, just as certain behaviors and customs are expected and appropriate in one culture but not in another. Exceptionality is generally defined through societal consensus; defining each separate area of exceptionality, however, is often controversial. Specialists also disagree about the criteria for diagnosis and classification. These problems are intensified for young children, since (1) some definitions do not apply until children reach school age, (2) developmental changes occur rapidly in the early years, and (3) young children often demonstrate more than one discrepancy from their peers. For purposes of education in this country, it is the law that defines exceptionality. Chapter 2 of this book provides clarification of these issues through a discussion of the appropriate public policy statements.

In general, exceptional children are those whose mental, communication, social-emotional, or physical characteristics require some adaptations in the educational program in order for them to learn optimally. With the single exception of gifted and talented children, these children display characteristics that involve disabilities or delays in one or more areas of functioning. Approximately 10 percent of all children of any given age are assumed to have disabilities significant enough to qualify them as exceptional; gifted and talented children constitute another two to three percent.

APPROPRIATE EDUCATION FOR ALL YOUNG CHILDREN

The key word regarding teaching exceptional children is not *mainstreaming,* but rather *appropriate.* The major policy document in this area, Public Law 94–142 (The Education for All Handicapped Children Act, 1975), is often referred to as "the mainstreaming law." In fact, however, the word mainstreaming never appears in it; the word appropriate appears repeatedly. The central purpose of the law is to ensure that all handicapped children are provided a Free Appropriate Public Education (FAPE).

P.L. 94–142 establishes that every handicapped child, regardless of the severity of the handicap, is entitled to a free appropriate education, but it does not provide a precise definition of the term *appropriate*. Instead, it requires that an appropriate education for each handicapped child be defined individually, in an Individual Education Program (IEP), the components of which are spelled out in the law. (See Chapter 2.)

An important requirement—and the one that has inspired this book—is that **every IEP must specify the Least Restrictive Environment (LRE) for each student's school placement.** As part of this requirement, the planning team, including parents, teachers and other appropriate professionals, must indicate **the extent to which the student will participate in regular educational programs.**

At first, the principles of least restrictive environment and appropriate education might seem to represent two different, potentially conflicting, values. Actually, they are inseparable: appropriate education is not being provided unless it occurs within the setting that is least restrictive for a specific student.

For children identified as handicapped, P.L. 94–142 requires schools to follow:

> . . . procedures to assure that, to the maximum extent appropriate, handicapped children including children in public or private institutions or other care facilities, are educated with children who are not handicapped. That special classes, separate schooling or removal of handicapped children from the regular education environment occurs only when the nature or severity of the handicap is such that education in regular classes with the use of supplementary aids and services cannot be achieved satisfactorily. (P.L. 94–142, 20 U.S.C. s 1412, 5, B)

The law does not state that every handicapped student must be or should be taught in a regular classroom, but it does assume the desirability of a regular classroom environment if the student can be taught there, possibly with "supplementary aids and service." The reason for emphasizing the importance of such a school setting is stated effectively by Vincent, Brown, and Getz-Sheftel (1981):

> The philosophical basis for providing least restrictive programs rests on the principle of normalization. The more fully a handicapped child's needs are met through typical service delivery, the closer professionals have come to best educational practices. Adapting the normal/typical service delivery system is always preferable to developing separate services. Providing service in the "mainstream" of society emphasizes the similarities rather than the differences of the handicapped individual. (p. 19)

For handicapped children, then, appropriate education is individually determined, individually designed, and depends upon placements that are least restrictive and maximally normal.

The field of early childhood education, like that of special education, has focused much attention on the issue of appropriateness. Many advocates for young children contend that teachers are sometimes constrained to teach in ways that are inappropriate to the developmental characteristics of their students. Early childhood educators have experienced pressures from many sources, sometimes having little or nothing to do with the needs of the children themselves (Doremus, 1986). The school reform movement of the mid-1980s, for instance, produced considerable fallout in early education, resulting in greater pressure for more academic skill training and formal instruction, including reading instruction, in the early years.

Leaders in early childhood education have responded eloquently and forcefully in asserting the need for developmentally appropriate practices in the education and care of all young children. The National Association for the Education of Young Children (NAEYC) has adopted position statements based on two key dimensions of developmental appropriateness: (1) age appropriateness, and (2) individual appropriateness. The NAEYC statements recognize the uniqueness of the early childhood years and the distinct developmental periods they encompass, as well as the uniqueness of each child's developmental characteristics and needs. They emphasize the interactive nature of young children's learning, the child's active role in learning, the facilitating rather than directing role of the teacher, and the unity and wholeness of all aspects of young children's development (Bredekamp, 1987).

As these statements stress, all young children are unique. The developmentally appropriate practices recommended by NAEYC are fully congruent with the special needs of most young children with handicaps.

As society changes, so do schools and other agencies that serve young children. Prevailing views among Americans have changed radically in recent years concerning the need for care of young children, including infants and toddlers, outside their own homes. Today, with more than half of all mothers of preschool children employed outside the home, the need for such care is a simple reality.

Should a young child be cared for by people other than parents? Beginning at what age? Who should provide this care? These are vitally important issues that the United States government has only recently begun to address in any systematic way through social child care policies. For any particular parent or any particular family, however, the concern is what is best for their individual child. As parents, we are concerned about how our own child's needs can best be served, given the realities of our individual situations.

Similarly, teachers and others who work with young children are fundamentally concerned with the well-being of the individual child. This profound respect for the uniqueness of each child has always been central to the role of the early childhood educator.

The philosophy of special education has also historically emphasized the value and uniqueness of the individual. Special education is a field fundamentally concerned with differences, both among students *(interindividual differences)* and within individual students *(intraindividual differences)* (Kirk & Gallagher, 1987). It is the uniqueness of each child's characteristics, abilities, and needs that is the principal consideration. Special educators are not advocating "sameness" when they advocate equal rights, equal access, and equal opportunities for children with handicaps. Rather, what has been underscored by the movement to serve handicapped children within the educational mainstream is this principle: *the differences among individual children, whether handicapped or nonhandicapped, must determine how children are taught.* These, which are not presumed to be group characteristics, are the differences that are educationally relevant.

THE RIGHTS OF CHILDREN

The fields of early childhood education and special education have a great deal in common because of their stress on children as individuals, and their recognition of every child's right to an education that is appropriate to individual and developmental needs.

Persons with disabilities have become a potent political force, advocating on their own behalf only in recent years. In the United States, these self-advocacy efforts were responsible for major antidiscrimination legislation, reflected in the Rehabilitation Act of 1973. Section 504 of that Act established that no handicapped person can be subjected to discrimination under any program or activity that receives federal assistance or support, ". . . a first step toward an expanded effort to establish civil rights for handicapped people" (Parker & Hansen, 1981, p. 24). Since children with disabilities participate in many "programs and activities" that are partially supported through federal funds, including public schools, day care programs, public transportation systems, public libraries, and other services, they too benefit from this national nondiscrimination policy.

Historically, as any particular group becomes empowered to advocate on its own behalf, reforms benefiting members of that group are likely to follow. Reforms that benefit young children, however, must of course be advanced by others on their behalf—that is, by adults. As controversies continue in the fields of day care and early education, and as we hear more plaintive expressions of concern for the taxpayer, the wage earner, and the economy in general, we need to keep always in mind: "What is best for the child? Who speaks for the children?"

ATTITUDES TOWARD PERSONS WITH DISABILITIES

Today we may find it difficult to believe the extremes of hostility that were commonly demonstrated toward persons with mental or physical disabilities in the past. A ruling of the Wisconsin Supreme Court in 1919 (cited in Hensley, 1973), for instance, stated that "a mentally normal, blind child could be barred from school since his/her handicap had a depressing and nauseating effect on teachers and children" (p. 3).

Such attitudes reflect a composite of fear, myth, and superstition, attributable directly to the segregation of disabled persons from the rest of society. In earlier periods, society often responded to disability by placing blame ". . . on the affected individual who was often shunned, feared and left to die or on the family who was viewed as suffering the act of a vengeful god for past misdeeds" (Safford & Arbitman, 1975, p. 3).

Dr. Bettye Caldwell, a contemporary pioneer in work with young children with special needs, identified three stages through which society has progressed in its treatment of handicapped children (1973): Forget and Hide, Screen and Segregate, and Identify and Help.

Forget and Hide

The first stage encompassed the attitudes suggested above: neglect, fear, blame of the victim and his or her family, and, from the standpoint of the child and family, shame.

Screen and Segregate

The second stage was marked by important changes. Attempts were made to identify the handicapped in order to provide services to them, but such attempts primarily emphasized how different these children were as a result of their disabilities. The field of special education was born, but the prevalent mode of providing special education was through special classes and sometimes special schools, segregated from the normal mainstream. Children whose handicaps were judged more severe, especially those labeled mentally retarded, continued to be excluded from public schooling altogether. Less severely handicapped children were often segregated within the public school setting, their classroom often located in the least desirable part of the building ("next to the boiler room," as many special education teachers recall) where interaction with nonhandicapped children was unlikely to occur. Sometimes segregated play areas were provided, and handicapped children typically rode separate buses and ate lunch in their own classroom or at a "special" time in the lunchroom. This kind of segregation kept handicapped children away from others their own age—and also, of course, meant that nonhandicapped children were deprived of the opportunity to know those in special classes.

We can easily recognize how separation of this sort would increase rather than lessen negative feelings and even fears on the part of the other children and their parents. As Caldwell suggests, it almost seemed as if people feared that a handicapped child could contaminate their own, that a disability might be somehow contagious!

Bad as this kind of segregation was, the handicapped children involved were at least provided the opportunity to attend schools also attended by nonhandicapped children (except in instances where the entire school was specifically for handicapped children). They lived at home rather than in institutions and participated, to the extent they were able, in their communities. Out-of-school experiences during this period sometimes actually approached "normalization." In fact, a panel charged by the President of the United States to study the status of retarded persons in U.S. society in 1968 coined a phrase reflecting this irony: "the six-hour retarded child" (President's Committee on Mental Retardation, 1968).

There were, however, less just and more harmful consequences to educational segregation. During the first decades of the 20th century, screening frequently led to exclusion of children from school altogether, and many times to their placement in institutions. Parents were urged to refer their children voluntarily for institutional placements if delayed development was suspected (Wolfensberger, 1969). Thousands of children, including many with mild delays, undiagnosed hearing loss, or what we would today recognize as a specific learning disability, were *made* retarded and deprived of the opportunity for a normal childhood (and adulthood) through institutional placement—all in the belief that society should be "protected" from mentally retarded persons. Today, institutionalization is rarely the recommendation, no matter how severe the disability. Instead, this country has attempted to effect *deinstitutionalization* through the development of community-based services and family support programs.

Identify and Help

In the last decade, we have passed into the third stage suggested by Dr. Caldwell. P.L. 94–142 (1975) specifically mandated the identification of handicapped children, and Public Law 99–457, signed by President Reagan in 1986, provided further and more specific criteria for identifying and serving handicapped and developmentally delayed children from birth to age five. The goal of these identification procedures is not to screen out or otherwise segregate young children with special needs as was done in the past but to locate children in order to provide appropriately for each child's unique needs. As Dr. Samuel Meisels (1986) points out, screening and assessment of young children should never be used to close educational doors for a child, but rather to open them. Early identification is effective only to the extent that it leads to the provision of services appropriate to the needs of the individual child (Keogh & Daley, 1983). For some children, a goal of total habilitation may actually be attainable (Drash, Raver, & Murrin, 1987).

AVOIDING IDENTIFICATIONS THAT CLOSE DOORS

Identifying young children with special needs is a necessary step in helping these children, but it should not result in excluding, segregating, or permanently labeling them as "deviant." Attention must be paid to potential problems that have been associated with the process of identifying handicapped children over the years. These include.:

> The incorrect identification of children who are not in fact exceptional—
> that is, "false positives" (Gallagher & Bradley, 1971).

The failure to identify children who do have special needs, resulting in their not getting the services they need.

The failure to identify accurately a child's special needs, (for example, identifying as mentally retarded a child who actually has a hearing loss resulting in language delays).

The inability to provide needed services for children who are correctly identified.

The *labeling* of an identified child, resulting in the expectation that the child will conform to the label.

These are all serious problems, but the last is especially so. Labels applied to groups do not fit individual members of those groups. Labels fail to account for the diversity of individuals—even those individuals who may share some single characteristic. In addition, labels have a symbolic, connotative quality, and people often interpret them in an evaluative way. Certain labels, particularly those connoting exceptionality, evoke emotional reactions or unconscious associations. The label *mentally retarded,* for example, is often associated with assumptions of differentness, slowness, dependence, or low levels of performance. Even labels applied informally, like "slow learner," have connotative properties.

Educators are particularly concerned about the possible harmful and lasting effects of labeling young children with special needs. In mandating services for young children, P.L. 99–457 does not require or emphasize categorical labels for the following reasons:

Young children's needs are difficult, if not impossible, to categorize with traditional labels.

Especially during the early years, these needs change rapidly.

Categorical labels have no utility for young children, since categorical programs may not be appropriate.

Early labeling of children may limit and restrict them, since others may respond to these labels in limiting and restricting ways.

Labels tend to follow the child, even after they are no longer applicable or appropriate. A label is a hard thing to lose!

Least restrictive services for young children, required by P.L. 99–457, are intended to foster the interaction of handicapped and nonhandicapped children. Labels tend to impede that interaction.

NORMALIZATION: THE PHILOSOPHICAL BASIS FOR MAINSTREAMING

Normalization, which has provided a rich source of insights concerning standards for all human services (Wolfensberger & Glenn, 1973), is both a simple, straightforward idea and a highly complex one. The normalization philosophy grew out of work with mentally retarded persons worldwide, but the term itself and the first demonstrations of its application originated in Scandinavia. Nirje (1976) defines normalization as ". . . making available to all mentally retarded people patterns of life and conditions of everyday living which are as close as possible to the regular circumstances and way of life of society" (p. 231), but it is Nirje's position (and the position of all advocates of normalization) that this philosophy is applicable to all persons with disabilities, irrespective of the type or severity.

The expert most often quoted in this country regarding normalization is Dr. Wolf Wolfensberger, whose applications of the concept pertain to persons of all ages with a variety of disabilities. Wolfensberger comments specifically, however, on the desirability of integration in programs that provide education and care for very young children, where the inherent benefits of normalization for both handicapped and nonhandicapped children can be maximized. Wolfensberger noted, for example, the benefits associated with peer models (see Chapters 4 and 11). "Particularly at this age level," he points out, "normal peers seem to constitute nonthreatening models from which the handicapped (especially the retarded children) learn much more than they typically do from their impaired peers" (Wolfensberger, 1972, p. 51). Happily, the benefits are reciprocal; children who are not handicapped gain from their experiences with handicapped children in ways they could not were they deprived of these associations.

THE VALUE OF INTEGRATION FOR ALL CHILDREN

For handicapped children, there are very specific and compelling reasons for integrated teaching approaches. Acceptance by peers and adults during the early years is of critical importance in influencing the handicapped child's subsequent adjustment, social development, and self concept (Horne, 1984). For nonhandicapped children, however, there are potential values that are equally compelling. A child's preparation to live in a heterogeneous society begins with experience in integrated educational settings (Bliton & Schroeder, 1986). Teaching handicapped children in settings that provide for personal association with nonhandicapped peers is based, then, on an "assumption of heterogeneity" (Brown, Nietupski, & Hamre-Nietupski, 1976). No learning group ever can be entirely homogeneous, consisting of children with identical characteristics and needs who can be taught effectively in exactly the same manner. The very diversity within a group of children enriches the experience of learning for the children and for those who teach them. The presence of children identified as "exceptional" underlines the principle of diversity but does not change the fundamental reality of heterogeneity that always exists in any group.

Beginning integrated learning experiences early in life maximizes their value in the promotion of positive attitudes about human differences. This implies potential ultimate benefits to society, as Dr. Diane Bricker (1978) notes in her summary of the social and ethical arguments for educational integration. Attitudes toward disabled persons can be favorably influenced by early integration, she argues, while the harmful effects of separation can to a large extent be eliminated. Additionally, such segregation in any form is not only ethically wrong; it is also economically costly.

Subsequent chapters in this book will address the specific implications of integrated teaching for nonhandicapped as well as handicapped children. In Chapter 3 you will find a discussion of the compatibility of "best practices" in early childhood education with those in special education. Chapter 4 reviews the evidence suggesting that integrated programs are effective for both handicapped and nonhandicapped children. Such evidence has been reported for mainstream early education programs as well as specialized early intervention programs in which nonhandicapped children also participate (Odom & Speltz, 1983). Finally, Chapter 11 considers the impact of group procedures, as well as how the group may be affected by the kinds of special interventions required by the needs of the disabled participants.

WHAT IS EDUCATIONAL MAINSTREAMING?

Integration in early education may occur either in regular or typical settings, or in settings specifically intended to provide early intervention. Whatever the setting, association with nonhandicapped children is essential to providing appropriate education for children identified as handicapped or developmentally delayed. It is mandated in P.L. 99–457 for that reason. Peterson (1987) recommends three criteria for interpreting the concept of Least Restrictive Environment for young handicapped children:

1. Can the setting provide an effective "intervention" through special services and individualized programs that will increase the chances that a child will be developmentally more capable of functioning later in a less restrictive environment?
2. Is the setting culturally compatible with the values and practices of the community or subculture of which the parents and family are a part?
3. Is the setting equipped to provide the forms of stimulation and care that are age-appropriate for the child and in harmony with the child's unique caretaking and educational needs? (p. 340)

None of these criteria requires that the setting in which young handicapped children are served be a "special" setting. They recognize the possibility, however, that standard early childhood settings may not be able to serve the needs of all handicapped children. For some young children with special developmental needs, only specialized intervention early in life can lead to maximum future participation in the mainstream. As long as they provide for interaction with nonhandicapped children, *specialized settings may represent least restrictive educational environments for some children with handicaps.*

Mainstreaming, however, occurs only within standard educational environments not specifically established for the purpose of intervention. These standard environments, we should note, have not been established to serve only children without disabilities! Having a disability does not make a child "ineligible" to be taught within a regular education setting. The important consideration is that the child's educational needs can be served. As Ann Turnbull and Jane Schulz (1979) have stressed, "Mainstreaming is the social and instructional integration of handicapped students in regular classes. It is not just their physical presence" (p. 56).

Mainstreaming requires certain active accommodations and, usually, specific and careful planning. According to Karnes and Lee (1978), mainstreaming is generally recognized to include temporal integration, instruction based on individually determined needs, social integration, role clarification for the professionals involved, and "de-labeling" of the handicapped child. A frequently cited definition of mainstreaming is the following:

> Mainstreaming refers to the temporal, instructional, and social integration of eligible exceptional children with normal peers based on an ongoing individually determined educational planning and programming process and requires clarification of responsibility among regular and special education administrative, instructional, and supportive personnel. (Kaufman, Gottlieb, Agard, & Kukic, 1975, pp. 40–41)

WHICH HANDICAPPED CHILDREN ARE MAINSTREAMED?

As we have noted, the law does not require that every handicapped child be educated entirely in regular classroom settings. The law does require, however, that every child's educational planning begin with an analysis of his or her special needs and a determination of whether, or to what extent, these needs can be appropriately met within the regular classroom. In other words, we begin with the assumption that the student will be placed in a regular classroom and removed from that classroom only if necessary and only for as long as necessary. The law specifically requires that each handicapped student's Individual Education Program (IEP) define the extent to which the child will participate in regular education. These requirements imply two basic assumptions:

1. Education in a typical, or mainstream, setting is preferable to education in a special setting and should be effected unless there are compelling reasons indicating otherwise.
2. No matter how severely handicapped the child may be, or to what extent he or she may have highly specialized needs, the child should have some degree of participation in regular education.

Determination of whether or not a child is to be mainstreamed is based on that child's individual characteristics, not on the type of disability the child may have.

Children may share a common diagnostic "category" yet be extremely varied in their social, motivational, intellectual, and physical abilities.

P.L. 94–142 defines areas of exceptionality in children for purposes of education. (See Chapter 2.) In addition, each state has established policies for identifying children who are eligible for and entitled to special services mandated under both federal and state laws. To use such definitions and criteria for identification, as required by both state and federal law, implies a categorical approach; we have already mentioned the limitations and problems associated with categorizing and labeling young children.

Frequently, broad distinctions are made based upon either the prevalence or the severity of disabilities. In general, the more severe the problem, the less prevalent it is; conversely, mild or moderate problems are more prevalent. Often distinctions of degree and prevalence are applied to the question of mainstreaming. Many educators assume that the more severe a child's impairment is, the less he or she might be expected to participate in regular education. Mildly handicapped children, on the other hand, are often expected to participate in more, and many times in all, aspects of regular education. Assumptions about mainstream participation for the mildly handicapped are generally warranted. However, the converse assumption is frequently not justified. Like many attempts to simplify complex issues by making broad, general distinctions—in this case between mildly and severely handicapped students—the assumption is flawed, misleading, and potentially harmful. Many severely disabled children—particularly those with disabilities affecting movement, communication, vision, or hearing—can indeed be very good candidates for full participation in the educational mainstream. (Examples are presented in the appropriate chapters in Part II.)

About 70 percent of all students identified as handicapped are mainstreamed for at least part of each school day (Reynolds & Lakin, 1987). In general, the less a child is educationally discrepant from other children of the same age, the more likely she or he can be taught with those children. In fact, many authors (for example, Wang & Birch, 1984) maintain that students with mild or moderate educational handicaps are not different in their learning needs from a great many other students who have not "qualified" as exceptional and thus are not eligible for special education. They believe that both "special education-eligible" and "special education-noneligible" students would be better served if the distinction between regular and special education were eliminated altogether. Their arguments are especially convincing in view of inconsistent and unreliable practices reported in determining special eligibility, especially in the area of specific learning disabilities (Ysseldyke, Algozzine, Richey, & Graden, 1982).

Young children with mild disabilities or delays are often difficult to identify since the severe problems are more likely to be apparent earlier. This is unfortunate, since early intervention can prevent secondary problems; enable the child to acquire compensatory skills and strategies; and close what might otherwise become a widening gap between the child and his or her peers as they progress through school.

WHO WILL MAINSTREAM YOUNG HANDICAPPED CHILDREN?

The most direct answer to this question is, "You will!" If you are, or intend to become, a "regular" nursery, kindergarten, or primary grade teacher, or to work with young children in day care, you, in coordination with parents and resource professionals, will be the mainstream early childhood educator. You can anticipate that your responsibilities will include young children identified or identifiable as handicapped. Most, especially those with more serious developmental problems, will also have had and may continue to have the services of specialists. In addition to physicians and other professionals involved in addressing medical needs, these specialists may include special educators, speech and language therapists, physical therapists, occupational therapists, and others. Rather than attempting to consider children with special needs based on the types of disabilities they have, you may prefer to consider them on the basis of the specialized intervention services they have received or may be receiving:

1. Some children will have previously been served through an early intervention program that included some nonhandicapped children. This program may have been similar in most respects to the one in which you teach, but probably included more emphasis on specific measurable objectives for individual children, more time devoted to highly structured activities, and more direct involvement of specialists (including therapists) in daily planning and program. Although children now in your program are considered skillful and mature enough to function within a mainstream classroom, their disabilities (as Turnbull & Turnbull point out [1985]) have not been "cured" or "fixed."

2. Some children may attend another program concurrently with yours to receive specialized assistance. They may spend part of each day in a resource or therapy program within your school building, or they may be transported elsewhere for such services. In full-day, school-based programs, children may be "pulled out" during the day; in half-day programs, some children may attend a specialized class during the other portion of the day. Nursery and day care children may also attend other programs, perhaps community-based. And some children may attend another "regular" or mainstream program. In any of these situations, communication among the various program staffs, and with parents, is obviously essential.

3. Some children with handicapping conditions will not have been previously served in special programs and will not see other specialists or be provided with special services while attending your program. For them, the least restrictive environment has been identified from the start as full participation in a regular classroom. Their placement in the mainstream does not mean that their special needs have not

been identified; it should mean that their needs can be fully met within the mainstream setting. In this situation, you may need resource assistance from specialists or therapists. Their expertise is used not for direct intervention, however, but, as Bricker and Sandall point out (1979), to respond to your questions, to help you plan, and to suggest environmental, curricular, or instructional adaptations that you may find useful.

A SUMMARY OF PUBLIC POLICY PROVISIONS FOR MAINSTREAMING YOUNG CHILDREN

Public Law 94–142

The provision for Least Restrictive Environment in P.L. 94–142 is intended to ensure that handicapped children participate to the maximum extent appropriate in education settings that are provided for all children. As Gilhool and Stutman (1978) stated:

> If a child can come to school at all, even to a self-contained class in a handicapped–only center, he can come to a self-contained class in a normal school. Any teaching technique that can be used in a self-contained class can be used in a self-contained class in a regular school building. There are few if any legitimate teaching strategies which require the complete isolation of a child from interaction with other children . . . (p. 215)

Thus, according to the LRE provision of P.L. 94–142, the minimum requirement is an opportunity for some degree of contact with children who are not handicapped. Without such opportunity, the LRE principle cannot be applied and the law is being violated. And unless it is applied, the *appropriate* education mandated by P.L. 94–142 cannot be achieved.

The problem in implementing Least Restrictive Environment for young children has in the past been the unavailability of public education preschool programs for all children. ("Preschool" in most general usage refers to programs for children in the age range three through five. Technically, it encompasses whatever occurs *earlier* than what the public school's responsibility is defined to include.

Thus, in some states, kindergarten is still considered "preschool," but in most states it is not. The unavailability of public school mainstream alternatives has been seen as posing a "dilemma" (Meisels, 1977) and "an educational conundrum" (Blacher-Dixon & Turnbull, 1979). According to Peterson (1987), it is still not clear what a "regular preschool environment" is. Turnbull (1982) has suggested that the Least Restrictive Environment principle, when applied with preschool-age children, frequently implies a *future orientation*: that is, children are being prepared to function successfully within maximally typical or normal school settings when they reach the age at which those settings become available. Lizabeth Vincent (Vincent, Salisbury, Walter, Brown, Gruenwald, & Powers, 1980) and her colleagues described this strategy as preparation of the child for the "next environment."

In summary, P.L. 94–142 provided an incomplete guide for least restrictive, integrated education of handicapped children younger than school age. The intent was clear, but the means of implementation was not. However, as other policy considerations complemented The Education for All Handicapped Children Act of 1975, it has become increasingly possible for that integration to be achieved within "mainstream" settings. Before describing the LRE provisions of the major recent policy "breakthrough," Public Law 99–457, we should summarize two other significant public policy provisions that have been in effect, like P. L. 94–142, for more than a decade.

Section 504 of the Rehabilitation Act of 1973 (P.L. 93–112)

The Rehabilitation Act forbids discrimination on the basis of handicapping condition and requires that any state that provides public school programs for five-year olds (that is, kindergarten) or, younger children must serve handicapped as well as nonhandicapped students. Since public schools are increasingly involved in providing programs for four-year-olds (see Chapter 3), four-year-old handicapped children are increasingly being provided with options for full or partial mainstreaming under public education's responsibility as well. Similarly, school-based or community day care programs that receive federal funds cannot deny services to children based on handicapping conditions (Cohen, Semmes, and Guralnick, 1979).

Project Head Start

The Head Start, Economic Opportunity and Community Partnership Act of 1974 (P.L. 93–644) requires that "for Federal 1976 and thereafter no less than 10 percentum of the total number of enrollment opportunities in the Head Start programs in each state shall be available for handicapped children . . . and that services shall be provided to meet their special needs" (U.S. Department of Health, Education, and Welfare, 1978, p. 1). Policy mandated not only enrollment of handicapped children, but also staff training and the provision of appropriate services. Staff development materials were created and disseminated, and the position of Handicap Coordinator was authorized for local Head Start programs. As a result, the Head Start programs have established a tradition and demonstrated effective practices for integrating handicapped children with those who are not handicapped.

To ensure that the 10 percent enrollment requirement is met, Head Start programs may admit handicapped children whose families do not meet the income eligibility requirement if an insufficient number of low-income handicapped children is identified. In fact, Project Head Start regularly exceeds its "quota," annually reporting an average 12 percent handicapped enrollment, the majority of these being mildly handicapped, especially speech-delayed.

Public Law 99–457

Federal legislation enacted in 1986 reauthorized 1975's Education for All Handicapped Children Act (P.L. 94–142) and extended its provisions to include younger children. Although the original legislation required public schools to identify and evaluate suspected handicapped students from birth and to serve handicapped students beginning at age three, it also included an important unless: service was to begin at age three unless that ran counter to an individual state's law of judicial ruling. Thus, whether handicapped children younger than age six were served by public schools or not was dependent upon state rather than federal policy. P.L. 99–457 offered incentives of continued and augmented federal funding for early childhood programs to states that adopted policies in compliance with the new federal legislation. As a result, nearly all states have done so. The law also provides additional incentives for providing direct services to eligible children from birth to age two, although requirements for this age group differ in that: (1) the state agency responsible for coordination does not have to be the state department of education but may be any appropriate agency so designated by the state, such as the department of health; (2) criteria for identifying eligible children may be set by the individual state in meeting the requirement that "developmentally delayed" infants and toddlers must be served; and (3) perhaps most importantly, the focus of the services is the family/child system, with services spelled out in an Individual Family Services Plan (IFSP).

In extending the provisions of P.L. 94–142 to all three- to five-year-old handicapped children, the legislation: (1) de-emphasizes disability labeling and categorical placement of handicapped children; (2) encourages creative partnerships and collaboration between the public schools and other agencies; and (3) requires involvement with nonhandicapped children. Agencies involved may include both public and private programs, provided that services are appropriate and of high quality, and provided that *integration is present*. Such partnerships may increasingly involve programs that in the past have served mainly nonhandicapped children, including proprietary, cooperative, and other community nursery schools.

For public policy to establish a basis for mainstreaming through "legal and legislative arguments" (Bricker, 1978) is extremely important. Such policy can enable mainstreaming through creation of mainstream alternatives (as discussed earlier), through mandating guidelines that facilitate rather than impede mainstreaming, and through creating funding incentives. These positive reinforcements represent an even more valuable basis than those aspects of public policy that compel compliance by punishing noncompliance, although the latter are also necessary. As with racial segregation, the *illegality* of segregation based on handicapping conditions must be clearly established.

Other arguments for mainstreaming provide the rationale for legally grounded policies, however. The ethical and philosophical bases have been introduced in this chapter and are discussed more fully in Chapter 3. Demonstrations of the educational and psychological effectiveness of mainstreaming in early childhood are reviewed in Chapter 4. The benefits for young, handicapped children are both personal-social and cognitive-instructional. Morgan and York (1983), for example, identify three basic reasons for mainstreaming a young handicapped child: to allow the child 1) to choose both handicapped and nonhandicapped children as friends; 2) to make use of materials not otherwise available; and 3) to learn from models provided by more capable peers. Garner (1986) elaborates on these benefits, explaining that the opportunities to model age-appropriate behavior are more likely to be available in a mainstream setting. Additionally, the expectations that adults—parents as well as teachers—have for a child will be more positive and less limiting, and any stigma associated with enrollment in a segregated program is avoided. Equally important, nonhandicapped children gain opportunities to learn about, get to know personally, and be comfortable with, children who have disabilities or are otherwise different from themselves.

THE VIEWS AND THE ROLE OF PARENTS

Public Law 99 – 457 identifies a more basic role for parents of young handicapped children than that stipulated in P.L. 94–142. This legislation not only renews commitment to the concept of equal partnership of parents and professionals, but also recognizes that it is primarily the young child's *family* that shapes his or her life experiences. The role of professionals, and the schools and agencies in which they work, is to support families, not attempt to supplant them.

Whether handicapped children are actually served within the least restrictive and most "typical" educational settings often depends upon the willingness and ability of parents to advocate such a placement. Some parents, of course, have concerns for their child in a mainstream setting. Parents often underestimate their child's ability to meet expectations of such a setting, and they may underestimate the receptiveness of other children, their parents, and the teachers. To expect the parent to bear the burden of convincing professionals that they should "accept" the handicapped child is unreasonable. Ethically as well as legally, it is the professionals who should make readily available to parents least restrictive educational placements. Parents should not have to fight for this; it is their right and their child's.

The "war stories" of parents of handicapped children could fill many volumes. One mother, anticipating by several years her child's school entry, volunteered to serve on a school district's "mainstreaming committee" and exercised leadership that paved the way for her own child's mainstream placement—as well, of course, as those of other children—beginning at the kindergarten level. Another, against the advice of professionals, removed her child from a specialized agency program, convinced a community nursery school to admit him, and then, faced with reservations among nursery school teachers (although not her own child's teachers), persuaded the agency to provide "awareness" sessions for teachers, children, and parents, as well as adaptive equipment and continuing support services! Generally, throughout history, it has been the parents of handicapped children who have led the way, who have been the most articulate and effective advocates in achieving policy reforms on behalf of their children.

In the past, many professionals interpreted parental advocacy for more normalized education as a reflection of the understandable wish, and unrealistic hope, that a handicapped child could be normal. Many physicians, psychologists, social workers, and educators felt that parents had difficulty accepting the fact that their child was *not,* and could never be, normal. Consequently, the professional's responsibility was seen as helping the parents to face and accept their child's limitations, and to plan a future that must be different from that of a developmentally normal child. Parental *denial* was seen as an understandable, but maladaptive, response.

Struggling through a grieving process that leads ultimately to an acceptance of the child as he or she is is certainly necessary for many parents (Bromwich, 1984). However, in emphasizing parents' difficulties in accepting the "facts" of their child's limitations, some professionals tended to overemphasize those limitations. Today, professionals recognize that to be different must not mean to be excluded. They share a new kind of relationship with parents in advocating *together* for those children whose experience of childhood includes confronting a disability (Turnbull & Turnbull, 1986).

They also share the realization that schools and community services can accommodate differences. That is a far more realistic expectation than the expectation that all children, in order to "fit," must be alike.

SUMMARY

Important changes in practices with young children who have handicapping conditions have occurred in recent years, culminating in the passage of Public Law 99–457, which extends mandates for free appropriate education in least restrictive settings to children aged three through five, while also providing incentives for services to even younger children, including infants, determined to be handicapped, delayed, or at risk. For the early childhood educator, these changes coincide with a renewed emphasis on the importance of early education policies, approaches, and practices that recognize both the uniqueness of the early childhood period of development and the uniqueness of each child.

Although increasing numbers of young children with special needs have been provided services, recognizing the critical nature of early experiences, these services often have been provided in ways that preclude opportunities for these children to interact with normally developing peers. By the same token, typically developing children have had limited opportunities to learn early in life that people with disabilities are people with individual personalities, likes and dislikes, skills and needs—just as they themselves are. Early childhood education presents the best place to start to enable young children to know and learn from each other. In classrooms and centers all over the nation, and indeed throughout the world, that opportunity is being made available. Making the most of it requires professional commitment on the part of the teacher, teamwork with parents, and an understanding and genuine appreciation of the diversity among young children.

CHAPTER 2

Identifying Special Needs in Young Children

Teachers of young children are very much aware of the uniqueness of each child they teach, and that a child's uniqueness implies the need to respond differentially. Quality early childhood education programs do not strive to make all children alike; rather, they nurture individuality. Quality early childhood programs also ensure that young children themselves will learn to respect and value the differences among people, and at the same time, come to understand the ways in which people are all basically alike. Children internalize an awareness that the other children in their classroom group all have their own wants, feelings, likes and dislikes; they also come to understand that all the others, even those who have something about them that is very different, are in many ways just like themselves.

Clearly that is a vitally important focus for us as teachers of young children: we are all alike—and we are all different! And we can help our students understand two particularly important aspects of that concept:

The differences that we can immediately see about a person are not the differences that make that person a truly unique individual.
In fact, the "differentness" that you can see immediately does not really make that person different at all!

The apparent paradox contained in these statements is not difficult to comprehend, especially if children's early socialization is characterized by two key factors:

Opportunities for shared experiences with others different from themselves.

Models—adults—who themselves demonstrate appreciation and respect for each child's individuality.

We often hear that handicapped children are more *like* other children than they are *different* from them. Handicapping conditions represent variations in the range of individual differences, but handicapped children differ from one another just as nonhandicapped children do. As K. Eileen Allen (1980) has noted, there are no well-defined boundaries between "typical" and "atypical," or handicapped, children. Additionally, a great many children viewed as "normal" may in fact have problems that are potentially handicapping.

If all young children are basically alike, except for the great many ways in which each child is different from every other child, then why do we need to talk about "exceptional" children? Every child is exceptional! A good early childhood educator is both sensitive to the individual needs of each child and responsive to those needs. As every teacher knows, however, that is less straightforward and easy than it sounds. The special needs of many children require more individualized planning and specific strategies than do those of others. Some children with particular and identified special needs are called exceptional.

Departures from the historical trend of "separating and combining" specific groups of exceptional children based on the "type" of exceptionality have come about as a result of several key realizations:

All children with the same type of exceptionality do not learn in the same way and cannot be taught most effectively in the same way.

Teaching arrangements and strategies that are effective for many exceptional children are also effective for most children who are not so identified.

Children taught in separate educational settings do not necessarily gain more, and frequently gain less, than children who are not separated from their peers.

Normalizing educational (and life) experiences are valuable for exceptional children. These children have a right of access to all the benefits of both citizenship and human experience.

Having learning experiences in common with those different from themselves is valuable for all children, and for society as a whole.

HOW DOES IT FEEL TO BE "SPECIAL"?

Very young children have not yet formed a clear idea of their own uniqueness. They see the world from what Piaget termed an egocentric perspective (1952, 1967). The notion that other people might have their own perspectives on things, their own thoughts, is grasped only slowly in the course of development.

As children come to an awareness of their own uniqueness, most value that special sense of individuality. The uniqueness suggested by the term *exceptional,* however, may not seem so desirable. Most children identified by others as exceptional would prefer to be like their peers rather than different from them, especially with regard to educational needs. This is certainly the case when those needs are associated with handicapping conditions. It is no less so, in the view of most advocates for gifted children (and indeed in the view of many gifted children themselves [Delisle, 1984]), when those needs are associated with giftedness.

Obviously there are many ways of being exceptional—different from everyone else—that children consider very desirable. Those differences that cause *others* to view a child as different, however, are not the kind that children enjoy. The consciousness of differences on both sides is intensified when children are separated from each other on the basis of those differences. As McCoy and Prehm (1987) observed, "It seems clear that segregation means different and that being different, when attached to a label like mentally retarded or learning disabled, is not highly desirable. Perhaps the safe harbors are not so safe after all" (p. 12).

THE LAW AND THE DEFINITION OF EXCEPTIONALITY

Whom shall we regard as exceptional? Exceptionality can be defined according to various criteria—medical, legal, sociological, psychological, educational. Except for the last, these may bear little relationship to the setting in which a child's impairments are most likely to be experienced: the school.

The fact is, however, that when we define exceptionality for educational purposes, we must look to the law. Laws determine which children are to be educated and, in the United States, because of Public law 94–142, that must include all handicapped children. Laws also determine *where* children are taught (that is, in what types of schools or school placements), *by whom* they are taught, and *with whom* they are taught. To some extent, laws also determine how the effectiveness of schooling is to be measured.

The relevant definitions for the groups of children affected by P.L. 94–142 are provided in the Rules and Regulations accompanying that law (Federal Register 1977, August 42 [163] 20 U.S.C. 140 [1], [15]).

Exceptionalities may be defined somewhat differently in different laws enacted for different purposes. The intent of Section 504 of the Rehabilitation Act of 1973 is to forbid discrimination against persons of any age who are handicapped. Thus, important definitions in this set of federal rules and regulations highlight potential issues with regard to possible discrimination.

Developmental disabilities is a related term that has been defined on the basis of legislation (Public Law 95–602, The Developmentally Disabled Assistance and Bill of Rights Act of 1977). As Wiegerink and Pelosi (1979) underlined, as defined in this law, the term refers to a severe chronic disability that:

1. Is attributable to a mental or physical impairment or combination of mental and physical impairments.
2. Is manifested before the person attains age twenty–two.

3. Is likely to continue indefinitely.
4. Results in substantial functional limitations in three or more of the following areas of life activity: self-care; receptive and expressive language; learning; mobility; self-direction; capacity for independent living; and economic self-sufficiency.
5. Reflects the person's need for a combination and sequence of special interdisciplinary or generic care, treatment, or other services that are individually planned and coordinated.

Although this law differs slightly from the definitions of handicapping conditions of children contained in P.L. 94–142, there are similarities in emphasis. What is important is (1) the specific ways in which an impairment may affect functional, adaptive skills in critically important areas, and (2) the implications for individually planned and implemented interventions, carried out through a team approach.

Whereas P.L. 94–142 pertains specifically to children and youth—and definitions refer to the effect of a handicapping condition on educational performance—P.L. 95–602 pertains to the full age spectrum, provided that the disability was incurred during the developmental period. At the same time, P.L. 95–602 defines disabilities themselves with more specificity and narrower scope. Many children provided for under P.L. 94–142 would not be encompassed within the Developmental Disabilities definition.

YOUNG CHILDREN AT RISK

This book frequently refers to children who are at risk for handicapping conditions. At-risk children have been defined (Keogh, Wilcoxen, & Berheimer, 1983, p. 1) as children ". . . with a higher than average probability of problems in development. Negative developmental outcomes are . . . viewed as ranging from life threatening or handicapping conditions to school failure." This concept of risk implies a particularly critical role for early childhood programs in the area of prevention: the opportunity to identify indicators of risk that might be present and, through early intervention, to ensure that the child's developmental progress is optimal.

Infants and young children at risk for developmental problems are considered to comprise three groups: (1) children at established risk; (2) children at biological risk; and (3) children at environmental risk (Tjossem, 1976). Much of the evidence that early intervention is effective in achieving its goals comes from work with young children, who, because of low family income and factors associated with poverty, are considered to be at environmental risk. (See Chapter 4.) However, there is also evidence of early intervention effectiveness with the other two groups. Much of this evidence has been obtained through the concerted and coordinated efforts of demonstration projects funded by the Handicapped Children's Early

Education Program (HCEEP), a division of the U.S. Department of Education, as well as by programs in other nations around the world. Early intervention as a means of enhancing the development of handicapped children is a worldwide concern. Least is known about the increasing numbers of children at biological risk, especially as medical sophistication has resulted in survival of children delivered significantly preterm and/or at significantly low birthweight (Ensher & Clark, 1986).

The three at-risk groups are not always clearly distinguished, since risk factors often interact in subtle and highly significant ways. What happens to a child born with certain characteristics, some of which might signal either biological or established risk, will greatly influence subsequent development. There is reason to believe that the majority of children born at biological risk (e.g., low birthweight, complications associated with delivery) develop normally (Ensher & Clark, 1986). Similarly, a situation of established risk, as in the case of Down syndrome, does not predict long-term outcome (Hanson, 1985).

According to Peterson (1987, p. 140), we can conservatively estimate that more than 2 million children in the United States under six years of age demonstrate one, or a combination, of these risk factors. That corresponds to the estimate usually suggested for the prevalence of handicapping conditions in children (i.e., about 10 percent of all children). Thus, if early risk indicators do not necessarily lead to handicapping conditions, possibly because of favorable early experiences for some children, the number of young children actually at risk would be much larger.

Identifying young children for whom effective early education is not only desirable, as it is for all young children, but possibly essential, is not, then, a matter of simply spelling out the various "types" of exceptionality. Young children do not come in "types." Nevertheless, when public policy is established to enable eligible children to receive services, efforts must be made to define eligibility.

THE PROBLEM OF LABELING

Labeling handicapping conditions and children who experience these conditions has long been controversial, and it is especially problematic with young children. Advocates for young children with special needs have tried hard to influence policy makers to require ways of identifying children without the use of labels.

This is difficult to do, however. The standard argument for the use of labels of any kind is that they are necessary in order to insure that the intended individuals receive the intended benefits. Some form of disability designation, or label, has been seen by families and by disabled persons themselves as a sort of "passport" to needed services (Hobbs, 1975). Without it, a person with a disability might be unable to gain access to certain educational, economic, vocational, and other benefits provided by legislation. One familiar example is the "disabled" windshield or license plate sticker or emblem entitling one to park where access to stores and shopping malls, public buildings, and offices is facilitated.

In summarizing the conclusions of a large-scale project in which 93 authorities and advocates explored issues of identification and labeling of children, Nicholas Hobbs (1974) listed the positive aspects of labels:

1. Obtaining needed legislation.
2. Facilitating communication among policy makers and practitioners.
3. Designing appropriate services.
4. Organizing volunteer advocacy agencies (such as the Association for Retarded Citizens, the United Cerebral Palsy Association, and others).

However, the negative consequences of labeling were also identified.

1. The possibility of permanent stigmatization.
2. Rejection by peers.
3. Possible assignment to inferior education programs.
4. Unwarranted, unnecessary institutionalization.
5. Misdiagnosis, especially of minority children, through the use of inappropriate tests.

Even before P.L. 99–457 was enacted in 1986, public schools were required to identify preschool-age (as well as school-age) handicapped children. Of course this required the application of criteria for identification. The need to define the population leads, apparently inevitably, to some form of labeling. This presents a dilemma. In order for a child's special educational needs to be appropriately met, an added risk must be imposed. The label may adversely affect a child's self-concept, the expectations of others, and the opportunities for normalized school and life experiences available to the child, who is thus at double jeopardy.

The problem is compounded for young children, since categorical definitions promulgated in federal legislation refer primarily to school-age children. *Learning disability,* for instance, is the most prevalent diagnosis for school-age handicapped children, but it is a condition that cannot be reliably diagnosed in early childhood. In a joint statement, the Division for Early Childhood of the Council for Exceptional Children (DEC/CEC) and INTERACT (The National Committee for Young Children with Special Needs and Their Families) have recommended a noncategorical classification for young children such as "preschool handicapped" (Statement, submitted to the Subcommittee for the Handicapped of the U.S. Senate, March, 1986).

As Robert Bogdan (1986) observes, labeling theory in the field of sociology concerns not the actual characteristics of people but rather their *attributed* characteristics—that is, the perceptions of others. When these perceptions involve stigmatization and social rejection, the individual is clearly harmed rather than helped by the label.

Labeling can be a self-fulfilling prophecy; we tend to "see" others acting in accordance with our expectations, and we base our expectations on the labels we have given them (Merton, 1967). This phenomenon has long been known to be influential in determining how teachers view children (Rosenthal & Jacobsen, 1968). Recent research also suggests that it is an important determinant of how well children actually achieve in school; specifically, teacher beliefs that children from low-income families can learn if they are taught effectively has been found to be one of the most critical characteristics of effective schools (Brookover & Lezotte, 1979; Edmonds, 1979).

If labels *do* create a self-fulfilling prophecy, teachers need to be aware of any expectations, and consequently any behavior of their own, that might be evoked by a "handicapped" label applied to a child. We may feel or act differently due to our perception of what a particular label suggests (e.g., Algozzine, Mercer, & Countermine, 1977). Young children are keen observers! Nonhandicapped students may readily sense the teacher's discomfort, concern, or fear (Cook & Armbruster, 1983) and reflect those feelings in their own responses to the handicapped child. The "labeled" child may then begin to act as expected, thus confirming the belief of the teacher and, consequently, the other children. Although messages of hostility are possible, avoidance is more likely, leading to the child's isolation or feeling of rejection. Oversolicitousness, on the other hand, conveys its own kind of message, that the child is less competent or worthy than others.

The important point is that many of the social difficulties and learning problems a handicapped child may experience are due, not to the objective conditions of a disability, but rather to the attitudes and behavior of important others. Although we use the term handicapped children because it is employed in legal policy, we need to remember that the response of others determines to what extent an individual is handicapped.

We are even more concerned about the long-term effects of labeling in the early years, for the labels tend to "stick!" Further, accurate diagnosis and classification are, for most young children, extremely difficult. Making predictions about the course of future development is even more difficult. Much may depend upon what we believe to be possible. Finally, some of the handicapped labels are simply inapplicable, since they refer specifically to school performance (Peterson, 1987). The identification of young children as learning disabled, for instance, necessarily involves predicting that the child will be learning disabled in school, rather than confirming the child's present status as learning disabled (Keogh & Becker, 1973).

Hobbs (1980) described the system of classification of exceptional children, based on categories that are defined by eligibility requirements, as ". . . a major barrier to the efficient and effective delivery of services to them and their families [that] impedes efforts to help them" (p. 274). Among the recommendations suggested in *Issues in the Classification of Children* (Hobbs, 1975) is that children could be better served if classification were based on needed services rather than on type of disability. P.L. 99–147 represents the intent to do precisely that for young children with special needs.

HOW SPECIAL NEEDS ARE IDENTIFIED

In many children, a handicapping condition is present and potentially diagnosable at birth. In others, conditions present at birth may potentially lead to a handicapping condition. In still others, there are no necessarily predisposing factors present at birth; whether the child acquires a handicapping condition in many instances depends on the circumstances of his or her early care.

In certain instances, however, a disability is necessarily present at birth, caused either by factors operating prior to birth (including genetically determined disorders, fetal injuries, or other causes) or factors associated with the birth itself (including injuries resulting in interrupted flow of oxygen to the brain). Specific types of biological impairments, including chromosomal abnormalities (as in Down syndrome), muscular dystrophy, and others, are known or presumed to have a hereditary basis. In addition, hereditary factors are likely to be involved in many instances of congenital deafness and, to varying degrees, other congenital problems. Some disabilities, such as Down syndrome, can be identified prior to birth by means of well-established procedures such as amniocentesis or more recently developed methods including ultrasonography, a blood sampling procedure (alpha-feto protein), and chorionic villi sampling (CVA). As many as 108 specific genetic disorders have been determined to be potentially diagnosable in utero (Globus, 1982). Fletcher (1983) listed 182 fetal conditions that can now be diagnosed prenatally.

Medical diagnosis is not synonymous with educational diagnosis, however. Knowing that a child is at risk, based on medical diagnostic procedures employed prior to or at the time of birth, rarely permits a confident educational prognosis. Some children who do not have currently identifiable biophysical abnormalities may later present educational problems. The first line of identification of handicapping conditions is the hospital [often the Neonatal Intensive Care Unit (NICU)], the clinic, or the physician's office. But the majority of educationally handicapped children are not identified at that point. For those who are, the educational ramifications of their medical condition are rarely known with any degree of certainty.

P.L. 94–142 specifically charges public schools with the responsibility to identify all children who may be exceptional and potentially eligible for special education. This responsibility includes not only children of school age, but also preschool-age children. The major means of identification used are (1) systematic screening procedures, (2) referral processes, initiated by anyone (including parents, teachers, and others) who suspects a problem, and (3) systematic review of school records for children who are in school.

We will only mention screening procedures briefly here, since hearing and vision screening are discussed in Chapters 5 and 6, and other forms of screening are addressed in other appropriate contexts. However, we need to note several important principles in connection with the identification process:

1. Screening, by definition, is a gross means for economically sorting possible "cases" from the general population. It does not constitute positive identification, and it is not equivalent to diagnosis.
2. Many screening procedures are not sensitive to potentially serious problems. Examples are the screening procedures used in public schools, community clinics, and doctors' offices for hearing and vision.
3. In some areas of screening, the measures used do not meet acceptable standards, yet they continue to be employed. Examples identified by Samuel Meisels include the national program for Early and Periodic Screening and Developmental Testing (EPSDT) and commonly employed school entrance screening. In the former case, Meisels (1985) found that only five of the many tests used meet essential psychometric criteria. In the latter, Meisels (1986)), found that some tests are used for screening although that is not their intended purpose, and that generally school-entrance tests are inadequate because of their lack of acceptably documented validity and reliability.

REFERRAL

Referral is a familiar concept in medicine, where doctors routinely refer patients to other physicians more familiar with specific problems. Referral is also a very important aspect of the teacher's role. Whenever a teacher calls some concern about a child to the attention of a supervisor, colleague, or other professional, a referral is being made. Most schools and centers have clearly defined procedures that must be followed when any staff member feels there is a potential need for the attention of others, usually involving a written statement of the reasons for referral.

There are special considerations if a handicapping condition is suspected. Since the referral *is not* a diagnosis, terms like "learning disability," "slow learner," "emotionally handicapped," should be avoided. Instead, the referral should be a simple factual statement of what the child does. The diagnostic process, involving multifactored assessment, cannot be carried out until the parents' right of informed consent has been honored. As a classroom teacher, you will not refer the child for "special education," but instead for a determination of whether diagnostic assessment is warranted. Such assessment might result in a team decision on the part of professionals and parents that special education services are indeed indicated—or it might not.

Since many handicapped children are not identified prior to their entering school, teachers play an important role. In fact, referral by teachers is the major means for in-school identification of students who may be eligible for and able to benefit from special education services. Generally, to be effective in identifying potential problems as a teacher of young children, you should be:

1. Familiar with "normal" developmental processes and sequence.
2. Aware of symptoms that might be associated with certain problems, such as hearing or vision impairments.
3. Skilled in objectively observing and recording behavior of individual children.
4. Able to employ informal procedures to pinpoint educational problems.
5. Familiar with the appropriate referral process and knowledgeable about school and community resources.
6. Able to maintain effective, ongoing communication with the parents of the children you teach.

A written referral should include a description of what attempts have been made to provide for the pupil's individual needs, through such means as (1) conferences with parents, (2) conferences with the pupil, (3) individual tutorial assistance, (4) modification of the pupil's daily schedule, assignments, seating arrangement, etc., or (5) any special motivational or management procedures that have been used.

Some teachers perceive "mixed messages" with regard to referral. On the one hand, there is national concern about "over-referral" of students who are hard to teach. Some elementary and secondary teachers believe they should be able to "handle" any problem—and some administrators directly or indirectly communicate that expectation. A great many students referred for suspected learning disabilities, for example, are determined to be ineligible; yet, it is widely assumed that more students are being identified and served through special resources for learning disabled students than is appropriate (Ysseldyke & Algozzine, 1982; Ysseldyke, Algozzine, Richey, & Garden, 1982). A very promising and effective means of response is the concept of the school-based Intervention Assistance Team (McGlothlin, 1981; Abelson & Woodman, 1983), which neither denies that a problem exists nor removes responsibility from the classroom teacher in those instances where a child is believed inappropriately identified as "handicapped," as defined in the law. (See Chapter 13 for fuller discussion.)

Teachers need to identify possible problems to employ the referral process. In some instances (for example, instances of suspected child abuse) that process is required by law. In others, especially those involved with problems in vision or hearing, teacher referral may be essential to the initial identification of a problem. Generally, teachers should regard identification and referral of possible problems, whether or not these are symptomatic of a handicapping condition, as an essential facet of their professional responsibility.

Parental awareness of a teacher referral is certainly desirable and may be required by local school district or center policy. An exception is suspected child abuse; child abuse laws require such reporting and protect the individual filing the report. In parent conferences prior to referral, the teacher:

1. Describes the presenting problem objectively, ideally with documentation such as work samples, brief anecdotal records, or quantitative observational records.
2. Asks, invites, listens, rather than simply informing, so that the discussion is truly mutual and "two-way" (see Chinn, Winn, & Walters, 1978).
3. Avoids offering gratuitous advice, especially concerning areas such as recommended medical or other diagnostic services or treatment, diet, vitamin supplements, or medication.
4. Avoids interpreting or presuming to diagnose the child with labels such as "hyperactive," "slow learner," etc.

In summary, the description of a presenting problem, both in consultation with parents and in subsequent referral, should be factual and confined to what is known. Do not speculate about possible etiology (cause), differential diagnostic category, or special services needed. Those interpretive judgments must be based upon an appropriately comprehensive, multifactored assessment process.

In addition to teacher referrals, other referral sources include parents, self, school personnel other than a teacher, or individuals outside the school. Out-of-school identification, especially for young children, relies heavily upon parent referral. A major goal of *Child Find,* mandated under P.L. 94–142, is to make parents aware of their child's right to individualized, appropriate special services, if needed, and of the availability of those sources. This dual goal of creating awareness and of eliciting parent referral also applies to parents of children in school.

In-school self-referral by a pupil is most often associated with needs for counseling and guidance, usually on the part of older children and youth. Elementary school guidance counselors, although long recognized as needed, are not as likely to be available as those at the secondary level. A student may bring to a counselor any of a wide variety of personal, family, or educational concerns, most of which are not related to special education. Self-referrals may also be made to other individuals, such as a school social worker, principal, or nurse, or may be initiated through the pupil's sharing concerns about a personal problem or learning difficulty.

MULTIFACTORED ASSESSMENT

Multifactored assessment is the procedure required by P.L. 94–142 in order to: (1) determine whether a child is eligible for special education because of a qualifying handicapping condition and (2) determine the contents of the child's Individual

Education Program (IEP) if eligibility is established. In the past, special education placement occurred as a result of assessment, but there were inadequate procedures for informing and involving parents, ensuring validity of the assessment procedure, obtaining a sufficiently comprehensive and educationally relevant data base, and monitoring and reviewing children's progress and changing needs. With P.L. 94–142, the following critically important reforms were mandated:

1. No single test or test criterion can be used as the sole basis for placement in special education.
2. Each child's needs must be individually analyzed and described in an individualized (IEP), together with specifications of how those needs will be met and how stated goals will be evaluated.
3. The IEP must be re-evaluaated at least annually, but a review may be initiated by parents or school personnel at any time.
4. No special assessment may be carried out without fully informed parental consent.
5. Assessment must reflect the perspective of more than one individual representing more than one professional discipline orientation (determined on the basis of the individual child's situation, as well as state and local school district policy regulations).
6. Any testing that is done must be non-biased and non-discriminatory, as well as meeting other standards for valid use with a specific child.
7. The assessment process provides a bridge to instruction by yielding information relevant to how, what, and by whom the child will be taught, as well as indicating the nature of any related services to be provided.

The critical need for a multifactored assessment process is apparent because

A single measure simply provides too little information concerning the child's present functioning, what services may be needed, and what objectives are appropriate. All test results are subject to error, and any single result has the potential, especially for young children, of being grossly inaccurate and misleading.
Many criteria besides simply a score on a test must be considered in determining an appropriate educational placement.

Thus, multifactored assessment means that all forms of assessment necessary to determine a child's needs must be carried out before a decision is made—mutually, by parents and professionals—to provide special education services. The law does not specifically state what types of assessment this must include; that must be determined individually, for each child. Nor does the law, except in certain instances, stipulate what specialists, in addition to teacher, school representative, and parent, must participate in the assessment process.

Because of problems in the past involving inaccurate and inappropriate diagnosis, labeling, and placement, the law also mandates that all assessment must be non-biased and non-discriminatory. In the past, disproportionately large numbers of children of Hispanic, Black, Native American, and other ethnic identification had received such labels as "mentally retarded," "emotionally disturbed," "language impaired" based on the use of assessment procedures with built-in discriminatory characteristics. Tests used to make placement decisions, for instance, had in most instances been standardized entirely with white, middle-class children. Use of such tests with children having characteristics different from those of the standardization sample is clearly in violation of established psychometric standards. Often, a child whose primary language was other than English was given an "intelligence test" by an English-speaking psychologist, or a language evaluation by an English-speaking speech and language specialist.

Finally, assessment is no longer viewed as basically a matter of determining a child's current "characteristics" and "ability to learn." We recognize that children do not function in a vacuum, and that no current assessment results are predictive of future functioning. These principles are especially true of young children. Lerner, Mardell-Czudnowski, & Goldenberg (1987) have identified five different approaches in the diagnostic assessment of young children possibly presenting special learning needs:

1. An *interaction or ecological approach,* to incorporate an understanding of both the child's unique characteristics and environmental influences affecting his or her development

2. A *developmental approach,* which considers the child's current functioning in relation to normative expectations for sequential accomplishment of developmental skills in such areas as concept learning, language acquisition, motor functioning, self-help skills, and social-emotional functioning.

3. An *information-processing approach,* emphasizing analysis of how the child approaches problems, strategies employed, and learning styles, based on a dynamic assessment model (Feuerstein, 1979); Lerner et al. (1987) note that Feuerstein's dynamic assessment concept has been applied in working with preschool children by Lidz, 1983.)

4. A *behavioral approach,* involving a functional analysis of the child's current skills in relation to the requirements of present and future environments in which the child must function.

5. A *neuropsychological approach,* involving analysis of evidence of underlying perceptual, motor, and sensory-motor integration characteristics.

In addition, assessment procedures are differentiated based on the source of information and/or the way in which assessment data are obtained. For example, Seibert, Hogan, and Mundy (1987, p. 41) identify three basic methods used in assessing the social-communicative behaviors of infants and young children: (1) Caregiver Interview, (2) Observation of the Child with Caregiver, and (3) Structured Assessment of the Child by a Trained Tester.

Teachers both contribute to the formal multifactored assessment process and have important responsibilities for assessment related to progress in attaining goals and objectives identified in the IEP. In addition, teachers must monitor progress on an ongoing basis as the plan is translated into day-to-day implementation. Although some use of formal testing may be helpful and appropriate, informal and criterion-referenced procedures have several very important uses, as summarized by Neisworth, Willoughby-Herb, Bagnato, Cartwright, and Laub (1980, p. 43):

1. Identifying absent, inconsistent, poorly developed, and excessive behavior patterns across multiple areas.
2. Identifying different settings, events, materials, and activities that appear to control both desirable and undesirable behaviors.
3. Identifying materials, activities, and rewards that stimulate desirable behavior by children.
4. Identifying prerequisite goals for children.
5. Identifying functional handicaps that will affect performance and learning and therefore require adaptive procedures and materials.

Since assessment is so integral to special education teaching methodology, other important aspects are described in more detail in Chapter 3 in connection with the philosophy, goals, and methods that characterize special education. This chapter will conclude by summarizing two centrally important, and closely related, elements that have been alluded to frequently throughout Chapters 1 and 2: the Individual Education Program (IEP) and alternative educational placements for children identified as handicapped.

WHAT DOES THE IEP INCLUDE?

Although each local school district establishes its own format for the IEP, the law clearly sets forth the basic requirements:

> The term "individualized education program" means a written statement for each handicapped child developed in any meeting by a representative of the local educational agency or an intermediate educational unit who shall be qualified to provide, or supervise the provision of, specially designed instruction to meet the unique needs of handicapped children, the teacher, the parents or guardian of such child, and, whenever appropriate, such child, which statement shall include (A) a statement of the present levels of educational performance of such child, (B) a statement of annual goals, including short-term instructional objectives, (C) a statement of the specific educational services to be provided to such child,

and the extent to which such child will be able to participate in regular educational programs, (D) the projected date for initiation and anticipated duration of such services, and appropriate objective criteria and evaluation procedures and schedules for determining, on at least an annual basis, whether instructional objectives are being achieved. (PL 94–142, Section 4 [19])

Examples in Parts II and III of this book elaborate on the components of the IEP. Perhaps the most important point to make concerning the IEP is that it represents the answer to that most elusive question posed in Chapter 1: What is an appropriate education for a handicapped child? Basically, each child's IEP defines his or her most appropriate education.

We should note that, under the provisions of P.L. 99–457, the individual plan for children in the birth through age-two range (the Individualized Family Service Plan or IFSP) is based on family needs rather than those of the child alone.

WHAT ARE EDUCATIONAL PLACEMENT ALTERNATIVES FOR HANDICAPPED STUDENTS?

The issue of educational alternatives for very young children was described in Chapter 1 as complex. In the case of handicapped children for whom the public schools have had responsibility, the range of alternatives has been associated with the "cascade model," developed by Dr. Evelyn Deno (1970) well before P.L. 94–142 was enacted.

Although the cascade model has provided a very useful means of conceptualizing placement alternatives as a *continuum,* and has emphasized the intent to *facilitate movement toward the mainstream* while striving to prevent movement in the other direction, school districts must be careful not to employ it in limiting ways. As Taylor, Biklen, and Searl (1986) have noted, the model implies potential dangers, including the possibility that the Least Restrictive Environment might be defined in terms of the placements a school district has available, rather than the needs of an individual child. Districts must also recognize that more restrictive settings do not necessarily prepare students for less restrictive ones; that is, segregated classrooms do not provide the best means to prepare children to function in integrated classrooms. For these reasons, this book is addressed primarily to early childhood educators who work, or will work, in mainstream settings.

SUMMARY

In order to provide services for young children with handicaps and for their families, we must first find them. That requires establishing some agreed-upon criteria for determining which children are eligible to receive special services. The first set of difficulties encountered in attempting to accomplish identification involves defining the population, determining criteria for inclusion, and, where appropriate, distinguishing certain types of special needs from others. These difficulties are compounded when we consider young children, since definitions may not apply to them, some criteria are specific to the school setting, young children are experiencing a time of rapid change, and measurement methods are less valid and reliable than for older students. Nevertheless, identification is a necessary first step in helping.

Federal legislation has enabled children with handicapping conditions to receive special education and other services that are specifically tailored to their individual needs. It is importnat to ensure, however, that the child is not *deprived* of benefits and opportunities by the very process that is intended to provide benefits and opportunities. Of particular concern are possible consequences of identification, classification, and educational placement. Special services should always be seen as a means toward the goal of full participation in the mainstream of society.

CHAPTER 3

Integrating the Intervention and Developmental Philosophies in Early Childhood Education

Although the shared focus upon the individual child in early childhood education and special education suggests strong parallels, there are also differences between these two fields. In this chapter, philosophical traditions, underlying psychological theories, and instructional practices typically identified with each are reviewed. *Early childhood special education* (ECSE) represents a synthesis of traditions, theories, and practices (Bailey & Wolery, 1984; Lerner et al., 1987; Peterson, 1987). However, for teachers principally oriented and prepared to teach young children with special needs in integrated special education settings, the balance "tilts" in the direction of special education methods and procedures. On the other hand, teachers in typical, or mainstream, settings must respond to the unique needs of children, including those with disabilities and delays, within the framework of the best traditions and practices of early childhood education—that is, *developmentally appropriate practices* (Bredekamp, 1987).

The philosophy of integrated teaching presented in this chapter is intended to suggest guidelines for both early childhood special educators and "regular" early childhood educators, but it is specifically addressed to the latter. *Best practice* in early childhood special education involves services provided through the regular education program structure (Vincent et al. 1981) and requires participation of nonhandicapped peers (Guralnick & Groom, 1988; Odom, Deklyen, & Jenkins, 1984). For these reasons, and also because of the inherent value of good early childhood practices for all children (Widerstrom, 1986), early childhood special education programs need to apply developmentally appropriate practices within an *intervention-oriented* context. For the mainstream teacher, on the other hand, the need is reversed: integrated teaching in regular preschool, kindergarten, and primary classrooms is achieved through combining child-specific adaptations and interventions with teaching approaches appropriate to the needs of all young children.

EARLY CHILDHOOD EDUCATION
AND THE CLIMATE OF CHANGE

Social historians will surely look back at the 1980s as a decade of searching analysis and major change in American education. Many of the concerns addressed are not new. Instead, they reflect renewed determination to resolve long-standing problems: school failure, low literacy, the perpetuation of the poverty cycle, the climate of schools as places in which to learn and to teach, and the preparation and status of teachers. These, in turn, have been seen within a broader social context involving the changed and still changing nature and role of the family in the society, the gap between rich and poor, and the impact of a radically changed culture upon children's physical and psychological safety and health. Within this cultural context, ever increasing numbers of children have been characterized as *at risk*.

In the 1960s the question posed for the schools was, "Can education solve the problems of society?" In no other area was there more optimism than in early childhood education. However, as problems persisted and worsened, it appeared to many (Jencks et al. 1972; Mosteller & Moynihan, 1972) that the impact of schooling could not compensate for home environmental influences. The long-range potential of early education, too, came to be less optimistically viewed (Cicerelli, Evans, & Schiller, 1969). Project Head Start survived, but for some time was itself "at risk." As public schools experienced ever growing financial stress, earlier hopes for the schools to extend their responsibilities to young children grew dim. Far more middle and upper income than low income families enrolled their children in pre-kindergarten programs, such as proprietary and cooperative nursery schools and Montessori programs (Schweinhart & Weikart, 1986). Quality day care or other outside-the-home child care provisions were increasingly in demand, hard to find, and harder still to afford.

Nancy Peterson (1987) in describing the significance of the current cultural context for early childhood education, has noted the importance of the *zeitgeist*—the spirit of the time—in determining whether new ideas are well received and adopted or are not. That has certainly been a most important factor in the area of early childhood. For example, President Nixon's veto of legislation for national child care policy in 1971 probably reflected an accurate reading of the sentiment of "middle America," if not of the majority of the American public. Despite the great and growing need for day care at that time, many people felt strongly that such a national policy could potentially threaten the role and integrity of the family, especially the mother-child relationship. However, in the 1980s, the national sentiment became much more favorable toward national day care policy, evidenced by the Action for Better Child Care (ABC) legislation.

Citing U. S. Bureau of the Census data, Schweinhart and Weikart (1986) reported that, as of 1985, 36 percent of American three- and four-year-old children were enrolled in preschool programs, while the majority of five-year-olds were enrolled in kindergarten. They also noted that one out of four children younger than age six is poor, and therefore at risk, with a much higher proportion of young children of poverty among Black and Hispanic children.

The school reform movement of the 1980s has impacted upon early childhood education in many ways. To the extent that early childhood education's role is seen as preparing children for subsequent schooling, it is potentially "at risk" for what James Hymes (1974) had earlier called "the dribble down disease." That is, there is a tendency to impose learning requirements upon children at increasingly younger ages. As Evelyn Weber (1984) cautioned, recent movements for educational reform pose inherent dangers, to the extent that developmentally inappropriate goals and practices are imposed on young children. Early childhood programs are essential elements of an improved, even transformed, system of public education. However, they are unique elements precisely because of the uniqueness of the early childhood period in human development.

THEORETICAL TRADITIONS IN EARLY CHILDHOOD EDUCATION

Changing views of the nature of childhood and of the learning process have been associated with changing trends in the nature of programs provided for young children (Weber, 1984). To varying degress, different approaches in the field of early education reflect different theories of child development and of learning (Evans, 1975). Lerner et al. (1987) identified six such basic theoretical positions:

1. *The philosophical or moral approach,* associated with the pioneering work of Froebel, "the father of the kindergarten."
2. *The developmental or normative approach,* most closely identified with the maturational theory of development and the description of age-specific norms provided by Arnold Gesell.
3. *The psychoanalytic approach,* influenced of course by Sigmund Freud, but more directly by Anna Freud, Erik Erikson, and other child analysts and ego psychologists.
4. *The compensatory education approach,* originally developed in England by the MacMillan sisters and most generally associated in the United States with Project Head Start.
5. *The behavioral approach,* mainly derived from principles articulated by B. F. Skinner and typically closely associated with practices in many early intervention programs and the concept of direct instruction.

6. *The cognitive psychology approach,* which in early childhood programs most generally involves application of Piaget's *constructivist*
   theory of development, reflected in the work of Constance Kamii
   (e.g., Kamii & DeVries, 1978) and David Weikart (Schweinhart &
   Weikart, 1980; Berrenta-Clement, Schweinhart, Barnett, Epstein, &
   Weikart, 1984) and their colleagues.

In general, theories of children's development differ in their relative emphasis
on either innate, biologically determined influences, or environmental influences.
The above positions are not mutually exclusive, but tend to be reflected in various
combinations in early childhood programs. Virtually all such programs reflect an
emphasis on the interactive relationship between innate influences and environmental factors. However, differences in emphasis are frequently identified in early
childhood programs for children who are at risk or who have identified handicapping conditions.

A key issue in the resolution of different "approaches" in the education of
young children is the concept of *readiness.* A maturational view of readiness is that
it involves biological influences intrinsic to the child. At the other extreme, a
radical behaviorist views children's readiness as determined by external, environmental influences. As opposite poles on a continuum, these two views would
appear to be irreconcilable. One position states that children's development is
entirely governed by biological growth and heredity. The other states that patterns,
accomplishments, and rates of children's learning are determined entirely by
environmental factors.

In practice, of course, there are very few advocates of either extreme position.
Developmental psychologists may emphasize one more than the other; however,
the core theoretical question in developmental psychology regarding "nature and
nurture" for some time has been neither "Which one?" nor "How much does each
influence children's development?" but rather "How do they interact?" (Anastasi,
1958). Both extreme views can be described as unduly deterministic and reduc-
tionistic. A central problem, however, is that maturationism-hereditarianism offers
little optimism concerning the potential of environmental (and consequently educational) intervention, while environmentalism may fail to consider sufficiently the
uniqueness of both specific developmental periods and of the individual child.

In general, the first three approaches (philosophical/moral or Froebellian
tradition; developmental/normative or Gesellian; and psychoanalytic) tend to emphasize common developmental themes. They imply a role for early childhood
education that involves sensitivity to the uniqueness of the early childhood period
of development and response to young children's developmental needs. The compensatory and behaviorial approaches, on the other hand, imply a different role:
that of altering the course of children's development.

In contrast, the *cognitive psychology* approach is based on an *interactionist*
view of children's development, mainly derived from the theory of Jean Piaget.
This orientation is represented among early childhood educators in very different

ways. Contemporary early childhood education, especially in nursery schools, has been significantly affected by Piaget's observations concerning how children learn, but not all applications depart significantly from the traditional, maturationist approach. The issue of whether, or to what extent, children's development can be significantly altered through early education may not be addressed in many programs influenced by Piagetian concepts.

Intervention-oriented programs for children at risk or with handicapping conditions have increasingly reflected Piagetian influences (e.g., Anastasiow, 1978, 1985; Bricker & Bricker, 1972, 1976; Schweinhart & Weikart, 1986a; Weikart, Rogers, Adcock, & McClelland, 1970). However, they frequently differ markedly from Piagetian applications in general early childhood education (e.g., Kamii & Radin, 1970) or eclectic versions influenced by both Piagetian and psychoanalytic theory (e.g., Shapiro & Biber, 1972). Resolution of such differences may hold the key to improved practices that give a more influential role to instruction, provide for a wider variety of individual differences in children, and operationalize Piaget's conception of readiness as "solving the problem of the match" (Hunt, 1961). Resolution may also lead to more normalized practices in intervention-oriented early childhood programs, which reduce the discrepancy between such programs and general early childhood education and better prepare children with special needs to function successfully in "mainstream" settings.

The basic principle of Piaget's theory that applies to young children's education is the concept of *constructivism* (Kamii & DeVries, 1978). We can use a familiar analogy in defining its opposite, that is, what constructivism is *not:* a child's mind is like a container, into which knowledge can be "poured." According to the "teaching-as-pouring-in-knowledge" idea, knowledge comes from the *outside,* with the child merely a passive receptacle. However, in Piaget's view children have a very active role: *the child "constructs" knowledge from within.* Experiences with the social and physical environment are important because they provide the occasions for the child to restructure knowledge.

The principle of active learning is expressed by the authors of *The Cognitive Curriculum* (Hohmann, Banet, & Weikart, 1979).

> The overriding implication of Piaget's work for educators is that the teacher is a supporter of development, and as such his or her prime goal is to promote active learning on the part of the child. (p. 3)

According to Piaget's theory, interaction with both the physical and social environment is important. Some areas of learning require child and peer group interaction. However, Kamii and DeVries (1978) advise the teacher, when planning direct experiential activities, to view them as providing the context for children's social interaction, rather than the reverse. They stress that social interaction and cooperation in the preschool occur as a result of activities that require children to be active in pursuing knowledge. That is, social interactive aspects are secondary, while individual and small group experiential learning are both important in their own right and also instrumental in creating a natural social context for learning.

PHILOSOPHY AND PRACTICE
IN EARLY CHILDHOOD EDUCATION

Early childhood education does not represent a philosophical orientation or uniform set of practices, since the field is composed of several different areas, each with its own origins and traditions. Broadly, we can distinguish four distinct areas: primary education, kindergarten, nursery or "preschool" programs (as well as compensatory programs, generally for three- and four-year-old children), and day care. As we shall see, however, these increasingly overlap, especially regarding the public school's involvement.

A common thread runs through early childhood programs, across types and settings: that is, a *child development,* or *developmental,* orientation. No specific curriculum or program design claims the title of "**the** child development approach," but such an approach is represented in a number of variations from one program or classroom to another (Roopnarine & Johnson, 1987). All share one central premise: *children are active learners who learn best through direct experience.* Barbara Day and Kay N. Drake (1986) have identified four major aspects of the developmental and experiential approach in early childhood programs:

1. These programs recognize young children's needs to practice developmental tasks associated with that developmental period.
2. They are characterized by teachers' understanding of developmental needs and characteristics of young children and teachers' ability to intereact appropriately with young children.
3. They are characterized by a curriculum that furthers cognitive development, based on academic areas, such as science, mathematics, language arts, etc., and based upon concrete experiences.
4. They are characterized by physical settings that are designed to stimulate curiosity and motivation, encourage independence, and enable direct experience with concrete materials.

Such features can most readily be provided, Day and Drake note, through the use of concurrent and simultaneous activities within the classroom, by means of learning centers. Taken together, assumptions about the nature of young children and their learning, the style of the teacher, the nature of the curriculum and learning materials, and attributes of the learning environment, all inherent in the above description, suggest the general theme of developmental appropriateness. The theme is reflected in all four of the areas of early childhood education: primary education, kindergarten, nursery or preschool, and day care. The following brief summaries of distinctive aspects of each highlight ways in which this theme suggests particular responsiveness to the differential needs of individual young children, including those at risk or with handicaps.

PRIMARY EDUCATION

Within the age-grade structure of American education, Grades 1, 2, and 3 have long been viewed as constituting a unique area where lasting patterns of learning, social skills, and self-concept are formed. Children are also expected to have mastered basic skills in reading, written and oral communication, and mathematics before moving on to the upper elementary level. Although practices vary, primary-level children typically identify at each grade level with a single teacher, who is responsible for their instruction in most areas.

Few major changes in standard primary education have occurred, although from time to time significant, even radical, changes have been proposed. No doubt the most significant of these were associated with practices in the British Primary, or "infant" school (Blackie, 1967; Brown & Precious, 1970; Rogers, 1970; Weber, 1971), which, for a time, were adopted in many American schools. Generally, experimentation in primary education, introduced in the late 1960s and early 1970s under the rubric "open education," did not bring about widespread, lasting change in the general character of American primary education. Nevertheless, some major elements of what many (e.g., Silberman, 1970) saw as a radical modification in design and practice continue to be found. These are elements that could be viewed as developmentally appropriate for all young children and especially capable of accommodating a wide range of pupil differences, including differences associated with exceptionality. They include:

1. *More open physical settings.* In many communities, schools were actually constructed without interior walls separating instructional areas, and/or with more flexible space utilization capability achieved through such means as movable partitions. This trend affected the entire elementary school, rather than the primary level alone. However, more recently many districts have provided for the primary grades in separate buildings.

2. *Ungraded or combined-grade arrangements.* Influenced by the British concept of "vertical" or "family" grouping, as well as long-standing concerns about artificial, "lock-step" grade structure, some schools organized into ungraded primary units, building in both large and small group instructional options, and often using team teaching. More commonly, however, combination Grade 1–2 units have been used, and differential instruction according to grade level is typically followed for most curricular areas.

3. *Use of learning centers.* The concept of learning centers has gained

favor among many primary grade teachers, who believe they provide for: more direct involvement of children with learning materials; individual and small group learning; differential pacing based on children's differences in learning style and time requirements; fostering of application, generalization, and transfer of concepts and skills introduced in the various curricular areas; and peer-mediated and cooperative learning. Learning centers may be constant or variable with respect to theme, and they may or may not be identified specifically with curricular areas (e.g., reading and writing center, math center, science center.)

4. *Use of more concrete materials and "hands-on" experiences.* In this respect, Piaget's influence on primary education has been felt, both through the English Primary model and in its own right. In addition to concrete materials, tasks are provided that require children to identify "real" problems and experiment with solutions, involving such processes as measurement, and including divergent as well as convergent thinking. Increasingly, primary children use microcomputers as a standard means of solving problems and experiencing direct, active involvement in learning.

5. *Integration of curricular areas.* The term "integrated day" was used to describe the British Primary instructional program (Brown & Precious, 1970). It was based on recognition that curricular "area" distinctions are often artificial, for children's learning is not naturally "compartmentalized." Additionally, the arts, composition, science, mathematics, "practical arts," and physical education can complement each other, with instructional unit themes applied across curricular areas.

Other significant changes harmonious with accommodating pupil diversity have focused upon specific areas of instruction. Notable among these are the areas of reading—now increasingly integrated with writing experiences (Vacca, Vacca, & Gove, 1987)—and mathematics (which has been greatly influenced by increased use of microcomputers, general availability of pocket calculators, and adoption of the metric system of measurement.)

Another important dimension of primary education, broadly described as *affective education,* is probably in transition. For a time, human relations programs, substance abuse prevention programs, and guided discussion of life situations and problems were frequently included in the primary curriculum. Greater stress in the 1980s on basic academic skills, as well as controversies about "secular humanism," schools' assuming parental prerogatives in such areas as sex education, and the appropriateness of "moral education," have tended to crowd out or discourage stress on the affective areas. Increasing societal problems and cultural diversity continue to imply some important role for schools in such areas as these. However, what schools actually do, or should do in the areas of attitudes, beliefs, and values remains controversial. Successful mainstream participation of handi-capped children requires that children discuss and understand human differences, but that focus of discussion is far more effective and natural in classrooms in which human relations, attitudes, and feelings are addressed as an integral part of the standard program, rather than handled as an isolated topic (Sapon-Shevin, 1983).

KINDERGARTEN

Unique among the levels of schooling, kindergarten has a distinctive tradition about which much controversy has developed in recent years. Unlike other levels of public education, kindergarten may or may not be required, and if required, may or may not be scheduled as a full-day, daily program. As of 1984, only 22 states mandated kindergarten programs, and the age at which school attendance was required varied from five to eight (Glazer, 1985).

Kindergarten has traditionally been regarded as serving a transitional func-tion for children, representing their first formal school experience. As society changes, however, the concept of kindergarten is also in transition. Kindergarten is no longer the first school experience for most children; data gathered by the National Center on Educational Statistics for 1980 and summarized by Judith Glazer (1985) revealed that more than half of all three- to five-year-olds were enrolled in preschool programs, including 85 percent of all five-year-olds, 46 percent of all four-year-olds, and 27 percent of all three-year-olds. As a result, educators have increasingly called for public schools to formalize full-day pro-grams, and even to begin serving four-year-olds.

Traditionally, half-day kindergarten programs were established so that teach-ers could visit pupil homes during the afternoon (Lazerson, 1972). Teachers in half-day programs today, however, typically teach both a morning and an afternoon group. Some school districts assign students to full-day programs on alternate days. Generally, the trend is toward full-day daily kindergarten, and research evidence (Gullo, Bersani, Clements, & Bayless, 1985) suggests that this option need not imply developmentally inappropriate demands upon children. In fact, more time available for learning may benefit academic and social skills prepara-tion.

In addition to the accumulating evidence that full-day, compulsory kinder-garten is beneficial, not harmful, to children, other important societal factors are influencing policy decisions, including (1) families' needs for all-day, daily care for their children; (2) experimentation with alternative or transitional kindergartens resulting from concerns about children's differential readiness and increasing incidence of kindergarten retention; and (3) increasing public school involvement in providing formal programs for four-year-olds, as well as school-based child care for both very young children and school-age "latchkey" children.

Concerns do exist about the purposes of kindergarten and the type of empha-sis kindergarten curricula should reflect.

Paramount among these concerns is the issue of developmental appropriateness and the "fallout" of school reform that has tended to make kindergarten increasingly academic skill- and future-oriented:

> The kindergarten of today is being beckoned in two opposite directions. To some it seems that kindergarten can and ought to be strengthened in the direction of supporting more effective total learning and growth for young children in ways that matter to children yet are significant in the eyes of adults. This approach does not focus on specific academic skills but supplies the ground for them. To others it seems appropriate to hasten children's entry into formal skill learning by borrowing from the grades and turning the kindergarten into a watered-down version of first grade (Rudolph & Cohen, 1984, p. 6).

For example, realization that many kindergarten-age children are "ready" to learn to read, and *do* read, prompted efforts to begin formal reading instruction as part of the kindergarten curriculum. In the view of many, however, the appropriate question is not ". . . *can* we teach formal reading skills in kindergarten, but *should* we?" (Ballenger, 1983, p. 186). As Barbara Bowman (1986, p. 8), a former president of the National Association for the Education of Young Children (NAEYC) has stated, the ethical responsibilities of members of that organization indicate that "We should . . . speak out more frequently against practices that are recommended for children and families which are not consistent with our understanding of their needs." Such practices in the kindergarten would include activities that place children in a passive, receptive role rather than an active, exploring one; expectations for formal academic instruction in skill areas such as reading; and use of "seatwork," such as workbooks and worksheets, rather than direct involvement of children with real objects and situations (Moyer, Egertson, & Isenberg, 1987).

Although such concerns have been expressed with more urgency than in the past, they are not new. Bernard Spodek (1986) summarized changes that have occurred over time in the nature of the kindergarten and recurrent tensions and conflicts concerning what kindergarten should be. He observed that, although much recent concern has focused upon the apparently increasing "one-sidedness" of today's kindergarten, and the early introduction of reading and other academic skills, such presses and resultant concerns have characterized the history of kindergarten education. Educators have never resolved these conflicts totally. Many early childhood professionals would add that educators have never understood fully the learning process in the early years of life.

These tensions are directly relevant to the mainstreaming of children with handicapping conditions in kindergarten. In terms of the integration of the developmental and intervention philosophies—basic, respectively, to early childhood education and special education—they suggest a paradox. The more rigorous the performance demands placed on kindergarten pupils, the more difficulty some children with handicaps may experience. Yet, the more direct instruction toward specific objectives is used, the more congruent kindergarten instructional procedures become with those typically associated with standard special education practice. However, direct instruction, in itself, is not necessarily *individualized* instruction. Moreover, the overriding concern is developmentally appropriate practice for all young children, whether handicapped or nonhandicapped. The most important characteristic of five-year-olds with handicaps is *not* that they are handicapped, but that they are five years old! When substantial numbers of young children who are "typical" are not considered "ready" for kindergarten, are required to repeat it, or are placed in a remedial or transitional class, we have good reason to question the appropriateness of kindergarten curricula for all children. By the same token, inherent in special education philosophy is the belief that *failure to learn reflects failure to teach.* Both of these key ideas are elaborated in the final section of this chapter, toward an integration of developmental and intervention philosophies.

There is some misunderstanding concerning the "traditional" kindergarten, especially the original concept of Froebel and his followers. Although Froebel is generally assumed to have advocated free play for kindergarten children, he actually prescribed a quite structured and closely supervised program of specific activities (Weber, 1969, 1971). Children's training in desirable personal habits, such as cleanliness and courtesy, was emphasized, and children were taught specific skills in these and other areas. Although Froebel considered creativity important, most educators today would not agree with his notion of creativity in young children. For Froebel, creativity meant producing imitations of the teacher's model, rather than spontaneous or original work that was the child's own (Rudolph & Cohen, 1984).

Mrs. Carl Schurz, Froebel's student, brought kindergarten to the United States in 1855, establishing a German–speaking kindergarten in the Wisconsin town where she lived. In Boston, Elizabeth Peabody founded the first English–speaking kindergarten (although she maintained the German name, which means "children's garden"), and helped establish a training center for teachers, based on Froebellian principles. Susan Blow later developed the structure of kindergarten as a component of the public schools and, through her prolific writing and lecturing, effectively advocated for its adoption (Weber, 1969). The Froebellian model was not always adopted in its "pure" form, however. Early U. S. kindergartens often found it necessary to compromise Froebellian principles when confronted with societal problems in America, and especially the actual and urgent needs of children of poverty (Rudolph & Cohen, 1984).

Another source of dissent was based upon the emerging field of child psychology and new ways of viewing the educational process. G. Stanley Hall, often called "the father of child psychology," criticized the Froebellian approach. Hall and John Dewey introduced attempts to apply scientific modes of study to learning and teaching. This led to reform efforts, consonant with the Progressive Movement in education and a new understanding of the nature of childhood itself. Dissenting kindergarten educators, especially Anna Bryan and her student, Patty Smith Hill, were attracted to these views. They argued that the American kindergarten should be more culturally relevant, encourage greater freedom for children, and demonstrate far more awareness of and respect for individual differences among children than the Froebellian model was able to do (Weber, 1969).

Although the American kindergarten has retained elements of the original creation of Froebel, including the name itself, the approach advocated by Patty Smith Hill has been very influential. At the same time, kindergarten has been ever more affected by changes, trends, and conflicts in elementary and secondary education. Most educational innovations, ranging from "the New Math" of the early 1960s through computer-assisted instruction have touched kindergarten curricula. Most of all, concern for children's subsequent school failure has tended to result in ever greater pressure for "more, better, faster, and earlier." Increasing pressures for more teacher-directed, structured, and academically oriented programming have been seen not only to increase difficulties experienced in mainstreaming special needs children, but also as comprising a growing problem for many children not identified as handicapped (Salzer, 1986; Walter & Vincent, 1982).

Although kindergarten programs are quite variable, features common to most can be identified. First, virtually all involve a fairly predictable and consistent daily schedule of activities. Although there may be periods of time when several different activities occur, often using learning centers, these are interspersed with periods when the entire group is engaged in a common activity. The extent to which free and spontaneous play is emphasized is also variable, although nearly all kindergartens make some provision for: *sociodramatic play,* involving dress-up materials, a housekeeping corner or center, or other elements intended to encourage and support small-group or individual role-taking, narration, and other dramatic play activities; *constructive play,* involving materials such as blocks, sand, water, or other materials used by children individually or used through parallel or cooperative play modes; and *teacher-led or teacher-guided group games,* within the classroom and on the playground.

Typically, schedules provide for teacher-led large group activities including a beginning sharing time; a period for listening to a story, sometimes combined with music, rhythms, verbal participation activities, or discussion; and a closing time. Large group modes may also be used for instruction in some academic skill areas.

Learning center-based small group experiences with mathematics and science-related activities are a standard part of many kindergartens. The degree to which centers are organized and provisioned to permit and encourage peer cooperation, peer direction, spontaneous discovery and problem-solving, step-by-step teacher demonstration and guidance, etc., varies according to the nature of the activity and the philosophy and style of the individual teacher. The alternative instructional modes possible through learning centers enhance the ability to provide effectively for individual differences among children, including those with special needs.

Experiences in graphic and plastic arts, using diverse media, are standard as well, although how these are provided varies. Finally, well-illustrated books, both familiar and new, are important in the provisioning of every kindergarten. A reading and writing center, a quiet/relaxation center, or other way of making these available and attractive to children may be present, and books appropriate to center or unit themes may be found in all or most centers. Whether or not formal reading and writing instruction occurs, the availability of books is standard.

Increasingly, kindergarten children use microcomputers, which have greatly expanded the possibilities for individualization and discovery learning, as well as possibilities for introduction of formal instruction in mathematics and other areas. Electronic or other media frequently found in the primary grades, such as listening centers, may be standard in the routine of many kindergartens. Finally, as has been noted, formal instruction, involving reading materials, writing practice, and even published or teacher-made seatwork materials has tended to characterize the kindergarten program.

The Problem of Kindergarten Readiness and Kindergarten Failure

At the point where the "two worlds" of early childhood and public school education meet (Safford & Rosen, 1981) wide differences among children are observed. At this point also many children encounter situations in which they experience failure for the first time, and some of these children are identified as potentially educationally handicapped. Of these, significant numbers may come to be labeled as learning disabled, developmentally delayed, or having behavior problems.

There are many popular views, no doubt shared by numerous parents, as well as educators, of warning signs that might suggest that a kindergarten child is at risk for educational failure. Screening and readiness testing—two areas of assessment that are often confused (Meisels, 1986)—as well as less formal "kindergarten roundup" procedures typically incorporate skills traditionally viewed as important predictors of success or difficulty in kindergarten. However, as one analysis of research literature suggests, we may often be looking for the wrong things! Based on a review of studies correlating skill performance in kindergarten with academic failure, Simner (1983) concluded that kindergarten children who are at risk for school failure

> . . . are not necessarily lacking in many basic motor, language, drawing, and copying skills when compared to the average kindergarten child. Nor are these children necessarily shy, lonely, withdrawn, or uncooperative. Instead . . . these children are far more likely to display attention or memory problems, lack verbal fluency, be disinterested in school-related activities, have difficulty identifying letters and numbers, and produce a fairly large number of form errors when printing. (pp. 23–24)

The growing problem of kindergarten failure is of great concern to early childhood educators, as it is to the entire education community, including officials and administrators at state and local levels. Long-standing questions concern relationships between chronological age at entrance and developmental readiness.

Of more recent concern are the apparently increasing demands of the kindergarten curriculum. Considering both, Uphoff and Gilmore (1986) summarized possible options that might be taken in order to counteract or lessen the problem of kindergarten failure:

1. Changing cutoff dates for entrance, based on beliefs that the youngest children enrolled are least likely to succeed or at least to be judged successful by the teacher;
2. Adopting better and more commonly employed developmental assessment processes to determine readiness;
3. Urging parents to hold back young children and enroll them instead in a more play-oriented preschool program or, if eligible, Head Start;
4. Changing the curricular trends, delaying the beginning of formal instruction in mathematics, reading, writing, etc. (as is done, for example, in the Scandinavian countries);
5. Adopting a transitional kindergarten as a "pre-first grade" option, as an alternative to retention in kindergarten and repetition.

Related to the last option is the concept of a "junior kindergarten" as part of a "two-tiered" kindergarten structure (e.g., Galloway & George, 1986). However, close scrutiny should be given the expectations and requirements of the regular kindergarten curriculum (Option 4 above), based on the criterion of developmental appropriateness, before alternatives are adopted.

Paradoxically, high rates of kindergarten failure and retention may have resulted in an even greater tendency to adopt developmentally inappropriate practices. Salzer (1986) has asserted that the very elements of kindergarten most beneficial to young children, and most congruent with the way they learn, tend to be eliminated in the erroneous belief that earlier formal academic instruction will lessen subsequent school failure. Literacy is surely a major and growing societal problem; however, "literacy behavior" in young children should not necessarily be defined in the same manner as for older students. Alternatively, The Early Childhood and Literacy Development Committee of the International Reading Association (Vacca et al., 1987, p. 65) have made recommendations believed appropriate to the developmental characteristics of young children; they emphasize the active and creative role of the individual child as a language user, the need for young children to enjoy language and integrate literacy with all aspects of development as well as to experience success, and the importance of developmentally appropriate language learning experiences at home as well as in school. They also stress the importance of appropriate evaluative procedures.

Measurement of kindergarten readiness is problematic at best, complicated by the fact that the most commonly used readiness measures do not meet acceptable standards of validity and reliability (Meisels, 1985). The use of tests with no demonstrated validity for the purposes for which they are employed is untenable (Salvia & Ysseldyke, 1981). A related problem involves what is done with the results obtained from readiness tests. As Shephard and Smith (1986, p. 85) stated, ". . . school districts must think again before screening children into unsuccessful programs on the basis of fallible tests." They refer to identification for special class placement, kindergarten retention and repetition, and to the variety of alternative or transitional programs that have been proposed.

Identification of children for special class placement based on unsound measures is inappropriate and unwarranted, and there is no convincing evidence either that potential benefits positive to most children outweigh potential harmful effects. Concerning simple retention and repetition as an option, there is little if any evidence that many children benefit from "more of the same." For example, Leinhardt (1980) found at-risk children who received extra help in the next-level regular classroom did better academically and socially than did children retained for a second year.

The issue of entrance age and associated differences in readiness has been frequently discussed but little researched. However, Shephard and Smith (1986) reported results of one comprehensive study of children's age in relationship to kindergarten success. They indeed found evidence that older children do better in kindergarten. However, they stressed that the difference, on average, is not educationally very great and ". . . unless it is cast in stone by a learning disability label or grade retention, in most cases it will disappear entirely by about the third grade" (p. 85).

In summary, unique stresses and divergent views are associated with the American kindergarten. As transitional kindergarten options are considered, the kindergarten itself is "in transition." As kindergarten becomes more formally structured and academically demanding, increasing numbers of "normal" children experience difficulty and even failure. Alternatively, the kindergarten program itself may be in need of "remediation" so that it can: (1) implement expectations, educational goals and instructional practices appropriate to the developmental characteristics and needs of young children; (2) respond more effectively to young children's individuality and diversity, rather than imposing common expectations and using group-efficient, but not individual-sensitive instructional modes and procedures; and (3) avoid, where possible, labeling practices that lead to segregation, exclusion, or stigma for nonhandicapped as well as handicapped children.

NURSERY SCHOOL

Paradoxically, the historical roots of the nursery school, unlike kindergarten, are closely associated with the concept of compensatory education, but most modern American nursery schools tend to reflect the developmental/normative or the psychoanalytic approach. The two general "types" of programs are both strongly influenced by the cognitive psychology (Piagetian) approach, yet they are quite different in application. Programs that do not intend to *alter* the course of children's development differ from those (such as Head Start), which focus specifically on the needs of children at risk, with respect to teacher-imposed and materials-imposed structure, monitoring of children's progress, and nature of parent involvement. Frequently, however, such differences are not readily apparent.

The major differences involve the issue of self-motivated learning vs. direct instruction—perhaps the most critical issue for us in attempting to resolve differences in philosophy and practice between "mainstream" early childhood education and early childhood special education. We shall return to it following a brief overview of the history of nursery school education.

The English Nursery School and Montessori Traditions

The emergence of the nursery school came about much later than the kindergarten. The work in England of Rachel and Margaret MacMillan in the late 19th century is generally cited as marking the origin of the nursery school (Evans, 1975; Hendrick, 1986; Hildebrand, 1981). They coined that term for the group program that had evolved from what they actually began as a clinic for the prevention of health problems among poor children. Sanitation, proper nutrition, and hygiene were emphasized in response to the sisters' concerns about the spread of disease, general poor health, and vulnerability to illness among children of the poor. Meanwhile, Dr. Maria Montessori had also pioneered a form of preventive and developmental education based on her belief in the unity of all aspects of children's development—physical, mental, and spiritual. Her approach initially derived from her work with mentally retarded children in institutions. She then applied her methods with children in the slums of Rome. Montessori was actually following a tradition that had provided the origins of the field of special education—that of physician-turned-educator. Her predecessors included other pioneers who brought their medical training and philosophy to bear in work with mentally retarded, deaf, blind, and otherwise impaired children, such as Itard, Seguin, and Howe (Safford, 1983).

While kindergarten was influenced by the work of Froebel, the efforts of both the MacMillan sisters and Montessori drew heavily from the work of Seguin with mentally retarded persons, which especially stressed sensory experiences, functional self-care skills, and personal responsibility. From these early beginnings, however, emerged quite different approaches. "Mainstream" nursery schools have traditionally reflected an eclectic blend of pschoanalytic, maturationist, Progressivist, and Piagetian thought, while Montessori programs tended to retain intact the whole system conceived by their creator, although differences are also found among Montessori schools.

In England, the writing of Susan Isaacs (1929, 1933), based on her work with children in The Malting House School, as well as her study of the emerging field of child psychology, had great influence. Isaacs and others advocated a flexible, child-centered approach, recognized the importance of play in children's learning, emphasized the social context of learning, and reflected an awareness of and concern for the child's inner life of emotion, fantasy, and imagination. The child's natural curiosity and need to discover were made the cornerstone of the nursery program, rather than adult-imposed rules and rewards. The teacher was a respected, trusted, and loved model. While emphasizing the "wholeness" of children, Isaacs did not ignore intellectual development. However, many nursery programs, in their focus upon social and emotional aspects and emphasis upon free play, probably tended to de-emphasize cognitive learning. In the words of Millie Almy (1968),

> . . . it is true that, for a time, in some nursery schools and kindergartens, one sought vainly for some evidence that teachers, however concerned they might be with the children's emotional and social development, had any notion of their intellectual power. Susan Isaacs, with her belief that the intelligence and power of observation of young children are generally underestimated, could only have been appalled at the intellectual sterility of some of these programs. (pp. ix–x)

The Montessori approach is actually imbedded within a philosophical system based on faith in the child's innate will to learn, belief in the unity of knowledge, and recognition of the integrative nature of learning (Montessori, 1912, 1949). In general, the Montessori approach differs from others in its emphasis on formalized, prescribed and especially designed materials. Montessori also tended to emphasize individual rather than group activity, implying a lesser focus on language-related activities. Generally, less emphasis is found on creative use of art media, music, and spontaneous dramatic play. Montessori materials have been designed to facilitate self-directed and self-paced learning, following a sequence presumed to parallel children's development. The teacher arranges the environment, models a profound respect for the materials of learning as well as how they are used, and guides only as necessary. The approach is both highly structured and based on principles of self-guided learning.

Despite the worldwide appeal of her system, Maria Montessori's approach did not gain acceptance in the United States during her lifetime. By midcentury, however, independent Montessori schools providing for a range of ages from preschool through adolescence began to appear. Her approach seemed to appeal especially to a clientele quite different from that with which it was developed; in many U.S. communities, the impetus for Montessori programs came from middle- and upper-income families. The inevitable costliness of these programs, with their special materials and especially trained teachers, no doubt accounted for their adoption by families with means. Nonetheless, Montessori also came to be included among the various preschool intervention "models" federally funded as compensatory programs.

Certain aspects of the Montessori system, especially the environmental arrangement so fundamental to it, seem particularly appropriate to meet the needs of handicapped children in both special and mainstream classes. The especially adapted materials, many of which are self-correcting, and the opportunities to work with these materials individually and at a child's own pace are particularly appealing (Krogh, 1982). Importantly, the Montessori philosophy does not emphasize distinctions among children based on categorical "labels," but instead stresses the individuality of each child. This approach is viewed as appropriate to the needs of children who are intellectually gifted or delayed, as well as those within the average range of functioning.

Nursery schools are either proprietary or cooperative, the major differences being the degree of parent involvement and the cost, since coop nursery parents establish policy and select teachers, as well as generally helping out in the classroom or otherwise. Many communities have special purpose nursery programs, emphasizing the arts, theatre, dance, or other such areas.

Head Start

Since its origin in the summer of 1965 as a critically important component of the War on Poverty, Project Head Start has involved a much more comprehensive approach than other preschool programs. Health, nutrition, and family needs have been emphasized, and parents have been encouraged and helped to break out of the poverty cycle through employment in centers or elsewhere. Parent involvement has been especially important, and in many instances parents were genuinely empowered to participate in the governance and policy decisions of their own programs. Since Head Start is not exclusively an educational program, *multi-disciplinary* staff and services are considered essential.

Significantly, Head Start has been the only "regular" public early childhood program required on a national basis to include handicapped children. As was noted in Chapter 2, it has demonstrated convincingly that young handicapped children can be successfully integrated with nonhandicapped peers at the preschool level. In that respect, as in others, the story of Head Start is indeed a "success story."

However, Head Start may be seen as a special case, not precisely representative of typical early childhood programs. It was conceived as a means of intervention in the lives of children, a way of changing life opportunities for them and altering the course of their development. General nursery school education, its historical origins notwithstanding, espouses no such goal.

Head Start is the best-known component of what was a network of federally initiated and supported efforts on behalf of young children at environmental risk and their families. These included Follow Through, Parent and Child Centers, Home Start, and developmental screening through a program known as Early and Periodic Screening and Developmental Testing (EPSDT), created in 1967 as part of Medicaid and The Maternal and Child Health Program.

Locally, Head Start programs may be administratively tied to public schools or they may be quite distinct. The funding structure, implementation guidelines, and accountability procedures for Head Start are separate from those of the public schools; however, various models for coordination with schools can be found. The issue of availability of Head Start as a free, public program for lower income families and also for parents of handicapped children eligible to participate is a very important one. As Winton, Turnbull, and Blacher (1984) point out to parents searching for a good preschool program, publicly supported mainstream pre-schools, excepting Head Start, have been rare.

Although general policies govern practice in Head Start programs, wide variation exists among individual centers, since local initiative is important and encouraged. Superimposed on these individual program differences are alternative "models" or general approaches. A number of specific models have been developed and, in both Head Start and Follow Through programs, tested on a national basis to determine their relative effectiveness in achieving goals that are important both nationally and locally. Perhaps the major conflict concerning alternative models involves the issue of direct instruction vs. child-initiated active learning. Each has its strong advocates, and each is concerned with the long-range impact of compensatory early education with young children at environmental risk. Neither perspective is specifically confined to Head Start, however.

Engleman (1966) and others advocated identifying and systematically teaching specific skills required for school success. Others, especially David Weikart and his associates (Schweinhart & Weikart, 1980; Weikart, Rogers, Adcock, & McClelland, 1970) designed and advocated an approach intended to foster the development of cognitive processes. According to Piagetian theory, cognitive structures that children develop are the product of their active learning through transactions with the environment. It is these that form the base for later learning, rather than specific skills that can be taught directly.

Evidence suggests the long-range superiority of active learning designs (Schweinhart & Weikart, 1986). However, the conclusions have been severely attacked by some critics who favor the direct instruction approach (Bereiter, 1986; Gersten & White, 1986). These critics cite efficacy data obtained through the national Planned Variations study of the effectiveness of Project Follow Through (Kennedy, 1978; Meyer, 1983), revealing more consistent positive findings associated with direct instruction, despite differences among individual centers. The argument for direct instruction focuses on the greater efficiency of systematic procedures that target specific skills needed by children to meet academic demands (Roehler & Duffy, 1981). At first look, this controversy concerning early education for children at environmental risk—child-initiated active learning vs. direct instruction—seems to capture the essence of the differences between the developmental and intervention philosophies. However, as has been noted, the major, perhaps dominant, force in this area has been the cognitive developmental approach.

Preschool Programs under the Auspices of Public Schools

As discussed previously, kindergarten is becoming established only now as a standard component of public education. Yet, public schools have become involved in recent years in providing services for even younger children, through: (1) programs for preschool-age children identified as handicapped, which until P.L. 99–457 was enacted were mandatory in about half the states, permissive in the others; (2) school-based day care; (3) public school-based or affiliated Head Start programs; and (4) programs in some school districts for four-year-olds, not tied specifically to Head Start.

Increasing public school involvement in programs for young children may be mainly responsive to societal and family needs, rather than those of young children (Doremus, 1986). However, the schools' increasing involvement in serving four-year-olds may reflect an extension of the philosophy of compensatory education through early intervention. One concern about this development involves the need to coordinate with other agencies, especially Head Start. Another concern involves the issue of developmental appropriateness: such programs might be seen within the context of school reform as a downward extension of the increasing academic demands and pressures in the kindergarten (Morado, 1986). Some of the studies, reports, and proposals generated in connection with the school reform movement of the 1980s suggested that such need not be the case. For example, Mortimer Adler (1982) recommended flexible practices, geared to individual needs of students, with regard to both age of school entrance (from four to six) and length of schooling (10 to 14 years). John Goodlad's (1984) extensive study of American schooling led to recommendations for fundamental restructuring, beginning with a primary school for four- to eight-year-old children that would combine nursery school and kindergarten within a single year.

Public schools' involvement with very young children will surely be furthered in response to P.L. 99–457, and demonstrations had been provided previously indicating that public schools can provide effective programs even for infants (Turner & Rogers, 1981). Identifying the school as the most appropriate agency for serving young handicapped children is based on several considerations, especially its historical commitment to educating handicapped children as an instrument of social policy (Behr & Gallagher, 1981). The need to provide for least restrictive placements for three- to five-year-old children with handicaps, mandated under P.L. 99–457, suggests the possibility that schools may be encouraged further to extend programs to those who are not handicapped, as well.

DAY CARE

Although day care is generally viewed as relevant to the needs of working parents, rather than inherently desirable for children, that does not necessarily mean it is a "necessary evil." Potentially, good quality, professional child care can be an effective area of early childhood education. Ideally, day care is developmentally oriented, rather than custodially oriented, although the quality of day care in the United States has been highly variable. That is just one of the reasons that its impact upon the development of young children has been difficult to determine (Belsky & Steinberg, 1978).

Day care also presents another area in which young handicapped children can be integrated with their nonhandicapped peers. As Klein (1981) has observed, the need for quality day care is shared by parents of children with disabilities:

> The economic pressures experienced by families of young nondisabled children today are also experienced by families of disabled children. In fact, families of disabled children frequently face extraordinary medical and related expenses which strongly impact on the need for a second income in the family. As a result, more and more mothers of disabled young children are seeking employment and quality extended daycare for their children. (pp. 50–51)

Day care staff must realize, as they approach serving handicapped children, that many of these children will also be participating in some other type of early childhood program. Involvement in a mainstream setting is seldom an "either-or" proposition. The model that Klein (1981) suggests emphasizes the need for coordination between a specialized early intervention program that some young children may need, the regular (mainstream) day care program, and of course the family.

Despite variability in licensing requirements and caregiver qualifications, proponents of quality, developmental child care believe that day care can do much more than simply care for children. Some see a fine line separating center-based day care, especially, and community nursery school programs. We should note that day care is provided not only for preschool-age children, but also for those of school age, during periods of the day (and/or night) when parental employment requires separation. All states have differential licensing requirements, depending upon the ages served, specifically in such areas as adult-child ratio.

The developmental potential inherent in day care has been increasingly recognized as our understanding of young children has changed. Educators had long assumed that experiences in group programs would not be meaningful for children younger than age three, based on observations that cooperative play, conformity to group conventions, and empathetic concern for others seemed to emerge at about that age. "Two's" were thought to be not only too socially immature to interact with peers but virtually lacking in responsiveness to peers. Although two-year-olds are rapidly developing language capabilities, language use is dyadic, employed interactively with a significant adult, generally the mother.

Group programs for very young children began to proliferate in response to changes in the society, then, rather than changing views about children. Interestingly, opportunities to study children in such group contexts has resulted in altered views concerning their social responsiveness. A major area of child development research that has subsequently emerged has focused upon peer interactions among very young children (e.g., Mueller & Brenner, 1977), and convincing evidence has been obtained that toddlers do interact meaningfully with each other (Bronson, 1975; Lewis, Young, Brooks, & Michalson, 1975). Even within the first year of life, social learning apparently occurs as a result of contact with other infants (Becker, 1977; Vandell, Wilson, & Buchanan, 1980).

The history of day care in the United States, prior to the Act for Better Child Care, has been divided (Steinfels, 1973) into three general periods. First, in the early years of the present century, child care was provided during a period of rapid industrialization in order to enable women to work. The second period, from the 1920s to the 1940s, saw day care provision limited to cases of special need, with a very significant increase during World War II, under government sponsorship, to free women for war industry work. Federal subsidization ceased following the war, however, and a stigma developed, associating day care with mothers who were unwilling to do their "proper" job, which was child-rearing. During this same period, the day care that did exist came under the influence of the nursery school movement, resulting in more developmentally oriented programs. The other side of that coin, however, was a growing imposition of developmental requirements— being toilet-trained or able to dress oneself—that effectively excluded many children with handicaps or delays.

In the third period, beginning in the 1960s, the federal government again became involved with day care, leading to a "revival" of the field, mainly in terms of emerging compensatory programs. As Peterson (1987) observed, day care services, in contrast to nursery or kindergarten education, have emerged in response to social needs rather than the insights of educational pioneers, which may explain the absence of a well-articulated philosophy or consistent curriculum.

Day care, like other areas of early childhood education, is at a crossroads. In addition to concerns about *availability* and *affordability,* society is concerned about the *quality* of the care it needs and supports. This last concern bears directly on the status, recognition, and remuneration of child care providers. With the professionalization of day care providers, better strategies for performance evaluation and more effective training will be required. These need to be based on a better understanding of the components of good day care than was possible until recently (see, for example, Greenman & Fuqua, 1984). The goals of availability, affordability, and quality associated with the Act for Better Child Care (ABC) appear to be within reach at last.

Licensing standards in many states make specific reference to requirements applicable when children with certain handicapping conditions or medical needs may be involved. In themselves, these do not imply a requirement that handicapped children will be served, however. The policy requirement to include handicapped children specifically affects programs that receive federal funds, under Section 504 of the Rehabilitation Act of 1973, as explained in Chapter 1. Some projects in specific communities have been notably successful in encouraging and enabling community day care programs to include children with handicapping conditions, as illustrated in the final chapter of this book.

EARLY EDUCATION: IN SUMMARY

A considerable amount of discussion has been devoted in this chapter to the scope of "regular" early childhood education, with particular stress given to two major considerations:

1. *Philosophical assumptions, goals, and undergirding theories* associated with early childhood approaches followed in four distinct areas: the primary grades, kindergarten, nursery or preschool programs, and day care;

2. *Typical or standard practices* that appear to have specific implications for young children with handicapping conditions and/or the integration of the guiding philosophies associated with early childhood education and with special education—the developmental orientation and the intervention orientation.

Although the legally mandated character of special education was described in Chapter 2, and aspects of special education practices are illustrated throughout Parts II and III as these can be implemented within mainstream classroom or center environments, the next section briefly summarizes philosophical positions associated with special education and the methods and practices they imply. The final section is an attempt to present an integrated view of early childhood education and special education.

PHILOSOPHY AND PRACTICE IN SPECIAL EDUCATION

What is "special" about special education? This question began to be asked seriously during the period of social upheaval and unrest of the 1960s and early 1970s. It was raised in part due to the lack of any compelling evidence that, for many mildly handicapped students, special class placement was more effective than regular class placement.

Disturbingly, research also suggested that, to an inordinate degree, minority students tended to be identified, labeled, and placed in special classes (Dunn, 1968; Mercer, 1973). At a time when the civil rights movement was arousing the national consciousness concerning racism, it was becoming apparent that some degree of institutional racism was reflected in special education placements, although such practices would be directly counter to special education philosophy. The mandate to "identify and help" (Caldwell, 1973) certainly does not imply practices of discrimination and segregation. The mainstreaming movement, as well as due process safeguards under P.L. 94–142, brought about corrective measures.

Historically, special education has been characterized by a high degree of optimism. During periods when that optimism has waivered or been replaced by pessimism and fear, persons with disabilities have suffered. The most powerful example involves that period in American history, traced by Wolfensberger (1969), when what had begun as schools for the education and training of mentally retarded persons became instead crowded, dehumanizing institutions. The loss of humanity that results from such a loss of hope has been unforgettably depicted by Dr. Burton Blatt in the pictorial essay titled *Christmas in Purgatory* (Blatt & Kaplan, 1966).

The Medical Model

One explanation for the historical shift from the optimism of Samuel Gridley Howe, Seguin, and other pioneers was the growing involvement of medical practitioners and the application of a medical orientation, which sought cure. Throughout history, the inability to cure people with handicaps has led to a fatalistic acceptance, profound pessimism, and even to blaming and punishing the individual with a disability. During the late 19th and early 20th centuries, the segregation of disabled persons, especially those labeled mentally retarded, increased at an alarming rate. The dominance of hereditarian views of human intelligence, the Eugenics Movement, and misuse of intelligence tests, in combination with race and ethnic prejudice, contributed to irrational fears concerning human differences. These led even respected scientists to advocate segregation, institutional incarceration, sterilization, and denial of human rights to persons even suspected of being mentally retarded, based on the unfounded and scurrilous belief that they were a threat to soceity. Such shameful developments in the history of society's treatment of mentally retarded persons have been traced by Wolfensberger (1969), and the misuse of science and the dominance of prejudice over reason have been traced by Stephen Jay Gould (1981) in his book titled *The Mismeasure of Man*.

During this same period, however, other more positive developments affecting societal attitudes were occurring. One of the most influential involved a single blind and deaf individual, Helen Keller, and her teacher, Ann Sullivan. A truly gifted although disabled person, Helen Keller inspired people all over the world. Public schools began to provide for handicapped children. Special education (as a component of public education, as well as a specialized profession) grew, and specialized services, such as speech therapy, counseling, and school psychology emerged as professional fields with roles in the school.

The Educational Model

Application of an *educational* model, in the tradition of Itard, Seguin, Howe, and Gallaudet, implied greater acceptance of diversity and a more realistic optimism. That education could not "cure" deafness, blindness, cerebral palsy, or other organically-based disabilities was generally accepted. Children with such disabilities could, however, learn through compensatory, special education to function as independently as possible, and to avoid experiencing secondary problems. That did not imply that the search for means of prevention or cure should not continue, for such efforts have been very successful in the areas of both physical and mental disability. However, the teacher's role is to teach those children based upon understanding of both their individual difficulties and their individual strengths, working to enable each to attain the optimal degree of independence, accomplishment, and quality of life that might be possible.

Hopes for educational "cures" have persisted, particularly with students having specific learning disabilities. Increasingly, however, we are recognizing that, for many students, a specific learning disability is no more remediable than *general* learning disability (as we might characterize mental retardation.) That does not mean that effective teaching cannot significantly change either a child described as learning disabled or a child described as mentally retarded. Children who have been given either label can be enabled to function educationally, vocationally, and socially within the normal range, for **retardation is a description of one's functioning at some given point in time, not an explanation or a prediction.** Through effective educational intervention, especially if begun early in life, children with either general or specific learning difficulties can be expected to function much more capably—cognitively, emotionally, socially, vocationally—than when instruction is not optimally matched to the individual needs and characteristics of the student. However, we now recognize that many individuals with specific learning disabilities are likely to experience some difficulties, and need to compensate for these difficulties, throughout their lives. Today, colleges and universities are likely to provide assistance for learning disabled students, as well as other handicapped students, through an office for disabled students, ensuring them access to educational programs under the same mandate (Section 504) that forbids discrimination against persons with other disabilities.

Individualized Teaching

The guiding principle in special education practice is individualized teaching (Strain, 1988), frequently involving a combination of compensation and secondary prevention of problems for which a disability places one at risk, rather than remediation or cure. Special educators do not restore sight, hearing, sensation to touch, or destroyed or diseased tissue. What they strive to do, however, in working with a student with a disability, whatever its cause, is to help that student to: (1) learn to use the affected mode of functioning optimally; (2) learn to use other modalities optimally in order to compensate for an affected modality; (3) experience a sense of competence, positive self-esteem, and an appropriate level of self-confidence required to undertake new experiences and to risk failure; and (4) avoid secondary problems—in school, in family and other social contexts, and in the workplace—for which a disability may place one at risk.

CURRICULUM AND INSTRUCTION IN SPECIAL EDUCATION

As established in Chapter 2, special education cannot be defined as education that takes place in special classes or special schools. These are possible placements for students identified as handicapped, but the majority are assumed to be able to have some or all of their teaching within the regular classroom. That implies the need to consider the elements that do define special education: the goals and content of teaching and the strategies or techniques that are used.

A major issue with specific implications for early childhood is the basis of the curriculum to be followed in teaching exceptional students. For many years, the dominant view was that the curriculum should be based on developmental concepts; that is, learning activities should be sequenced in a manner that parallels the order and schedule by which learning accomplishments occur in the process of normal child development. Major considerations for determining *what* to teach were: the developmental level a child had attained; and what developmental theories, age-scales, or even simply beliefs dictated ought to be next in order of difficulty.

However, what may at first seem an obvious guide and set of principles is not without problems. Indeed, the developmental curriculum orientation has been the subject of much controversy in special education. The difficulty special educators have with the developmental orientation lies in four related areas: (1) the assumption of normality; (2) the issue of age-appropiateness; (3) the issue of functionality; and (4) the problem of readiness.

The *assumption of normality* reflects the fact that the major theories and normative descriptions of children's physical and psychological development are based on children who are physically and psychologically intact, typical, or "normal." Indeed, we speak of age norms and normative scales and in many ways stress that the frame of reference is the sequence of stages, milestones, and skills that children normally follow. Developmental assessment measures are called developmental *schedules:* children's progress in any particular domain of development, such as language or motor skills, is described based on age-equivalence. "Mental age," "social age," and "language age" are measurement indices derived from age-normed scales. Problems with an age-normed model are: (1) it is based on evaluative tools standardized with nonhandicapped, rather than handicapped children; (2) it does not account for possible qualitative differences in how children with specific disabilities accomplish developmental milestones, compared to typical children; and (3) it may lead to erroneous and limiting descriptions of a child's current status and likely future accomplishments, since specific skills may be masked by overall depressed scores due to a sensory, communication, mobility, or coordination difficulty.

The *problem of age-appropriateness* follows, in that, if a person "scores" on some measure at the level of age one, three, five, etc., but is chronologically older, we may assume that the individual should be given tasks typically associated with the age level implied by the test score, based on the belief that, in a sequential pattern of development, children must first master certain skills before encountering more advanced ones. Thus, older students and adults have been given unmotivating, unrewarding, and stigmatizing tasks because they are assumed to function at the level of a younger child. In reality, performance of many tasks appropriate to their chronological age is quite attainable.

The *issue of functionality* defines the essential difference in viewpoint concerning what is to be taught. Those who advocate teaching functional skills, rather than skills that, in themselves, have no demonstrable function, are clearly dominant in special education today. The older the handicapped student, the greater may be the discrepancy between what the student needs to be able to do and what the developmental model may imply the student is "ready" to do. The functional orientation involves identifying skills actually needed to function within present and future environments and teaching those skills. Numerous effective demonstrations have provided convincing evidence that even severely handicapped persons, if effectively taught, can learn skills required to do significant work, maintain friendships, and function generally much more competently than their scores on age-normed measures would suggest (e.g., Brown et al., 1979; Gold, 1980). Functionality has been most effectively and urgently addressed concerning students with severe handicaps, but it has influenced practice in special education generally. Therefore, although the mainstream teacher is more likely to work with children within the context of the typical curriculum, the concept of functional skills is explained here as an important issue in special education curriculum.

The *problem of readiness* is indeed a problem if it reflects maturationist and age-equivalency assumptions. For young children, a totally maturationist (rather than interactionist) view of readiness would actually *prevent* many children from becoming "ready," since it would suggest delaying instruction, rather than providing it. A fundamental tenet of special education practice is that "readiness" is a thing to be taught, not a thing to be awaited.

Learning from the Severely Handicapped

Prior to the present strong emphasis on a functional approach, special educators generally identified learning objectives on the basis of standard curricula but assumed that learning would be more slowly paced. However, they realized that certain areas of the curriculum would be inappropriate to the needs of some students, especially those with severe handicaps. With these students, attention was focused on preacademic or readiness skills. Although precise, systematic instructional methods were suggested (e.g., Bricker, 1976; Snell, 1983), the *content* of instruction was drawn from normative sequences of children's development and the typical progression in successive mastery of skills and concepts. For example, Cohen, Gross, and Haring (1976) developed a system of "developmental pinpoints" to provide for sequencing instruction. Instruction was seen as a process of guiding students (irrespective of age) through successive developmental stages in a specified sequence corresponding to the skills acquired by typical children.

Despite the apparent reasonableness of this approach, there are disadvantages. Even if a severely handicapped student could ultimately progress through an entire developmental sequence, the rate of progress might make completion impossible during the period when the student is served by the school. The result of rigid adherence to such a model would be, in a great many instances, adults confined by skills inappropriate to their chronological ages, as well as age-inappropriate expectations and demands (Wolfensberger, 1980). Although a hierarchical structure of prerequisite concepts and skills is assumed under this model, it is really not known which of these skills are in fact essential. As presumed prerequisites receive attention, skills required for ultimate functioning in the society may be postponed indefinitely (Baumgart et al., 1982).

The alternative, functional approach to curriculum development and task selection grew in part from successful demonstrations of the application of behavior analysis procedures in teaching individuals with severe handicaps, many of whom had been believed incapable of learning. These provided demonstrations of the feasibility of the *zero-exclusion* mandate of P.L. 94–142, since they showed that even the most severely handicapped student could learn if provided appropriate and systematic instruction. However, behavioral procedures do not define the content, or *what* is to be learned; rather, they suggest the *how*. The functional approach extends the behavioral orientation by addressing the content of instruction. Important principles for identifying what is to be taught derive from a future orientation: what will the student need to be able to do to function as independently as possible as an adult? This is generally referred to as the *criterion of ultimate function* (Brown et al., 1976).

A procedure used to determine what skills the individual needs to learn is the *ecological inventory* (Brown et al., 1979), useful not only for school and work, but also for recreation and leisure contexts (Ford et al., 1984). Targets for instruction are selected by analyzing environments in which the person will need to function. Next, discrepancies between the student's present skills and those required by the environments are identified. Then, these specific skills are taught, whether or not they might be considered part of a "typical" developmental sequence or of their placement within that sequence. The need for "prerequisite" or readiness skills is not assumed.

Nonetheless, especially when working with young children with handicaps, functional approaches can be integrated within a developmental framework (e.g., Bricker, Macke, Levin, & Campbell, 1981; McCormick & Noonan, 1984). Such integration providing for the needs of individual children, both typical and handicapped, would appear essential within a mainstream early childhood setting.

SPECIAL EDUCATION: IN SUMMARY

The essential element of special education is individualized teaching (Strain, 1988). Although for the vast majority of students with handicaps, the standard curriculum and typical modes of teaching (adapted as indicated by the needs of individual students) provide the basic framework for instruction, insights gained from work with those who pose the greatest instructional challenge—students with severe handicaps—are useful in understanding similarities and differences between regular early childhood and special education. Since the zero-exclusion mandate associated with P.L. 94–142, a scientifically based set of concepts and procedures for systematic instruction (Snell, 1983) has emerged. Attention has focused upon identifying best practices in teaching students at all age levels, including effecting positive transition to adult living and vocational skills. Age-appropriateness has been identified as among the most important elements, with respect to the nature of the task, the setting in which it is learned, the materials used, and other considerations (Brown et al., 1979). A closely related issue is the functional utility of the skills to be taught, and the potential for generalization of those skills in various environments in which the student will need to function. There is evidence (Hunt, Goetz, & Anderson, 1986) that "best practice" considerations such as these are more likely to be reflected in the IEPs of severely handicapped students served in integrated, rather than segregated school settings. That does not necessarily mean placement within the mainstream classroom for students for whom that is not instructionally appropriate, but it does require location of special classrooms within the regular school. For those children with handicaps—the majority—for whom the mainstream curriculum and typical modes of instruction are appropriate, concepts, principles, and strategies derived from special education can be integrated after determining individual strengths and needs of each child.

The late Dr. Burton Blatt (1977) expressed the real contribution of special education, historically and today, as the application in practice of a set of fundamental values and beliefs:

> The promise of special education was not a special curriculum, or special methods, or even special teachers. It was to demonstrate that each person can contribute to the larger society, that all people are valuable, that a human being is entitled to developmental opportunities, and that development is plastic. The gifts that this movement was to bestow were optimism and belief in the human ethos, charity and love for our brothers, and the conviction that our work is not to judge who can or cannot change, but rather to fulfill the hope that all people can change; each person can learn. (p. 6)

EARLY CHILDHOOD EDUCATION AND SPECIAL EDUCATION

Peterson (1987) describes early education for young handicapped children as a blend of special education, early childhood education, and compensatory education, each of which has its own unique philosophical traditions and distinct methodology. Although parent involvement is important in all three fields, it may have a somewhat different character in each. In early education for handicapped children, parent involvement is perhaps most comprehensive. As Peterson asserts, early childhood special education ". . . is unique in its extensive options and alternative ways for assuring parental involvement in the child's intervention program" (p. 85). This area is pursued in Chapter 12 of this book.

Early childhood education and special education, despite philosophical similarities, also reflect differences, some of which may be quite basic. Both emphasize the value and worth of the individual child, and in both fields the optimal development of the individual child is the major goal. On the other hand, the nature of the program designed to meet that goal is often quite different for children who are physically intact and whose social, emotional, communicative, and conceptual development are within "normal" limits than for children for whom that is not the case. Some authors (e.g., Kaufman, 1980) have seen in such differences a basic incompatibility between the "two worlds" of early childhood and special education. Mowder and Widerstrom (1986) identified what they saw as distinctly different perspectives:

> Early childhood educators hold the belief that a child-directed and child-oriented curriculum is crucial, that group activities are highly beneficial, and that firm teacher control of the classroom is unnecessary. Special educators, in contrast, tend to adopt a deficit model on which to base goal development. This model leads to a teacher-directed curriculum, an emphasis on individualistic learning, and a high degree of teacher control in the classroom. (p. 173)

Discussions among teachers experienced in the two areas also reveal frequent differences in perspective, and certainly in terminology, understandable in light of inherent philosophical differences and different historical traditions (Kaufman, 1980). Special education has roots in the field of medicine, and many of its pioneer figures, such as Itard, Seguin, and Howe were themselves physicians. The "medical model" tradition is reflected even today in the use of such terms as *diagnostic teaching, educational prescriptions,* and the like (Kaufman, 1980; Safford, 1983). Early childhood educators, in contrast, are not likely to refer to "diagnoses," "prognoses," or "prescriptions" in talking about the children they teach. They do not view their children as "sick" or as manifesting "deficits" that need to be "remediated" or "compensated." Consequently, teachers view their role in a different way.

One obvious difference in how teaching is conceptualized is in the area of precision and systematic instruction, characterized by objective observation, measurement of observable behavior, manipulation of environmental variables under the teacher's control, and measurement of the behavior in question to determine its response to the environmental manipulation. Widerstrom (1986) argues for greater recognition that *young* children, handicapped and nonhandicapped, have more in common than do young and older handicapped children. In her view, early childhood programs should reflect that reality. This suggests that good standard early education practices are frequently more appropriate for young children with special needs than some of the diagnostic/prescriptive practices typically applied with older handicapped students.

Differences can also be observed in the physical classroom environment. In typical preschool and kindergarten settings, classroom arrangement and provisioning is extremely important; in some specific approaches such as Montessori, the environment and instrumental materials within it are central to the program's philosophy. Classroom arrangement is also accorded an important role by Piagetians, since it is children's interaction with the environment that enables them to construct knowledge.

In early intervention settings strongly influenced by behavorial principles, environment is also centrally important, but that importance is reflected differently. In a comparison of early intervention and typical preschool environments, Bailey Clifford & Harms (1982) found similarities, but also identified several standard elements that were frequently lacking in the special programs. These included furnishings for relaxation and comfort, child-related display, a dramatic play area, areas for sand and water play, areas for free play, and space for children to be alone if they so chose. Not every early intervention classroom lacked such provisions, of course, but the study did reveal apparent discrepancies between the "typical" and the "special" classroom in these respects. Whatever other positive benefits were provided in the early intervention settings, features considered important in regular early childhood classrooms were not nearly as likely to be present. Yet these features, the researchers believed, were appropriate for all young children. "Deficiencies in environments," they argued, "are difficult to justify based on the argument that handicapped children require something different in the absence of supporting data" (p. 98).

From the reverse perspective, what elements of programs provided for young children with handicaps could profitably be integrated within typical programs for young children? That is the area specifically addressed in Parts II and III of this book. As described in previous sections of this chapter, certain pioneers in early childhood education, such as Susan Isaacs, the MacMillan sisters, and Maria Montessori, specifically addressed special needs of young children, and Montessori developed a general approach, applicable to all children, directly from her work with those with special needs. Some excellent nursery schools were conceived as therapeutic programs or were at least strongly influenced by child psychoanalytic insights (e.g., Furman & Katan, 1969). Some leaders in early childhood special education, such as Dr. Bettye Caldwell, have had similar influence and leadership in general early childhood education. In this text, the position is taken that the two fields are actually not necessarily that different and what differences there are can be resolved. What is advocated is an integrated approach, suited to the diversity among young children, but also to the uniqueness of early childhood itself.

INTEGRATED TEACHING APPROACHES
IN EARLY CHILDHOOD EDUCATION

Teaching that successfully integrates young "exceptional" and "typical" children generally also integrates the two approaches—early childhood education and special education. This integration leads to an interactional or *transactional* view of young children's learning, in contrast to either a strictly maturationist or strictly behavioristic conception. The developmental theorist most generally associated with such a view is Piaget, and interestingly both fields have been strongly influenced by Piagetian concepts.

Certainly, the Piagetian influence has been felt in the field of early childhood education. Paradoxically, Piaget's insights focused upon cognitive aspects of development, and formal academic instruction is viewed as reflecting a cognitive emphasis; however, Piagetians view cognitive development as more of an "inside-out" process, governed by natural interests and inclinations of the young child. An academic skills focus fails to sufficiently take into account either the affective nature of young children's learning or how children structure their own learning. Piaget's influence provides a resolution of disparate and conflicting educational philosophies and views of children's learning, according to Spodek (1982), since the child's own mental activity and the learning environment are understood in a transactional, rather than a one-sided, way: "Knowledge is neither simply the accumulation of sensory experiences nor the accumulation of innate ideas but a human creation using sensory data—information resulting from experiences—to create ideas that can be tested against additional experience, discarded, elaborated, modified, or affirmed" (p. 6).

Behavioristic learning theory has been highly influential in special education, in part because of the inherent optimism in such perspectives, stressing the potential of the individual to change in response to the environment and the actions of others—parents, teachers, and therapists, for example. Although behaviorism had been the dominant force in American academic psychology, it has in recent years given way to cognitive theories, as the complexity of human learning has come to be more fully appreciated and better understood (Bell-Gredler, 1986). In particular, cognitive developmental and information processing models have come to the fore. According to a leader in the area of early intervention for children with handicaps (Anastasiow, 1981), "This shift is occurring in social psychology, personality and learning theories, child development, and in preschool education . . . (although) . . . the impact of this trend has not been felt broadly in education but will be in the near future" (p. 277). Near the end of the decade concerning which Dr. Anastasiow made these predictions, the 1980s, there is considerable evidence that he was correct. Cognitive perspectives have been influential in the growth and expansion of the use of microcomputers in schools, for example, and to some extent cognitive perspectives have been associated with concern for "excellence" in education, associated with school reform movements of the 1980s.

Whereas cognitive developmental theories, especially that of Piaget, have been dominant in general early childhood education for some time, that has not been the case in programs for young children with handicaps. Anastasiow (1981), who had earlier noted attempts to meld cognitive and behavioral perspectives (1978), saw this as the trend of the future:

> . . . cognitive learning programs will be used as models for a new generation of early childhood programs. That is, behaviorism (task analysis or applied behavior analysis) will be used as a technology of program construction and implementation while cognitive theories will be used as the theoretical basis to account for

and describe human behavior. Teachers need to understand that handicapped children have more in common with normal children in terms of basic needs than is currently believed, particularly in the areas of emotional development and the need for creative play. . . . In essence the content of the future coursework in special education must be broadly based in child development and learning theory. (pp. 277–278)

Among early pioneering efforts in applying cognitive developmental theory and a research orientation in early intervention programs was the work of Drs. William and Diane Bricker at the Kennedy Center of George Peabody College for Teachers, beginning in the late 1960s and early 1970s. It was possibly the first and best-known attempt to integrate Piagetian insights and applied behavior analysis strategies. It was also among the first major efforts to successfully integrate nonhandicapped peers within a program of early intervention for handicapped, including severely handicapped, infants, toddlers, and preschool age children. They showed that the integration of young handicapped and nonhandicapped children is entirely consistent with the integration of developmental theory and behavioral strategies (Bricker & Bricker, 1976). Their application of key Piagetian concepts associated with the sensorimotor (infancy) period of development, as well as the general transactional perspective of Piaget, was termed the constructive interaction-adaptive approach, later (Bricker et al., 1981), as CAIT—Constructive Adaptation-Interactive Teaching.

Such *cognitive-learning* approaches (Anastasiow, 1978) have attempted to reconcile principles of child development with the differences in developmental patterns characteristic of many young children with handicapping conditions or delays. They reflect the interventive character of special education required by the inability of many handicapped children to progress optimally in the normal course of exposure to their environment with the need to approximate normal developmental experiences in their education.

Teaching, at any level, is always a transactional process if it is effective, and this means that the learner has a central role, for in Piaget's view, to learn is to construct knowledge. But all children do not do this readily without help from adults, such as parents and teachers. It is important to judge accurately what a child is ready to learn at any given time. A cognitive-learning approach suggests a framework for determining possible points of entry in teaching a child and for identifying next steps.

In brief, **a philosophy of integrated teaching asserts the centrality of the role of the young child as an active learner, but implies a very active role for the teacher as well.** In addition to being an arranger and facilitator, a guide and a model, the teacher provides effectively for special needs of young children through selecting from a broad range of *interventions* that are congruent with an underlying developmental philosophy. Parts II and III provide specific examples of methods and procedures for accommodating special needs of young children considered exceptional within the framework of programs that are considered developmentally appropriate for all young children.

In Chapters 5, 6, and 7, children are considered whose interaction with their physical and social environment is affected by an impaired sensory modality (vision or hearing), impaired mobility, and/or by chronic health problems. For these children, aspects of the environment itself can be modified, adaptive materials can be used, and special attention can be given to the child's need to communicate within her or his environment.

Many of the children considered in Chapter 8 have difficulty in acquiring knowledge through *incidental learning,* that is, through the normal course of classroom events. Many also have difficulty *generalizing* learning to other settings and situations. Differing individual needs for practice opportunities, and also differing time requirements, must be considered. Although for children described in this chapter play is a centrally important learning mode, as for all young children, many need specific guidance in how to play. Social skills and effective use of language, both to mediate learning and to communicate with others, represent areas of special need as well. In Chapter 9, guidelines are suggested for ensuring that special needs of intellectually gifted and highly creative young children are addressed, and young children who are both gifted and handicapped are considered.

In Part III, *generic* guidelines for integrated teaching within the mainstream early childhood classroom are suggested. The focus of Chapter 10 is upon strategies for responding to individual needs and for individualized teaching within the context of developmentally appropriate group instruction. Chapter 11 concerns the group setting itself, emphasizing peer interaction, social behavior, and attitudes. The final two chapters, respectively, concern the role of parents and parent-teacher communication and the wide variety of school and community resources that can be accessed and used for effective integrated teaching.

SUMMARY

Although the traditions of early childhood and special education differ in some respects, the development of these fields has converged at certain points in history. Both have been strongly marked by a sense of advocacy for children, both focus upon the individual child, and both have drawn from theory and research in child development. However, differences must be noted as well. One difference frequently noted is use by special educators of *direct instructional approaches,* congruent with a view of education as intervention. To the degree that providing for young children with handicaps within mainstream settings implies the need for more direct instruction than typical children may require, it is essential to adapt such instruction so that it is congruent with developmentally appropriate practices.

Neither extreme behaviorism/empiricism nor extreme maturationism/nativism would appear to satisfy the two basic criteria for developmentally appropriate early childhood education practice: appropriateness to the unique elements of the early childhood period of development, and appropriateness to the differing characteristics and needs of young children. Instead, an *interactionist* approach recognizes the young child as an active learner, underscores the critical role of the environment as it is experienced by the child, and recognizes and values, the individuality of young children. Programs that are developmentally appropriate for young children reflect a philosophical orientation and basic pedagogy capable of accommodating the needs of most young children considered exceptional. They need not become special education settings to do so. At the same time, some of the provisions required to ensure *individual* appropriateness of the program for children with specific handicaps offer the potential to enhance learning experiences for typical children as well.

CHAPTER 4

Why Integration in Early Education Works

Is integration of handicapped and nonhandicapped children in early education settings an effective way to teach? Evidence suggests that it is, but before we turn to that evidence, we should note certain points:

1. *All* early childhood settings, mainstream and special, are in fact "integrated," since all children are different and all classrooms heterogeneous.
2. We do *not* assume that every young child who is handicapped would appropriately be served in a mainstream classroom.
3. The arguments for integrated teaching come from a variety of different sources—value positions and philosophical beliefs, as well as scientific exploration.
4. Before we explore the effectiveness of integration, we must define "effectiveness" and agree on its meaning.

First, let's imagine a nursery program enrolling, say, ten four-year-olds. To increase the likelihood of similarity among the ten, assume that all the children have passed their fourth birthdays, and that all ten live in comfortable, suburban homes with both their parents (all of whom are in their thirties, with all fathers employed in professional capacities and all mothers college-educated and currently unemployed outside the home). Finally, assume that all the families are

Caucasian, have lived in the same geographic region for some time, and include no other children or family members (such as grandparents) living in the same home.

You are no doubt already smiling at the mythical "homogeneity" of this class. But look more closely. Even a short time spent as an observer in this class would demonstrate to you that the ten children are in fact ten very different individuals, despite their similarities in background. Assuming that the classroom program allows expression of individual traits, behavior patterns, likes and dislikes, special interests, fears, and styles of interacting both with one another and with the classroom materials, you would see an *integrated* group of ten very different individuals. The group would have certain distinct characteristics, determined by the distinctive individual personalities of its members, by the adult leadership, and by the interaction of all the determinants. The point is that no matter how we construct a hypothetical class, making it absolutely homogeneous is simply impossible.

Although several of the examples of mainstreamed handicapped children presented throughout this book involve moving *from* a special *to* a regular class setting, many children begin their schooling within regular settings and can be consistently maintained there. Mainstreaming does not always involve a change in placement. Further, we should not assume that mainstreaming can be considered only after a child's special needs have been "remediated," since in most instances, those needs will continue and many children will continue to need special services. These may be provided within the regular classroom, may be supplemental to the child's full participation in regular education, or may comprise a part of the child's schedule, so that mainstreaming is partial.

We have seen that the basis for mainstreaming comes from diverse sources (Bricker, 1978). Although we need to document the effectiveness of integrated arrangements (as we do all educational practices), principles of nondiscrimination and equal access, respect for and valuing of human diversity, and recognition of the inherent worth of each child transcend many other issues. Academic benefits to both handicapped and typical children should be *at least as great* in integrated settings; however, we do not need to document that integrated learning arrangements lead to *greater* educational gains than segregated ones.

In summary, every learning group is highly diverse, and each member brings to that group setting the unique blend of characteristics that defines every individual human being. For some members of any group of young children, some of these individual characteristics may be associated with a handicapping condition. The teacher's concern is to respond effectively and appropriately to the uniqueness of every young child in ways that nurture each child's development and learning.

Early childhood education of good quality is considered potentially important for all young children, but it is of critical concern for the young child with special needs. Effective early intervention can make very significant differences in the lives of young children who are handicapped or at risk. Without the opportunity to participate in good early childhood programs, many children of low income families and children with disabilities would be deprived of services demonstrated to be effective in optimizing their development and their access to the mainstream of society. These programs benefit children indirectly as well as directly, through attention to parents and other family members. We should review briefly the evidence for that assertion before returning to the issue of how to integrate the goals of early intervention with the goals of early education for all young children.

EFFICACY OF EARLY INTERVENTION FOR CHILDREN AT ENVIRONMENTAL RISK

Much interest in the possibility of breaking the poverty cycle and preventing school failure in young disadvantaged children developed during the 1960s. The scientific basis for this interest was closely related to changing views about human intelligence, influenced particularly by the publication of *Intelligence and Experience* by J. McV. Hunt (1961). The Civil Rights movement was clearly influential in creating the *zeitgeist* for the War on Poverty and associated federal initiatives, most notably Project Head Start.

Head Start was initiated in the summer of 1965, the culmination of previous demonstration efforts by a few pioneering projects, undertaken in both urban settings and the rural South. An important early example of the latter was the DARCEE Project, undertaken to determine whether the progressive educational retardation observed in children of deprived circumstances could be offset. The term *cumulative deficit* had been coined by Deutsch (1965) to describe the widening gap that these interventionists sought to prevent. Intervention provided through the DARCEE Project produced gains but these then leveled off and declined once intervention ceased. The project leaders (Gray & Klaus, 1970) concluded that a preschool intervention program alone may be insufficient to offset progressive educational retardation. In order to have lasting effects, they believed, intervention needed to be both comprehensive and continuing.

The impact of Project Head Start upon the development of children from low-income families was initially difficult to evaluate, especially in light of the high hopes with which it began. Some disillusionment resulted when a Westinghouse Learning Corporation evaluation (Cicerelli et al., 1969) reported that IQ gains made by participating children were eroded by about the third grade. Reaction to this disappointing finding, similar to that of Gray and Klaus, was summarized by another pioneer, Dr. Merle Karnes (1973), who stated that "There is general agreement that one year is not sufficient to stabilize gains" (p. 62).

Although support for the concept of early intervention was momentarily jeopardized, this did not curtail studies to determine whether *continuing* efforts (through Project Follow Through), as well as *earlier* and *more comprehensive* approaches (Project Home Start, Parent-Child Centers, etc.) could achieve more lasting results. Additionally, more searching analyses of what did occur through the Head Start effort were initiated. In particular, the almost exclusive focus upon IQ was criticized, especially in view of the very positive reports from individual programs. In an important book edited by Edward Zigler and Jeannette Valentine (1979), a number of authors described positive outcomes for participating children, in terms of physical, social, and emotional development, as well as for their families. Such outcomes are not necessarily reflected in scores on IQ tests.

Additionally, carefully controlled early intervention efficacy studies focused upon more meaningful indices of impact. Important among these was a longitudinal study of the effectiveness of the Perry Preschool Project in Ypsilanti, Michigan, reported by Schweinhart and Weikart (1980). This study demonstrated that compensatory intervention during the preschool years resulted in higher academic performance in school, lower delinquency rates, and better prospects for earnings for disadvantaged children who participated, compared to a control group who did not. Specifically by age 15, preschool participants were at least one grade ahead of the control group on the average, scored higher on reading, mathematics, and language achievement tests at every grade level, displayed less antisocial behavior in school, and were more likely to hold after-school jobs as teenagers. In summary, they found that:

> Two out of three preschool participants graduated from high school, compared to one out of two in the control group.
> At age 19, 61 percent of the preschool participants, compared to 38 percent of controls, scored average or above average on a test of functional competence.
> The rate of enrollment in post-secondary education was nearly double the rate for control students.
> On the average, preschool participants required special education class placement for two years, compared to three years, six months for controls.
> The detention and arrest rate for participants was 31 percent, compared to a 51 percent rate for controls.
> Teenage pregnancy occurred at a rate about half that for controls.
> At age 19, 50 percent of the participants were employed, compared to 32 percent of the controls.
> Only 18 percent of the participants reported that they were currently receiving welfare assistance, compared to 32 percent of the controls.

Schweinhart and Weikart (1980) summarized cost benefits of the program, demonstrating that the financial investment required for preschool intervention resulted in cost savings for society. He identified three major types of cost benefits: (1) a substantial portion of the total costs were recovered from savings that resulted because students who participated in the preschool program required less costly forms of education as they progressed through school; (2) preschool participants had higher projected lifetime earnings; and (3) the value of parents' time released as a result of the child's attending preschool was considered an economic benefit.

A later cost-benefit analysis, conducted when the students had reached age 19 and were out of school (Schweinhart & Weikart, 1986a) showed that: (1) the return on the initial investment was equal to three and one-half times the cost of two years of preschool and seven times the cost of one year of preschool; (2) major benefits were reduced costs of education and increased actual, as well as predicted, earnings; and (3) other benefits included decreased costs associated with delinquency, crime, and welfare assistance.

In addition to the longitudinal study of the Perry preschool program, two other in-depth, longitudinal studies reviewed the data from early model programs and reached more positive conclusions concerning the effectiveness of early intervention with disadvantaged children. Urie Bronfenbrenner (1974), reviewing data from 12 original model programs, again found that, almost without exception, children showed substantial IQ gains initially; however, regression occurred after they entered school. The decline was most severe for children who came from the most deprived social and economic backgrounds. Disadvantaged children living in most favorable circumstances appeared to maintain their gains.

Very importantly, however, Bronfenbrenner highlighted the role of parent involvement in the intervention process. He found that in the intervention programs that emphasized parent-child interaction, substantial gains were still evident for several years after the program terminated. Additionally, parent-focused intervention benefited siblings, as well as the target child, while also enhancing the self-esteem of parents who were involved. Zigler and Seitz (1980) viewed these gains in the area of social competence as being of more overall significance than increases in the children's measured intelligence.

The other important report was that of the Consortium for Longitudinal Studies (Lazar & Darlington, 1979), summarizing results of a comprehensive long-term follow-up of the graduates of 12 early intervention projects. The investigators used the original data, obtained when the children were enrolled in the respective programs. They also located the children during the 1976–77 school year and compared their status to that of control group members. Results showed that early education significantly reduced the number of children placed in special education classes and retained in grade. Children who had received preschool intervention scored significantly higher on achievement tests in math and reading as well. Contrary to the results of previous studies, children's IQ gains tended to be maintained, in some projects long after the program ended. Lazar and Darlington concluded that early intervention produced lasting positive effects and that it was cost-effective, as compared to later special placement or remediation.

The impact of the evaluation research carried out by the Consortium for Longitudinal Studies (Lazar, Darlington, Murray, et al., 1982) has been described as representing a "victory" for children and for the child development profession (Brown, 1985). But even more importantly, according to Brown (1985, p. 13), the results represent ". . . a victory for a compassionate and caring nation which has given the world a new standard of social progress. [The success of early intervention] stands as a tribute to a nation which is socially creative, optimistic, and dares to solve its problems."

Evaluation research concerning Head Start continues to reveal some unevenness and inconsistency in results, but overall there is clear evidence of effectiveness in achieving its goals (McKey et al., 1985). Therefore, Lawrence Schweinhart and David Weikart (1986b), principal spokespersons for early childhood programs for children at environmental risk, summarize the evidence to date:

> Good preschool programs for children at risk for school failure *do* better prepare them for school both intellectually and socially, *probably* help them to achieve greater school success, and *can* lead them to greater life success in adolescence and adulthood. (p. 54)

EFFICACY OF EARLY INTERVENTION FOR HANDICAPPED CHILDREN

There are two issues in the evaluation of early intervention programs for preschool-age children and special education. First, can early childhood programs reduce the impact of handicapping or at-risk conditions on later learning and personal-social development? In this section, we will review evidence that, for children who have identified, biologically based handicapping conditions, such programs *can* improve adaptive abilities and prevent secondary problems. Second, can early intervention prevent the need for subsequent special placement or other special services? Many children of economically disadvantaged families experience difficulties in school and many are labeled "mildly mentally retarded" or "slow learner" and placed in special classes. To what extent does early intervention work as a *preventive* strategy, to keep children from being labeled and assigned to special education programs?

Subsequent school placement has become a key measure of effectiveness in evaluating early intervention programs for young children at environmental risk (Schweinhart, 1986a; 1986b; Lazar & Darlington, 1979). The longitudinal research projects described above provide solid documentation that children who participate in good preschool programs are significantly less likely to require subsequent special education placement (Reynolds, Egan, & Lerner, 1983). Early intervention, then, *can* enable children who are at environmental risk for school failure to participate in the educational mainstream.

Evidence also suggests that early intervention for children who have *identi-*

fied handicapping conditions (that is, who are at *established risk*) can increase significantly the likelihood of subsequent mainstream participation. In a study of more than 2,700 handicapped children in Washington and Colorado who had participated in preschool programs, Eugene Edgar and his associates found that about a third of the mildly handicapped students from one state and about two-thirds from the other state went on to participate in regular class placements, with or without supplemental aids and services (Edgar, McNulty, Gaetz, & Maddox, 1984). Although the percentages were somewhat smaller for severely handicapped students, and those with severe handicaps were more likely to be placed in separate special classes for most or all of their schooling, some severely handicapped children were placed in regular or mainstream classrooms, usually with supportive assistance. The findings for both mildly and severely handicapped children provide evidence of the significant role of preschool intervention in preventing, for many of these children, the need for special education placement.

Although most of the efficacy evidence is relatively recent, two early studies were highly influential. Indeed, the research of Skeels and Dye (1939) changed beliefs about human intelligence itself! They placed an experimental group of orphans in cottages at a state school for the mentally retarded, where they received individual stimulation from the adult residents as well as from a half-day preschool program. A control group remained in the nonstimulating environment typical of orphanages at that time. After two years, the treatment group showed an average IQ gain of 27.5 points, while the initially higher IQ controls showed a *loss* of 26.2 points. Long-term follow-up of the children as adults (Skeels, 1966) revealed that the treatment group members had maintained these gains and were all self-supporting. Most control group members remained wards of the state or worked as unskilled laborers, with an average level of educational attainment of third grade.

The other pioneer study (Kirk, 1958), although less dramatic in its results, also provided convincing evidence of the effectiveness of early intervention for children identified as mentally retarded. Eighty-one children with IQs ranging from 45 to 80 were assigned to two intervention conditions and respectively matched control (no intervention) groups. Both preschool intervention groups (community-based and institution-based) made significant gains on measures of intellectual and social functioning, compared to their controls. These gains were maintained up to five years later, when follow-up testing was done. Since these two early studies, the results of numerous early intervention programs (e.g., Bricker & Bricker, 1971, 1972; Hayden, Morris, & Bailey, 1977; Heber & Garber, 1975) have been reported. Generally, findings have consistently documented the effectiveness of preschool intervention efforts with handicapped children.

As was noted earlier, many of these programs have been supported by federal funding, through the Handicapped Children's Early Education Program (HCEEP). An efficacy study of 40 of these programs, undertaken in 1972, resulted in the overall conclusion that ". . . educational programs for preschool handicapped children—whether they be infants or five-year-olds—can significantly improve the quality of the children's lives" (Stedman, 1977, p. 1). Results of a national evaluation study of 32 First Chance Programs, conducted in 1973, revealed that about two-thirds of the participating children were subsequently mainstreamed, compared to one-third in special education placement. Children's gains were one and a half times to twice what would have been predicted without early intervention, and positive changes in children were reported by 97 percent of the parents (Stock et al., 1976).

More than 200 First Chance Programs have been funded by HCEEP, and efforts have been made to determine which models demonstrated sufficient evidence of effectiveness to warrant replication. Seven programs were selected by a Joint Dissemination Review Panel of the U.S. Office of Education (now the U.S. Department of Education.) These seven models represent a variety of approaches demonstrated to be effective with diverse groups of handicapped children (Karnes, 1977). Ultimately, 21 projects approved by the Joint Dissemination Review Panel were analyzed, with further confirmation of their effectiveness (White, Mastropieri, & Casto, 1984).

About the evidence of efficacy of HCEEP-funded programs, former Director Jane DeWeerd (1977, p. 3) asserted that these programs were clearly ". . . reducing the number of children who will need intensive or long-term help." Alice Hayden (1977), a leader in the development of programs for early intervention for handicapped children, added comments suggesting necessary ingredients of effective programs:

> We do know that probably the most effective means of dealing with . . . handicapping conditions at present is through first-rate interdisciplinary, developmentally based programs that provide opportunities to work with these children and their families through early and continuous intervention (Hayden, 1977, p. 34.)

Hayden and her associates are in fact responsible for one of the best known reports of effective early intervention, based on the University of Washington Early Intervention Program for Down Syndrome Children (Hayden & Dmitriev, 1975; Hayden & Haring, 1976, 1977). Children who participated in this program approached developmental norms following intervention and maintained their gains several years later, continuing to progress rather than demonstrating the later declines frequently reported for children with Down syndrome. The success of this model carried over into the outreach phase, when it was replicated in other sites (Oelwein, Fewell, & Pruess, 1985).

Similar results have been found in other early intervention programs for Down syndrome children. For example, Clunies-Ross (1979) reported the effectiveness of intervention begun when children were 3 to 37 months old. The development of all participants was reported to have been accelerated, with attainments at and even above normal levels in some instances. Bricker and Dow (1980) showed that infants who were more severely handicapped could also benefit from early intervention. The 50 children studied showed significant gains in the *Uniform Performance Assessment System* (UPASS), and 88 percent of these children were subsequently placed in public school programs, rather than totally segregated ones.

Children who participated in the Carolina Abecedarian Project, an early intervention program for at-risk and developmentally-delayed children under age five, maintained their significant gains throughout the elementary grades. Their performance, following participation in this program which emphasized cognitive, linguistic, and social areas, was substantially superior to that of a control group, and at or near age norms (Ramey & Campbell, 1984; Ramey & Haskins, 1981).

Polloway (1987) summarized the major points relative to effective early intervention practices as follows:

1. Curricular models which stress cognitive or academic instruction and objectives have been associated with the most significant increases in intellectual functioning.
2. Programs found most successful tend to be structured with detailed outcome objectives tied to a specified plan of learning sequences.
3. The concept of "critical periods" of development has failed to receive consistent support in the literature. Nevertheless, programs which focus on younger children (e.g., 2–3 year olds) have a number of advantages over those geared to older children (e.g., 4–5 year olds.)
4. Home intervention efforts are most helpful as complements to short term preschool programs although there are equivocal findings regarding the degree of effectiveness of specific parent involvement components.
5. Since time is an important variable, the intensity of the program should be such that activities are selected and implemented based on their maximum contribution to a child's learning.
6. Programs of longer duration are justified because children continue to progress beyond the initial year of programming. Limited intervention efforts cannot be presumed to result in long term behavioral change.
7. School programs should be modified to capitalize on the skills that children who have benefited from quality programs bring to the classroom setting.
8. Programs are most appropriately evaluated by, for example. measures of academic and communication skills acquisition and the ability to cope with subsequent environments, rather than by IQ gains. The former are not only responsive to intervention but also more relevant to subsequent school performance. (p. 15)

We cannot assume that all early intervention programs are equally effective. Different programs are no doubt effective in different ways. Typically, those programs that have well-articulated goals and a clear philosophy are more likely to be effective. Strain (1986) has identified the following attributes in programs that produce long-lasting benefits:

1. *Timeliness*—responding to problems as they arise, rather than delaying intervention beyond the time when it might be maximally beneficial.
2. *Comprehensiveness*—responding to the needs of family as well as child.
3. *Normalization*—teaching children skills they will need in order to function successfully in future regular class settings, by enabling them to practice those skills in environments as much like those future settings as possible.
4. *Intensiveness*—devoting more time proportionally to actual instruction. (Research findings relating to the importance of "time-on-task" in early intervention are paralleled, interestingly, in general education. We are not referring to the length of time a child is enrolled in a program or the number of hours or days the program is in session, but rather to the amount of *planned teaching and learning* that is actually occurring. Unfortunately, both in regular and special education, the children who need the most often get the least.)
5. *Integration*—enhancing the social awareness and skills of both handicapped and nonhandicapped children by allowing them to share common educational experiences.

The stress on experiences with non-handicapped children in settings either in the mainstream or approximating the mainstream returns us to the question of how to most successfully provide these.

WHAT DO WE MEAN BY EFFECTIVENESS OF INTEGRATION?

There are two basic points that derive from legal and social-philosophical principles that must be made prior to considering what is meant by effectiveness of integrated approaches:

1. The educational placement of a handicapped child outside the regular classroom would have to be justified by compelling evidence that such placement is appropriate, rather than the reverse.
2. An educational setting that does not provide for at least some degree of integration of handicapped and nonhandicapped children can *never* be considered appropriate:

The least restrictive mandate of P.L. 94–142 can only be interpreted as being fulfilled if the programming is conducted in an integrated setting. The degree and type of integration needs to be individually determined for each young handicapped child, but whether integration is provided does not. (Vincent et al., 1981, p. 23.)

This means that educational integration of handicapped and nonhandicapped children does not have to be defended on the basis of research evidence that it "works"—just as integration on the basis of race requires no such support. The contributions of research and evaluation relate to the *how* of integration, not to *whether* we should have it or not. The real question about integration is not whether it works, but how to make it work optimally. In the words of Douglas Biklen (1985, p. 3), "It is a moral question. It is a goal, indeed a value, we decide to pursue or reject on the basis of what we want our society to look like." In terms of public policy, that decision has been made.

Dr. Vincent and her colleagues summarize the issues relating to research and practice with respect to integration in early childhood as follows:

> While certainly more research needs to be conducted which analyzes how to make integrated programs maximally beneficial to both handicapped and typical children, the current definition of best educational practice must be that integrated programming is always the first choice. Such programs have been shown to result in equal if not greater skill gain for the handicapped students involved than segregated programs. Even severely handicapped children have been shown to benefit from integrated experiences, although they need only to be shown not to be harmed to justify such programming. Philosophically, integrated programs come close to exemplifying the principle of normalization. They provide opportunities for both parents and children to acquire positive information and knowledge about handicapping conditions. They maximize the possibility that young handicapped children will be recognized to be normal in some areas of development and that this similarity between handicapped and typical children will be highlighted. (Vincent et al., 1981, p. 23.)

In general, research has established that young handicapped children progress cognitively and socially at least as well in integrated educational settings as in settings that are segregated. However, many studies demonstrate that, when interactions between handicapped and nonhandicapped children are systematically structured, cognitive as well as social gains for the handicapped child are significantly greater than in settings where there is no opportunity for peer modeling of more competent behavior to occur.

In integrated settings, then, young handicapped children can potentially experience benefits that are simply not available in separate programs. Guralnik (1976 p. 237) has especially emphasized the benefits gained from observing and interacting with more advanced peers. In order to describe how potentially important this aspect can actually be, he cited an early report of the pioneering work done by William and Diane Bricker (1971).

The ways in which a non-delayed child plays with toys and other objects in the classroom and playground provide greater variation in the types of activity available than that provided by the more limited repertoires of the delayed youngsters. This modeling of object-relevant play may provide a better instructional medium than a teacher demonstrating the same activity directly, since both approximations to relevant use and greater variations in the use of objects are evident in the play behavior of the non-delayed child. (pp. 3–4)

Vincent and her colleagues (1981) note that there is an ample research base demonstrating ". . . that children learn through observing, practicing, and modeling the more competent behaviors of their peers" (p. 21). Therefore, we need to ask how *typical* children will benefit from an integrated setting, and "a simple answer would be [from] the more competent or appropriate behavior shown by the student's handicapped peers" (Vincent et al., 1981, p. 21). This is a most important, and frequently overlooked, consideration. Many people tend to expect *generalized* limitations in children with disabilities, but most handicapped children are not delayed in all developmental areas. In fact, many children with handicapping conditions demonstrate *superior* performance in some or even all other areas. All children have a contribution to make that can benefit their peers.

Even children whose disabilities are severe and multiple, resulting in delays in communication as well as motor, cognitive, social, and self-care skills, can make positive contributions. The modeling effect does not work to the disadvantage or detriment of children from the standpoint of more advanced or more competent young children acquiring *less* adapative or appropriate behavior (Bricker & Bricker, 1972).

Opportunities for meaningful, personalized interaction between typical children and handicapped peers offers the potential for positively altering general societal attitudes toward persons with disabilities. For example, Voeltz (1980) demonstrated that contact with severely handicapped students resulted in improved attitudes on the part of their nonhandicapped peers, who developed more realistic perceptions of the abilities of students with severe handicaps through opportunities for interaction in a school setting.

QUESTIONS FREQUENTLY RAISED
ABOUT INTEGRATION EFFECTS

Teachers, as well as parents, have expressed understandable concerns about integration and mainstreaming at all educational levels. What research says to teachers of young children, specifically, is organized around the three basic concerns: personal-social development of young handicapped children, personal-social development of young nonhandicapped children, and cognitive learning and skill development of both.

Will Handicapped Children Be Ostracized because of Their Differences?

Children, especially young children, do tend to be curious, but they are usually not critical or judgmental. They might have questions about why another child uses a walker or a wheel chair, or otherwise appears different. A good early childhood classroom or center is one in which children are able to ask questions about things they wonder about and feel safe in doing so. Their questions should be encouraged, and they should be answered honestly and directly, as well as positively.

Teachers should be aware of the great influence of their own attitudes in communicating with children and in the models they present in this area as in any other. If the teacher demonstrates openness, security, and confidence in relationship to a young child with a disability, children are likely to respond accordingly.

There is some evidence (e.g., Guralnick, 1981) that physical attractiveness is initially influential in the acceptance of a young handicapped child by peers. Young children may also at first have fears that they will "catch" the disability, and they need to feel that it is all right to ask about them. Since such fears may not be consciously recognized, the nature of a child's disability and how it came about should be explained directly.

In general, a child's *disability* does not cause her or him to be ostracized or avoided. Peer acceptance and social interaction are influenced by the child's *social and communication skills* (Gresham, 1982), as well as other factors *indirectly related* to a handicapping condition. We need to remember that many of those indirectly related factors are things the teacher can influence significantly or even control; they are not necessarily intrinsic to the child.

Young typical children and their peers with severe handicaps may not automatically play together (Devoney, Guralnick, & Rubin, 1974). That is initiated by the teacher's structuring of play activities that result in more cooperative play on the part of children with handicaps, not only during the structured play but also during free play.

Will Children Who Are Developmentally Normal Learn Inappropriate Behavior from some of the Children with Handicaps?

The research evidence is very clear on this point: *they will not*. Socially unacceptable or immature behaviors of children with developmental delays or handicapping conditions are *not* adopted by typical children on a lasting basis. Children are more likely to imitate other children (handicapped or nonhandicapped) whose behaviors are more mature, competent, and appropriate. When they do imitate the behavior of children with handicaps, what they imitate is usually appropriate behavior. When imitation of a handicapped child's appropriate behavior occurs, increased social interaction results, since mutually appropriate modeling increases the likelihood that the children will interact with each other (Peck, Apolloni, Cooke, & Raver, 1978; Peterson, Peterson, & Scriven, 1977).

Is It Possible to Meet the Diverse Educational Needs of Both Handicapped and Nonhandicapped Children without some Detriment to Either?

Assuming positive teacher attitude and, consequently, teacher attention to the nature and quality of the social interaction between handicapped and nonhandicapped children in the classroom (Johnson, Johnson, & Rynders, 1981), children's self-esteem can be enhanced, not harmed. Given conditions for effective integration, rather than merely "mixing," research evidence indicates no detrimental effects to either (e.g., Cooke, Ruskus, Peck, & Appolloni, 1981; Hanline, 1985; Ispa & Matz, 1978) in the areas of language, cognitive, motor, perceptual, or social development. Typical children benefit academically to at least the same degree as would be expected had they attended nonintegrated programs (Spodek, Saracho, & Lee, 1984).

For example, Odom, Deklyen and Jenkins (1984) randomly assigned four nonhandicapped four-year-olds to each of four different special programs, so that a total of 16 children were integrated with handicapped peers. Each center enrolled eight children with mild or moderate handicapping conditions, identified as having communication disorders, mental retardation, behavior disorders, and physical disabilities or chronic health problems. Their findings supported the conclusions of earlier research (e.g., Bricker & Bricker, 1972) that even *reverse mainstreaming* to achieve integration has no detrimental effects on the typical children involved.

There is solid and consistent research evidence that young children with handicaps can benefit greatly from the opportunity to interact with typical peers in educational settings. However, we should also stress that mere mixing does not, in itself, result in optimal benefits. Temporal mainstreaming (Kaufmann et al., 1975), or mere physical proximity, is a necessary but not a sufficient condition for both groups to benefit to the extent possible or desirable.

Several approaches have been studied that involve more systematic structuring of the interaction between handicapped and nonhandicapped young children in the classroom or center. Jenkins, Speltz, and Odom (1985) have summarized these as involving three different models:

1. A "cooperative" model (Johnson & Johnson, 1975).
2. A systematic imitation model (Apolloni & Cooke, 1978).
3. A confederate model (Strain, Kerr, & Ragland, 1981).

Each of these has been implemented primarily in special early intervention programs for the most part, rather than in typical preschool, kindergarten, or primary mainstream settings. However, all three have been to some degree employed in the typical program environment, and all suggest specific "strategies that work" that teachers can employ. These possibilities are illustrated in later chapters, and especially in Chapter 11, which focuses upon the group context of early childhood programs.

Jenkins et al. (1985), in the belief that mainstream integration was frequently undertaken using a simple *proximity model,* attempted to replicate the "standard," rather than the optimal situation. They studied the effect of mere exposure to nonhandicapped children upon young children with disabilities when nothing was done systematically to structure their classroom interaction. The purpose was to determine whether, even under those conditions, handicapped children did at least as well as a matched control group of handicapped children enrolled in totally segregated programs designed primarily to provide direct, focused intervention based on careful assessment of their specific needs. Using measures of cognitive, pre-academic, language, and fine motor skills, they found no significant differences between the two groups. Special needs in these critical learning areas were met as effectively in regular settings as in specialized early intervention programs: both groups gained. What was "sacrificed" in the way of direct, structured programming was apparently compensated for by the setting itself. The results of this study also imply that if the possibilities for peer-mediated learning were to be more systematically exploited even greater gains might be possible.

CONDITIONS FOR EFFECTIVE MAINSTREAMING IN EARLY CHILDHOOD PROGRAMS

Research suggests the following conditions for successful mainstreaming:

1. The philosophy of the early childhood program must be comparable with mainstreaming and with including young children who are handicapped (Guralnick, 1976).
2. The handicapped child should be able to contribute to the program, and the program should be able to contribute to the handicapped child (Meisels, 1977).
3. The handicapped child's needs must be compatible with the instruction offered the other children, the teacher must be willing to modify some techniques, and support personnel must cooperate with the teacher (Guralnik, 1982).
4. If transition from one program to another is involved, continuing communication among the professionals concerned is essential (Hutinger, 1981).
5. In order for meaningful social integration to occur, situations need to be structured and arranged by the teacher that enable and facilitate social integration of handicapped and nonhandicapped children (Allen, 1980; Burstein, 1986; Cooke et al., 1981; Guralnick, 1978; Safford & Rosen, 1981).
6. Sufficient time must be allowed for children to learn to interact most effectively and to form relationships (Dunlop, Stoneman, & Cantrell, 1980).

The above does not make specific reference to two important areas, to be addressed in some depth in Chapters 10 and 11: preparation of the handicapped children, and preparation of the typical children. There are some observations concerning handicapped children who are candidates for mainstream placement that are important to make, especially in terms of characteristics that should be expected. What child "qualifications" are indicated? First, we need to recognize that a handicapped child can be a good candidate for inclusion in a typical program even though handicapping conditions are present. This may appear obvious; however, some people believe that only those children whose handicapping conditions have been "remediated" should be mainstreamed. Early beliefs in our ability to "remediate" educational handicaps have been, in many instances, overly optimistic. We no longer hope to effect a "cure" through specialized educational and therapeutic intervention for most disabled children, even if such measures are initiated early in life. Teaching cannot restore sight, hearing, or a missing limb, undo brain damage, or cure disease.

As teachers, we are charged with the responsibility to teach a wide array of children, all presenting unique needs. Some of the differences among children are associated with cultural identity and cultural patterns, others with biologically based characteristics that differentiate them markedly from many of their agemates. The differences are real. It is not the teacher's or therapist's task to eliminate these differences and to produce sameness. Rather, it is our task to gear instruction to the differential needs and strengths of learners, at any age or educational level.

Recognition that mainstreamed children will continue to be handicapped suggests to some authors (e.g., Tawney, 1981; Walker & Hallau, 1981) that mainstreaming be approached with caution. We must ensure that the *teacher* is ready, perhaps even more importantly than the child. Also, needs for appropriate supportive services must be identified and provided for. Specifically, Tawney (1981) identified these concerns: (1) regular teachers' lack of training in how to implement specific techniques appropriate to the needs of young handicapped children; (2) possible negative attitudes toward handicapped individuals on the part of teachers themselves; (3) concerns of the parents of other children; and (4) the difficulties for teachers that are involved in planning instruction to accommodate increased discrepancies in children's skill levels. These are all issues of which we should be aware, not reasons not to proceed. First, special educators may be inclined to underestimate the receptiveness of both parents and regular early childhood teachers, as well as the competence of the latter. Second, concerns about continuing specialized needs of some children can be alleviated because of the support system (Chapter 13) that can be brought to bear. Direct or indirect supportive assistance to the teacher provided by specialists may be, for some young children with handicaps, essential to their successful mainstreaming.

Lerner et al. (1987, p. 129), citing specific areas of concern identified by Zigler and Muenchow (1979), warn of possible "backlash" if mainstreaming is implemented without adequate planning. Specifically, they listed these cautions:

1. Appropriate training for teachers and other personnel who work with handicapped children is needed. In the case of preschool children, this includes volunteers, teachers, and related personnel.
2. Without adequate support personnel to assist regular class teachers with the handicapped, mainstreaming is doomed to failure. This means that preschool teachers, day care teachers, Head Start teachers, and so on need supportive help from special educators for handicapped children in their charge.
3. Mainstreaming should not be viewed as a way to save money. Properly conducted, a mainstream program will cost as much as the self-contained special education classes.
4. Mainstreaming and its evaluation do not take place in a social vacuum. The point here is that, for some children, "normalization" placement in a nonhandicapped setting is the wrong type of placement.

Some educators may attempt to implement a mainstreaming effort without sufficient planning based upon knowledge of the individual needs and characteristics of the children involved. Others, however, may be so cautious that anxieties become heightened and valuable time lapses before action is taken. "The basic principle is that educational placement decisions need to be made about *individual* children. We cannot think appropriately of mainstreaming in an abstract or general way. Additionally, we need to remember that P.L. 94–142, in defining the concept of Least Restrictive Environment, suggests that the *starting point* in examining alternative educational placements for any individual handicapped child is the *regular classroom*. Can the child's special needs be fully and appropriately met there (perhaps with supportive aids and services)? If the determination is that they cannot, then alternatives can appropriately be considered, provided that (1) removal from the classroom is only for specifically identified purposes, and then only for as long as is necessary to meet those purposes; and (2) some provision is made for continued involvement and interaction with nonhandicapped children.

You may have noted that most of the conditions for successful mainstreaming summarized earlier in this section and nearly all of the cautions identified above pertain in some way to the role of the regular teacher. There are implications in these conditions and cautions concerning three major areas: knowledge, attitudes and values, and skills.

Knowledge

What knowledge should a teacher of young children have in order to implement mainstreamed learning experiences successfully? This book reflects an attempt to respond to that question by summarizing relevant areas of knowledge. Clearly, however, it is not a complete source. In the Appendix, you will find additional resources—lists of printed materials, people, places, and national and community agencies. Much of the knowledge you will need is *child-specific;* you may wish to obtain detailed information regarding a specific chronic illness, for instance, or the nature of a particular child's hearing or vision loss or motor impairment. Or you may want to obtain precise information about certain adaptive equipment, such as an electronic communication system, that a child is using. There is no way that a teacher, regular or special, can learn in advance everything that she or he may need to know about every situation that may be encountered; for *specific knowledge,* you will need to continue to consult other sources.

As a well-prepared teacher of young children, however, you will already know a great deal of what you need to know, in terms of *general knowledge,* to work effectively with young children with special needs. This book attempts a comprehensive presentation of *complementary* information, which we believe is specifically pertinent to working with special needs children.

Attitudes and Values

We have stressed the importance of positive teacher attitudes, but this does not reflect a view that your attitudes toward handicapped children or toward people with disabilities generally are unfavorable or need to be improved. On the contrary, we assume that early childhood educators are more likely to be open, positive, and receptive to children with special needs than educators at any other level. There is a great need, however, for all of us to have greater confidence in our ability to put our beliefs into practice.

One point should be made about the role of *expectations.* Teachers' expectancies that children can learn have been documented as a key variable associated with effective schools (e.g., Edmonds, 1979). The relevant point here has two facets: (1) *Beliefs* that a handicapped child can succeed in a typical placement increase the likelihood that the child will, in fact, succeed; and (2) A handicapped child's *placement* in a typical setting is more likely to lead adults to expect that the child can succeed in the mainstream than his placement in a special setting. Personal observation suggests that public school personnel are influenced by their knowledge of a child's prior educational experiences. In fact, for many educators, the fact that a child is in a mainstream placement for his or her initial educational experience appears to be more important than performance on measures of developmental readiness. For a child who is in a mainstream nursery school, future educational placement is more likely to be predicted in the mainstream than for a child whose nursery school experience is in a specialized and segregated placement. Parents' as well as professionals' expectations are affected.

Are these predictions simply a reflection of the teachers' and parents' *desires* that the child can continue in the mainstream—a question of belief? Belief in itself is important. But more important, predictions in these cases can be based on *actual observation* of a child's success in the mainstream. For the child in a segregated placement, no such evidence exists.

Belief in mainstreamability is more influenced by observation of feasibility than by test scores or similar predictive measures. Although "actuarial" statistics suggest that a child should have a developmental age of five to succeed in kindergarten, little evidence actually supports that contention. To the contrary, Campbell (personal communication) reported instances of children for whom mainstream kindergarten success was predicted by regular nursery school teachers, despite the teachers' knowledge of the children's low scores. These young children with Down syndrome, who had spent a year in regular nursery school, had a mean Developmental Quotient of about 65—at the age of five, in other words, their *measured* average developmental age equivalent was that of a three-year-old. We cannot underestimate, then, the importance of these two implications:

1. Whatever developmental scales might (or might not) indicate, it is what the child actually *does* in the classroom setting that is most likely to influence the expectancies of teachers (and, presumably, parents and other adults as well).
2. *Starting* in a typical setting is more likely to lead to a child's continued mainstream placement than is starting in a segregated placement.

Skills

The relevant teaching practices that make integrated education effective in early childhood programs are outlined in the remainder of this section. Parts II and III of this book elaborate them more fully, first in connection with more specific areas of exceptionality (Part II), and then (Part III) more "generically," that is, as applicable to children with diverse special needs.

TEACHING STRATEGIES FOR EFFECTIVE INTEGRATED TEACHING

The basic requirement for teaching young handicapped children in integrated regular classroom settings is the ability, and willingness, to respond to specific individual needs. We should add immediately that that is also the basic requirement for teachers carrying out early childhood programs that are developmentally appropriate. By definition, teaching that is appropriate to a pre-kindergarten, kindergarten, or primary context is responsive to the wide range of individual differences among children in such a context. In good early childhood programs, the individual child is the basis for planning; that is why early childhood programs are uniquely suited to include young children whose individuality is *in part* influenced by a disability.

As is illustrated in the chapters that follow, provision for individual differences associated with *exceptionality* is accomplished by adaptations in one or more of the following areas:

1. The *social context,* including orientation or preparation of children in the class; specifically structuring the social interactive context of classroom, with respect to large group activities, small group arrangements, peer "confederate" strategies (buddy system, peer modeling, etc.); involvement of an additional adult (or older child) as aide or volunteer assistant; and use of group discussion.
2. The *curriculum* including decisions about what is taught, determination of child-specific goals and objectives, the sequence of intended outcomes.
3. The *physical context,* including design and development or provisioning of activity areas or learning centers; physical modifications required for safety, access, reduction of noise interference or other conflicting or interfering sources of stimuli; the use of specific adaptive equipment, prosthetic devices, communication systems, etc.; attention to seating for a specific child, as well as location of work areas, within the classroom.
4. The *instructional approache*s or methods employed, including provision for differential time needs, for sufficient frequency of trials for a specifically targeted skill, for probe, generalization, and fall-back strategies, etc.; and implementation of a specific contingency management system, reinforcement schedule, Premack application, time-out, or other child-specific behavior management strategies.

SUMMARY

Public Law 99–457, enacted in October, 1986, reflects recognition that early education for children at risk or with handicapping conditions is effective. That a base of evidence has been established demonstrating the efficacy of early education for handicapped or at-risk children was no doubt a critical factor in bringing about the dramatic changes in social policy associated with this legislation. One of the most important elements in early childhood programs for handicapped children is their opportunity to interact socially with, and to share learning experiences with, peers who are not handicapped. That can be accomplished in either of two ways: (1) early childhood programs for children with special needs in which non-handicapped children participate (integrated programs), or (2) enrollment of handicapped children in regular, or typical, early childhood classrooms or centers (mainstream programs.) Since this text is addressed primarily to the regular early childhood educator, we treat mainly the latter situation. Consequently, the efficacy issue of major concern in this chapter has involved, not *whether* early childhood mainstreaming works, but *how* to make it work. Parts II and III provide specific suggestions, guidelines, and examples intended to enable the regular classroom teacher in preschool, kindergarten, and primary grade settings to be effective in meeting special needs of young children.

PART II

Methods for Meeting Special Needs of Young Exceptional Children

CHAPTER 5

Integrating Young Children with Visual Impairments

Impaired vision is not an all-or-nothing phenomenon; impairment occurs along a continuum in both visual acuity and visual field. For legal purposes, the following definitions are generally used throughout this country.

> *Blindness* connotes visual acuity for distance of 20/200 or less in the better eye, with best correction; or visual acuity of more than 20/200 if the widest diameter of field of vision subtends an angle of greater than 20 degrees.
>
> *Partial sight* connotes visual acuity greater than 20/200 but not greater than 20/70 in the better eye with correction (National Society for the Prevention of Blindness, 1966, p. 10).
>
> *20/200* and *20/70* mean that a person can identify chart symbols at a distance of 20 feet that can be identified by a normally sighted person at 200 or at 70 feet. A normally sighted person has a field of vision, or can see peripherally, at a range approximating 180 degrees.

These definitions serve to qualify individuals for services, but they have very limited educational usefulness. They do not, for instance, discriminate those visually impaired children who can read print, nor do they specify how children use the vision they do have in other areas of learning.

Not all children who have vision defects are identified, for purposes of special education services eligibility, as handicapped. A 1980 publication of the National

Society to Prevent Blindness estimated the number of normal children in the United States who have visual problems to be 5 to 7 percent. However, only about one-tenth of 1 percent of all school-age children have visual impairments that warrant special education provisions. Serious visual impairment is a handicapping condition of low incidence in children, but there are indications of some increase in incidence, especially associated with other biological risk factors (especially extremely low birthweight and very young gestational age) or other impairments such as cerebral palsy (Ensher & Clark, 1986).

Importantly, the range of intellectual ability and learning potential is just as great among blind children as it is among children with unimpaired vision (Cartwright, Cartwright & Ward, 1985).

Like many other impairments, visual problems may be congenital or acquired, and congenital problems result both genetically and from fetal or perinatal injury. In general, prenatal, perinatal, and postnatal factors associated with risks for developmental disabilities are also linked with risk for vision impairment (Cress, Spellman, & Benson, 1984; Ensher & Clark, 1986). Vision impairment is often associated with other handicapping conditions, such as cerebral palsy, and is also often related to poverty. Problems for young children range from amblyopia, or wandering eye, which is relatively responsive to early treatment, to glaucoma and cataracts, visual problems more typically related to the aging process.

IMPACT OF BLINDNESS UPON EARLY DEVELOPMENT

Since you are no doubt quite familiar with Piaget's descriptions of early development, you can readily imagine the catastrophic effects that congenital absence of the ability to see would presumably imply. The fascinating thing, however, is that most congenitally blind children approach developmental norms in cognitive areas by the time they reach school age (Barraga, 1976). The presumed high risk for associated problems in learning and concept formation, communication, and social-emotional development is frequently not borne out. Despite the critical importance of vision, especially during the sensorimotor period of development, it appears that most blind children do acquire the concept of object permanence, an understanding of physical causality and of object relations, and the other "building blocks" of intelligence (Fraiberg, 1977).

There is a great deal of research literature in this area, and it is potentially misleading to summarize with the facile observation that blind babies learn and are consciously as well as unconsciously taught to employ other modalities in order to compensate for their lack of vision. At least the following caveats must be added:

1. Development may be uneven (Scott, 1982).
2. Development in the early years will probably be delayed (Fraiberg, 1977).

3. Compensation does not occur "naturally," nor do blind persons have innately heightened hearing, touch, or other modalities.
4. Early intervention efforts focus especially upon the mother-infant relationship and communication system. (Dubose, 1979; Fraiberg, 1974; Fraiberg, Smith, & Adelson, 1969).

For all young children, concept learning is based upon direct experiences with objects in the environment. Children discover relationships that lead to "hypotheses," which are tested, repetitively and in a variety of contexts. Blind children's concept learning depends upon the same processes as that of sighted children. Physically manipulating objects is essential for all young children, and this mode of discovery, so essential for the child without sight, in no way sets him or her apart in a child care nursery. The impaired child may simply need a greater variety of experiences with objects than do most sighted children.

Exploration is prompted by curiosity and leads to discovery, involving the senses in interaction with objects in the physical world. Olson (1983) compared the exploratory behavior with new toys of blind and sighted preschoolers. Blind children were found not to differ significantly from their peers on most of the variables studied, possibly because of their experiences in early intervention programs. The blind children did indeed make more use of their hands, however. Olson concluded that early intervention may be necessary in order for visually impaired young children to acquire exploratory skills equivalent in effectiveness to seeing children, as these subjects had.

It is a truism that young children learn through play, that "play is the young child's work." However, in addition to free play, the young blind child needs guidance in his exploratory play (Hutt, 1976). One important area involves the child's inability to see someone else interact with a toy or other object and to imitate those actions—one of the hallmarks of early development. *Observational learning* (Bandura, 1969), which is such an important mode for sighted children, is not as accessible to the child who cannot see. Therefore, another person must orient the child to play materials and guide her to participate imitatively with another. Congenitally blind toddlers generally learn to engage in representational play, but again, direct intervention may be needed to enable them to learn to do so. In summary, although play "comes naturally" to *all* young children, blind children generally need to be taught to use play as the significant learning mode that it is.

Children who are blind develop their own, individual styles and strategies for learning. This individuality also extends to discovering ways to gain information in the absence of one of the major modalities with which unimpaired children discover and interpret the things around them. Thus, some children will rely primarily on touching, while others will seem to employ their entire bodies. Still others will rely extensively on the mouth, and others will seem to need to touch everything to their cheek or forehead. Kastein, Spaulding, & Scharf (1980), noting these individual patterns in young blind children, suggest that parents should encourage them during early development, and that these patterns will be abandoned in favor of language as the most effective way of gaining knowledge and of communicating. Some authorities (Dubose, 1979; Kastein et al., 1980) have also noted that the olfactory sense, or sense of smell, is often overlooked as an important mode of learning for blind children, and as a potentially effective avenue in teaching all young children.

As in other areas of sensorimotor development, awareness of causal relationships is based upon observing and thus being able to predict events. Intentional behavior emerges as a hypothesis-testing process imposed upon observed events in the environment. Similarly, the ability to anticipate what will happen next is based upon observation of cues and signals that lead predictably to certain events in a rhythmic pattern and routine. The interactive patterns between the blind infant and caregiver involve a mutual cueing process: the mother must learn to interpret and respond to the baby's communication, and the baby to interpret cues and messages provided by the mother (Ferrell, 1985; Fraiberg, 1977).

For young blind children who are multihandicapped, this is more difficult, depending upon the degree to which other modalities are involved. The situation has been well described by Rogow (1984):

> Visually impaired multihandicapped children are not necessarily able to perceive social signals. Social routines that employ rhythmic changes and actions create awareness at a perceptual level. As the children become involved in the action sequences and sound patterns associated with the rhythmic change, they become increasingly aware of rhythmicity as well as of the actions, sounds, and adult roles. Social routines become identified by the distinctive rhythmic patterns incorporated in both changes and actions.
>
> In the context of the social routine, the child learns that what he does is important to the adult and that he can elicit a reaction from the adult. The desired coordinated actions are thus modelled and permit and encourage imitation of actions and sequences of actions. In the course of games with adults the visually impaired multihandicapped child acquires meaningful social signals. Perhaps the most important learning is that actions produce results; that is a realization that is at the heart of intentional behavior. (p. 69)

Because of the extreme importance of the parent's role in facilitating the early learning of children born without sight, or who lose sight early in life, the child-parent and child-family interactive relationship is the focus of early intervention efforts. As with other areas of disability, other parents of blind infants and young children provide especially sound and valuable insights and guidelines. An example, in addition to the parent's account of a mainstreaming experience later in this chapter, is provided by a mother of a partially sighted child and details specific activities for parents in systematically assessing and guiding their child's development (Barry, 1973). Some excellent materials have been developed for use by parents, all stressing that early education programs only complement and support what parents and other family members do. (See Appendix for organizations that produce these.)

EARLY EXPERIENCES OF MAINSTREAMED
VISUALLY IMPAIRED CHILDREN

Prior to participating in a regular preschool, kindergarten, or primary program, the child will have had a good deal of preparation, whether through guidance from parents, direct involvement in a special program, or a combination of these. Early intervention will have focused upon parent-child interaction, as noted, but will also have introduced orientation and mobility training. (Such training will not have involved use of a guide dog, or in all likelihood, the use of the long cane. Even older children do not have the strength or maturity required to use a guide dog, and both professionals and parents differ about when cane training is appropriately introduced [Dickstein, 1976]). For younger children, training to permit independence in mobility emphasizes the child's use of specific *trailing* techniques. The child learns to use the wall, large objects, and environmental cues suggesting, for example, doorways as guides in walking about a room, from one room to another or to or from a corridor, down a corridor, up or down steps, and so forth.

The appearance of awkwardness in a classroom situation or reticence to participate does not imply a motor impairment, nor does it suggest that the vision-impaired child is slow to learn or unmotivated. Rather, as Eileen Scott (1982, p. 25) points out, the likelihood is "that he has never had the opportunity to learn that particular skill or to practice it until he has gained proficiency in it."

Early intervention will also have focused upon helping the child to use effectively the sight that he or she has. The importance of working with the child, beginning very early in life, to exploit remaining vision has been especially emphasized and documented in the work of Natalie Barraga and her associates (Barraga, 1976; Barraga & Collins, 1979). The principles their research suggests for the mainstream teacher working with a young, visually impaired child are included in Guidelines for Teaching at the end of this chapter.

The other area of special emphasis in early intervention programs will have been communication and the use of spoken words in helping the child orient to the environment, learn about objects and events, sense feelings and interpret social cues, predict events, be aware of attributes, and interact socially with others. Communication continues to be central for the child who is integrated into a regular program with young sighted children. We need to be conscious of the role of visual information in communication in order to ensure that the child gains the needed information through other channels. We must not overlook the critical importance of body language, facial expressions, and gesture to make sure that important cues to meaning, which sighted persons take for granted, can be provided in other ways. As Scott (1982) reminds us, the blind child ". . . is completely unaware of the visual aspect of communication. He is restricted to receiving information from the actual spoken words and the tone of the speaker's voice, both of which may be open to misinterpretation" (p. 31).

When we stop to realize how much of the communication process involves visual messages and cues, which extend or modify the meaning of what is said, we begin to understand the importance of providing additional information in communicating with a blind child. Not being able to see facial expressions and body language (unless it involves tactile contact for the child), the blind child at times requires more verbal information about, for example, the feelings of the person speaking. By the same token, the child must realize that his or her own feelings are recognized (Kastein et al., 1980). Introducing experiences, new materials, or new skills, as one teacher observed, basically involves "talking it through" with the child. We can imagine how that principle might be applied in locating something in the classroom, block construction, using a toy, or removing and hanging up a coat. Other children readily model the way a teacher accomplishes this to help a blind classmate with the sometimes difficult transition during the classroom routine or in cooperative play.

The vision-impaired child's needs for a great deal of specific verbal orientation will not constitute undue demands on time and attention, not only because of the help other children, or possibly another adult in the classroom, can provide, but also because talking effectively to a blind child simply involves good teaching principles. Teachers and parents often observe that a blind child heightens their own awareness of and sensitivity to the world; they learn to look at the world in a different way. They also become skilled in describing things, noting subtle distinctions based on sound and touch cues. At home, for example, water running in the kitchen sink has a different sound quality from water running in the bathtub. In school, such distinctions are important for daily adaptive functioning for the blind child, but they are also critical for *all* young children in grasping same-different, classification and seriation, and relational concepts.

Visually impaired children often have special needs with regard to self-awareness and self-esteem and adaptation to social situations. This dimension of the identity of the young blind child that is different from those of other children is not as straightforward as one might assume, as Kastein et al. (1980) have described:

> Since the realization that they are blind is generally very gradual, it may seem as though children understand, yet will respond in a manner which makes it doubtful. For example, one bright five year old, who appeared to know he was blind, still could not understand how his teacher knew he had a new haircut without touching his head. This confusion is common in young blind children and shows their struggle and efforts to understand. (p. 190)

As a teacher with visually impaired students, you may initially be inclined to undue and unnecessary overprotection (Gearhart & Weishahn, 1976). You need to recognize such potential tendencies in yourself and overcome them, to allow the disabled child opportunities to grow in independence. Frequently expectations of what an impaired child will be able to learn and do independently are too modest and tend to limit the child unnecessarily. At the same time, the child needs to feel confident that she is safe—just as all young children do. A blind child in the classroom implies the need for certain precautions that, although more critical, are no different from those constituting good physical management practice in any setting where young children learn. The floor should be free of objects on which a child could slip, doors should not be left ajar, and other similar hazards should be avoided (Schultz & Turnbull, 1983).

We should all heed this advice, offered by Patricia Maloney (1981) to other mothers of blind children:

> Nearly every parent of a child who is different fears that the child will be made fun of or teased. Such fears are almost totally unjustified. It will happen but far less often than you might think. Actually, the opposite is true. Other children tend to be overly helpful and must occasionally be reminded that a blind child can manage independently in most situations. (p. 29)

CASE HISTORY 5.1:   MARANA

The path is certainly never easy for any child born blind, but in Marana's case it has been especially difficult. Because some of her functional difficulties are associated with a rare medical syndrome—which is frequently associated with mental retardation—the professionals who have worked with Marana have not been able to agree about the significance of many of the skills she learned during her two years in a special nursery school program. Although she is blind, having only some light perception, this program was not specifically geared to serving young children with visual impairments. Her other medical problems, together with the lack of an alternative available for her at that time, led to her placement in this center where, in addition to classroom experiences, she received physical therapy, occupational therapy, and language therapy.

Although Marana has been blind since infancy, this was her first early educational intervention experience. She lives with both her parents, and both work. However, the total family income is low, and their rented home is in an inner city location. With medical costs associated with Marana's problems, the family has experienced difficult times. In fact, prior to their daughter's enrollment in this program, most of their contact with professionals has involved doctors, nurses, and social workers.

None of these had conveyed a very optimistic picture of Marana's future, and her mother's own observation of Marana has convinced her that her daughter is, and will always be, very "slow." Although Marana had been well cared for, nicely dressed, and loved, there had been little effort to provide stimulating learning experiences at home. Marana had not talked, and so her mother saw no reason to talk to her. In short, despite a potentially nurturing home situation, Marana did not have a lot working for her to encourage her potential for learning and developing.

When she entered the program, the few words she uttered were echolalic; that is, she would simply "parrot" a word someone used, whether or not that person was addressing her. She did not connect words with anything—objects, events, actions, or people (with the exception of her mother). (Her medical record explained that echolalic speech is frequently found in children with this same syndrome. However, it is also a phase in normal speech development that may persist in children who are blind or who have certain other developmental problems longer than is typical.)

An orientation and mobility trainer in the public school district that would ultimately be responsible for her placement was consulted. He advised Marana's teacher and the speech and language pathologist and physical and occupational therapists who would be working with her to focus on teaching her to use words in order *to get things to happen.* This strategy produced almost immediate results. The physical therapist found that she liked the movement sensation experienced in an improvised swing. She soon grasped that this could be initiated by her saying *swing,* and when she wished, saying *stop* produced the result she wanted. Staff members observed how the orientation and mobility trainer would play with her, holding her in a position in which she felt secure, and producing squeals and laughter with familiar movement patterns. She could initiate the game by saying "Airplane!" and then request familiar variations by name. This approach was carried out in many activities, both in the classroom and in her individual therapy sessions. Little success was seen in encouraging Marana's mother to carry over the strategy at home; she did not appear much impressed by the importance of this first "breakthrough" in getting Marana to employ language to communicate in a rudimentary way. She would need far more evidence to convince her that Marana could learn to talk and, with that skill, could learn many other things and develop a number of other skills, as well.

Previously inexperienced with other children, Marana related readily to the other children and they to her. Sometimes, two children would fight to be the one to hold her hand and help her find her chair or go to the door. One little boy, whose aggressiveness with peers was a constant concern, was especially fond of, and helpful to, Marana. This child's speech was also delayed (although it was soon to "take off"), and they "conversed" with mutually imitated non-verbal vocalizations. Soon, Marana was able to identify each of her classmates' voices and name whatever child was speaking. She could also identify each by touching their heads.

The orientation and mobility trainer also recommended that Marana learn to identify and name body parts. With the use of a familiar nursery record, this was accomplished rapidly. Movement-to-music activities became favorites, and Marana rapidly learned the words to songs and would request specific songs, both recorded and teacher-led. Tactile books were obtained from a community Vision Center, but the supply could not keep pace with the demand, so her teacher would make her others, to touch when singing certain songs, such as "Mary Had a Little Lamb."

Marana's insecurity and fearfulness in new situations reflected a combination of experiential deprivation due to blindness with that of a young child of the inner city. Her mother had neither attempted to expose her, gradually, to new experiences nor to "talk her through" situations that were in any way novel. In the center, professionals found her responsive and made more secure and willing to venture out with this kind of guidance.

Eventually, she would go to the bathroom, adjoining the classroom, on her own, find her own cubby in the cloakroom, and go to the door and down the hall without assistance. She readily oriented to the classroom and therapy rooms, and in the classroom would count the steps in climbing to and descending from an elevated playhouse area. Toilet training and wash-up routines were taught through task analysis procedures, and she could name the water, sink, toilet, and so forth. Similarly, she learned to ride a tricycle, bounce and catch a ball, and participate in all other large muscle activities.

Initially, Marana would not touch sand or paint. Besides the unfamiliarity of the sensation, she seemed to want her hands free, and she did engage in the self-stimulatory "blindisms" observed in some children. In fact, some of her hand movement patterns were self-injurious, in particular hitting her own forehead until it was quite bruised. The self-injurious behavior was stopped without having to use restraint, as she increasingly experienced environmental stimulation. Sand play became a favorite activity, and it was difficult to get her to paint with a brush, as she came to like the feel of the paint and the sensation of spreading it on paper.

Counting skills were transferred spontaneously to a variety of situations once they were learned. Her teacher guided her in counting pennies as she dropped them through a slot in a bottle lid, counting accurately the number of pennies up to 20. Finding, on her own, a pegboard in the game and puzzle area, Marana would count the pegs as she removed and inserted them, and this "counting approach" characterized her exploration of a great many new items when she encountered them for the first time.

Considering her virtual lack of communicative language when she began, her progress in this key area was very gratifying. She had indeed come a long way in a short time! Her teacher believed that, with supportive guidance to the teacher by a specialist, and continued direct speech and language therapy, regular class placement could be a possibility. At this point, however, that seems less likely than it had seemed earlier. Her placement at age five, based on a formal measure of IQ, continued special needs, and lack of advocacy on the part of her parents, is in a totally segregated setting. Her classmates' communication skills are, generally, far less advanced than hers. Her promised "special therapies," assumed to be more readily available in this setting than in the public schools, have either not materialized or have been far from adequate. The special preschool staff members fear that she will have regressed, or at least the rapid learning that characterized her behavior once the "key" was found, will not have continued. In particular, given her responsiveness to other children, there is concern about the absence of peer modeling opportunities to continue to stimulate her learning.

LEARNING ABOUT THE CHILD

Young children entering a nursery or kindergarten classroom, or beginning in a day care center, have had widely varying previous experiences. Although they will very likely have experienced some form of professionally guided early intervention, the same principle is true of young children with significantly impaired vision. The first principle, therefore, is to determine *what the child can do,* what skills and understandings he or she already has, and what strategies and techniques are used in approaching new situations and in communicating with others. For teachers of young children, teaching always begins with learning about the individual child, and such learning is critical in beginning to work with a young visually impaired child.

As with all young children, studying the blind or vision-impaired child involves more than verbally probing, despite the extremely important role of vocal interaction. The "verbal facade" (Almy, 1966) present in many young children is particularly likely to be present in young children who are congenitally blind. That is, the child's conversation, including vocabulary and syntactic structures, may suggest greater understanding and sophistication than the child actually possesses. The child's fluent, even glib, speech may bely lagging development in certain specific conceptual and problem-solving areas, resulting from early interference with sensorimotor development (Truan, 1984). However, gaps or what appear to be isolated "splinter skills", should not lead us to infer that the child is actually a "slow learner." On the contrary, the skills and accomplishments provide the base on which instruction can be built to help the child fill out the conceptual matrix necessary to gain solid understanding.

It may be helpful to describe how a resource teacher or consulting specialist is likely to proceed if asked to observe a visually impaired child within the classroom or child care setting.[1] The specialist will probably both question adults, and observe the child directly, in order to form and to test hypotheses before making suggestions specifically applicable to the particular child. The kinds of information sought include:

> *How* does the child use his or her eyes?
> *What* does the child see? (Things at a distance? Things close at hand?)
> *Where* does the child sit, for example when watching a television screen?
> How good a *listener* is the child?
> Does the child frequently trip or bump things?

---

[1] The author is indebted to Janet Stone, Children's Services Coordinator of the Cleveland Society for the Blind for these and many of the other suggestions included in this section. This agency, which provides a wide variety of resource services, is located at 1909 East 101 Street, Cleveland, Ohio 44106 (phone: 216-971-8118).

Does the child appear to become confused when moving from a well-
lighted to a darker space?

Is the child's behavior on the playground noticeably different than in the
classroom (that is, any more than for all children?)

Is there acting out, possibly fighting, on the playground? Does the child
seem not to want to go out?

Occasionally, a teacher will raise concerns about perceived behavioral problems, rather than focusing upon learning needs associated with the visual impairment. The teacher may not have connected a certain behavior pattern or tendency
with the child's vision problem at all. The discovery, for example, of a great deal of
light sensitivity may yield insight and understanding concerning the child's response, enabling a constructive rather than a punitive response.

It is important for you to know the nature of the child's vision loss, and a
resource specialist can assist in this area as well. Such knowledge has very
practical utility in terms of knowing what orienting behaviors to anticipate, as well
as knowing how to involve the child optimally in classroom or playground activities. For example, if the child has a *field* (peripheral) loss, we can avoid
throwing a ball from the side affected; or the child can be positioned in a circle
game to make most effective use of the vision he has. We can help the child learn
to track the sound of the ball, in order to be aware of its location and the direction
from which it may be coming. We can instruct *all* children to first say the name of
the child to whom the ball is going to be thrown.

Corroborate your impressions about the child's use of sight based on apparent
orienting behavior by consulting the eye chart contained in the vision reported.
This enables you to combine data sources and confirm or reject hypotheses
concerning how the child uses his or her vision. The child who holds his head up or
down rather than looking directly at a speaker may be using available sight when
there is a field loss; we shouldn't harshly correct these mannerisms, which may
have great functional utility, but we can help the child learn to normalize physical
attitude by striking a compromise between optimal posture and the more typical
posture of a sighted child.

CLASSROOM ENVIRONMENT AND LEARNING MATERIALS

A blind child can participate fully in virtually all activities involved in the classroom program, including individual, independent, small group, and large group
activities. The modifications needed are essentially matters of common sense and
will be apparent if you simply consider the situation from the child's perspective.
Marilyn Swieringa, who lost her sight in her thirties, asks sighted persons who
wish to be helpful in everyday situations to *See It My Way* in an effectively

illustrated book of that title (Swieringa, 1972). Helping a blind child or adult orient to their surroundings, avoid minor embarrassing mishaps, and feel secure participating in social situations involves taking the perspective of the other person. The blind individual is not helpless; without sight, however, he or she has a continuing need to orient to the environment. With this in mind, we can help the blind person obtain needed information (who you are, who else is present, where the chair, drinking glass on a table, step, or obstacle is) in a natural and unobtrusive manner.

As a classroom teacher you need to ask yourself questions such as:

Does the child have access to various activity areas?
Does the child know where to go; that is, where centers, doors, etc. are located and what "markers" can be used to proceed toward them?
Are objects that a child could fall over in the path of any access routes?
Have other potential hazards such as half-opened doors been eliminated?

These questions, of course, are relevant for any classroom, but they are particularly important for classrooms including blind or sight-impaired children. The physical environment is always important in programs for young children. Many teachers prepare approximate scale drawings of possible classroom arrangements; you may find this a useful technique in designing a stimulating and responsive learning environment, and one that also helps the children organize their learning. Such preplanning allows you to consider questions of specific access, space availability, furniture arrangements, and the like that may be required by the disabled children in your group, including children with low vision or blindness.

If your class does include a visually impaired child, we suggest that once you have implemented an appropriate room arrangement, you leave it alone. If you do make changes, make sure you communicate verbally precisely what is different— whether it be the furniture or center rearrangements, newly introduced materials, learning aids, or new persons. Children need to know who is present as well as what.

There are many specific ways in which the teacher can help a visually handicapped child with orientation and mobility in the classroom. Eckstein, Reilly, Sicnolf, and Wilkinson (1981) suggest techniques such as:

Describing a location by using words like up or down, right or left, and front or back.
Using a clock face, by identifying location in comparison with the numbers.
Letting the child feel the walls and identify objects such as a light switch, windows, bulletin boards, or any objects that help them see a pattern.

Encouraging the child to identify classmates' desks and their relationship to objects in the room.

Enabling the child to locate potentially hazardous objects, such as electrical outlets, or any items on the floor.

Guidelines for Provision and Use of Activity Centers for Vision-Impaired Children

1. Make working materials safely accessible to the visually impaired child, so that they can be accessed through reach or by search.
2. Use materials that are stimulating to touch, smell, hear, and taste in centers, as well as large group learning activities.
3. Limit the number of children, or the size of small groups working in centers at any given time. (This is a principle used by most teachers, but it is especially important in terms of the learning context for a visually impaired child: too many noises, and too many voices at one time can be very confusing.)
4. Stay in sufficiently close proximity to the child at all times to assure adequate hearing distance.

In summary, the way the environment of the classroom is organized, and the way the classroom is provisioned, enable the visually impaired child to be oriented, to be safe, to access activities and materials, and to capitalize on all learning modalities.

SPECIAL AND AUGMENTATIVE MATERIALS

The most familiar specialized materials employed by many blind persons enable reading and writing in braille. However, the majority of young children with special vision needs are not blind but partially sighted, and they can read print. For many of those children, other forms of augmentation may be appropriate and effective. In general, such augmentation with regard to print materials involves *heightened contrast* or *enlargement*. Necessary accommodations need to be made for a child to store, access, and use bulky items such as large print books, as well as materials prepared in braille or a brailler, should those be used.

Use of braille is fully compatible with mainstreaming. For older students, mainstreaming criteria involve specifically determining the student's academic capability, not the type or degree of vision loss or ability to read print. Braille can readily be accommodated within the mainstream in all academic subject areas, and experienced braille users function independently. Vision centers, metropolitan libraries, and special education resource centers facilitate the acquisition of text and other materials printed in braille. For as long as the student requires instructional guidance in braille, the school can contract with a braille teacher by contacting a vision or resource center if a specialist is not employed full-time by the school district. Two modes of writing in braille are commonly employed: the brailler, which involves the use of a small typewriter-like keyboard, and the slate and stylus, which has the advantage of greater portability. Transcriptions of print materials into braille are made by appropriately qualified braillists (Cargill, 1987).

CASE HISTORY 5:2:   MAINSTREAMING A YOUNG BLIND CHILD

"How is your daughter doing in school?" is a question I am asked frequently. Nicole is in the fourth grade at our neighborhood elementary school and I believe she is the youngest blind student ever to be mainstreamed in Shaker Heights. At the current time, she is the only totally blind child enrolled in our entire district. Parents, especially those with a handicapped child, are always interested in how we arrived at our decision to mainstream Nicole and the results of that decision.

Although blind since infancy, Nicole showed herself to be intelligent, articulate, and outgoing from an early age. In the years before formal education she had numerous group experiences—playgroup, story hours, Dalcroze class—all of them with sighted children. These had been successful and enriching. At the same time she was ready for nursery school no preschool for visually impaired youngsters existed, so we investigated schools for both special needs and regular populations. We finally chose a regular Montessori nursery school that Nicole successfully attended for two years.

Then she was ready to enter kindergarten. Shaker Heights recommended enrolling Nic-

ole in the class for the visually impaired housed at A. G. Bell School in Cleveland. Shaker would pay her tuition and provide transportation. Sending her out of a district did not please us. We worried about the possible long ride to school and the isolation from neighborhood friends.

So I went to visit the class for the blind at Bell and my observation convinced me of two things: (1) This was a suitable place for Nicole to begin her education, and (2) I did not want her remaining in a special education classroom throughout her schooling. I feel that the most important things for any child to gain from the primary grades are a proficiency in the three R's and a sense of confidence about his own ability to learn. It seems to me that these goals are best accomplished with a skilled teacher of the blind in a classroom where others are learning in the same mode (braille). At Bell I had observed a fine teacher, a caring environment, a small class, plus extras such as mobility training, adapted physical education, and home economics offered right in the building. Nicole began school at A. G. Bell the following fall.

There were, of course, trade-offs. The small

class size (10 students of mixed grade levels, K–3) was often as big a disadvantage as it was an advantage. The school itself is a conglomeration of handicapped populations: the deaf, the autistic-like and one class of visually impaired. These groups could rarely interact in any meaningful way. The transportation service was often a source of aggravation and Nicole was isolated socially from the kids in the neighborhood.

We had always hoped that after a good grounding in basic skills in a special primary classroom, Nicole would be ready to be mainstreamed in the upper elementary grades. Then, in the middle of her second grade-year, Nicole's teacher moved away and Cleveland had trouble finding a suitable replacement. The class hit a stalemate, Nicole seemed bored and was clearly not being challenged. So we began discussions with Shaker about mainstreaming Nicole in the third grade.

We were met, if not with enthusiasm, at least with cooperation and sincere good will. This was uncharted territory for them and the biggest stumbling block seemed to be a lack of knowledge about what the necessary resources, materials, and support personnel were and where to locate them. With a lot of prompting from us, most of the materials were eventually ordered and mobility was contracted for.

The transition went very smoothly in the fall. Nicole spent one day prior to the opening of school becoming familiar with the building with the help of her mobility instructor. Within a few weeks, she knew her way around quite well and was confident traveling without a sighted guide. Socially, Nicole was happy to be back in the neighborhood school; she said it made her feel "like a regular kid." She was accepted by the staff and students, she made friends and joined a few extracurricular activities, had dependable transportation, and although she had to work hard, she found the class stimulating intellectually. The principal and classroom teacher were always available and willing to help when small problems arose.

The most serious problem we encountered in mainstreaming Nicole was the inability of Shaker to find an itinerant teacher of the visually impaired to continue Nicole's braille instruction. With help from home, Nicole did well in school mastering the regular curriculum, but her special skills needs were being neglected. So at the end of the third grade, we were glad we had mainstreamed Nicole but were worried about the braille deficiencies.

This year has been a much better mainstreamed situation because a highly qualified, dedicated itinerant teacher was located. She has been an invaluable resource for the classroom and special subject teachers and us. This person truly is the key to successful *academic* integration of a totally blind elementary school student. (Ideally, the itinerant teacher would be available several half-days a week for work with the student and/or staff. Because of scheduling difficulties this is not the case—Nicole works with her itinerant teacher for nearly the entire day once a week).

From our experience, I would cite the following realities of mainstreaming:

1. This is a team effort involving equal commitment on the part of all three parties, the child, the parents, and the school.

2. Mainstreaming demands more parental involvement (time) and support than special education placement.

3. The classroom teacher has to be more organized and thoughtful when planning his lessons and assignments.

4. The child will have to work harder, concentrate more, and have more homework than he did in his special class. (These inconveniences will no doubt accompany him in all of life.)

5. The child will be tired and sometimes frustrated by working differently than his classmates.

6. Social adjustment/acceptance may present a challenge.

So, to the question "How is your daughter doing in school?", I have to reply: She has some friends, feels a part of the school community, she is being challenged, and she has to work very hard to get the good grades that she does but, on balance, mainstreaming has been a success.[2]

If braille instruction, mobility training, or special tutor services are identified as necessary *related services* on the student's IEP, they are provided at no cost, whether the child is in a mainstream or specialized classroom setting. Similarly, paraprofessional assistance in preparing, copying, recording, or reading materials may be provided. Informal arrangements for voluntary assistance by parent tutors or others may be made if appropriate, as can peer-tutor arrangements with the classroom or involving older student helpers.

Certain specialized equipment is also employed in special education resource programs that translate print into braille and even into sound. Another fascinating area, in addition to reading and writing provisions, involves recreation. Most people have become aware of the extent to which, with sound augmentation, blind persons have been enabled to participate in recreational activities, including competitive sports, such as softball, basketball, and soccer. Volunteer organizations, including telephone system employees called "Telephone Pioneers," provide valuable resource assistance in these areas. These groups design and construct, or will acquire, "beeper balls" and other ingenious items. On a less technically sophisticated level, items can also be improvised for use in the classroom, gymnasium, and playground. For example, a nerf ball, or other type of ball, can be cut open and a bell inserted.

One of the critical functional skills nearly every blind child must acquire, irrespective of communication mode used, is to sign his or her name. This may be done through the use of a *signature frame,* and requires practice in holding a pencil and paper and in making the necessary letter forms.

The tape recorder is a useful and, for some children, essential augmentative aid. In addition to commercially available materials for listening, or those prepared and supplied by a vision center or special education resource center, stories, lessons, and other items can be especially prepared for the child by a paid or

---

[2] Susan H. Kahn, (1987, May). Mainstreaming a young blind child. *Parent Forum, 6* (4), Margery Buxbaum (Ed.). Reprinted by permission.

volunteer "reader" or other student. Listening centers, with individual or multiple headsets, are standard in many primary and some preschool classrooms. This is an activity in which the visually impaired child may participate as a member of a small group, or one in which he or she can work independently with minimal or no direct assistance.

For children with low vision, materials must have high contrast. For example, the child can use a black felt marker, rather than a pencil, on white paper. A problem in many primary classrooms involves the practice of using ditto work sheets or workbooks with tearout ditto pages. Many early childhood and primary educators are concerned that such materials are overused or are actually *developmentally inappropriate* for all young children. Concrete materials more nearly match the learning styles and needs of young children than do two-dimensional "seatwork" papers. But where these materials are employed, children with low vision may participate if the dittos are darkened and/or enlarged. A copying machine with the capability to darken and enlarge is generally available, if not in every elementary school, then in the central office or resource center for the district or region. Vision centers are readily accessible by mail, and they provide many services including enlarging and taping, as well as braille translation.

A great many minor adaptations of standard learning materials within the classroom are possible. Yellow acetate over print improves contrast, and this technique can be employed conveniently and independently as a standard adaptation by the disabled children themselves. Where pencil is necessary, use soft lead; a black broad-tipped marker may be preferable in most situations.

Room lighting is a vital consideration for children with limited vision, but it usually requires no special or unusual arrangements. Effective use of natural light and avoidance of glare are desirable for *all* children but are especially important for the visually impaired. A sight-impaired child should be seated so as to minimize interference from glare and shadow and maximize desirable levels of lighting. The child should not: face the light; be seated so that his work is in his own shadow; or have the light source blocked by people or things. Generally, in a room with one windowed side, the child should be seated as near the front or focal point of the classroom (chalkboard, chart, etc.) as she finds most comfortable. Permitting the child to move or adjust desk, chair or table placement is both appropriate and typically nondisruptive.

The following are adaptive or augmentative devices and materials that enable teachers to help children use within the classroom:

Hand-held and stand magnifiers, which many children with low vision have been trained to use and carry with them. Each child must determine the optimal distance to hold a magnifier in order to obtain a clear image, through experimentation (Dean, 1982). A child's use of a magnifier involves initial difficulties: things may appear inverted or get out of focus, finding the next writing line may be difficult, and insufficient light may be a problem. However, these can be overcome with guidance and practice (Dean, 1982).

A *telescope* for distance viewing, which also involves correctable problems of focusing (Dean, 1982).

An *abacus,* useful for computation.

Bold-line paper or *raised-line paper* (Eckstein, Reilly, Sicnolf, & Wilkinson, 1981).

A *braillewriter,* a braille-typing machine operated by the student.

Slate and stylus, a small metal frame, able to be carried, for writing braille by punching the six dots.

An *Opticon* translates printed materials into braille.

Talking calculator.

Writing guide, a rectangular form with open space, with which the child can learn to write within boundaries.

Tactile maps and globes, as well as other tactile items, such as numerals.

Tape recorder, commonly found in a regular classroom, and one of the most helpful items for a visually impaired child.

Adjustable-top desk or *desk-top easel,* to enable the child to adjust distance from materials without the strain and discomfort of constantly bending over.

Special paper for low-vision students, with widely-spaced green lines and a dull finish.

Felt-tipped or nylon-tipped marker, pen, or soft lead pencil, with which a child can experiment to determine which is preferred.

CASE HISTORY 5.3:   A TEACHER TELLS ABOUT A NEW STUDENT

Near the end of the school year, I had a new student assigned to my classroom, an eight-year-old girl, whose family had just moved into our district. She looks and acts like any of my other students. However, she is labeled visually impaired.

Karen came to our school very well prepared. She does have light perception and uses a hand-held magnifying frame for reading. She has never been in a special classroom. Fortunately, her parents were able to provide her with special training before she entered school. She can read braille but prefers the use of her magnifying frame.

I was amazed that after only two days she was very familiar with my classroom. After about four days in our school she asked if she could play kickball with the rest of the class. She explained how her father had taught her and we gave it a try. The first few times I would tell her when to kick and then as time went on she would just listen for the balls. She knew where to run by turning her feet a certain degree. This was amazing! Naturally, we had to help her when she arrived at the base, but the students were so thrilled that she could join in they were right there for her.

THE BLIND CHILD AS LISTENER

We need to remember the extent to which a blind child relies on other modalities to compensate for the inability to see. Certainly, the child needs to be allowed to use touch in lieu of sight. As a teacher, you can be very verbal about what is taking place at all times in the classroom. Remember, however, that this need not involve artificial, contrived, or unnatural verbal behavior on your part. Persons unaccustomed to speaking to someone who is blind may speak loudly and in an exaggerated manner; needless to say, that is neither necessary nor appropriate. Auditory information should be clear, specific, and employ (where indicated) directional words (e.g., to your right, or in front of you, rather than over there or up here.)

Children's librarian Jean Brown (1972) has observed, "When telling stories to blind children a veteran storyteller soon realizes that his voice is the only instrument upon which he can rely to convey moods and tones and to describe actions and incidents as they unfold. He realizes that his narration must not only appeal to the aural sense, but also to the other senses—touch, taste, smell, and general awareness" (p. 356).

She also vividly described the perspective of the adult in terms of expectations of "feedback" from one's "audience" in recounting her first storytelling experience with a group of blind children:

> To look into the faces of a blind audience while storytelling may not always provide clues as to whether the child is actually enjoying the story, although in actuality he may be thoroughly engrossed by the tale. My first encounter with such an audience made me feel ill at ease. Even though I was well prepared, I was conditioned to the responses of a sighted audience, with the usual facial expressions, the bright flashing eyes, and alert faces and bodies turned in my direction while listening to every word. Instead, some blind children were facing me, but some were not; most, however, seemed to be completely relaxed. Those not facing me sat sideways with their ears directed toward me listening to the story. (p. 356)

Although it is "natural" (at least in Western cultures) to look directly at a person speaking, that is actually learned behavior, based on observation, which enables the listener to receive the visual information that is part of discourse. The blind child has neither observed that others face a speaker nor profited from the information others acquire from so doing. For a child with visual field impairment, the visual information can often best be gained when facial attitude is slightly averted.

Part of the development of social skills involves learning to adopt behaviors that are consonant with what is expected by others. In our society, a person speaking to another expects the listener to look at the speaker, to provide "eye contact." Similarly, we expect that when someone is speaking to us, the speaker will indicate that by looking at us. As Kastein et al. (1980) note, even young sighted children sometimes need to be reminded of these communication conventions. For a child who has had no experience in seeing a speaker, or listener, it is necessary to teach these patterns, which are not intrinsically important to the child without sight. Early in development, gentle physical prompts can begin so that this socially expected "looking" behavior can become habitual.

General Guidelines for the Teacher of Sight-Impaired Children

1. Encourage and enable the child to use the sight he has.
2. Instruct the child in the most effective use of available vision.
3. Provide opportunities for normalization, both in terms of activities and experiences and the manner of the child's participation.
4. Challenge the child equally with other children.
5. Use language as effectively as possible, especially in giving information or directions.
6. Explain any changes in where things in the room are.
7. For many preschool-age children, a quick, daily verbal orientation may be necessary.
8. Provide a verbal orientation whenever the child appears momentarily confused, and sensitize other children to do the same.
9. Use directional words (such as right, left, behind, in front, etc.) when orienting and describing.
10. Remember that, for many activities, learning by modeling must involve touch (for example, in group movement activities or games such as "Eensy Beensy Spider").
11. Blind children need to acquire as *social skills* behaviors such as facing a speaker or a book being read aloud, even though doing so may have no functional utility.
12. Children must be able to communicate with peers.
13. Be comfortable in using words such as "see" and "look" in talking with the child.

SUMMARY

Not only is visual impairment a matter of degree in young children, but different types of visual problems may be present. In the classroom, as well as at home and in the community, the important issues are: determining how the child uses his or her vision; helping the child orient to the environment; facilitating compensatory use of other modalities; ensuring safety and a sense of security and confidence, and communication. In addition to the physical environment of the classroom, adapting instructional activities and materials is frequently important. Resource persons and resource materials can readily be accessed by the mainstream teacher, but the child himself or herself, together with parents, is the teacher's best "consultant."

ADAPTING INSTRUCTIONAL ACTIVITIES FOR THE VISUALLY IMPAIRED

This section is intended to present a number of examples of the ways in which teachers might adapt typical learning activities planned in conjunction with each of several major early childhood curriculum areas of focus. They have been developed by Maria Sargent, a teacher of young children with special expertise in working with handicapped children in integrated early childhood classrooms.

Color Concepts

Children with impaired vision may experience varying degrees of difficulty within this area. The use of additional cues such as shape or size may aid the child having difficulty. For those children in which color discrimination is not an expected achievement, the activities can be structured in such a manner that the child is practicing tactile discrimination skills at the same time the other children are working on color discrimination.

GOAL:
To provide a child with no color discrimination ability with alternative activities in conjunction with color matching activities.

OBJECTIVE:
The child will be able to match (or sort) colors by relying on tactile discrimination markers pre-set on the materials to be used.

MATERIALS:
Various objects or printed materials. Glue, yarn, or small beads.

PROCEDURE:
1. Prepare the objects with a specific set of consistent tactile cues.[3]
2. Introduce one color to the child at a time. Have child note the particular marker used and stress that this marker represents what is known as a color. An alternative at this point is to also introduce the child to a sensory stimulus that will help the child gain a sense of the color word (e.g., blue-ice, yellow-the sun's warmth, etc.)
3. Introduce the child to tactile discrimination of one color by using *one* distractor color and increasing the number of distractors as mastery is gained.
4. Continue to add more colors to the child as each color is fully mastered through the above process.

Number Concepts

The child may need to rely on tactile manipulation of concrete materials to take part in number-related activities. Various concrete number activities can be designed and concrete or tactile cues can be added to activities in which concrete forms are not to be used. Small adaptations to written materials are also a possibility.

GOAL:
To assist the child in completion of paper activities requiring visual skills the child cannot meet.

OBJECTIVE:
The child will use tactile cues to count objects and complete a work sheet.

MATERIALS:
Work sheet; glue; small cards[4]

PROCEDURE:
1. The work sheet should be adapted in the following manner. For counting

---

[3] Possible tactile markers: Small dots of hardened glue in patterns, shapes, or number sequences; yarn glued into place in specific geometric shapes; small beads used in the same manner as the glue dots (held with glue) or in specific braille-related patterns.

[4] For activities of an independent nature, small cards can be made using yarn and/or glue. The cards should provide tactile representations of the actual number of items, the number itself, the number word, or the braille representation depending on the child's level. These cards can then be placed on the work sheet to show the desired answer. If there is danger of the sheet being disrupted before a teacher can see it, the small cards may have small magnets attached to the backs and the work sheet can be placed on a metal tray and secured. Any answer cards then placed on the sheet cannot be disrupted when the sheet is moved.

activities place a large drop of glue on top of each picture to be counted in the correct quantity (e.g., four pictures, four drops of glue). If the pictures are simple in nature, an attempt to actually outline them can be made.

2. The child can then be shown how to count the object using the sense of touch. The child can then give the answer in written or verbal form according to ability.

Letters

The child may have difficulty developing the concept of the different letter shapes. For the child with limited vision, a mental concept of the letter shape must be developed to aid the child in later work. For the child with little or no vision, letter activities can provide practice for the later use of braille.

GOAL:
To assist the child with limited vision in the recognition of various letter shapes.

OBJECTIVE:
The child will be able to visualize the letter shapes after repeated tactile practice using sandpaper letters.

MATERIALS:
Sandpaper; scissors; smooth paper; large alphabet of same size as sandpaper letters.

PROCEDURES:
1. Introduce the child to two letters at a time. Show the child how to outline the shape of the letter using her fingers. Once the child has felt the letter, discuss the various aspects of the letter formation the child can see to help the child develop a certain set of cues to help letter discrimination based on her available sight.
2. Have the child give you the letter requested out of a series of letters (number of distractors based on child's ability). Then have the child place the letter over the written alphabet provided. Use black letters on white paper for best results.
3. This activity can be developed into a group activity by giving each child three written letters. During their turn, they must try to find the letters they need through touch alone. A shorter method is to let each child choose a letter, try to name it and if correct, keep it. The most letters at the end wins.

Some children dislike the rough texture of sandpaper. Other items can be used: wood blocks, fur, or other materials with a definite texture. Yarn held in place with plenty of glue is another option.

Shape Concepts

The child may find it difficult to distinguish among shapes in general or shapes with similar attributes (e.g., square versus rectangle). Concrete representations should be used to help the child develop a visual concept of the shape being referred to.

GOAL:

To assist the child with visual needs to develop the concept of square versus round and oval versus circle.

OBJECTIVE:

The child will be able to match a concrete representation of the shape to a drawn shape using sponges and paint.

MATERIALS:

Firm sponges; paper; paint

PROCEDURE:

1. The child will be shown the two shapes to be used (circle and oval, square and rectangle). Allow the child to examine them and describe in her own words any differences between the two.
2. Give the child a paper with the two shapes drawn or preprinted on them. With the paint, the child can cover the preexisting marks. Separate colors of paint and corresponding colors on the sheet can provide additional cues for the child who needs them.
3. Variation   For a child capable of following simple tracks or designs, the paper to be painted can include these items thus giving visual tracking practice at the same time.

Caution: If too soft a sponge is used, pressure may distort the print, further confusing the child.

Direction and Sequencing

The child may feel uncomfortable when experiencing various directions physically. The loss of orientation occurs easily and therefore, the child may shy away from experiencing many different activities involving concepts of relationship, sequencing, or directioning. Safe ways to give the child experience with these concepts may eliminate many fears and at the same time provide practice with direction-related vocabulary words.

GOALS:

To assist a child with visual needs in the exploration of direction-related words.

OBJECTIVE:

The child will be able to demonstrate various direction-related words using his body.

MATERIALS:

Cards showing pictures of objects in different direction-related situations (above, beside, under, etc.).

Large pillows; stuffed animals

PROCEDURE:

1. Show the child one picture at a time and have the child place the stuffed animal in the same position using the pillows (e.g., put the dog under the pillow).

2. Next invite the child to participate using one of the safer words such as on "top" of the pillows. Make sure to stress how comfortable and soft the pillows are to alleviate the fear of falling.

3. Progress to more "daring" concepts such as under and upside down as the child seems ready. Going through the activity with the child physically may eliminate fear.

4. Whenever a child is in a position, ask them to point which way is up, down, and to the side to help them find their orientation in space.

Social Skills

Children with limited or no vision lack the social cues that can be gained visually in social interactions. Teaching a child to be able to predict outcomes of certain actions based on their own feelings may help them judge the feelings of others in social interactions.

GOAL:

To help a child predict the outcome of a social interaction using their own reactions as a guide.

OBJECTIVE:

The child will be able to predict another's feelings in various social interactions based on their own feelings in similar situations.

MATERIALS:

Any in the room

PROCEDURE:

1. Set up a situation of your choice and discuss with the child several different courses of behavior available. For some children actually acting out the situation with dolls may be helpful.

2. Discuss the reaction of the other person to the various solutions the child offers. Have the child imagine how they would feel in the same situation if they are having difficulty predicting others' reactions.

3. Since the child may have no visual cues such as facial expressions to go on, they may rely on verbal cues alone. If this is the case, they may be taking advantage of children who do not react in a verbal manner. Be sure to point out to the child that we can feel a certain way without expressing

it verbally. Try to help the child see that they can't rely on cues from others because not everyone reacts in a way we can hear.

Motor Skills

The child with impaired vision may lack the confidence to rely on her own physical movement. Developing games in which partners are utilized and at the same time introducing new physical skills, the child may have more confidence to try the skill. In such games speed should never be the factor. Rather have stickers or small prizes for each pair that completes the task. Giving each pair a different task will also eliminate any self-initiated races.

GOAL:
    To help a child gain new physical skills in a non-threatening environment.

OBJECTIVE:
    The child will try new skills by participating in a physical activity with a friend.

MATERIALS:
    Hoops; ladder; rope; balance beam, etc.

PROCEDURE:
    1. Design several activities such as stepping through hoops, walking a balance beam, etc., which must be completed with a friend. Set up the activity so the peers are always assisting each other so that asking for help will not be avoided.
    2. Have each pair pull a cord from the pile and explain the task if necessary. In some cases pictures can be drawn of the task eliminating the need to read.
    3. Have each pair complete the task together in order to achieve their prize.

Feelings

The child with impaired visual needs may lack the visual cues that normally show us the emotions of others. To help the child develop a mental concept of these emotions, concrete forms that the child can examine may be used. Exploration of another's face as they mimic certain emotions can also be effective.

GOAL:
    To help a visually impaired child develop a mental picture of various emotions using concrete representations of different facial expressions.

OBJECTIVE:
    The child will be able to describe the feeling they are exploring using the concrete medium and provide an appropriate antecedent to that emotion.

MATERIALS:
 Two different textures of yarn; two different sizes or textures of buttons; round
 pieces of cardboard

PROCEDURE:
 1. Use one type of yarn to depict the eyebrows and the other to depict the
     mouth. Use one type of button for the noses and the other for the eyes. In
     this manner the child will have consistent cues about the spatial setup of
     the faces.
 2. Glue the various features onto the cardboard circles to depict various
     emotions.
 3. After the faces are dry, the child can feel the outline of the fact and can try
     to reproduce the expression with their own face.
 4. Have the child describe how they feel when they usually make that face
     and possible things that may have precipitated that feeling.
 5. Describe a situation and have the child choose the most likely resulting
     facial expression and feeling.

Body Image and Self-Concept

The child with impaired vision may not have a complete concept of his or her body.
Specific exercises in which the child explores her own movement potential are
appropriate to help the child gain a better understanding of the range of movement
of which she is capable.

GOAL:
 To help the child gain better understanding of her body and range of movement.

OBJECTIVE:
 The child will be able to move a particular body part upon various commands
 and describe the movement being made.

MATERIALS:
 Mirror; completely flexible doll or stuffed animal

PROCEDURE:
 1. Have the child look at and manipulate the doll provided. Discuss the
     various parts of the doll being handled and the specific movements being
     made. Note the differences and similarities in movements people can
     make.
 2. Initially start this activity seated on the floor to provide balance. Have the
     child point to and then move a requested body part. Continue until the
     whole body has been covered.
 3. Next focus on one body part and have the child move the part in as many
     ways as possible. Have the child verbalize her actions as she does them.

Turns can be taken between child and teacher or another child. One will move a certain body part and the other must do the same.

4. Eventually go through the process standing up and explore the range of motion that can be accomplished. Have the child notice that most of the movements made sitting down can be done standing up.

Discrimination Skills

Children with visual needs rely on tactile discrimination to varying degrees. For the child who will be relying on this mode of discrimination for later reading, practice in this skill is essential in the early years. Many activities in the normal curriculum can provide this experience.

GOAL:
To provide tactile discrimination practice.

OBJECTIVE:
The child will be able to match items through the sense of touch from two piles of objects.

MATERIALS:
Materials of various forms, sizes, and textures (pairs). Two trays

PROCEDURE:
1. Have the child choose an item from one tray.
2. Have the child describe the object verbally as it is felt.
3. Have the child find the matching object in the other tray. The child should be questioned as to the reasons for rejecting any object picked up and discarded. Encourage the child to verbalize what was wrong with her choice.
4. The game can be increased in difficulty by using one hand for one tray and the other hand for the other.

Perceptual Skills

The child with visual limitations may find it difficult to participate in putting puzzles together in free play. The use of tactile discrimination may not be enough to allow the child to complete puzzles successfully, especially ones with a number of pieces. Small adaptations can provide assistance and allow the child to participate fully in an activity that is enjoyable and will contribute to tactile skills.

GOAL:
To assist the child in completing puzzles in an independent manner.

OBJECTIVE:
Using her fingers to follow the glue outline of each piece, the child will complete the puzzle.

MATERIALS:
Glue; a puzzle; a pencil

PROCEDURE:
1. Remove all the pieces of the puzzle and replace one at a time. As each piece is replaced, trace around it with a pencil. When all pieces have been traced, remove the pieces once again.
2. Using a very fine stream of glue, outline the lines drawn. Going through this glue procedure twice is better than getting too much glue on the puzzle (too much glue will disrupt the set of the pieces).
3. By following the now complete boundaries for each piece, the child will be able to complete the puzzle by matching the puzzle shape to the glue outline. This adaptation will not prove distracting for other children using the materials and may provide an exciting challenge for other children as well.

Reading

The child with limited vision often misses out on the most enjoyable part of the books that are read to them: the pictures. Placement of the child can greatly facilitate what sight they possess. Also, the use of duplicate materials during group activities can provide non-obtrusive help. If the child has no functional vision, other adaptations can provide tactile stimulation pictures to correspond with the items used.

GOAL:
To provide alternative materials suitable for the visual capacity of the child when using reading materials.

OBJECTIVE:
The child will be able to follow the story using tactile representations of the pictures being shown (during a group story-time).

MATERIALS:
Paper; glue; various appropriate materials; masking tape

PROCEDURE:
1. Decide on the degree of assistance needed by the child. Slight limitation may need only thoughtful seat placement. Moderate to severe may require a copy of the book for personal use. Severe loss can require special adaptations.

2. Choose the book desired and determine pictures, characters, and actions necessary to the story.
3. Choose a symbol to represent the picture when possible. (e.g., cat could be represented by a piece of fur.)
4. For pictures that do not lend themselves to symbols, try to draw representations using heavy glue that, when dry, the child will be able to feel with her hand.
5. As the book is read, the child can hold her book of pictures and follow along. Page turnings will not correspond, so cue the child by pointing out the picture to the whole group. Whenever a picture is pointed out, the child will know that the picture mentioned is the next in *her* book, also.

Masking tape (wide variety) can be folded on itself along the center (leave a small edge on each side so it can be stuck to the paper) and used to develop raised pictures for the child. If desired, books to be used directly by the child can have pictures outlined in clear glue. In this manner, the child can feel the pictures and later users will not have their vision obscured.

Science

Many young visually impaired children often miss the fine details of objects around them. Often only the outline is the picture their eye receives. In the area of science, the use of magnifying glasses and microscopes can provide for some children pictures with a degree of detail normally missed.

GOAL:
  To provide experiences in which details of objects can be seen more clearly through magnification.

OBJECTIVE:
  The student will use the magnifying glass to examine objects in the environment and will then describe their appearance verbally.

MATERIALS:
  Magnifying glasses of different strengths; various objects of potential interest

PROCEDURE:
  1. Introduce the use of magnifying glasses and demonstrate the different results of the varying strengths.
  2. Show the child an object and point out the progressively larger and more detailed picture that can be achieved without successive glass strengths.
  3. Let the child explore, using the glasses, different objects in the room. Tell her to choose three she especially liked and have her show them to you and describe the detail verbally.

Music

Children with special visual needs usually require little adaptation in the area of music. Movements for songs may require special means in order for the child to fully understand the sequence. Music can also be used to advantage to enhance body awareness and spatial orientation through dance.

GOAL:

To assist a child with visual limitations in the sequencing of hand motions to simple songs.

OBJECTIVE:

The child will actively participate in the production of the hand movements to a simple song and will be able to repeat them in sequence.

MATERIALS:

A song

PROCEDURES:
1. Introduce the song to the children and teach slowly without the use of hand motions, or use a song familiar to the children.
2. Go back through the song and have the children make suggestions for appropriate hand motions. In this manner, the process moves at a slower pace so the child has time to grasp the motion, and, in the discussion of the movements, they are being explained verbally and tried out by the children around the student in a non-rushed manner, giving the child closeup models to copy without falling behind. Lastly, suggestions by the student herself will obviously be picked up quickly.

This procedure can be done by a small group or as a pair exercise with the finished product being shared with the class. In this manner, the child with difficulty gets to teach others.

Art

Children with special needs find non-limiting art activities like fingerpainting especially enjoyable. This activity provides tactile stimulation and is open ended so all results are perfect. The child with limited vision may have some difficulty in distinguishing the edges of the paper in activities like this. This can result in comments from other children about the mess, paint on the table, etc. To avoid this, and also to help a child learn to control arm movements within a boundary, special adaptations can be made.

GOAL:

To assist a child with limited vision in distinguishing the boundaries of the paper used in finger painting.

OBJECTIVE:

By feeling the boundaries of the paper, the child will be able to control her arm movements so that work takes place within the boundaries.

MATERIALS:

Masking tape; paper; paint

PROCEDURE:

1. Lay the sheet of paper on the table and place the edge of a piece of masking tape over it. Once the one edge is fastened, fold the center of the tape over on itself and then stick the remaining small edge on the tape on the table. The tape should then form a raised boundary that is securely fastened to the table.
2. By feeling the boundaries (created around the edge of the whole paper), the child can keep her work on the paper.

The use of old shirt boxes is also a viable alternative to this method and may be a great time-saver when it comes time to clean up.

CHAPTER 6

Integrating Young Children with Hearing Impairments

Historically, hearing impairment has inspired pioneering efforts to develop specialized educational approaches. The first systematic compensatory approaches were designed to enable persons with impaired hearing or vision to learn through other sense modalities. In many respects, these strategies provided models for educational techniques subsequently developed for other handicapped children. Deaf children were the first for whom residential schools were established, and later among the first to be taught in public school special classes (Kirk & Gallagher, 1987). Very significantly, long before the "mainstreaming movement" in public education, many students with hearing impairments received part or all of their formal education within regular classroom settings, frequently with special assistance provided by itinerant or resource specialists (Stuckless & Castle, 1981, p. 16). One survey of 557 hearing-impaired adolescents (Libbey & Pronovost, 1980), about two-thirds of whom had severe-to-profound hearing loss, revealed that more than half had been mainstreamed for some or all of their schooling for seven or more years. In this area of exceptionality, there is also a long history of cooperation and collaboration among families, schools, and community agencies to promote optimal educational opportunities and normalization. Early intervention has also long been known to be critically important for children whose hearing is impaired, since hearing is of critical importance in early development.

Hearing impairment, like visual impairment, presents a paradox: both are considered "low-incidence" handicapping conditions, yet both are extremely common in the general adult population. With the aging process, nearly all adults experience lessened acuity in either or both areas of function. Fortunately, effective means of correction, through corrective lenses or hearing aids, enable most of us to compensate for these problems. The concept of correction actually has very different ramifications for these two areas, however. Corrective lenses, for the majority of people who use them, effectively compensate for the vision difficulty. That is not the case with the use of hearing aids.

Children with impaired vision or hearing present a very different set of concerns, because of the important role these modalities play in development. The importance of early childhood educators cannot be overestimated. Their involvement is critical in:

> Identification of vision or hearing problems in young children.
> Using educational procedures that can enable a young child who has a visual or hearing impairment to participate fully and optimally in the classroom program.
> Developing effective and ongoing communication and a partnership relationship with the child's parents.
> Working, as needed, with appropriate specialists.

YOUNG CHILDREN WITH HEARING IMPAIRMENTS

An inability to hear well or clearly is frustrating for anyone. For an adult, lessened acuity creates a sense of missing things that are interesting and might be important, of being left out. It greatly interferes with the ability to converse with others or to understand the dialogue in a film or television show, the information provided by a news announcer or commentator, or a joke or amusing anecdote. Embarrassment and self-consciousness, coupled with frustration, unfortunately lead some of us to avoid associations and experiences we would enjoy. Rather than admitting we missed something in conversation and asking the speaker to repeat, we nod, smile, pretend we heard. Often we will wish that the person would just speak a little more clearly or face us when speaking. A noisy setting, or any setting in which we must discriminate what a person is saying from a background of other sounds also makes conversation difficult.

Frustrating as are these experiences—common to millions of middle-aged and elderly adults, even to many who use hearing aids—they do not parallel the situation of a young child lacking normal hearing acuity. Young children's acquisition of language itself normally depends upon their ability to hear the speech of others and their own speech as well. That explains why, in the case of hearing impairment, the *age of onset* is an extremely important consideration affecting the extent of handicap a child may experience, as well as influencing the nature of the intervention approach used (Northern & Downs, 1974).

Most children of preschool age who have significant hearing loss, with concommitant speech and language delays, need a systematically structured and relatively intensive program. That need has been known and provided for for many years, evidenced by the fact that seriously hearing-impaired children were the first group to be provided early childhood programs. However, an important component of early childhood programs for hearing-impaired children is the opportunity to interact with hearing agemates. The important decision for an individual pre-school-age hearing-impaired child is whether that child's needs for appropriate early intervention can be met within a *mainstream* preschool setting, whether those needs require more specialized instruction within an *integrated* preschool setting, or whether concurrent participation in both types of programs is indicated. That decision is not made "once–and-for–all" for the child during his or her preschool years; it must be continuously reviewed by the child's parents, teachers, and other professionals involved.

Hasenstab and Horner (1982) have described the practices adopted in the Comprehensive Services Program for Hearing-Impaired and Language-Delayed Infants and Preschool Children in the Speech and Hearing Center at the University of Virginia. This program enrolls a maximum of three hearing children in each nursery and pre-kindergarten class of about 10 children at the Center. According to Hasenstab (1982):

> This situation has been beneficial to all concerned. The handicapped children are receiving necessary interaction experiences with hearing peers; the hearing children receive a richly educational preschool experience; parents feel that the small groups, comprehensive curriculum, and extensive individual attention are beneficial to all the children; and teachers and teachers in training are constantly made aware of appropriate developmental behaviors at all ages. (p. 356)

She stresses that, for young hearing-impaired children, "The reason for integration is at least twofold: the presence of normal peers in a nursery setting provides age-appropriate language models, and it also provides play and social behavior in line with developmental age" (p. 356).

Ideally, most children with significant hearing loss that was incurred early in life or present congenitally will have had a great deal of prior experience in group educational settings before they enter a typical kindergarten setting; as a result, they may appear—and may even be—more "ready" than many of their hearing peers. However, as Ross (1978) has noted, that is a double-edged sword. What children may be demonstrating, because of their extensive prior preparation in educational settings, is optimal linguistic performance; however, the language-related demands increase rapidly in kindergarten and the primary grades, and children may soon find themselves experiencing failure for which they, their parents, and their teachers were not prepared.

MAINSTREAMING HEARING-IMPAIRED CHILDREN: NOT A NEW IDEA

Although the special needs of hearing-impaired children, especially in the early years, have long been recognized, there is a well-established tradition of promoting normalized learning experiences and participation in the regular school program.

This is no doubt due to the fact that the full range of human abilities, including average, above average, and superior intellectual potential, is represented among hearing-impaired persons (Cartwright et al, 1985, p. 198).

One of the strong advocates for appropriate mainstreaming for hearing-impaired children, Dr. Winifred Northcott (1973), recommended a continuum of educational placements, including full-time regular class placement, before Public Law 94–142 was enacted. The need for a range of alternatives was based upon a realistic appraisal of the differential needs of individual students. As Northcott stated, ". . . partial or full-time integration in regular classes is not a realistic goal for *every* child; nor is a policy of automatic self-containment from kindergarten through grade 12 . . ." (p. 6).

Northcott (1972) believed that hearing-impaired children who were "good candidates" for mainstreaming in early childhood were those whose loss had been identified early; who had received early intervention; who had been fitted early in life with hearing aids and used aids full-time, rather than irregularly; who had available a multidisciplinary team for support to both child and family; who had received early oral-aural training; and who were neither severely multi-handicapped nor extremely immature in their social and emotional development. According to Northcott (1973), hearing-impaired children who had been successfully integrated into regular classes shared the following characteristics:

1. Active utilization of residual hearing and full-time use of hearing aids if prescribed.
2. Demonstrated social, academic, cognitive, and communicative (auditory and oral) skills within the normal range of behaviors of hearing classmates at a particular grade level.
3. Intelligible speech and the ability to comprehend and exchange ideas with others through spoken, written, and read language.
4. Increased confidence and independence in giving self-direction to the task at hand. (p. 3)

Two especially critical elements highlighted by Northcott and emphasized by other professionals advocating mainstream options, when appropriate (e.g., Nix, 1976) were the multidisciplinary support team and strong parent involvement.

There has been a significant change within the decade or more since Northcott and others first formalized suggested criteria for mainstream participation. Educators assumed that the ability to participate, through both listening (augmented by speech-reading) and speaking, in the classroom setting *in the same manner in which hearing children participated* must be a "bottom-line" criterion. Clearly, the ability of a hearing-impaired individual to speak and to understand the speech of others continues to be seen as highly desirable. However, alternative modes of communication are now more generally recognized as legitimate, acceptable, and viable for persons whose disabilities make such modes more feasible and more effective. A deaf child who communicates manually may potentially be a good candidate for mainstreaming, provided the child receives *interpreter services.* Underlying language skills, rather than speech per se, represent the critical factor (White, 1981).

FORMS OF HEARING IMPAIRMENT IN YOUNG CHILDREN

As with adults, there are two broad classifications of hearing loss in young children, *conductive* and *sensorineural.* The term *mixed hearing loss* is used when both types are present. Conductive losses involve interference with the passage of sound waves to the inner ear, which may be due to fluid, impounded wax, or foreign objects, or to bone malformation. Many conductive losses may be medically, or sometimes surgically, treated. Additionally, amplification through the use of hearing aids is more likely to be beneficial. Sensorineural losses involve inner ear, generally, cochlear, or auditory nerve dysfunction. Such losses are much less likely to be ameliorated, and hearing is much less likely to be improved through amplification.

The *degree* of loss is also an important determinant of the extent to which hearing impairment is a handicapping condition. Degree of loss can best be understood in terms of a continuum, rather than as an "either-or" distinction, and most important is the degree of loss within the frequency range associated with human speech. The frequency range for speech is between about 500 and 2,500 Hertz (Hz), a measure of cycles per second. An audiogram reveals response to sound within the total range of human hearing capability (about 250 to 8,000 Hz (Dubose, 1979). Within a particular frequency range, the degrees of sound intensity, or loudness, are reported in terms of decibels (dB), scaled according to standards of the International Standards Organization (ISO) or American Standards Association. Degree of loss is reported separately for each ear, since an individual's functional hearing level may differ in each. A loss in only one ear is termed a *monaural* loss, whereas if hearing is impaired in both the loss is *binaural.*

Classification of level of hearing loss involves more subtle distinctions than simply differentiating children who are deaf from those who are considered hard of hearing. Most individuals considered deaf have some ability to hear, and many have some ability to hear human speech. It is only for a very small number of children that ". . . any sort of hearing is totally impossible" (Northern and Downs, 1974, p. 251). Various authors have suggested somewhat different classification systems regarding degree of hearing loss and its functional implications. Rebecca Dubose (1979, p. 366) has suggested a classification that is particularly helpful in considering the educational ramifications for children with various levels of hearing loss.

Finally, because of the potential impact of hearing loss on language development and speech, age of onset is an important determinant. Like other handicapping conditions in children, a hearing loss may be congenital or acquired (or

TABLE 6.1   RELATIONSHIP OF AMOUNT OF HEARING LOSS TO COMMUNICATIVE EFFICIENCY

Decibel Loss in Speech Range (ISO)	Degree of Impairment	Effects
0–15	Insignificant	Only difficulty will be with faint or distant sounds.
15–25	At Risk	Without awareness of hearing needs, problems in language and speech may emerge.
26–40	Slight	Has difficulty with whispers and faint speech; understands conversational speech at 3 to 5 feet. Will need auditory training, language training, and hearing aid.
41–55	Mild to Moderate	Has frequent difficulties with normal speech with sufficient training and no other impairments will function in regular classroom with minimum support.
56–70	Moderately Severe	Conversational speech must be loud; will experience difficulties with classroom discussions and telephone conversations; will need considerable support in acquiring speech; many will use total communication systems.
71–90	Severe	May hear voice a foot away; difficulty with consonants; some understand strongly amplified speech; many will use total communication systems.
91–	Profound	Maximally amplified speech is not understood; most will use total communication systems.

Dubose, R. F. (1979). Working with Sensorily Impaired Children Part II: Hearing Impairments. Adapted from *Educating Young Handicapped Children: A Developmental Approach*, 2nd ed., by S.G. Garwood, 258, with permission of Aspen Publishers, Inc., © 1983.

adventitious). A congenital loss or one acquired prior to the completion of critically important early stages in the development of language and speech, is termed a *prelingual hearing loss*.

IDENTIFICATION OF HEARING PROBLEMS IN YOUNG CHILDREN

The principle of earliest possible identification is especially applicable to hearing problems because of the important role of hearing in young children's language development. Yet, tragically, although the means for very early identification are available, delays continue to occur for many children in positive identification of a hearing problem and/or in acting upon diagnostic information once it has been provided. These delays can prove extremely costly as opportunities for timely intervention when it can have the most lasting positive impact are missed or deferred.

CASE HISTORY 6.1:   BRIAN

Brian, now five years, six months of age, was born with a congenital sensorineural profound hearing loss in both ears, as well as a cleft palate and lip. He was fitted with ear-level hearing aids at six months. His mother began learning sign language when Brian was about 12 months old, and Brian, with his mother, began to participate in an early intervention Total Communication program when he was two years old. To date, three surgeries have been performed for repair of the cleft palate and lip.

After showing good progress in the pre-school Total Communication program, Brian was mainstreamed into a regular kindergarten, with a sign language interpreter, during the morning. In the afternoon, he attended a hearing-impaired kindergarten class in the same building. He made excellent use of his residual hearing, with his speech ability improving more slowly than his receptive language skills. He continues to receive private speech therapy two hours each week, and he communicates with his mother and brother using Total Communication. His current receptive language level is with the four-year range and his expressive language is at about the three-year age equivalent level. Brian is currently repeating kindergarten for the second year.

There are still instances of a family member suspecting a problem, based on the child's unusual or delayed early speech, yet not acting on that concern, or acting but receiving advice to "wait and see." Some standard preschool or school screening methods are insensitive to mild losses, particularly those associated with *otitis media* (middle ear infection) (Cass & Kaplan, 1979), and many children who experience recurrent middle ear problems before reaching school age do not participate in such screening programs at all (Zinkus & Gottlieb, 1980). Even routine checking by the young child's pediatrician or the family doctor will not always detect a problem.

Provisions of Public Law 99–457 have made it more likely that, once a young child demonstrates delays in any area of development, including speech and language, early intervention can be provided immediately. Positive diagnosis of a hearing loss can now result in optimally timely response, including provision of amplification, if indicated, and provision of appropriate services for the infant or young child, and for the family as well. Previously, many prelingually deaf children were not served through early educational intervention until much later than would have been optimal, often not until age three or even later.

As noted above, undetected chronic or recurrent middle ear infection (otitis media) in young children may represent a significant cause of subsequent hearing and language-related learning problems in later years. Some research (Naremore, 1979) suggests not only that many children with language problems have un-detected hearing loss, but that this is true for a significant number of children who have been labeled learning disabled. Most frequently, Naremore reports, in these instances there is a history of otitis media.

This serious problem has many ramifications. First, most children up to about age seven are quite vulnerable to ear infections associated with viral upper respira-tory problems; therefore, all children are at risk during the early years for otitis media. Additionally, some children experience more risk associated with other health and anatomical differences. Third, a child may "pass" screening both because of the characteristically fluctuating patterns of hearing acuity associated with otitis media and also because routine examining procedures are not sensitive to low-level loss. Even when the infection is treated, residual fluid may still result in temporary or fluctuating hearing loss. According to Lerner et al. (1987, p. 360) 25–65 percent of children under age two have had at least one ear infection involving some hearing loss. The hearing loss, even if fluctuating, undoubtedly interferes with language development.

Lerner et al. (1987) suggest that teachers be alert to the following signs of potential hearing difficulties. The child

1. Does not respond to sound.
2. Does not talk or even attempt to talk.
3. Uses indistinct speech.
4. Is unusually attentive to facial expressions and lip movements.
5. Is unduly sensitive to movement and visual clues.
6. Has a perpetual cold or runny nose, frequent earaches, or is a mouth breather.
7. Has recently recovered from scarlet fever, measles, meningitis, or from a severe head injury.
8. Needs much repetition before demonstrating understanding.
9. Is unusually active, running about and touching things.
10. Does not respond to being called in a normal voice when out of sight.
11. Requires many activities and visual cues before responding.
12. Uses a voice that has a nonmelodious quality.
13. Does not moderate his or her own voice and either talks too loudly or too softly. (p. 36–37)

TEACHING THE HEARING-IMPAIRED CHILD
IN THE MAINSTREAM CLASSROOM

Where the child sits is extremely important. You should assign seats to hearing-impaired children with attention to the total room arrangement. Children need to be able to see the teacher comfortably, so they can more readily "speech read," which means using *all* the visual cues a speaker provides when talking, including lip movements. You must also pay attention to what is *behind* the speaker. Even a person with normal hearing can be fatigued by looking at a speaker who is standing or seated in front of a window through which light glares; for a hearing-impaired person, this is infinitely more difficult. A seat near the front, although not necessarily in the front row, is usually best if the room is arranged in rows. Whatever the room arrangement, the child's better ear should be toward the teacher and other children.

Guidelines for Arranging a Classroom to Accommodate the Hearing-Impaired

1. Seat the hearing-impaired child near the front and center of the room, always facing the person in charge of an activity, and with the better ear toward that person.
2. Keep room lighting in mind when you and the hearing-impaired child are in different parts of the room. (Remember, if the speaker is standing in front of a window or bright light, speech reading is made extremely difficult. Light reflected on the speaker's face facilititates speech reading.)
3. Do not seat the hearing-impaired child near windows or heating or air conditioning units. Extraneous noise is picked up and amplified by a hearing aid more strongly than speech is.
4. If the child uses a *sign language interpreter* for class time, seat the interpreter so that the interpreter, as well as the teacher and appropriate visual aids (such as a chalkboard, charts, or a film) can be seen easily.

Having a hearing-impaired child in the group can make you a better teacher in many ways! Many of the "little" things that facilitate the learning of a hearing-impaired child are actually helpful for everyone. Teachers of older students, for example, may have to "unlearn" some of the mannerisms they have developed in lecturing, including pacing back and forth, turning one's back to the class to write on the board while *continuing to lecture,* holding an opened book in front of one's face, stroking one's beard, twiddling a mustache, or otherwise obscuring one's lips. Some of us have adopted such mannerisms quite unconsciously, and are totally unaware that they interfere with *all* our students' ability to follow what we are saying. Although people whose hearing is normal don't actually lipread, sighted people constantly interpret visual cues. Most of us are relatively unconscious of the extent to which our listening skills are augmented by vision.

We assume that teachers of young children seldom if ever use the lecture method! But they are likely to:

Lead group discussions and "class meetings."
Tell stories or recite poetry to the group.

Read aloud to the whole class or a small group.

Direct children's attention to the "News Corner" of the chalkboard, the calendar, or other displays on a bulletin board.

Work with language experience charts in the front of the room or in a center.

Invite children to share experiences or ideas with the class.

And in many other ways have occasion to be certain that all the children—including anyone with a hearing difficulty—are in positions where they can comfortably see as well as listen.

With a hearing-impaired child in the class, teachers may become more conscious of the importance of clarity in their enunciation, inflection, and tone. Speaking clearly is essential; speaking loudly is not, although an appropriate volume should be maintained. In conversation, many people have certain elliptical mannerisms, fading out or omitting altogether some parts of their message, especially of the beginning or ending of a sentence. As models for good speech, in addressing any group or in conversation with individual children, we as teachers should avoid these "lazy" patterns; when a hearing-impaired child is our listener, we need to work even harder to ensure that the entire speech message is received.

We can also attend to the needs of hearing-impaired children—and all children—by being an interesting speaker. Young children will enjoy listening and pay better attention if the teacher

Speaks in an animated, though not exaggerated, fashion.

Uses inflection, rather than speaking in a monotone.

Employs visual aids such as pictures, a doll, or other appropriate objects.

Is conscious of the importance of gesture, body language, and facial expression in augmenting the verbal message.

Uses direct, clear sentences of appropriate length, with appropriately inflected questions and exclamations interspersed with declarative sentences.

Introduces interesting new words, but explains or illustrates their meaning, adding them to the children's "collection."

Provides a clear indication when the topic is shifting, to enable all children to establish the appropriate "learning set."

All young children have some difficulty "paying attention," especially if paying attention means remaining physically in a chair or seated on the floor and listening to an adult speak for long periods of time. For a child with a hearing impairment, this is particularly difficult. The hearing-impaired child may tire with the additional effort required in listening and speech reading. Verna Hart (1981) suggests that, to understand what the hearing impaired child may feel, we remember when we ourselves were studying a foreign language, and the sheer exhaustion we no doubt felt at the end of a class period conducted entirely in that language.

Recollections about school experiences from a professional in an area of exceptionality, who is disabled herself, can be particularly—and poignantly—interesting. Beth Froehlinger Powell (1981), severely hearing-impaired from birth but mainstreamed throughout her school career, introduces a discussion of the concept of *oral interpreting* (for hearing-impaired students who communicate orally, rather than in sign) with these thoughts from her own elementary school days:

> "Today we had a movie in class. It was about the Second World War. I recognized some faces since I have pictures of them in my history book. I did not understand what the dark-haired man with the mustache was talking about all during the movie. Sometimes I wish I could just read something that will help when I watch it. I hope we're not going to have anything from the movie on our test Friday."
>
> "Today we had slides about plants. I could hear the teacher talking the whole time, but I did not understand a word she said. I feel so left out. Why doesn't she use a flashlight or something so I can watch her face, too."
>
> "We had class discussion today. We were supposed to take notes. I didn't take much. I spent a lot of time trying to see who was talking. Why doesn't somebody just raise his hand longer when he's talking, or stand up or something? Even sitting in a circle would help. I wish I had just one person who would let me know who is talking and tell me what he says if I miss it." (p. 180)

You should remind the hearing-impaired child to attend visually, but also expect and accept some occasional inattentive behavior. It is simply too tiring for young hearing-impaired children to look at their teacher for extended time periods. There is an important difference, however, between setting expectations that are too modest and limiting (making excuses for the child because of the handicap) on the one hand, and having an appropriate degree of understanding on the other. What is appropriate for a hearing-impaired child is often quite similar to what is appropriate for his or her hearing classmates.

While we need to speak clearly and in well-modulated voices, we do not need to speak loudly. Increasing the volume to a level that is uncomfortable for both teacher and other children is neither necessary nor desirable. Proximity can make the difference in enabling a child to hear; try to stay fairly close and to face the child. Staying close is always preferable to shouting! A shouting adult is undignified, extremely unpleasant to hear, and a very poor model for young children.

The hearing teacher's ability to understand the speech of the impaired child typically improves with experience and practice; and communication with peers frequently progresses even more quickly. To be certain that the child understands you, you may simply ask that he or she repeat your directions. In time, you and the child will find yourselves able to take each other's cues and mutually monitor your conversation. Remember that hearing aids amplify *all* sound, but they do not eliminate distortion. As Rebecca Dubose (1979) explains:

Simply put, hearing aids are tiny amplifiers. They make all sounds louder, including extraneous noises to which most of us selectively fail to attend. The deaf child is bombarded with all environmental sounds and must be carefully and laboriously trained to distinguish speech sounds from environmental noises. (p. 369)

Since hearing aids operate by means of batteries, batteries must of course be working. Batteries need to be checked each day at the beginning of the day, and parents should see to it a supply of fresh batteries is available. A battery tester is a necessary equipment item. Ear molds need to be kept clean and properly adjusted; a loose earmold may result in acoustic feedback, that is, a squeaking nose audible to others, but not to the child. Often you simply need to tell the child so that he or she may adjust the ear mold. Most children learn to manage their own hearing aids, including testing the batteries and keeping the ear molds clean. For children who benefit from amplification through the use of hearing aids, regular use of the aids is obviously important.

White (1981) concludes:

You don't want to risk "oversell," but you do want to create an atmosphere in which the hearing-impaired child feels comfortable and accepted as an individual and as an equal, judged on abilities, not disabilities. To your students you are the model. Their understanding and acceptance of the hearing-impaired child will be a direct reflection of your own. (p. 119)

Guidelines for Mainstream Teachers of Hearing-Impaired Children[1]

1. Accept the child positively.
2. Remember that the hearing-impaired child is a child first.
3. Face the child when talking.
4. Use normal speech.
5. Encourage speech development.
6. Explain the hearing impairment in objective terms (to the normally hearing children in the class.)
7. Determine the best seating arrangement.
8. Remember that distance increases listening difficulty.
9. Consider a student helper.
10. Present information visually when possible.
11. Be aware of special language needs.
12. Help the child develop responsibility.
13. Remember that concentrated learning and listening are tiring.
14. Noise will interfere with listening and understanding.
15. Use resources.
16. Parents are part of the team.
17. Give praise when deserved.

---

[1] Synthesized from White, 1981, pp. 115–118.

Guidelines for Facilitating Acceptance
of the Hearing-Impaired Child[2]

1. Talk with the class about the child's special needs. Point out that some people wear glasses to help them see, and some wear hearing aids to help them hear.
2. Be responsive to questions about hearing impairment. Present information simply and objectively.
3. Help the students understand how to communicate with the hearing-impaired child.
4. Let the students know that you think each one is important.
5. Talk about individual differences and abilities. Compare their ideas about what they do well and what they don't do as well (bowling, swimming, etc.)
6. Have consistent expectations for all students regarding classroom rules and limitations. The hearing-impaired child's sense of responsibility can affect his acceptance.
7. Encourage the hearing-impaired child to participate in class activities and not be just a spectator. His motivation and determination to become accepted are important.
8. Don't overuse the "buddy" system. Encourage independence and self-reliance.
9. Carefully plan the hearing-impaired child's first day in your class to ease his introduction and initial adjustment.
10. Plan a mini-course on communication and/or on hearing impairment. This might blend very well with a particular social studies or science unit. Let the hearing-impaired student help plan and present.
11. Invite guest speakers to create interest. Hearing-impaired adolescents or adults might be interesting visitors.

SOCIAL INTERACTION OF MAINSTREAMED HEARING-IMPAIRED CHILDREN

Communication is essential for social interaction. Consequently, advocates of oral-aural methods with hearing-impaired children have stressed traditionally the need for children with impaired hearing to acquire the means to communicate within a hearing society—and emphasized speech skills as a fundamental criterion for mainstream placement in school (e.g., Northcott, 1970, 1973). One study supportive of the important role of speech skills for meaningful social interaction of young children is by Brackett and Henniges (1976), conducted with hearing-impaired children who were integrated within a nursery school setting. They found that those children with the least speech skills tended to segregate themselves, interacting only minimally with hearing classmates. However, there have also been reports (e.g., Ezold & Boss, 1978, in an article describing a mainstreaming program with older elementary school students) documenting the formation of friend-

[2] White, 1981, p. 119.

ships and meaningful interaction when strong teacher leadership, commitment, and planning were present. A study by Antia (1982), reporting that mainstreamed hearing-impaired children (in a sample representing grades 1–6) interacted more frequently with each other than with normally hearing peers, concluded that mode of communication (speech or sign language) was less important than teacher leadership and planning: ". . . it may be possible, through carefully planned situations, to encourage and increase social interaction between hearing-impaired children and their peers" (p.24)

Principles and practices of planning and implementing situations and activities that promote interaction of hearing and hearing-impaired children are essentially the same as those applicable to all exceptional children. These can be followed in all instructional areas and in the ongoing schedule of classroom activities. The expressive arts offer excellent opportunities for meaningful social interaction, especially since overt teacher direction can be minimized, in order to encourage children's self-expression and peer interaction (James & James, 1980).

Griffith, Johnson, and Dastoli (1985) have noted an important factor concerning the communication patterns of hearing-impaired children in school, whether in special or regular class settings: they generally tend to interact communicatively more with the teacher than with classroom peers, to a far greater degree than typical hearing children. They have suggested strategies for teachers to use in analyzing the communication context of the classroom, and they suggest that "conversing can be taught:"

> Conversation should no longer be thought of as simply the medium through which lessons are accomplished. Conversational skills must be incorporated into the goals of the lesson. Most especially, language time in classrooms for hearing impaired students must focus on dialogue. Teaching syntactic skills may have to be postponed until students are able to master the interactive requirements of their language. (p. 174)

Although, for many students with significant hearing impairment, conversational skills may need focused attention as part of preparation for mainstreaming, these skills may be learned best within a social context in which the student acutely experiences the need for communication with peers. Griffith and her colleagues (Griffith et al., 1985) suggest specific emphases in a critically important area of programming for hearing-impaired children: language. As a regular classroom teacher, you can expect future specialized intervention for hearing-impaired children to prepare them better, for example, to participate in class discussions or to engage optimally in other activities in which *communicative interaction among students* is required. For your part, you can continue to encourage and promote interactive communication among students as a focus in teaching that is important in itself.

A continuing need for hearing-impaired students, at all educational levels, is for opportunities to communicate with others. Culhane and Mothersell (1981) explain this in the following "reminder" to regular classroom teachers:

Because a hearing impairment can so easily produce isolation, hearing-impaired students need many opportunities to communicate with family, peers, teachers, and other significant people in their environment. Students need them to help with schoolwork, to answer questions, and to offer information which the normally hearing student picks up incidentally about current events, personal hygiene, occupations, consumer economics, community resources, government, peer norms, slang, etc. (p. 101)

CASE HISTORY 6.2: MARY ELLEN AND SANDY: TWO DIFFERENT BUT SUCCESSFUL MAINSTREAMING SITUATIONS

Possibilities for successful mainstream placement of hearing-impaired children using either major communication mode, speech, or sign language, are illustrated by the stories of two nine-year-old girls who were successfully integrated in regular third grade classrooms for certain subjects.

Mary Ellen had a bilateral sensorineural hearing loss, moderate in her right ear and severe in her left ear. Mainstreaming consideration was clearly indicated on the basis of her good language skills and intelligible speech, with excellent use of residual hearing and also lipreading. In addition, she was a very outgoing and personable girl, comfortable in social situations. The difficulties identified were that, since she was new to the school, forming friendships might be difficult at first, possibly more difficult to form with hearing than with other hearing-impaired peers. Both third grade teacher "candidates" were also hesitant because they feared that she might have difficulty understanding them, but more that they might have difficulty understanding her speech. Her parents opposed providing an interpreter, not only because they thought that would accentuate her "differentness," but more because they considered interpreter services for their daughter a possible "crutch" that would lessen her own independent communication effort.

With the agreement that the resource specialist would meet with them daily during an initial trial period of two weeks, both teachers agreed for Mary Ellen to be in either of their classes. Based on her test scores, placement was made, with Mary Ellen participating in the lowest reading group and the highest math group in one of the third grade classrooms. Following the specialist's suggestions and parents' requests, seating was rearranged so that Mary Ellen was seated in front, to the left side of the room. The teacher understood the importance of standing when speaking to the children with sunlight to her side, rather than behind her. She was relieved to discover that Mary Ellen could detect when a hearing aid was not working and take care of it herself.

During the two-week trial, daily meetings, which soon included Mary Ellen herself, revealed very few problems. The teacher recognized an ongoing problem that *she* had was to: (1) remember to stand still when talking; (2) always face the class when talking; and (3) make sure she had Mary Ellen's attention before beginning to talk. All of these improved with practice. By the end of the first week, the teacher found that she could easily understand Mary Ellen's speech nearly all the time, and, when she couldn't, other children in the class could. Mary Ellen's main difficulty was feeling comfortable enough to ask questions, but this too improved with time. At the end of the trial period, the teacher asked to have her mainstream participation extended to include social studies as well. Soon, she was fully mainstreamed, only receiving tutoring from the hearing-impaired resource teacher as necessary, along with twice-weekly sessions of speech therapy and aural rehabilitation.

Sandy's situation differed primarily because of the greater severity of her hearing loss. She had a profound bilateral sensorineural hearing loss, with virtually no speech. However, Sandy, described as "proud to be who she is, just the way she is," was friendly, with an outgoing personality. Although she was enrolled in a special education special class for hearing-impaired children, using a total communication approach, she also had good friends in both of the mainstream third grade classes who had learned some sign language. Between that and her good speechreading skills, she could both understand and, to some extent, be understood by, hearing peers. Her academic skills were good as well, and the fact that she was reading nearly at grade level suggested above average intellectual ability.

Mainstreaming for some "special" activities, such as art, presented no problem whatsoever. Sandy was not only very attentive, but also demonstrated possible talent.

However, mainstream placement for the regular subjects was another matter; although they were aware of the art teacher's very positive response to Sandy, both third grade teachers initially refused to take her. The resource specialist, considering alternative ways to proceed—Sandy's reading level was higher than that of many of the hearing children!—determined that simply to "push" the teachers would be, in the long run, counterproductive.

I decided instead to meet with both teachers on a Monday morning before school (before they were tired or frustrated) to discover why they didn't want her in their classrooms. Both expressed concern about their ability to understand her questions or make themselves understood. I explained the use of an interpreter and assured them that we would have one available at all times she would be in either of their classes. I also explained that supplementary tutoring would be provided, in the resource room, as needed.

That was acceptable to them, but they identified another problem. Between their two classes, they had a total of seven children who had come only recently from Viet Nam and who spoke little or no English. As yet, they had received no help with or support for these children, and they were frustrated. It seemed to them that adding Sandy, with or without an interpreter, would increase their already overwhelming "language barrier" problems.

So we worked out a trade. One of the teachers took Sandy into her classroom, and I took their Vietnamese students into my classroom for speech and language time each day. There were difficult times for all of us, but we all benefited greatly in the long run. After a one-month trial, we all agreed that things were working out better than we possibly could have anticipated, for all concerned.

However, some of the other third-graders had become interested in learning to use sign language so they could talk to Sandy more easily. The interpreter was asked, and agreed, to teach a sign language class after school once each week for all those interested. She had a large class! Thirteen students, four teachers, and the principal participated. Fortunately, however, she had an assistant—*Sandy.*

SPECIAL ASSISTIVE SYSTEMS AND RESOURCES

A very promising approach introduced into elementary schools in recent years is *classroom amplification*. The teacher wears a small lavalier microphone, and the sound of her voice is amplified while allowing her to use a normal and comfortable tone. As educators become aware of the substantial numbers of young children who may have slight hearing loss, especially associated with chronic or recurring otitis media, amplification in the classroom may become more common. It is, relatively, quite inexpensive, potentially beneficial to all children as well as those with impaired hearing, unobtrusive, and conducive to more comfortable, and less fatiguing, speech effort on the teacher's part.

Sign language *interpreter services* may be provided for a deaf child if indicated on the child's IEP. An interpreter does exactly what the term indicates: translates oral speech into sign language so that the child who does not hear speech can understand what is being said. *Reverse interpreting* means translating into speech what the deaf individual expresses manually. However, most classroom interpreting is provided mainly for the former purpose. If an interpreter is provided for a child in your classroom, you will be oriented concerning the interpretation process. You and the interpreter will discuss how the process can be facilitated in terms of seating arrangement and other logistical matters. You will find that the other children will of course be very interested in the signing, but that they will soon become accustomed to it. Their interest is an asset that can possibly lead to their learning to use some signs to communicate with the child who does not use speech.

Increasingly, special education teachers are specifically trained to facilitate the transition of students with handicaps into the mainstream classroom. That is certainly the case with specialists in teaching hearing-impaired students. A special education teacher can be an especially helpful resource person, guiding you to apply the general principles discussed and illustrated in this chapter to the unique situation of individual children with impaired hearing.

Even a fully mainstreamed hearing-impaired child will continue to be seen by a speech and language pathologist for speech therapy. As with other areas of disability, you will need to plan with the speech and language pathologist how the child's individual communication goals can be furthered in the communicative context of the classroom.

Although *audiologists* are correctly identified as playing an absolutely essential role in assessing children's hearing characteristics, they may also be helpful in implementing intervention in the classroom. Audiologists not only provide guidance concerning hearing aids, they also can suggest approaches to help children enhance listening abilities. Clinically, audiologists work individually with children and their parents, but some auditory training procedures may have implications for classroom implementation.

SUMMARY

Like young children with visual impairments, those with hearing impairments present a wide range of abilities, styles, personal characteristics, and emotional as well as cognitive and academic needs. However, the overriding and common concern is communication. Many children with hearing problems, and especially those with severe, prelingual hearing loss, require specialized early intervention, at least when they are very young. They need to be taught very specific skills to enable them to communicate and also to develop the language base for reading and other academic skills areas. At the same time, interaction with hearing children is critically important. Mainstreaming for each child requires careful individual planning and a team approach. Teachers, especially those in early childhood, need to be aware of how frequently hearing problems are undetected and also of the great disservice to a child when communication needs are neglected.

ADAPTING INSTRUCTIONAL ACTIVITIES
FOR THE HEARING-IMPAIRED

In contrast to children with visual or motor impairments, many children with impaired hearing require few specific classroom, curricular or instructional adaptations that are not equally appropriate and desirable for all young children. Creative and responsive teachers who understand the special needs of hearing-impaired children can enhance the learning of those children in all the curricular areas encompassed within early childhood education, nonetheless. This chapter concludes with suggestions developed by Maria Sargent for adapting typical learning activities.

Color Concepts

Children with impaired hearing may find it difficult to discriminate among colors referred to in the verbal mode only. The use of concrete materials should accompany the verbal instructions as much as possible. Symbolic cues will also aid the child with hearing difficulty (signs, gestures, etc.) The use of these signs or gestures can be easily taught to all the children, which will aid communication among peers allowing for full participation in group activities.

GOAL:
>   To assist the child with hearing needs to discriminate among colors referred to verbally.

OBJECTIVE:
>   The child will use predetermined cues to assist in discrimination of color words.

MATERIALS:
Various colored objects

PROCEDURE:
1. The child will be introduced to the specific cue to be used whenever the color is referred to in the course of a lesson. The color will initially be present in concrete form and eventually this concrete aid will be faded.
2. Various games can then be introduced to the child. The teacher can give the cue and the child will have to find the color or the color can be shown and the specific cue then given.
3. Games using this format can be used for group activities if the cues are taught to all the children. The child has the choice of giving one of three clues to the color: the actual concrete object with that color; the verbal color name or the sign/cue used for that color. Another child, using that cue must provide a different answer (e.g., if the child gives the visual cue of the concrete object, the other child must provide the color name or the sign). In this manner the children can use the color form they are comfortable with while providing the needed assistance for those with hearing problems. This procedure also provides alternative answers for the student experiencing difficulty with correct pronunciation of color words.

Number Concepts

The child may lack the basic vocabulary needed to understand fully math-related concepts. Physical experience with concepts such as more, less, bigger, smaller, etc. should be provided to assist the child in the symbolic representation of these concepts math will later require. Also needed may be concrete representations of various math-related terms including the area of geometry and measurement.

GOAL:
To assist the child in understanding the symbolic concepts of same, more and less through direct experience.

OBJECTIVES:
The child will be able to represent the concepts more, equal (same), and less than by using play dough "cookies."

MATERIALS:
Play dough; paper plates; several dolls or stuffed animals; cookie cutters; paper plate "models"

PROCEDURE:
1. Introduce the child to the play dough and cookie cutters and show him how to cut out cookies if he does not know how.
2. Open up a "cookie store" and use the dolls as customers. Have the first

doll order three cookies and let child cut them out and place them on the plate.

3. Have the next doll order, "more cookies, less cookies, or the same amount of cookies," as the first doll. If the child has difficulty filling the order, have him use the paper plate models (these models should have circles corresponding with the number desired). The child can then fill the order by placing a cookie over each drawn circle. Point out the differences verbally to the child as the game proceeds. Roles may be switched so the child can get the chance to use the concepts in a verbal manner. Also, this game can be used as a small group activity.

4. If the paper models are used, gradually phase out their use as the child begins to understand the concepts without the cues.

Letters

Some children with speech disfluency may run words together or speak in a mumbled manner. For others, the main concern will be the recognition of the letter signs to be used for speech purposes. Activities to help either group of children can be developed easily. Most activities will require little or no adaptation needs. Teaching the letter signs can be an enjoyable activity for all children as most find the activity fascinating.

GOAL:
   To assist the child who is developing the habit of rushed or slurred speech to speak slower in a nonthreatening manner.

OBJECTIVE:
   To provide a situation that requires the slow, clear pronunciation of the alphabet.

MATERIALS:
   Alphabet bingo cards, chips; alphabet; tape recorder

PROCEDURE:
   1. Have the child be the caller for an alphabet bingo game with a small group of children.
   2. Stress the need for the caller to say each letter chosen in a clear manner and to pause after each so the players may lay down their chips.
   3. Tell the child to hold up the letter as he says it so any difficulty with pronunciation will not elicit a chorus of questions that might embarrass the child.

If the child feels uncomfortable about speaking in front of the group, he can pre-record a randomized alphabet sequence in private. He can then merely turn on and pause the tape recorder after each letter during the course of the game.

Letters

GOAL:

To provide practice in the alphabet and the corresponding letter sign in a group setting.

OBJECTIVE:

The children will have the choice of providing one of three cues to the letter they want. They may give the sign, show the letter, or say the letter out loud. The child will then answer in like form using one of the two remaining modes.

MATERIALS:

Chart of the alphabet; pictures of the finger signs for each letter

PROCEDURE:

1. One child will pick a letter to use. He will then pick one of the three cues detailed above and use it. The child will then call on another and that child must identify the letter using one of the two modes left. In this manner, the child can use whatever mode he feels comfortable with and the child with hearing difficulty will be able to participate fully.

Shape Concept

A hearing-impaired child may have difficulty understanding the concepts inherent in basic shapes. Verbal descriptions normally used with other children may be lost to them without the use of concrete materials. Activities in which the child constructs the shapes for himself are essential for complete understanding of the differences among the shapes referred to.

GOAL:

To assist the child in visualizing geometric concepts using a concrete mode.

OBJECTIVE:

The child will be able to place several pieces of wood (or other children can be used) in the shape requested.

MATERIALS:

Wooden planks; nails and hammer (optional); several friends; concrete representations of geometric shapes as models; plastic animals or blocks in geometric shapes

PROCEDURE:

1. Introduce the game of "house builder" to the child. He should be told that he needs to build houses for some friends or for the animals or blocks (depending on the variation used).
2. Have the animals or one of the other children pick one of the shape models and ask the child to build a house in that shape (foundation only).

The pieces of wood can be nailed together if desired. The child can continue to build houses in the various shapes requested.

3. Variation: If desired, the child can build houses for "block people" but should be told that the blocks will only live in houses the same shape as they are. The child can build the required shape and then place the blocks inside. This will provide additional practice in shape discrimination through matching.

Direction and Sequencing

The child with a hearing problem may have difficulty following directions. So much effort is put into the processing of the first part of a direction that the later portions may be missed. Children with speech difficulty find it difficult to verbalize the action they wish others to take.

GOAL:

To assist the child in developing the ability to remember and carry out two- and three-step directions.

OBJECTIVE:

The child will carry out a one-step direction given in a progressively closer sequence until the child can follow two or three of the directions at once.

MATERIALS:

Anything in the room

PROCEDURE:

1. The child will be told he is a robot that must follow every command of his owner. Give the child simple commands with a great deal of time between the commands.
2. Gradually shorten the span between commands until the child seems able to handle two commands at one time. If the child cannot complete the task, move back and re-institute the pauses and slowly progress downward again.
3. This activity can be conducted as a small group situation. Since children often cannot produce a two-step command on their own, two children can give one command each and the child must carry them both out.

GOAL:

To give a child practice in the production of exact commands to others.

OBJECTIVE:

The child will be able to describe a picture and issue directions to another child in such a manner that the child ends up with the same picture.

MATERIALS:

Colored felt shapes of different sizes; two felt boards

PROCEDURE:

1. Have the child construct a simple design on his felt board (out of the other child's sight).
2. The child must then tell his friend exactly what to put on his board in order to construct the same design. Have the child start with only two- or three-piece designs and progressively become more complex.
4. If the child seems stuck, assist by giving clues such as, "You must tell him what color, shape, size, or place you want." "Should that piece go on top of the circle or next to it?"
5. This activity can be slanted to give practice in an area of visual discrimination the child is having difficulty in. If the child is having difficulty with the color blue, for instance, let squares be blue only so the child has another cue to fall back on.

Social Skills

Children may tend to avoid group social interactions due to the problems with basic communication. Setting up situations in which physical expression and not verbal expression is required may aid a child in making that first step toward developing friendships.

GOAL:

To set up situations in which a child can participate in social interaction without the use of verbal interaction.

OBJECTIVE:

The child will participate with a partner in a game in which the only mode of communication is physical.

MATERIALS:

Six pictures of people with various occupations or activities which can be easily acted out; props if desired

PROCEDURE:

1. Give each child a set of six pictures and the props to be used.
2. Tell the children they will take turns picking a picture (with their eyes) and acting out the action of the picture. They may use no words.
3. When the child is finished, the other child must try to pick out the picture of the action just acted out. The picture should be pointed to. They can then change places and repeat.

Motor Skills

The child with hearing problems will often experience no difficulty in the area of motor control. For some, however, the presence of inner ear problems may affect balance. While most of the difficulty cannot be avoided, practice in balancing activities can provide some measure of self-confidence.

GOAL:
To provide practice in balancing for the child experiencing inner ear balance deficiencies.

OBJECTIVE:
The child will be able to walk across a balance beam set a few inches off the floor.

MATERIALS:
Green paper; balance beam; blue pillows

PROCEDURE:
1. Draw large alligators on the green paper and place under the balance beam.
2. Take the children on a jungle safari that will include the need to cross the bridge over the "alligator" river.
3. If the child exhibits a great fear of falling, pillow rocks can be added to the river to make the child feel more secure.

During the safari, other balance-related activities, like stepping in and out of tires, can be included.

Feelings

Children with speech or hearing difficulty may have difficulty describing their emotions. Activities can be developed for these children in which they learn to verbalize their emotions to the extent possible and develop appropriate alternatives when words cannot be used.

GOAL:
To assist children in the expression of their feelings in an appropriate manner.

OBJECTIVE:
The child will be able to describe the emotion that goes with the facial expression they are mirroring from a card. Alternative means of relaying that emotion other than speech will be elicited where appropriate.

MATERIALS:
Pictures of people showing various facial expressions; props as needed to act out situations

PROCEDURE:
1. Show the child a picture of a emotion and have the child mimic the emotion with his own face.
2. Have the child describe how he would feel if he had that expression. Acting out a scenario appropriate to that feeling may help the child in his description.

3. Help the child find as many ways to express his feelings verbally as possible.
4. Discuss appropriate (moving away) and non-appropriate (hitting) ways to communicate one's feeling without using words.
5. In classroom situations remind the child to take his time and use words to describe how he feels.

Body Image and Self-Concept

The child with impaired hearing may feel frustrated and have low self-esteem. Awareness of self centers too much on his problems and not his skills. Provide a situation in which the child is the expert at some activity. Any hobby or skill that he possesses to a great degree would be fine. Being placed as the center of interest for a skill instead of a difficulty, the child may begin to see himself in a more positive light. From the perspective of the other children, he is the boy with the great comic book collection instead of the boy who can't talk right.

GOAL:
To provide an experience that focuses on a speech- or hearing-impaired child's unique skills.

OBJECTIVE:
The child will demonstrate to the group via a presentation, table setup, or bulletin board a specific, unique skill, hobby, or accomplishment he possesses.

MATERIALS:
Whatever is appropriate

PROCEDURE:
1. Discuss with the child his unique experience before the presentation.
2. List the points the child wishes to make and let him choose the manner in which he wishes to make them.
3. Provide the set-up materials and assistance and assist in its presentation to the degree needed.
4. Encourage the other children to follow up any questions and further interest one-to-one with the child.

Discrimination Skills

Some children with special speech and hearing needs may benefit from practice in auditory discrimination. Various noises can provide close listening requirements that may be beneficial to the child. The child can also develop his own tape of noises to use with other children thus providing practice and at the same time a natural leadership role.

GOAL:
To provide practice in auditory discrimination.

OBJECTIVE:
The child will be able to identify objects by the sound they make.

MATERIALS:
Tape of everyday sounds (appliances, animals, etc.); tape recorder; blank tape; pictures

PROCEDURE:
1. Have the child listen to each sound and identify its source.
2. Provide pictures of the various objects if the child is having difficulty identifying the sounds.
3. Discuss some of the sounds the child can hear in the classroom.
4. Allow the child to tape some of the sounds in the room. The tape can then be played to a group of friends with him acting as the "teacher." (Voices of people in the room are also a possible source of sounds).

Perceptual Skills

The use of puzzles can provide auditory discrimination practice in a new format for young children with special hearing needs. Activities can be structured for work in pairs or work with tape recorders. Adaptations to the puzzles will not distract other children and may be an exciting challenge for all children needing auditory discrimination practice.

GOAL:
To provide practice in auditory discrimination or direction following using the activity of puzzle completion.

OBJECTIVE:
The child will listen to the directions given by a peer or by a tape recorder in order to locate the next puzzle piece to be placed in the puzzle.

MATERIALS:
Marking pen; puzzle; tape recorder

PROCEDURE:
1. Tell the child that the peer or tape recorder will give directions needed in order for him to locate the next puzzle piece to be used. Use puzzles that have no inherent sequence so the child must rely on the directions. (If peers are used, activity will vary according to child's directions)
2. Have the child listen to the tape recorder direction for the first piece (tape-recorded messages can be developed as desired; be sure to include pauses between directions). Once the child has heard the direction, have him locate the piece requested and place in the puzzle. Show the child how to pause and unpause the machine if he needs more time.

3. If desired, the prerecorded instructions may contain an answer symbol after each pause. The symbol given will correspond with a symbol on the back of the puzzle piece. In this manner, the child can self-correct his own work.

Reading

Reading (an aspect of communication, which is the key problem area for hearing-impaired children) has traditionally posed difficulties for many children with significant hearing disabilities. Changing trends in reading instruction that emphasize the language base and communicative context for reading (e.g., Vacca, Vacca, & Gove, 1987) may portend more relevant and effective approaches for all young children, including those who are hearing impaired. As Degler and Risko (1979) recommend, teaching reading to hearing-impaired children in the regular classroom simply involves paying greater attention to those "best practices" that guide reading instruction for all young children. First, the reading curriculum should be part of a meaning-based, total language approach; consequently, the major goal is comprehension. Skill acquisition is important only insofar as it is instrumental in achieving that goal. Second, children's learning to read builds upon the language competence that they bring to reading. Third, instruction, including the introduction of new sight words, is most effective when it is context-based rather than removed from context.

The young child with hearing-impaired needs may find the area of reading bothersome in varying ways. The child may often miss parts of a story that are read out loud, lack comprehension skills, or feel uncomfortable about his speech and reluctant to "read" his stories in front of other children. These problems, among others, can be eased with the use of special activities and a little care.

GOAL:
To help a child become more comfortable reading his language experience stories in front of a group.

OBJECTIVE:
The child will use a tape recorder to "practice" his story and will eventually read it to the group itself.

MATERIALS:
Paper; crayons and pencil; magazine pictures; tape recorder

PROCEDURE:
1. Have the child draw a picture of something he likes or is interested in. Pictures from magazines can be substituted for this step.
2. Have the child make up a story or tell about the picture he has drawn or the picture he has chosen.
3. Write down exactly what the child says when he speaks. Go over what was written and encourage the child to share the "story" with others.

4. Provide a tape recorder so the child can practice reading his story.
5. Let the child present the tape while holding the picture if he is still reluctant. Continue with other stories at various times until the child is ready to try it on his own.

Books that have prerecorded stories that require only the turning of pages at a bell, can also provide nonthreatening "reading" experiences in front of a group. The child can hold the book and turn the pages for the class.

GOAL:

To assist the child with hearing difficulty in catching the important points in a story being read to the group.

OBJECTIVE:

The child will use his normal hearing plus the repeated cues to provide information about the story to be used in a variety of comprehension questions.

MATERIALS:

Book

PROCEDURE:

1. Read through the story prior to presentation and decide on the main actions and characters that are essential to comprehension. Note or mark these for easy reference.
2. When reading the story, make comments or ask questions structured in such a manner that the points desired are restated for the child to hear again. For example: if the action essential to the story was a rabbit stealing a frog's hat, you could say, "Where do you think the rabbit will hide the hat he stole from the frog?" In this manner the whole group of children are being involved in the story, and, at the same time, the child will get a second chance to catch the needed points.

Science

The child with a hearing problem may find it difficult to follow directions, a skill that is required for conducting many scientific experiments. Providing extra cues for these children using visual sequence steps can promote independent investigation without the chance of failure due to misfollowed directions.

GOAL:

To assist the child with a hearing impairment to follow the steps of instructions needed to conduct a simple scientific experiment.

OBJECTIVE:

Using the visual sequence cards, the child will be able to conduct a simple science experiment.

MATERIALS:
    Objects for experiment; colored trays or pieces of paper; masking tape; large
    cards

PROCEDURE:
    1. Sequence the steps required for the experiment and decide on the means
        to symbolize each step (drawings, actual models, etc.).
    2. Put one step on each card. Use color coding to show the child which
        material to use and have those materials placed on that color tray
        or paper.
    3. On each card draw a picture (place picture in a box or next to a model), so
        the child can compare the result of each step for correct procedure.
    4. Before allowing individual work, go through all but the last step of the
        experiment to help explain procedure and generate interest.

Music

The child with speech/hearing needs may rely a great deal on visual cues and
vibrations for guidance when dealing with music. The child may need extra time to
grasp the words of the song. Several methods can facilitate and maximize their
participation.

GOAL:
    To assist children with speech or hearing needs in the full participation in
    music-based activities.

OBJECTIVE:
    The child will participate in music activities to the fullest of their capacities.

MATERIALS:
    Percussion instruments

PROCEDURE:
    1. Use percussion instruments that vibrate in order to provide cues to
        sounds being produced.
    2. Use arm motions to depict the rise and fall of the tone and the beat.
    3. In experiences in which a child will move to music, always move your
        arm, a scarf, or beat a drum so the child has a sense of the rhythm.
        Providing pictures that give a sense of the music will help set the mood.
    4. Placement of the child during teaching of a song may facilitate the grasp of
        the words. Speaking each line before teaching the melody may help.

Art

Children with impaired hearing will need little or no adaptation for the majority of
art projects. The essential point is to progress through any directions slowly and
concisely. Many art activities can provide tactile stimulation that is beneficial.
With the use of the right materials, auditory stimulation may occur as well.

GOAL:
To provide an art activity that provides auditory stimulation.

OBJECTIVE:
The student will use varying sizes of beans to create a collage and will describe the differing sounds they make.

MATERIALS:
Paper; glue; various size beans; rice; sand; strainers; shirt box; brush

PROCEDURE:
1 The student will apply a small portion of glue to a paper placed within a shirt box using the brush provided.
2. The child will decide on the object group to be placed and will use the strainer (for sand and rice) or will use a spoon to place the objects in the box. Let the child discover on his own which items will go through the strainer.
3. The child can then cover the glued area by tilting the box back and forth.
4. Point out the different sounds made. Have the child describe the differences heard between the various objects.

Many objects will provide the same results. Heavy plastic, wax paper, styrofoam, etc., are all materials with potential for auditory-based art-project development.

CHAPTER 7

Integrating Young Children with Motor Impairments and Other Physical Disabilities

This chapter presents a wide range of concerns and describes a wide range of strategies. Quite simply, that is because the children who experience physical or health problems present an extremely wide range of characteristics and needs. The only unifying factor is the likelihood that each of these children, and their families, will have had a great deal of involvement with doctors and hospitals. Like sensory impairments, physical impairments and health problems are experienced by many, if not most adults. Yet, as a "group" of exceptional children, children with physical handicaps comprise a low-incidence category.

In this context, the distinctions suggested by the terms impairment, disability, and handicap are especially relevant. *Impairment* refers to a medically diagnosed structural defect or loss of physical function that in certain instances can be restored, as for example, with a prosthetic limb (Love & Walthall, 1977). To the degree that a person's life functioning is affected by an impairment, a *disability* is present. Whether the child is *handicapped* depends upon the child's own psychological adjustment (Langley, 1979) and the response of others (DeLoach & Greer, 1981). This distinction is extremely important to bear in mind. Nevertheless, the term *physically handicapped,* as well as other similar terms (orthopedically handicapped, crippled and other health impaired) are employed in national and state policy documents to attempt to define a "group." As in other areas of exceptionality, the purpose of that attempt is to ensure that the rights of individuals are established—to appropriate education, in the case of children, and to access to services, employment opportunities, and all benefits of the society for adults.

A great many children may have physical or health problems and may require long-term or ongoing medical care, yet are not considered handicapped for purposes of education. As a group of exceptional children eligible for special education services under P.L. 94–142, orthopedically and health-impaired children are defined as follows:

> Orthopedically impaired means severe orthopedic impairment which adversely affects a child's educational performance. The term includes impairments caused by congenital anomaly, impairments caused by disease, and impairments from other causes such as fractures, or burns that can cause contractures. Other health impaired means limited strength, vitality or alertness due to chronic or acute health problems such as heart condition, epilepsy, tuberculosis, rheumatic fever, nephritis, asthma, sickle cell anemia, hemophilia, lead poisoning, leukemia, or diabetes, which adversely affects a child's educational performance. (p. 42478)

EFFECTS OF DISABILITIES ON EDUCATIONAL PERFORMANCE

For some children, having a physical problem may have pronounced adverse effects on educational performance; for others, that is not the case at all. Among the latter group are a great many children whose learning ability is in no way affected, who can be and are fully mainstreamed in school, and who can participate fully in all aspects of the standard school program, requiring no special adaptations or adjustments. Also included are many children who can participate fully, but only if certain adaptations and adjustments are provided; their situations require attention to the distinction between disability and handicap. Failure on the part of the school program to accommodate the physical situations of these children results unnecessarily—and *illegally*—in handicapping them. The most familiar example concerns sheer physical access to the school itself, the classroom and other necessary school resources (such as the library), rest rooms, and learning facilities within the classroom. Other examples pertain to instructional adaptations that can be implemented by a teacher, involving materials, scheduling of activities, seating assignment, and the incorporation of assistive aids, devices, and alternative provisions (if needed) for communication. This chapter will focus primarily upon these areas.

There are indeed children whose physical disability can adversely affect educational performance in any of a variety of ways. Of principal concern would be children whose cognitive skills are impaired to such an extent that curricular goals and instructional methods in some or all areas of learning are appropriately different from those employed for nonhandicapped children. That may be the case if brain function is involved, but is certainly not necessarily the case, since individuals with cerebral palsy, for example, represent the full gamut of intellectual functioning, including superior intellectual ability. In general, all children with physical or health impairments should have, are entitled to, and can benefit from educational experiences in which they are integrated with "typical" children.

Peterson (1987) has described four general areas in which a child's physical disability may impact upon his or her development. First, the child may have experienced a great many medical procedures, often including multiple surgeries and repeated or prolonged hospitalizations, involving separation from family and interruption of normal home, school, and peer group experiences. Second, where abnormal reflex patterns are involved, as is the case with cerebral palsy, the child experiences interference with movement and with motor skill performance. Third, abnormality in tone affects not only movement but frequently physical growth. Fourth, restricted movement can interfere with the child's mastery of motor skills as well as cognitive skill learning. According to Peterson (1987), serious health problems may potentially impact upon the development of a young child as

1. Social isolation and disruption in normal life experiences that promote early learning.
2. Physical limitations and reduction in energy level.
3. Potential disruption in interpersonal relationships.
4. Effects upon parent's child rearing practices.
5. Alterations in a child's level of dependence/independence.
6. Side effects of medications.
7. Potential emotional effects of illness. (p. 222–223)

For some children with physical disabilities, *communication* is a major concern. Abnormal speech patterns or significant difficulty in speech are present to the degree that voluntary muscles affecting speech production are involved, frequently the case with cerebral palsy. Children who are severely speech-involved experience great difficulty in communicating their needs and desires.

Impaired mobility may affect early psychological development to the extent that the young child's physical transactions with a responsive environment are impeded, for it is through such transactions that young children develop concepts of causality, physical attributes, and self (Langley, 1979). Children with disabilities have the same needs for mastery as do other children, and difficulties in experiencing control over the environment make achievement of a sense of personal competence more difficult.

In summary, children with physical disabilities may but do not necessarily have special learning needs. Children's intellectual ability may or may not be impaired, and associated *secondary impairments* affecting communication, perceptual processes, or social-emotional development may or may not be present. Diagnosis and description of children with physical disabilities is based on a medical model and on medical, rather than educational, criteria. This tends to result in an emphasis upon the child's limitations and differentness from the norm, rather than upon the child as a whole person, with characteristics in common with all other children, and also with specific strengths (Best, 1978). Children with physical disabilities comprise an extremely heterogeneous group. The only common denominator is a medically diagnosed, biologically based problem, which generally requires ongoing medical attention. Some ameliorative procedures, such as physical therapy, although medically prescribed, comprise a critically important element in the educational program designed for many children. For other children, medical and therapeutic needs may be addressed independently of the school, rather than considered *related services* required by a handicapped child in order to benefit from special education. For some children, their medical problems require informed awareness of school personnel and cooperation in areas such as those involving medication, special dietary considerations, allergies, the possibility of seizures, any restrictions in physical activity, mobility, and self-care areas.

TYPES OF PHYSICAL DISABILITIES IN YOUNG CHILDREN

Physical disabilities in children encompass a great number of identified medical *syndromes,* some extremely rare. Listing all known forms of physical disability would be of questionable value here. There are, however, some excellent references for educators, some of which are listed in the Appendix of this book.

Excepting certain chronic health problems, most young children with a physical disability are impaired with respect either to mobility or to manual skills, or to both. The source of impaired movement or manipulation may reside in the bones or muscles (musculoskeletal impairments) or in the brain or central nervous system, where damage or dysfunction may result in impaired voluntary control of muscle groups or sensation (neuromotor impairments). Most common among the latter, and the largest single medical classification, is *cerebral palsy.* Cerebral palsy is a *nonprogressive* condition in which voluntary control of involved muscles is impaired as a result of brain injury incurred either during the fetal period (prenatally), at the time of birth (perinatally), or during the developmental period (postnatally).

Although cerebral palsy is commonly thought of as a specific type of impairment, the term actually encompasses a broad range of causes, functional levels, and degrees of intellectual, sensory, motor, and communication involvement. The most visible characteristic is likely to be impaired movement due not to bone or muscle malformations but to problems in the control center for muscle activity, the brain. The nature, extent, and severity of the resulting disability depends upon the location and extent of the brain lesion. Some individuals are very mildly and focally involved, while others are multi-handicapped, with associated problems in communication, sensory, perceptual, and intellectual functioning.

The more common forms of cerebral palsy, *spasticity* and *athetosis,* are characterized by abnormal muscle tone. *Ataxia,* a less common form, involves problems associated with gait and balance. Use of or control over arms and legs is most commonly affected, but other muscle groups may also be involved. Some children with severe involvement may be unable to sit unassisted, or may have minimal head support and lack the ability to turn their heads from side to side. Chewing and swallowing may be affected, and even less severely involved children may have abnormal speech patterns. Physical and occupational therapists can provide invaluable help in showing you how to position a child, or even physically support a child suffering from cerebral palsy, in order to normalize muscle tone and thus facilitate optimal classroom participation.

Epilepsy or *convulsive disorder,* although also of neurological origin, is not reflected in chronically impaired movement, nor is it actually a discrete disease. Epilepsy refers to a predilection to seizures or convulsions; many children with cerebral palsy or other problems also have a history of seizures. Although epilepsy cannot be cured, seizures frequently can be controlled through medication. Children who may experience seizures present two very important requirements for school personnel: provisions to ensure that the child's specifically prescribed medication is available and taken as prescribed and awareness of proper handling of a seizure incident should one occur. Both are addressed in subsequent sections of this chapter. Every teacher should understand what seizures are and know what, and what not, to do when someone experiences a seizure. A third type of physical impairment frequently encountered by mainstream teachers is *spina bifida* (technically, *myelodysplasia*), which identifies a range of congenital malformations of the posterior vertebrae that may or may not result in significantly impaired sensation and movement. Generally, however, we use the term spina bifida to refer to the condition in which spinal cord damage has occurred.

Medical advances have profoundly changed the prognostic picture for children born with spina bifida. *Shunting* procedures can now relieve the accumulation of cerebrospinal fluid in the brain *(hydrocephalus)* that would previously have led to retardation and, typically, death. With newly developed surgical procedures, a child born with spina bifida may have normal intelligence, but may still never be able to walk or control bladder or bowel functions (Batshaw & Perret, 1981, p. 42). A child may need repeated shunt operations as he or she grows, and may also need orthopedic surgery. Bladder and kidney infections may occur, requiring programs of bowel and urinary management including catheterization. Obviously, these self-care concerns are important in terms of the child's adaptive functioning, at school as well as at home.

Clean Intermittent Cathetherization (CIC) is a procedure by which a person with spina bifida (as well as other symptoms relating to difficulty with bladder control) can empty the bladder. As a result of a Supreme Court decision (Irving Independent School District v. Tatro), it is considered a health service, rather than a medical service, since it can be provided by persons other than a physician, or by the individual himself or herself. The Tatro decision established that CIC can be identified on a child's IEP as a related service necessary for the education program to be provided, just as physical, occupational, or speech and language therapy may be so identified if they are needed. Related services must be provided by the school.

CIC is termed "clean" because simple cleanliness, not sterilization, is required. The most important aspect of catheterization is that it is done frequently and regularly. Typically, it is carried out every three to four hours (Stauffer, 1983). Obviously, privacy is required for the child to catheterize (or "cath"). Most children will have learned, or will be learning, to handle the process themselves. It is important, however, that if someone else must catheterize a child, more than a single adult in the school setting be prepared to handle the catheterization. That is because frequency is the most important factor, and it is essential not to delay because of a nurse's, aide's, or attendant's temporary absence.

Among the advantages of CIC, and especially self-catheterization (CISC), are its normalization aspects. The child can avoid the embarrassment of wetting incidents, be responsible for carrying (very compactly and inconspicuously) the tube and collection container, and experience a degree of significant self-care control otherwise impossible.

Arthrogryposis is a congenital, nonprogressive stiffness of the joints associated with defective muscle tissue but only rarely with intellectual impairment. Other orthopedic impairments include *juvenile rheumatoid arthritis,* involving inflammation of joints; *osteogenesis imperfecta,* sometimes called brittle bone disease, where children are highly susceptible to fractures; *Legg-Calve-Perthes disease,* which involves diseased bone tissue at the hip; and *achondroplastic dwarfism,* characterized by increasing body disproportion as growth progresses and caused by diseased cartilage.

Limb deficiency (congenital or surgical amputee, or congenitally foreshortened and abnormally structured limb, termed *phocomelia*) is most familiar to many people through media attention to thalidomide babies, individuals whose mothers used during pregnancy a prescribed drug that was later found to cause birth defects. Other factors result in limb malformations as well, and sometimes a limb may be surgically amputated as a drastic measure required by disease. Some but not all children use a *prosthesis* to approximate normal use of a limb.

Among the great many other disease entities and chronic health problems are several conditions that the early childhood teacher is very likely to encounter. These include: *congenital or acquired heart conditions; cancer,* which in children occurs most commonly in the form of leukemia and tumors of the eye, brain, bone, and kidneys (Bigge, 1982); *hemophilia,* a sex-linked hereditary blood disorder, requiring vigilance to note even the most minor injury; and *chronic respiratory disease* (allergies and asthma.) In all of these, and other situations in which a chronic health problem is present, the *child-specific* implications for school functioning must be known, especially where precautions or medications are involved.

Certainly the most common of all these are allergies. Allergy and asthma are related, in that the latter represents a chronic pattern of respiratory distress, potentially very serious, in reaction to the former. An allergy is a dysfunction of the immunological system and may be associated with asthma or with other familiar forms of reaction, including hay fever, eczema, and behavioral patterns such as apathy, fatigue, and irritability. A child may have highly specific allergies in reaction to dust or molds, foods, chemicals, animals, or season-related substances such as ragweed. Many allergic persons have multiple allergies. Asthma is a chronic lung disease associated with hypersensitivity in the airways. It is usually precipitated by an allergic reaction, with symptoms involving recurring episodes of breathing difficulty, which may be acute, due to constriction or blockage of bronchial tubes.

CASE HISTORY 7.1:   THERESA

At age 6, Theresa was enrolled in a primary-level special class for children with multiple handicaps. She was diagnosed as having mild motor delays, epilepsy, moderate speech and language delay, and mild mental retardation. It was believed that Theresa could function within a mainstream class and that such a placement would be very desirable from the standpoint of her learning and social skills development. However, there were concerns about seizure occurrence, as well as difficulties associated with the anticonvulsant medication. Her doctor had not as yet been able to determine an appropriate medication program that would be effective in controlling both her petit mal and gran mal seizures. The petit mal seizures occurred from 5 to 18 times daily, with gran mal seizures occuring between 1 and 6 times each day. In addition, her medication involved side effects, including frequent drowsiness and sometimes even deep sleep, as well as slurred speech and, infrequently, loss of fine motor coordination.

The resource teacher briefly discussed Theresa's situation with each of the three first grade teachers in the building, and then called Theresa's mother. This was not a mother whom the school team had found to be especially cooperative or involved in planning Theresa's school program. She had waived her right to participate in the IEP conference each of the last two years. A single mother, she appeared to be overwhelmed with other concerns, and in fact her response to the proposition that planning might evolve toward mainstream participation was neither enthusiastic nor oppositional. She did not wish to attend any meetings or be otherwise involved.

The receptivity of the teachers was more encouraging. All three had some children with special needs in their classes; however, one,

Ms. Walton, thought her current group of 22, although diverse, posed fewer special concerns of a highly demanding nature. Her concerns focused upon the children's response to Theresa's seizures, but she thought it would be potentially in their interests, as well as Theresa's, to try. It was determined that planning would begin with an analysis of Theresa's medical situation but, just as importantly, a review of her current educational functioning including her strengths as well as weaknesses; Ms. Walton's classroom program; and ways of helping the other children to gain an understanding of, and be prepared for, seizure episodes should they occur.

Ms. Walton shared the resource teacher's general impression that Theresa was a child who could benefit from and contribute to a typical first grade situation, although she did indeed present special needs. The planners focused first upon the strengths she demonstrated, even within the more restrictive situation of her current placement. These included the following:

1. She was very cheerful and personable, readily liked by both other children and adults.
2. She demonstrated good play and social skills with other first graders on the playground, though these were slightly delayed in comparison to typical peers.
3. She loved to pretend and displayed an active imagination.
4. She was easily interested in a wide variety of things first graders do in school.
5. Once interested in something, she was very determined to follow through and complete it.
6. She was physically able to do nearly

anything required without special adaptations.

7. She liked books.
8. She enjoyed learning new things through both doing and listening.
9. She displayed good retention of new information and skills learned.
10. She displayed good self-help skills and personal hygiene.

Theresa's current weaknesses were identified as the following:

1. Once frustrated with a task, she would remember her frustration and would not want to attempt that same task again.
2. She found writing difficult and did not like it.
3. She would sometimes react to frustration in an unduly emotional manner, and her feelings were easily hurt by others.
4. The side effects of her medication were difficult to predict.
5. Theresa's doctor believed that Theresa's mother "played with the drugs," making it hard to tell whether she was getting proper amounts at consistent intervals for both seizure control and prediction of the timing of side effects.
6. Seizures occurred frequently.
7. Seizures were usually followed by sleep, typically for 1–2 hours.

It was determined that the first objective must be to control the one major weakness that could be controlled: proper medication dispensing. The resource teacher called the physician to discuss the problem and seek advice. He suggested that two of the three daily doses of medication prescribed could be timed to be dispensed at school, which would provide more consistency, and that he would continue to stress the importance of proper medication doses and intervals to Theresa's mother. At his request the school nurse called Theresa's mother to ask that the medication be sent to school so that she could dispense it twice each school day. Observing that it would be "one less thing I'll have to do," the mother readily agreed to this. At the doctor's suggestion, the resource teacher and aide recorded data for two weeks to determine any pattern of side effects in connection with times the medication was dispensed. At first, no particular pattern was evident. However, during the second week, Theresa was more consistently alert and had clearer speech from noon until 2:30 p.m., which was the period after lunch and before dispensing of her second dose. It was concluded that that would be the optimal time period for initial classroom mainstreaming. Theresa already participated in morning recess with the first graders, as well as lunch (11:20–11:45), lunch recess (11:45–12:00), and afternoon recess (2:00–2:15). This plan for classroom mainstreaming would both make possible a continuous period of time each day for participation with her regular class peers and take advantage of her period of optimal functioning each day for learning.

Ms. Walton provided her present classroom schedule for the afternoon, which was:

12:05–12:30 *Story Time* (Teacher read to the class and the children, seated at their desks, could just listen or quietly draw while listening.)

12:20–1:00 *Social Studies or Science* (Both usually involved small group activities based around a unit theme.)

1:00–1:10 *Clean-up*

1:10–1:40 *Specials* (Monday: gym; Tuesday: art; Wednesday: library; Thursday: music; Friday: movie, with other two first grade classes)

1:40–2:00 *Finish-up time* (This time could be used to complete work from earlier in the day or play related games in small groups.)

2:00–2:15   *Recess*
2:15–2:45   *Language* (Format varied.)
2:50   *Dismissal*

Both teachers agreed that there wasn't really anything in the afternoon schedule that Theresa couldn't manage. It was determined that she would go to the first grade classroom for lunch and stay for the remainder of the afternoon. Should any difficulties arise, Ms. Walton would note times and situations.

During the observation and preparation period, Ms. Walton had contacted the county chapter of the National Epilepsy Foundation, which sent a staff member three times weekly to teach the class and teacher, during Social Studies time, about seizures. Through demonstration and film, she illustrated what a gran mal seizure typically looks like, explained why it happens, and discussed how medication can usually control the seizures. She also explained what to do if they thought a person was having a seizure: *don't panic, move things away if possible, call an adult*. She provided Ms. Walton more specific information. All learned something about the brain and how it controls the body, or possibly, for a short time, puts the body out of control. They also learned how a person might get hurt during a seizure, from striking objects or falling to the floor, and they practiced bandaging pretend hurts and calling adults to help.

The Foundation's representative was not only very knowledgeable, but also skilled in establishing rapport with the children, who listened all the more attentively because they liked her. Since Theresa's mother refused involvement, the representative said that she would like to bring in a parent on the last day to talk to them about having a child with epilepsy. She continued to refer to that, stimulating the children's interest and curiosity, as they thought of questions to ask, She also encouraged them to invite their own parents to attend on that day. Ms. Walton had sent home a letter with each child explaining the two-week program. She received 10 responses expressing positive feelings about it, with one expressing negative sentiments.

On the last day, five of the children's parents attended. The parent of the "child with epilepsy" turned out to be the representative's own mother! The children's responses were very positive. They indicated changes in attitude from fear of the unknown, and the belief that a person who had a seizure was "weird" and should be avoided, to the belief that people with epilepsy are actually normal, although their brains sometimes make their bodies do strange things.

Theresa did have seven gran mal seizures throughout the remainder of the year while in the first grade classroom. Each lasted less than three minutes. After each seizure, Theresa was carried to the nurse's office to sleep and did not return to school until the next day. Ms. Walton reported that she felt that each time she was more alarmed than the children. To the best of her knowledge, no child ever remembered to mention it to Theresa by the time they saw her the next day. However, after each seizure occurrence, she did spend a few minutes talking to the children, reviewing what the Epilepsy Foundation representative had said, and answering questions.

Overall, Theresa got along quite well in the classroom. She did exhibit some overly emotional reactions and occasionally some aggressiveness when frustrated. However, Ms. Walton dealt with this in the same way she would with any other child.

MEDICATIONS, MEDICAL PRECAUTIONS, AND SPECIAL PROCEDURES

The teacher or caregiver must be aware of special considerations associated with any child's medical or health needs. In schools, important health-related information is generally maintained and communicated to teachers by the school nurse, especially for those children who have ongoing special needs in this area. In community preschool and day care settings, such information may be maintained by the director. Transient, situational concerns that bear on the child's physical and psychological well-being are known, in either case, to the degree that effective communication between parent and teacher is present.

Specific considerations and procedures associated with the needs of a handicapped child are identified in the child's IEP, which also specifies who is responsible for providing any *related services.* Examples include catheterization for many children with spina bifida, provisions for a child identified as *medically fragile,* and measures to be taken should *suctioning* or other special intervention be required. For a child using a shunt, having hemophilia, or with *osteogenesis imperfecta* (brittle bone disease), precautions may be noted to avoid injury and to recognize when injury may have occurred.

You need to be prepared to handle a seizure episode properly should it occur. Remember that a child may have had seizures without other manifestation of a developmental disability, so that the child may not have been regarded or served as handicapped.

Specific allergies, especially food allergies, must also be known. Again, many children not identified as handicapped have allergies, and your knowledge of these may prove critical if they involve substances encountered in school or if the potential exists for severe reactions, such as an asthma attack.

Children who require administration of medication while in school should not present special worries for the teacher, although teacher awareness of medication type, schedule, and possible side effects is important. It is generally recognized, and has been well established by policy and court rulings, that *the teacher should not be the individual responsible to keep and administer medications* (Thomas, 1987). In most instances, medication schedules are established to minimize or, if possible, eliminate the need for medications to be administered while the child is in school.

Medication prescribed for seizure control is fairly frequently noted for children with disabilities not specifically described as epilepsy. Again, your responsibility is not to administer the medication but, with the child's parents, to keep especially close track of behavior for children who take anticonvulsant medication. You should also monitor behavior of children on other medications, including stimulant-type drugs prescribed to control hyperactivity. With young children, there may be particular concerns about side effects of *ritalin* and other related substances, since social skills, emotional security, and functioning in cognitive skill areas tend to be adversely affected (Zentall, 1983). You should record specific behavioral observations for medicated children, precisely noting time of day and activity context.

Guidelines for Medication Administration

1. Parents should be required to administer medication at home when possible.
2. Educators may not medically diagnose ailment or prescribe medication, but may administer medication.
3. Medication administration at school may be required as a related service for specific handicapped children.
4. Prior to medication administration at school, written authorizations from both the parent and the physician must be signed and on file, even if the medication is to be self-administered.
5. Self-administration should not be in the presence of other children.
6. Children responsible for self-administration should not be permitted to carry the medication. All medication should be stored by school officials.
7. If possible, the authorization from the physician also should include a description of the probable reactions to the medication, as well as any side effects or emergency treatment.
8. The label on the medication should include the student's name, date of expiration, and directions for use (i.e., dosage, when to consume, what if anything to eat or drink when consuming).
9. Also on file should be the student's home or emergency phone number; the name, strength, and serial number of the medication; the names and phone numbers of the physician and pharmacist; and storage instructions (e.g., avoid sunlight, store between 60 and 75 degrees).
10. Storage compartments should be locked.
11. Records must be maintained regarding receipt, use, return, and disposal of drugs, syringes, and needles.
12. Educators should observe, record, and report unforeseen medication-related changes in behavior.
13. Educators responsible for medication administration should receive in-service training.
14. School districts should indemnify their employees who are responsible for medication administration.
15. School districts should carry adequate insurance to cover possible suit for negligence, or should self-insure.[1]

PAST PRACTICES IN MAINSTREAMING PHYSICALLY DISABLED STUDENTS

Mainstreaming of students with physical disabilities has had an almost random character in many instances. Many of you may recall one or more classmates from your own school days who had significant physical impairments. This author

---

[1]Thomas, S. B. (1987). *Health-related legal issues in education* (pp. 33–36). Topeka, KS: National Organization of Legal Problems of Education. Reprinted by permission of author.

knows a number of adults with disabilities, such as cerebral palsy, whose entire school career was in the mainstream setting. In many instances, special medical and therapeutic needs required by the disability were provided in settings separate from the school. Accounts of their experiences provided by disabled adults typically refer to the desire to be "like everyone else" and their families' encouragement of that attitude. As a friend with cerebral palsy, now in his early thirties, recalls, "I didn't think of myself as 'different' or especially 'handicapped'".

The community in which a family lived, as well as the policies and attitudes of school personnel in that community, were frequently major determinants of whether a child was in a special class or special school, or was treated as a "regular" student. In times before architectural barriers were recognized as such, and the right to access established in statute, individuals made adaptations in the best way they could—or simply assumed that no adaptations needed to or could be made.

Dr. Gary Best (1977), a leader in the field of education of students with physical disabilities, reported the results of an early survey of characteristics of mainstreamed orthopedically handicapped students in California, conducted in 1975. The date is important, since P.L. 94–142, enacted in 1975, had not yet been implemented. Best found that the percentage of students who were mainstreamed increased dramatically at the secondary level. Nearly half the junior high students and nearly two-thirds of the high school students were mainstreamed, whereas only 14 percent of the elementary school students were in regular classes, and about half that number totally mainstreamed. There were indications that the availability of special programs might have been a factor in many instances, accounting for what could be ". . . mainstreaming by default rather than by design" (p. 209).

This and other more recent surveys (e.g., Gans, 1987) have revealed considerable teacher receptiveness to the idea of educating students with physical disabilities within the regular classroom. Respondents to the California survey were asked to consider criteria for mainstreaming relating to students' mobility, speech, academic achievement, and personal-social adjustment. Interestingly, although moderate or even more severe speech or mobility involvement was perceived by the majority of respondents as acceptable, and even some discrepancy in academic skills, "acceptable social behavior" was considered essential by nearly all survey respondents (Best, 1977).

In many instances, whether a child is mainstreamed has depended primarily upon preference, and often assertive action, of parents. A mother of a child with spina bifida and significantly impaired movement who is currently succeeding well in a mainstream fifth grade classroom, described the decision she and her husband had made that their son's mainstreaming should begin early, in the face of professionals' disagreement:

> We found that Carl [not his real name] was, at that point in time, intellectually much beyond the other kids in his [special preschool] class. Not physically,

because he was barely walking, but intellectually and verbally he had achieved much more age-appropriate skills. And even beyond, especially his verbal skills. Although Carl was stimulating a lot of positive behavior in the other children, he was not necessarily being stimulated himself. Also, he was learning some manipulative behaviors, because he was verbally able to give commands to classmates—"Go get this for me, go get that for me"—and at that age they did. Our feeling was that putting him in with his normal peers would create a real challenge.

It was a very difficult decision. One of the social workers asked me if I was doing this for myself, or for my son. And my answer was, "Both! Yes, I want him to be more normal, and yes, I'm doing it for Carl." She said, "Well, how do you know you're doing the right thing?" And I said, "I don't, and I still won't know until we try it." That was kind of scary, because I was kind of hoping they would say, "You're right! Try it! Go for it!" But that's not what happened. They really implied they didn't think this was a good move. But what I had—that a lot of people don't have—is other parents of older kids with spina bifida saying to me that they've got to learn to function in their world at whatever level they can.

And starting in preschool is starting at an age when kids are so egocentric it seemed better than keeping him in the special nursery school and then putting him in regular kindergarten. What would he think? He wouldn't have had interaction with normal peers up to that point, and at age six kids are a lot more perceptive about how people are looking at them than they are at three.

Our older children had gone to this same nursery school, so this was not our first experience there. The teacher said, "Let's give it a shot and if it works out it does, and if it doesn't, maybe we'll have to do something different." Also, the Director was studying preschool mainstreaming in graduate school, so her reaction was "Great!" What was really good about that was, since we did know her and we were just very open about it, we all said, "We don't know what's going to happen but at least we can talk about it."

ADAPTATIONS IN THE CLASSROOM

Simply knowing the nature of the physical impairment a child may have is not, in itself, enough to determine what specific adaptations, if any, may be required. Each individual child is different. What is needed is a functional analysis of the child's situation in light of the task and environmental demands. A good rule is that adaptations should be as unobtrusive as possible. In some instances, advances in technology have made possible adaptive modifications previously unimagined, but in the majority of cases, "high-tech" solutions are not necessary. The determination of whether electronic or mechanical devices are indicated should be made on the basis of a thorough study of the child's functioning within a specific environmental context, such as the classroom or day care center. Use of unnecessary equipment should be avoided, since it simply calls attention to a child's differences (Hart, 1981).

Verna Hart (1981) summarizes the individually determined character of adaptations to accommodate the needs of children with impaired motor functioning in this fashion:

> Classroom adaptations for the children may be as minimal as taping their papers to the table so that their papers won't slide and they are able to use all their energies to write. Or it may mean that head sticks must be attached to a band around the children's heads so that they can operate electric typewriters on which a special template has been placed to prevent several keys from being pressed at one time. Obviously, those in need of the former adaptation will need no extra space around them, while those who need the latter will require room for the typewriter, books, headstick, and so forth. The needs of the children will determine the amount of space needed for their mobility and adaptive equipment. (p. 84)

Basically, any form of adaptation in the classroom involves a problem-solving orientation. Teachers need to know that they are not expected to undertake this process alone, however. Clearly, in this area, problem analysis and solution are a team undertaking. Specialists can provide information and insight about the individual child's physical status and its implications, as well as about any special equipment the child uses, such as braces. You should become familiar with any orthotic or prosthetic devices or appliances an individual child may use, since they must be used and fitted properly and not restrict the child's range of motion, cause discomfort, cause abrasions, or interfere with circulation. A very young child may not be able to communicate directly the source of discomfort, and adults need to watch for signs and interpret cues.

You also need information and guidance concerning helping the child from the standpoint of physical management. As Verna Hart (1981) suggests:

> Whenever you have motorically handicapped children in your classroom, you should immediately contact the physical and occupational therapists to obtain from them the things you will need to know about positioning, carrying, lifting, and so forth. Some children who have a lot of extension in their body movements will literally be unable to move themselves when placed in certain positions. The therapists can demonstrate the right kinds of positions, and you should practice using them while the therapists are still there. This will give you greater confidence when you are alone. (p. 85)

The term *related services* means transportation and such developmental, corrective, and other supportive services as are required to assist a handicapped child to benefit from special education, and includes speech pathology and audiology, psychological services, physical and occupational therapy, recreation, early identification and assessment of disabilities in children, counseling services, and medical services for diagnostic or evaluation purposes. The term also includes school health services, social work services in schools, and parent counseling and training.

The term "medical services" means services provided by a licensed physician to determine a child's medically handicapping conditions that result in the child's need for special education and related services.

The term "school health services" means services provided by a qualified school nurse or other qualified person. (Federal Regulations, 34 C.F.R. 300.13)

INTERDISCIPLINARY TEAM APPROACH AND INTEGRATION OF SPECIAL THERAPIES

Among the *related services* that may be identified on a physically handicapped child's IEP are: special transportation arrangements, physical therapy, occupational therapy, speech and language therapy, and adapted physical education. A child's needs for these services may change, and certainly not all physically handicapped children will require all these services. Some children participate in special therapies outside the school program, either by parental choice or in situations where it has been agreed mutually that the services do not fit the legal definition of related services. In any case, some children who participate in special programs are likely to be seen by several adults, each having a defined responsibility for working with the child in a specific area of function. Whether or not various professionals, representing diverse disciplines, continue to provide direct services to the child, they are likely to be involved in two other important ways: (1) contributing to a multifactored assessment, and (2) providing indirect service to the child through teacher consultation, parent consultation, or both, as well as participating in ongoing meetings to monitor the child's progress and evaluate the effectiveness of programming.

You may be familiar with the role of a speech therapist, but less so with those of the physical therapist and occupational therapist. In general both have special expertise in the area of motor functioning, as reflected in movement, balance, coordination, and activities of daily living (ADL). By tradition, physical therapy is a medically based, and medically prescribed form of intervention. It is defined as a related service when it is determined necessary to enable a handicapped child to benefit from special education. Occupational therapy may be similarly defined as a related service.

In a school or agency setting, the roles of the special therapists are to some extent interchangeable, for they share many of the same competencies (Campbell, 1987). However, the traditional distinction assumes that the physical therapist will provide intervention and consultative assistance with regard to optimal positioning for a child, mobility-enhancing procedures or equipment, and other areas relating especially to large muscle function and tone. The occupational therapist's role with young children (unlike his or her role with many older clients, with or without motor impairment) emphasizes helping the child with tasks requiring fine motor control, perceptual-motor coordination, and functions required by environmental demands. For young children, these include dressing and undressing, eating, washing, toileting, holding play materials, etc.

Whether either type of specialist will be available to interact regularly with teachers depends upon the individual school or center. Schools typically obtain the services of physical and occupational therapists in any of several ways: (1) employing them directly as full-time professional staff members (which would be their capacity in special service or rehabilitation agency settings, hospitals, etc.); (2) participating in a consortium (a group of cooperating school districts) that collectively employ special therapists to work with children in schools in a multi-district region; (3) contracting for therapy services with another agency, or with private practicing therapists. For children who receive therapy independent of their school programs (by parental choice, or if the therapy is not defined in a child's IEP as a related service), communication must still be maintained between the therapist, clinic, hospital, or community agency and the school. The parent is the vital link, and exchange of reports and records requires signed release by the parent.

As was noted, the traditional difference between physical and occupational therapy relates mainly to the focus of their respective contributions to a multi-disciplinary, or preferably an *interdisciplinary,* approach. It is an oversimplification to state that the physical therapist works mainly in the areas of gross motor function, balance, and mobility, while the occupational therapist's focus is on upper extremity function (hand and arm), head stability, perceptual-motor coordination, and activities of daily living. In practice, the two typically work together with a particular child, so that their contributions to assessment and programming are complementary. Increasingly, the terms *developmental therapist* and *pediatric therapist* are used to refer to members of both disciplines who have special expertise in working with children. The mainstream teacher can expect to be in consultation with one or the other, rather than both, in learning how to implement physical management practices in the classroom that are indicated for a particular child.

Both groups of professionals who work with children are guided by knowledge of central nervous system organization, with special training in neuroanatomy and neurophysiology. Both have been especially influenced in their work with children by certain theories and associated clinical approaches, probably most notably *neurodevelopmental training* (NDT). This is an approach for which therapists must be specifically trained through approved courses following principles based on the work of Dr. Karl Bobath and Berta Bobath (Bobath & Bobath, 1972, 1975). Therapists with training in approaches that emphasize facilitation and greater volitional control of movement, helping the child to learn to counteract primitive reflex patterns that have been maintained, and normalizing tone typically can apply these techniques within natural environments of home and classroom, enabling parents and teachers to optimize a child's position for balance and mobility. Highly specialized and bulky equipment is de-emphasized in favor of portable adaptive equipment, such as bolsters, where indicated.

In recent years many occupational therapists have developed particular interests and expertise in another approach, known as *Sensory Integration* (S-I). Key concepts in this approach, based on principles associated especially with the work of Jean Ayres (1972), involve children's processing of sensory information and obtaining proprioceptive feedback from voluntary movement and tactile experience, as well as movement experiences that are provided for the child, such as swinging.

ADAPTIVE EQUIPMENT

The first consideration for any special equipment a child may require is mobility. Equipment specifically designed to permit mobility includes varieties of leg casts and braces, the ankle-foot orthosis (AFO), crutches and walkers, and many different types of wheelchairs, including powered chairs, the last of which a child must be helped to learn to use. Even young children today can be expected to have and operate powered mobility equipment.

A therapist can often adjust standard equipment to permit its use for mobility and for play. A tricycle, for instance, may be adapted by moving the handlebars to an upright position (so that the child does not need to lean forward and perhaps look downward) and by securing the child's feet on the pedals with Velcro straps. Classroom chairs aid mobility, if the floor is uncarpeted, since a child can often push the chair in front of her to different locations.

Mobility equipment, like equipment designed specifically for positioning children who are unable to position themselves, also serves the following purposes: to normalize muscle tone; to reduce the influence of abnormal or primitive reflex patterns; to increase range of motion; to increase stability of head and trunk; to facilitate components of movement in a developmental sequence; and to decrease postural and position tendencies that might lead to deformities. This last is critically important. Clearly, then, motor therapy and the provision of proper equipment properly used has a *preventive* as well as a *therapeutic* function.

A wheelchair may play an important positioning role for many children. Position can be facilitated through a number of adjustments—lateral trunk supports, Velcro strips to secure feet or ankles—and some of these same adaptations can be made with an ordinary classroom chair. Often the simple addition of foot supports and a Velcro seatbelt can enable a child to participate in table activities along with other children.

Special adaptive chairs may be extremely useful. Two familiar types are *corner chairs* and *bolster chairs*. Both usually have removable trays; however, you should try to pull the child's chair up so that the table top can be used as a work surface or place for eating. In that way, the child can participate along with the other children and is not physically separated by the tray, and visible differences are minimized. Corner chairs provide support at both sides; the child sits astride a bolster chair.

Adaptive equipment may also be used to enable a child to stand. Supported standing forces weight-bearing that is necessary for the normal formation of hip joints. *Prone standers* support forward-inclined standing, possibly with the top of the board secured to a table top, permitting visual range and hand use on the table; *supine standers* support an upright position that may incline slightly backward; *freedom standers* are self-contained and enable the child to work in a supported standing position. Choice of a stander is based on the child's specific tone and reflex pattern, as well as weight-bearing capability and needs. Once you learn how an individual child will use a particular piece of equipment, how velcro straps are secured for that child, and how the equipment can be arranged to allow the child to participate in particular classroom activities, the therapist no longer will need to make these arrangements on an ongoing daily basis.

For floor activities in the classroom, a child may need to be supported in a lying position. The two most typical positions are *prone* and *side-lying;* for both, adaptive boards, wedges, and supports are available.

Other adaptive equipment may be used to facilitate hand activities. These include adapted scissors and other hand-held implements that enable a child to write, draw, paint, or color. Some children particularly need adapted implements for eating. Adapted spoons may have a built-up handle or a swivel so that gravity can right the spoon and prevent spilling. Scoop dishes and cups with a cutout side also facilitate independent eating. For children who cannot eat independently, adult help in actually placing chunks of food on the child's molars for chewing may be needed.

CASE HISTORY 7.2: CHRISSIE

Chrissie is a four-year-old girl who has spina bifida. The location of the lesion in her spine is such that she has no sensation in the lower part of her body and cannot voluntarily move her legs to walk, or stand without support. However, with short leg braces and crutches, she can move skillfully about the room. Nora Gage, the physical therapist working with Chrissie, has helped her to learn to coordinate her movements, so that she can now approach a work table, move a chair into place (turned out at a slight angle), rest one crutch against the table while steadying herself on the other so that she can steady the chair with a free hand (so it won't slide on the linoleum floor when she sits), swing safely into the chair, rest the other crutch, and slide her own chair up to the table. Also, if the chair must first be moved to the table, she drops both crutches and pushes the chair, using it as her "walker."

When the chair is in place, she supports her weight by holding the table edge with one hand and the chair with the other. This is a standard adaptive maneuver, which Chrissie and most other children with similar motoric impairment have learned, in the course of therapy, to perform totally independently. The typical preschool or kindergarten classroom includes a table with movable chairs and a floor surface permitting chairs to slide. If the floor surface of a classroom is carpeted (or the table for certain activities is in a carpeted area), or if desks with attached seats must be negotiated, children transfer the basic pattern and adapt to the requirements of that situation.

Nora has been working with Chrissie on climbing and descending stairs as well. Life would certainly be much simpler if everything were on one level, as is the case in both her home and in the special preschool she has been attending. However, she frequently encounters curbs to be negotiated, and she can anticipate stairs as well. In fact, she has begun to divide her school experience between the special setting and a community preschool program that does have a short flight of stairs. Clearly, the goal of totally independent mobility for Chrissie must involve dealing with stairs.

Since Chrissie has very normal verbal skills, she has not required special speech and language therapy. Her current IEP includes direct physical therapy and, until recently, direct occupational therapy as well, since she does experience some difficulty in tasks requiring visual-motor coordination. Also, through the coordinated work of Sally Thomason, an occupational therapist, and her mother and her teacher, Chrissie has learned to dress herself with minimum assistance.

Chrissie's folder contains the step-by-step procedures for performing Clean Intermittent Catheterization. Her teachers, as well as classroom assistants, in both preschool settings help her cath, but Sally Thomason and her mother anticipate that, within a year, she'll be able to self-cath. A bowel management program has just been implemented, and this will make it probable that, when in school, neither Chrissie nor her teachers will have to be concerned about this.

Chrissie's teacher feels strongly that Chrissie should be totally mainstreamed, since she actually has no special instructional needs. However, she does need to be challenged more, and also exposed to children her own age who model the level of intellectual, verbal, and social skills that Chrissie is very capable of demonstrating herself. Her teacher sees her as comfortable with other children and comfortable with herself, braces (and thick glasses) and all—but sometimes lapsing into dependency upon others and even inclined to be somewhat manipulative. Some of the group activities in the special preschool do not stimulate her interest and active curiosity as much as standard preschool activities do. Also, her teacher and mother have both become aware that, since attending the regular preschool program, she has started to engage in imaginative play, something she had not done before. Chrissie has an imaginary friend, Sara. Sara is four years old and, like Chrissie, has brown hair, and likes to play with Chrissie's dolls. Although, there are real friends—two girls from Children's Town have engaged visits with her, and there are neighbor children with whom she plays—Sara is a nice companion for the other times.

Her school district is anticipating that Chrissie will be fully mainstreamed next year, participating in an all-day kindergarten program. She can continue to have direct therapy service as long as it seems needed to help her maintain her progress in independent mobility. Indirect assistance to the teacher will help to ensure that she continues to compensate for her eye-hand coordination difficulties, that she has enough time to move about in the room and building on her own, and that the catheterization is done regularly.

Experiencing control over one's own environment and the opportunity to influence the environment through one's own actions are basic to self-esteem and the "sense of competence" (White, 1959). Not experiencing such control leads to feelings of "learned helplessness" (Seligman, 1976). In the case of severe motoric impairment, technological interventions may provide ways to enable a child to experience control over his or her environment. However, professionals who work with such children must discern those situations that can be helped best through a technological solution and select the type of intervention that is optimal for each child (Campbell, Bricker, & Esposito, 1980).

Microswitches enable some individuals with severe motor impairment to gain environmental control. Again, it is important to be able to discriminate and select, based upon the requirements of the task and the functional characteristics of the child. Campbell, McInery, & Middleton (1982) have developed a manual for selection and use of devices of this sort. York, Nietupski, & Hamre-Nietupski (1985) have developed a decision model for the use of microswitches in working with students who have severely impaired motor functioning. This model addresses the series of decisions which must be made, beginning with the question of whether it can be taught directly. If adaptations are necessary for the student to learn the activity, the next question is whether a microswitch adaptation would be appropriate. If appropriate, next decisions involve selecting the appropriate type of switch, instructional procedures, motor behaviors involved, positions, etc., all of which go into developing the instructional program. The last part of this decision model pertains to evaluation of the intervention program and determining whether changes in the program are needed.

Although physical and occupational therapy may be thought of specifically in connection with children who have motor or other physical impairments, the service that is actually most likely to be needed is speech and language therapy. Substantial numbers of children with cerebral palsy, the most frequent diagnostic group, as well as many children with other impairments, are likely to demonstrate special needs in the area of communication. Young children in early intervention programs are likely to have both one-to-one and classroom-based language programming under the direction of a speech and language therapist. Increasingly, speech and language programming for young handicapped children is incorporated within the context of the classroom, capitalizing on the ongoing communication required in the peer setting.

Additionally, however, the speech and language therapist, frequently in collaboration with an occupational therapist, teacher, and parents, may need to develop a means that will permit a child with severe language delays or impaired ability to produce speech to communicate. This may sometimes involve another form of adaptive equipment. Advice about various kinds of adaptive equipment may be obtained from the organizations listed in the Appendix.

INTEGRATING CHILDREN USING AUGMENTATIVE COMMUNICATION SYSTEMS

One of the most striking illustrations of the positive impact of technology on reducing handicap is in the area of communication. Augmentative communication systems are used to enable communication between children who are unable to use speech and their peers and teachers (Bottorf & DePape, 1982). Until recently, early childhood educators were unlikely to encounter children employing an augmentative communication system, since such systems were introduced only after all efforts to enable the child to learn to speak had failed, not before about age 8 or 9. However, within the last decade, evidence has grown suggesting that providing a supplementary communication system can motivate a non-speaking child to attempt further communication (Nietupski & Hamre-Nietupski, 1979).

Augmentative communication systems have been used primarily in three situations: (1) individuals whose speech communication is impaired due to hearing impairment; (2) individuals with severe language deficits including those associated with mental retardation; and (3) individuals with severe neuromotor or other physical impairments affecting the ability to produce meaningful oral communication. Systems are of two general types: unaided (for example, manual sign language) and aided, which includes communication boards or other means, often used in conjunction with mechanical or electronic devices. In general, your role as a teacher involves three major responsibilities: (1) contributing, as a team member, to the decision-making process about the supplementary aid needed and the vocabulary content, based on the functional demands of the child in the environments in which communication is important; (2) helping the child to implement the system within the classroom environment; and (3) monitoring and maintaining observational data on the child's communicative activity and progress and communicating such data to parents and other team members. Typically, key team members with whom you will work closely are the speech and language therapist and occupational therapist.

Unaided systems are essentially gestural, while aided systems are characterized as symbolic. They have been classified (Vanderheiden & Grilley, 1978) as requiring any of three basic strategies: (1) direct selection, (2) scanning, or (3) encoding. In direct selection systems, the individual selects, by pointing, touching, or visually focusing, a picture or other symbol from an array displayed, for example, on a board. Pointing may be accomplished through an adaptive device, such as a head pointer. In a scanning system, all possible stimuli are presented and the individual responds only when the desired item is indicated. Encoding is both most efficient and most abstract, for it employs a code system (e.g., number, letter, or color) to denote a wide variety of messages, either memorized or listed on a chart. Variations and combinations of the three basic approaches may be used with individual children, and the appropriate clinical specialist enables the teacher to learn the system and provides guidance in its use in the classroom.

CASE HISTORY 7.3: PETER

Peter was a five-year-old who participated in a special preschool program, located within a regular elementary school building. His cerebral palsy was associated with quite abnormally high muscle tone (spasticity) and motor involvement affecting both upper and lower extremities, as well as speech. However, his head and trunk stability was good, sufficient to enable him to remain unsupported in a sitting position, although he could not come to a standing position or, when standing, walk, even with the aid of crutches or walker. Peter was alert and quietly socially responsive. He vocalized, approximating certain typical word sounds, most frequently "Yehhh!" However, he would often respond with this to almost any question asked him, apparently to be agreeable and satisfy the adult. Since he had difficulty chewing and swallowing, as well as articulating words, an occupational therapist, speech and language therapist, and special preschool teacher were conducting a program cooperatively with him.

In the meantime, however, it was felt that the regular kindergarten setting would both offer him greater challenge and provide peer modeling opportunities. Having observed Peter in his special classroom, the regular kindergarten teacher agreed to this, but with some initial reservations. She felt it important that, with 26 kindergartners, some very bright and a few presenting needs for a good deal of individual attention, another adult in the room would really be necessary to ensure both that Peter could benefit optimally and not require an undue portion of her time and attention because of his behavioral and physical management concerns. Initially, a graduate special education student shared this responsibility with a resource teacher, so that an adult was present at all times Peter was in the kindergarten specifically to assist him if needed, while recording data on his social involvement with peers and task performance.

As the time required for data decreased, it became apparent that Peter needed very little individual direct help from an adult—his classmates were more than willing—and the support role became more generalized. Eventually, it was determined that a classroom aide for general assistance, rather than an especially trained resource person assigned to

Peter, was what was needed. A schedule was designed whereby undergraduate teacher education students completing field experience requirements in their early childhood education program could fill this need; thus, the role of the special resource person was phased out. Within a few weeks, Peter was participating in all facets of the full-day kindergarten program, pulled out for individual work incorporating occupational therapy and speech therapy goals. However, his eating program was implemented in the lunchroom, during the regular daily lunch period with the other children.

During her participation with Peter in the kindergarten, the resource teacher maintained a log, noting especially his adjustment to the social requirements of the classroom situation and his interations with other children, as the following excerpts illustrate:

Peter played with the bucket containing blocks and put it on his head. I took the bucket away and showed him how to put the blocks together. He tried but doesn't have the hand strength to manipulate them. He then tried to grab Kelly's and Carl's constructions. Carl said "No, Peter," in a patient voice.

Later, at the opening circle, I helped Peter with the hand motions of a song which he enjoyed. During "News and Views," Peter's attention was fair, but he kept trying to leave the group, so I sat behind him.

Peter crawled over to the shelf and took out the domino blocks (which he's able to manipulate and use to construct.) He then went to take something else out, and I told him he had to put the dominoes away first, which he did. He took out a number puzzle. I asked Joanna, Mary, and Julie to help him put it together. I showed them how to "help" Peter (not do it for him!) they did a very nice job of showing him where the pieces go and helping him move the pieces to the right place. They really enjoyed playing "teacher!"

Peter played with some lego-type blocks

with Jason and Jonah. Jason would ask Peter questions such as, "Peter, does this go here?" and Peter would answer "yes" or "no." Jason would respond like a game show host—"Right you are, Peter! It goes here!"—and Peter would get excited and clap his hands. Jason has become Peter's really good friend. He has figured out how to ask Peter questions that he can answer (yes/no questions, like "Peter, do you like my new shirt? Did you have a nice birthday?" etc.)

At Opening, Peter is also doing really well cleaning up his toys when Mrs. Brown plays the piano (the signal to clean up and come to the rug for circle time). Of course, he gets many reminders from the other kids, but today he put his puzzle away and came to the rug without any reminders at all. For "News and Views," Peter told everyone he lost his tooth and couldn't find it.

AN ACCOMMODATING CLASSROOM ENVIRONMENT

The classroom environment is an essential component in all early childhood programs. Many of the same principles apply equally for young children with physical disabilities and all young children, as this "checklist" proposed by Ann Rogers-Warren (1982) illustrates:

_____ How does the setting appear at a child's level? Are there interesting things to see and touch, such as windows, mirrors, aquariums, and toys?

_____ Is there room for a wheelchair-bound or awkwardly mobile child to negotiate in and out of spaces and turn around?

_____ Are shelves and tables at a comfortable level for a child's height? Is there a place (preferably more than one) that you accommodate a child in each activity area?

_____ Are shelves, tables, sinks, and other fixtures sturdy enough to hold the weight of a minimally mobile child who may need special support?

_____ Are prosthetic devices (such as a standing cuff) easily accessible in the areas where children might gain practice standing or sitting without an adult's assistance while engaged in an activity?

_____ Are some of the materials and toys accessible to a child without assistance even if he or she is minimally mobile?

_____ Are the sound level and acoustic arrangement of the room satisfactory for a child with a hearing impairment or hearing aid? Are there some special quiet areas for children to work with minimal noise distraction?

_____ Does the environment contain sufficient contrasts to attract the notice of a visually impaired child? Does color and light contrast corroborate texture and height contrasts?

_____ Are the cues (use of color, change of levels, dividers) that designate different areas clear and consistent?

_____ How much of the environment is designed for self-management or self-engagement? How frequently do children use these opportunities? Does a child need training to use these opportunities?

_____ Does the arrangement of the room allow for quiet places and social places to meet the changing moods and needs of children? (pp. 29–30)

For children who require assisted mobility, using a wheelchair, walker, or crutches, the following general guidelines for arrangement and management of the classroom environment are useful. Your goal, of course, should be to allow the child to participate totally in classroom activities.

1. *Desks or tables and chairs and all working areas in the room should be arranged to provide ample room to accommodate the child's equipment used for mobility.* Consider the space the child needs in order to turn around, as well as the space required for stationary activity and direct movement from one point to another. If the classroom has desks, these can be arranged in rows of pairs, with a wide aisle between rows. Leave an area free of furniture for play, floor sitting for certain activities or movement activities. Or arrange furniture around the periphery of the room, leaving the center free. Make sure any free-standing furniture such as bookcases or toy shelves is heavy enough and secure enough to withstand being pulled up to by a child without toppling!

2. *Working materials should be accessible for one-hand use if the child needs to stand up for an activity.* For example, for painting involving an easel, secure the paper to the easel and place paints in opened, non-spillable holders in the easel tray. Place one brush, long enough to be grasped without much leaning over from a walker, in each paint color container. The activity time should be reasonably short, based on a young child's ability to maintain upright balance with one arm, while using the other arm to paint. If the child cannot stand and paint, use a stander and adjust the easel to the child's body level, or allow the child to remain in a wheelchair, if appropriate, with the tray removed and the height of the easel adjusted as necessary.

3. *Activities involving movement should allow the child to be involved as much as possible without accentuating his or her inability to move well.* For example, in Follow the Leader, the leader can combine sitting and movement activities with floor locomotion activities such as clapping hands, blinking eyes, rolling on floor, combat crawl, lying down and raising hands, scissoring hands, and rolling back to the starting place. Such movement activities are best done to music, which both motivates continued involvement and helps guide and regulate participation.

4. *Make the child with a disability inconspicuous.* When the other

children are standing, the child with a disability should also be standing, using adaptive equipment as needed. When the others are sitting in chairs, the child with a disability also should be sitting, either in a chair or, if more adaptive or necessary, wheelchair with the tray removed to permit proximity to other children and/or table or other center, depending upon the activity. When the other children are moving, the disabled child should be moving as well.

Minimize the physical demands of a situation, but remember that the discrepancy between what the child with a disability is doing and what the other children are doing should also be minimized. The goal is to maximize both instructional and social involvement; therefore, any barriers that prevent proximity to other children should be eliminated. Sometimes, this requires adjusting equipment—removing wheelchair trays, providing support with velcro straps. Tray substitutes such as Triwall can be placed at the appropriate level between the wheelchair arms, without extending outside the chair. (Physical and occupational therapists are extremely good at working with teachers to devise means of both permitting more normalized tone and optimal positioning for children with cerebral palsy, and maximizing access and participation.)

5. *Working materials should be accessible to the child at appropriate body level.* This principle is based on another: the child should use the same materials as all the other children, unless specific modifications are indicated. A child seated in a chair needs to be able to reach independently and to manipulate objects necessary for participation. Materials should be kept within reach considering *the individual child's height in the chair* and also *reach distance.*

6. *All children, including the child with a disability, need to be aware of safety rules.* The kinds of safety precautions needed for a child with a disability, who may use a walker, crutches, or a wheelchair, are appropriate for all children. Children need to know that spills must be cleaned up immediately, and the floor should be clear of pencils, crayons, erasers, and other dropped items. Also, the familiar classroom rules—walk in the classroom, no pushing, and the like—are essential for the safety for all young children, including the child with impaired mobility.

7. *Materials in the classroom can be organized according to their use within distinct areas, to reduce the requirement for unnecessary movement.* This principle is entirely congruent with classroom designs making use of learning centers, such as an art corner, science center, play area, and so forth. When specific centers can be designated as specific locations, all children's learning time and energies are more constructively invested than when this is not the case.

SUMMARY

Children discussed in this chapter represent a wide variety of characteristics and needs. Even children with the same medical diagnosis may be less similar than a disabled child and a nondisabled child in learning style, characteristics, and special needs. Many children with physical disabilities or health impairments actually require no "special education" at all since their educational performance is in no way impaired. Others, however, may experience difficulties in cognitive areas. Children with cerebral palsy comprise the largest single group; however, these children range from essentially no disabling effects to very severe motor involvement and multiple difficulties. Many young children with chronic health problems or impaired mobility have already had experiences in their lives quite different from those of most of their peers, possibly including numerous or prolonged hospital stays (perhaps with multiple surgical procedures), and having to learn to use orthotic or prosthetic equipment. Some of these children may not have had opportunities to move about and explore freely. Yet they, like all young children, need to experience mastery and control over their own bodies and their environments. Adults sometimes have to be reminded not to overprotect or help too much.

Increasingly, day care centers, nursery programs, and public schools—like society as a whole—have become aware that children with disabilities are, first of all, children and that they are also *children with abilities*. Providing them opportunities to use and develop their abilities is first a matter of providing access. That may involve providing for transportation, as well as ensuring that the physical design and arrangement of buildings, rooms, corridors, etc., do not impose barriers to access. Additional considerations, based on individual needs, may include adapting instructional activities, classroom furniture, or specific materials used for play, learning tasks, and self-care functions. For some children, adaptations may be introduced to facilitate communication. Technology continues to open new doors for children, as well as adults, with physical impairments. Professionals with special expertise in these areas—including physical and occupational therapists, rehabilitation engineers, and speech and language pathologists—are likely to play extremely important roles in planning and problem-solving, working closely with teachers and parents. Even children regarded as *medically fragile* are increasingly being enabled to experience normal childhood activities as ways to provide for specific medical needs within the school setting are implemented.

ADAPTING INSTRUCTIONAL ACTIVITIES
FOR THE PHYSICALLY DISABLED CHILD

Adapting the curriculum *per se* is not usually indicated based on a child's physical disability, although some adaptations in certain classroom routines, time provisions, etc., may be necessary. For the most part, however, the child with a physical impairment can participate in all learning activities that are part of the regular classroom program.

For some children, the same problem-solving approach used in determining ways to maximize the child's general classroom participation can lead to ingenious, practical adaptations for purposes of specific learning activities. Given the individuality of each child's functional characteristics, the following ideas suggested by Maria Sargent can only be illustrative of adaptive instructional strategies teachers can develop.

Color Concepts

Children with motor impairment often experience difficulty in the physical aspects of color discrimination tasks. Various adaptive devices or modes of communication can assist these children in color activity games. Of special consideration in these cases are the patterns of movement any adaptations will require. These patterns may be contrary to the good motor patterns of the child. Any questions or concerns with specific adaptations should be related to the physical therapist working with the child or the child's parents.

GOAL:
> To assist the child with limited movement to participate in a color matching activity.

OBJECTIVE:
> The child will use an adaptive device to obtain and sort the various colors.

MATERIALS:
> Shapes of different colors; strong magnets; pieces of velcro; glue; sorting trays; elastic band

PROCEDURES:
1. Cut elastic band and fasten velcro to ends in such a manner that it fits over the palm of the child's hand snugly.
2. Sew velcro securely onto the palm portion of the band so the velcro faces outward when worn.
3. Glue or use self-sticking velcro to attach velcro pieces to the various color forms.
4. Attach magnets to the opposite sides of color forms.
5. Attach magnets to the bottom of the various sorting trays.
6. By applying slight pressure using the velcro band, a child lacking fine motor ability may pick up the pieces and transfer them to the appropriate tray. By then placing the magnets together, enough of a pulling force can be exerted to pull the velcro apart leaving the band (and hand) free to find another piece. Of consideration in this process should be the amount of control and, therefore, pressure the child will exert. Different strengths of

magnets may need to be experimented with to provide enough force to break the velcro bond. Once this procedure is perfected, however, it can be used for any activity: shapes, letter discrimination, sorting of concepts, number activities, etc.

Number Concepts

The child may find it difficult to participate in number activities requiring fine motor control. For this reason, counting may be difficult until the child develops enough of a sense of one-to-one correspondence to be able to keep track of the objects visually while counting. Various adaptations to assist the child who does not have one-to-one correspondence are possible.

GOAL:
To assist the child in counting activities in which, due to lack of fine motor control, he loses his place.

OBJECTIVE:
Using this adaptation, the child will be able to count and pick up objects at the same time thus eliminating some of the difficulty experienced with one-to-one correspondence.

MATERIALS:
Elastic band; velcro; pieces of cloth or other items that velcro will pick up; magnet wand (used for bingo) with push release; magnetic bingo chips

PROCEDURE:
1. Make an elastic band to fit over the child's hand on which velcro has been sewn (velcro should face outward).
2. Lay the pieces to be counted on the table and show the child how to pick them up by brushing his arm across them. (Make sure pieces are big enough that they can be pulled off the bank by using pressure from the other arm.) The child can then count the pieces and maintain his place in a concrete manner.
3. Lay the magnetic bingo chips on the table. The child can then pick them up one at a time using the magnetic wand. All the chips can be released after counting by pushing the button on the end of the wand. Children using this method must have a wide arc of motion due to the great strength of the magnet used. The chips must be placed far enough apart that they will remain in place until the wand is over it. A child with a very limited arc of motion would only be able to pick up a few chips due to this problem.

For independent work, number cards can be made with velcro attached or with a magnetic chip attached so the child can count the items, place them in a pile, then find the corresponding number and place it on top. In this manner, the child can work on his own, and the work can be checked later.

Letters

A child may find it difficult to control a pencil in the manner needed to draw letters initially. Guides can be used to assist the child until he can work on his own. The child who will be using a typewriter or computer as a communication mode can be included in activities in such a manner that the muscle skills he will need are practiced. For instance, a child who will be using a joystick for a computer in the future may be provided with an alphabet stamp and an ink pad to facilitate his grasp. Specific goals and strategies can be discussed with parents or the physical therapist.

GOAL:
To assist a child in the early formation of letters.

OBJECTIVE:
The child will be able to form the letter desired by using a plate with raised guides that contribute to pencil control.

MATERIALS:
Cardboard; popsicle sticks; glue; paper

PROCEDURE:
1. The child will be given a stencil plate made in the following manner. The letter will be drawn on the piece of cardboard and the interior of the letter cut out with an exacto knife. If desired the cut edges can be reinforced with glue or glued on popsicle sticks to lengthen the life of the stencil.
2. Paper can be taped to the back of the whole setup (the paper with the stencil over it) and can be fastened to a piece of cork with long pins.
3. The child can then follow the outline of the letter by placing his pencil against the edge and following it. Special grips (elastic band with a elastic loop to hold pencil) can be placed over the hand or wrist if pencil holding is also a problem.

Shape Concepts

The child with impaired motor functioning must have the experience of shape construction in order to fully understand the difference in the shapes themselves. Construction of these shapes can be completed when other children are drawing the shapes. In this manner the child is "drawing" the shapes in the way he or she can.

GOAL:
To assist the child unable to hold a pencil and draw in the construction of shapes similar to those drawn by his peers.

OBJECTIVE:
> The child will be able to construct the shape requested using a long, straight stamp and ink.

MATERIALS:
> Popsicle stick; glue, masking tape, or adhesive putty; strong ink pad or very thin paint soaked sponge

PROCEDURE:
1. The popsicle stick must have a handle built up from its base at a right degree angle. The handle should be appropriate for the child's grasp. Possibilities include pencils, another popsicle stick and long round cylinder, shaped block, etc. Glue, tape, or putty and then tape the handle to the stick. The child can then grasp the stick or it can be placed into a hand grip of elastic placed over the child's hand or wrist.
2. By pressing the stick onto the ink or on the sponge, the child can construct any shape in which straight lines are used. For shapes such as rectangles shorter sticks can be used or the extraneous lines should be discussed as unavoidable problems and ignored. The child can construct the shapes and gain practice in the features that make up the shape (number of lines, number of corners, etc.).
3. Circles can be made using the rim of a hollowed-out coffee can lid with a portion of the center left and bent up to form a handle. This handle can be built up to fit the child's grip needs.

Direction and Sequencing

Some children may be able to perform movements in a singlar fashion, but they may have difficulty sequencing movement. Open-ended activities that allow a wide range of movement are ideal to facilitate movement sequence. If the child is on a therapy program, specific movements may be detailed by the therapist. If not, sequences of movements used in the classroom would be ideal.

GOAL:
> To provide practice in left to right then up to down movement needed for writing.

OBJECTIVE:
> Using colored shaving cream, the child will reproduce patterns from model cards.

MATERIALS:
> shaving cream; food coloring; old shirt; cards with lines drawn showing left to right and up to down motion

PROCEDURE:
1. Have the child put on the old shirt to protect her clothes.

2. Place a mound of shaving cream on a tray or table and place the desired color of food coloring on top of the cream (only a few drops are needed).
3. Have the child mix the color into the shaving cream and then show them that by smoothing the cream out into a thin layer they can draw designs.
4. Show the child the design cards and have them try to reproduce the design in the shaving cream (assist as needed).

Social Skills

Children with motor impairment may often be left out of activities that are normally conducted on the floor. By structuring the activity in such a manner that it is on the child's level, children who cannot participate in floor-based activities easily will be able to work with everyone else with no obvious adaptations.

GOAL:
> To provide a normally floor-based activity at a level appropriate for the child's full participation.

OBJECTIVE:
> The child will participate in the building of a town and castle high upon a "mountain."

MATERIALS:
> Pictures of castles in Europe built upon mountains; large table; various shaped small blocks; brown paper; tape

PROCEDURE:
1. Show the children the pictures of the castles built on the mountains and introduce the activity.
2. Cover the bottom of the table with the brown paper so the table becomes a mountain.

The children can now build a town and castle and all will be working at a level appropriate for the special needs child.

Motor Skills

The child may be unable to participate fully in large motor play. By introducing themes in the large motor area and including props and roles to assist the child, participation in these activities can be enhanced.

GOAL:
> To develop activities containing roles and props to assist in the participation of child with a motor impairment.

OBJECTIVE:

The child will participate in the thematic play using the props or roles designed for him.

MATERIALS:

Carts; bags; food; money; cash registers

PROCEDURE:

1. Set up a shopping mall with various stores around the play area or room.
2. Weight one shopping cart with a milk carton filled with sand to help the child maintain his balance while shopping.
3. Guide the children when needed in their various roles as shopper, bagger, or cashier.

Cashier or bagger roles are ideal for the nonmobile child. For the child in a wheelchair, the chair can be designed into a truck with paper and the child can deliver papers, milk, flowers, etc. to the others.

Feelings

Children with impaired motor functions may feel a great deal of frustration in their everyday activities. Conversely, other children may be curious about the braces, crutches, and wheel chair the child must rely on. Activities can be developed that will enable the disabled child to describe his feelings and, at the same time, familiarize the children with the equipment he lives with.

GOAL:

To help a mobility-impaired child describe his feeling and frustrations due to his handicap and at the same time familiarize the other children with the equipment he uses.

OBJECTIVE:

The child will describe his feelings about using a specific piece of adaptive equipment and at the same time introduce the other children to its use.

MATERIALS:

Crutches; casts; wheelchair; dolls; various materials

PROCEDURE:

1. Go through an activity in which the children raise their hand when they possess a certain characteristic. Make it clear that we all have eyes and noses, some have glasses, etc., and one person has crutches.
2. Have the child show the others how his crutches work and how he uses them. Have him describe how it feels to use crutches. Don't dwell on the things he can't do, but the things he can. Try to elicit the child's feelings about having to use crutches.

3. In the housekeeping area show the children the dolls and other materials. The children can make casts, crutches, etc. for the dolls with the materials provided. If possible, the availability of the real equipment to try out would greatly enhance the children's understanding of their friend's feelings.
4. Encourage the motor-needs child to be the natural leader in this activity by helping the children, letting them look at his braces closeup, etc.

Body Image and Self Concept

A child with motor problems may have a distorted view of his body. Placement in crutches and wheelchair may contribute to this problem. Concrete experiences to help the child view his body as a whole, without the trappings of the disability, can be beneficial.

GOAL:
To provide an activity in which the child can view his body in a concrete form without the hindrance of his adaptations.

OBJECTIVE:
The child will see that his body is basically the same as everyone else's. He will recognize that it is the function of his body that is different.

MATERIALS:
Large sheets of paper; marking pen; crayons

PROCEDURE:
1. Have the child lie down on the paper. Remove braces, etc.
2. Draw the outline of the child's body.
3. Discuss the differences and the similarities in his outline with everyone else's outline. Emphasis should be on the similarities in the various pictures.
4. Allow the child to color in his picture, add features, etc. Encourage the child to add his braces to the picture so he sees that the braces are only additions to a body like everyone else has.

Discrimination Skills

A child with motor impairment may often be in situations in which tactile stimulation to the feet is reduced (wheelchairs, heavy shoes, etc), although he or she can experience sensation in the lower extremities. Providing tactile stimulation to the feet may be a novel experience for the child and one he may enjoy. Caution: Because more children have never had this type of foot stimulation before, they may find it uncomfortable. If this is the case, the degree of stimulation can be reduced by varying the materials.

GOAL:

To provide tactile stimulation to the feet.

OBJECTIVE:

The child will use his feet to paint a picture.

MATERIALS:

Large piece of paper; basin of soapy water; towel; chair; newspaper

PROCEDURE:

1. Place the paper to be painted on the floor and surround with newspaper.
2. Place the child in a chair in which his feet can easily reach and move about the floor.
3. Place some paint on the paper and place the child's feet in it (roll up pants, remove shoes/socks).
4. The child can paint a picture by moving his feet over the paper.
5. When the child is finished turn him sideways in the chair so his feet go directly into a waiting basin of soapy water. Wash and dry feet. Replace shoes, etc.

For children who are not ready for the sensation of the wet paint, dry sand, styrofoam pellets or pieces of cloth are less bothersome to most children.

Perceptual Skills

The child with motor problems may find it difficult to pick up puzzle pieces in the normal manner. Some puzzles are equipped with handles or knobs but they are often designed for younger children. Those designed for a special needs population are often expensive and may lack the appeal of the puzzles used by the other children. A simple adaptation can help the child who lacks fine motor control use all types of puzzles without damage to the materials themselves.

GOAL:

To assist the child who lacks fine motor control in the manipulation of puzzle pieces.

OBJECTIVE:

The child will be able to grasp the handle of the adaptation on each puzzle piece and transfer it to the puzzle board.

MATERIALS:

Suction cups with hook (used to hang sun catchers on windows); masking tape; strips of paper; puzzle

PROCEDURE:

1. Attach a suction cup to the table and build a handle around the hook portion located in the center of each one. Use tape to form small handles or, for larger ones, alternate tape and small paper strips to make the handle. Any material that suits the child's needs should be used.

2. Press one suction cup into the center of each puzzle piece. Make sure the cup is secure. These should hold for all but the heaviest wooden puzzles.
3. The child can then hold the handles to move the pieces and manipulate them into place. The suction cups should be removed by placing the fingernail at the base to break the suction (don't pull on the handles, they may not be able to take the strain). The cups can be moved from puzzle using this method.

Reading

The child with motor impairment may find the physical activity of reading a book frustrating. They may often have to rely on a friend or adult to assist them. This cuts down on the time spent reading while thwarting the desire to read. Adaptations can be bought to hold book and turn the pages, but adaptations that cost much less can be made and may be more suitable for a child in the early years.

GOAL:
    To assist the child with motor needs in the physical aspects of reading a book.

OBJECTIVE:
    The child will be able to read a book at the highest level of independence possible.

MATERIALS:
    Book; clamps for holding papers (strong clasp); clear lucite chips or pennies; elastic band; tray

PROCEDURE:
1. Choose a book that the child will enjoy.
2. Let the child try to read it on his own. Note his arm movements, the range of his grasp, the movement of the book, etc.
3. If needed, use elastic bands over both covers of the book to secure it to a small tray or lap stand.
4. Place clips along the edges of the pages (one per page) in a staggered arrangement to facilitate grasp or provide level for arm (wrist) use.
5. Let the child try to turn the pages using these clamps only. Adjust clamp of any page beyond his grasp range.
6. If pages are making it to the midline and then falling back, attach clear lucite chips or pennies (if pennies are used, place so pictures aren't too obscured) to the front of each page in the middle. This will facilitate the force of gravity and make the picture turn over if midline is reached.

The key to this process is repeated trial and error. The specific limitations of the child may require different clamp use or weight placement. This adaptation, once placement is verified, is easy to switch to another book without damage to materials used. It is also less obtrusive than most purchased adaptations.

Science

The child with impaired motor functioning may find the ability to cause things to happen, inherent in science experiments, a welcome change from the normal reliance on others he may experience. Such cause/effect relationships may provide keys to adaptations and means of creating action on a self-initiated basis. A magnet experiment is an excellent way to introduce this concept of control over the environment.

GOAL:
> To provide an experience in manipulation and control of the environment.

OBJECTIVE:
> Through the exploration with magnets, the child will develop a use for magnets within the classroom.

MATERIALS:
> Magnets of varying strength; objects with different material compositions; two trays

PROCEDURE:
1. Introduce the child to the use of magnets. Through guided discovery, let the child see that not all materials are attracted to magnets.
2. Let the child explore with the magnets and attempt to come up with the basic rules that govern their use. Elicit a listing of materials he sorted (into the trays) that the magnet will or will not pick up.
3. After the child has worked with the magnets, illustrate some ways magnets can be useful (collecting fallen pins, etc). Help the child to discover some ways to use the magnets to help himself (retrieve objects, turn pages, etc.) Whatever adaptation he comes up with, let him try it out in the room and continue to use it if he wishes.

Music

The child with motor needs can participate with little difficulty in the area of music. Those with limitations may have their movement and participation enhanced by small adaptations. Movement for these children should never be in an overly structured manner. Free expressive dance will best fit the needs of the child who has a limited range of movement.

GOAL:
> To assist the child in the full participation of music-based activities.

OBJECTIVE:
> The child will use various adaptive instruments to provide accompaniment to various songs.

MATERIALS:
Velcro; elastic; instruments

PROCEDURE:
1. Select an instrument with the child.
2. Using velcro, make an elastic band that will fit over the child's palm or wrist. Attach velcro to the band so it faces outward. Attach velcro to the instrument to be played (if light enough) and stick to velcro.
3. If instrument is too heavy to be used in this manner, a loop of velcro can be attached to the band and the instrument's handle placed through it.
4. Instruments such as drums can be weighted down with various objects or secured with velcro to a tray.

Art

The use of scissors has always been a problem area for many young children and may be especially difficult for the child lacking hand strength or coordination. The child often has the ability to close the scissors but must use two hands to open them. A small adaptation can assist this process.

GOAL:
To assist a child lacking hand strength in the use of scissors.

OBJECTIVE:
The student will be able to work a pair of scissors with one hand when cutting thin paper.

MATERIALS:
Scissors; thin wire; masking tape; small spring; thin paper; strong glue

PROCEDURE:
This procedure is varied by the type of scissors used. For best results, use plastic ones that have a flat portion between the joint of the scissor and the finger hole. The spring helps the scissors reopen, making cutting easier.
1. Open the scissor and place the small spring on the inside portion of the joint (on the side of the finger holes, not the cutting edge). The spring should have the open ends toward the two handles.
2. Attach the spring to the two handles by running a thin wire through the last few loops on the end and then winding around the handle. This can then be secured with very strong all-material glue. Cover the handle and the finger loops with the tape so no sharp edges can cut fingers. (The tape will provide extra support as well). This is suitable for use with thin paper.

If this procedure breaks apart with your scissors, you can try opening up the spring partway and rewinding over the handle (so the handle actually runs through the spring). This should then be taped and glued as before.

CHAPTER 8

Integrating Young Children with Developmental Delays and Behavior Problems

The three preceding chapters dealt with young children who have objectively defined biological impairments that may or may not interfere with their educational performance. Such children account for a small proportion of those who are, for special education purposes, considered handicapped, and the considerations for teaching them in regular classrooms are to some degree disability-specific. For the children discussed in this chapter, distinctions based on the type of disability are not particularly useful, especially in early childhood. Therefore, even though these children represent the vast majority of those considered handicapped, our discussion is mainly generic or cross-categorical.

Another point may be surprising: Although the children discussed in this chapter are, for the most part, mildly or moderately impaired compared to many children with visual, hearing, mobility, or health impairments, among them are the children believed by many teachers to be the least readily integrated into mainstream classrooms. Surveys of elementary teachers' receptiveness to mainstreaming generally reveal that the two groups perceived as "least favorable" are (1) children labeled "behavior disordered," and (2) children labeled "mentally retarded." The children discussed in this chapter also include, however, the two groups invariably found to be considered "most mainstreamable:" (1) children with speech impairments, and (2) children with specific learning disabilities.

We should remember two guiding principles in understanding this apparent paradox:

1. The severity of a child's disability does not, in itself, determine how readily the child can be accommodated and taught within a typical setting.
2. The labels that are applied to exceptional children often serve to generate and perpetuate beliefs and myths, irrespective of the evidence in an individual situation.

The feasibility of full or partial mainstream school placement is influenced not by the type of disability, or even its severity, but by the effect of that disability on school performance. That may explain why some teachers are concerned when they hear the labels "behavior disorder" or "mental retardation." The first label suggests possibilities of disruptive behavior in the classroom, motivational problems, noncompliance, or emotional fragility. The second label suggests that the child may be unable to learn the same material, acquire the same skills, or perform at the same pace as the rest of the children in the classroom. Both may suggest to an already stretched and "frazzled" teacher special needs for teacher time and individual attention.

This chapter mainly concerns young children whose delays in one or more areas of development suggest that they are at risk for school failure. It also concerns young children who manifest special difficulties with regard to autonomy and independence, constructive and cooperative interaction within a social group setting, appropriate compliance with adult expectations, and management of fears, feelings, or impulses—that is, who are developmentally delayed in the personal-social domain. Many of these children present special needs in the areas of communication, motivation, and social skills, although the needs of each individual child are unique. Ultimately, at least based on past practice, many of these children may eventually be "sorted" into special education classifications identified by "high-incidence" handicap labels: speech and language impaired, mentally retarded, learning disabled, and behavior disordered. Such "sorting" has increasingly been attacked as arbitrary, potentially harmful, unnecessary, and inefficient (Reynolds, Wang & Walberg, 1987; Stainback & Stainback, 1984; 1987; Ysseldyke & Algozzine, 1982).

LANGUAGE AND COMMUNICATION: A FUNDAMENTAL CONCERN

Although controversies exist with respect to physical and sensory disabilities in children, they are verifiable objectively: vision, hearing, motor, and health problems can be medically defined; their existence can be established based upon agreed-upon criteria; and children with these problems can usually be distinguished from those without. That is not the case with most children classified as mentally retarded, behavior disordered, learning disabled, or language impaired.

(Children with speech difficulties but intact language constitute a special case. They are discussed in this chapter, even though most young children who can benefit from assistance specifically with speech difficulties would not be considered at risk for school failure. Also, most speech problems can be defined and identified more reliably than the other areas discussed in this chapter.)

The most common and pervasive special needs of young handicapped children, including low incidence as well as high incidence impairments, are in communication skills, one of the most important areas of children's development. Some children have problems specifically in the area of speech or language. Others, whose "primary disability" is identified as something other than a speech or language impairment, experience problems in language and communication that are associated with, or secondary to, their disability. For educational purposes, it is the difficulties in speech or language, rather than their presumed cause, that are specifically relevant to teaching.

It is difficult, if not impossible, to separate language from two other developmental domains of great importance in early childhood: cognitive development and personal-social development. A child described as mentally retarded will actually experience the most difficulties in formal learning with language-related tasks. A child who does not use language appropriately in social interaction will be perceived as experiencing difficulties in interacting with others; conversely, children who have difficulty in interacting with others may not be adept in the social function of language.

Handicapped children comprise just as varied a group as nonhandicapped children, and few useful generalizations can be appropriately applied. Handicapped preschool and primary children have many different needs, learning styles, strengths and weaknesses; what they have in common is what they share with all young children. Language and communication skills, however, represent particular needs for a great many young children identified as developmentally delayed. Virtually every "category" of disability is likely to imply significant risk for problems in language and communication skills. Consequently, this is a priority area for early childhood classrooms where handicapped children are mainstreamed (Spodek, Saracho, & Lee, 1984).

PROBLEMS IN COGNITIVE DEVELOPMENT

We can say that young children whose achievement of developmental milestones involving cognitive skills is significantly delayed are at risk for school failure and at risk to be labeled mentally retarded when they begin formal schooling. Mental retardation does not explain delayed development or problems in school learning. Instead, it is a term used to describe (and label) individuals who meet certain criteria: *"Mental retardation refers to significantly subaverage general intellectual functioning existing concurrently with deficits in adaptive behavior and manifested during the developmental period"* (Grossman, 1983, p. 1). This official current definition, promulgated by the American Association on Mental Deficiency (AAMD), implies several questions, including what is "general intellectual functioning," how do we measure it, and what is "significantly subaverage."

The definition says nothing about cause or duration. The cause of mental retardation can be determined in only about 15 percent of all cases (Lerner et al., 1987), and special education on the basis of mental retardation must be determined through an annual review of the child's IEP (although formal tests of intellectual functioning and of adaptive behavior are not necessarily readministered every year. A child may be classified as "in or out of mental retardation," in the late Burton Blatt's (1977) telling phrase, depending upon either or both of two important considerations, changes in the child's functioning, or changes in the eligibility criteria. To remind us of the influence of the second factor, Blatt (1977) observed that, with "a single stroke of the pen," the prevalence of mental retardation was significantly reduced when the AAMD definition stipulated that two standard deviations below the mean (i.e., an IQ lower than either 69 or 70, depending upon the test used) rather than one standard deviation (i.e., an IQ lower than 84 or 85) would satisfy the general intellectual functioning criterion.

The vast majority—more than 70 percent—of persons identified as mentally retarded are mildly retarded (based on IQ and adaptive behavior scores). It is the intellectual functioning status of these children that is particularly subject to fluctuation "in and out of retardation." Educators now generally agree that mild mental retardation is simply not an appropriate label for children of preschool age and, as Polloway (1987) notes, it is rarely applied to young children:

1. Mild retardation is related mainly to academic functioning in school, and thus is not likely to be apparent prior to school entrance.
2. Because of concerns about possible limiting and stigmatizing consequences of labels, professionals appropriately avoid applying such a label in situations where future possibilities depend greatly upon early experiences.

Tests of intellectual potential have little, if any, predictive usefulness for most young children (Sattler, 1988). One reason for this is that tests for infants and young children necessarily involve skill areas different from those measured in tests designed for older children or adults. Another reason is the belief, well supported by evidence (Bloom, 1964) that undergirds early intervention: *the future abilities of young children are greatly influenced by their early experiences.*

These same points apply to the label *learning disability* (Leigh & Riley, 1982). A great many young children who cannot and should not be identified positively as "handicapped" and diagnosed differentially as either mentally retarded or learning disabled do manifest delays in certain aspects of development, or disparities among areas of skill development. Effective early education for such children has the potential to enhance development; enable them to acquire compensatory skills; establish patterns of success and expectancies for functioning within typical, rather than special or segregated, educational environments; and reduce the likelihood of future specialized services.

Beliefs about mental retardation are based in part on beliefs about human intelligence: persons labeled as retarded have been presumed to "have" less of "it." A basic tenet of certain theories is that a person's "level" of intelligence is fixed at birth and remains the same throughout life. There are four basic fallacies that have had especially handicapping consequences for persons throught of, or formally identified as, mentally retarded:

1. The *reification fallacy* (Gould, 1981)—the belief that intelligence is a "thing."
2. The *measurement fallacy*—the assumption that the psychometric construct IQ is synonymous with intelligence, based on the beliefs that intelligence can be defined independently of IQ tests and IQ tests are accurate measures of intelligence.
3. The *unity fallacy*—the belief that persons are equally capable or equally limited in all areas of intelligent behavior.
4. The *immutability fallacy*—the belief that intelligence is fixed, unchanging, and unchangeable, despite alternative life experiences and opportunities.

These fallacies explain, though they do not excuse, past practices in public education regarding students identified as mentally retarded. These practices, now seen as untenable and unjustifiable, included:

1. Excluding some children from school based on IQ scores that were believed to imply "uneducability" or "inability to benefit from education."
2. Assigning students to alternative, segregated tracks and assuming (and ensuring) permanency of such segregated placement.
3. Assuming homogeneity among students labeled as mentally retarded, within each of three classifications: "educable," "trainable," and "custodial," or in alternative terminology mild, moderate, and severe/profound retardation.
4. Developing "standard" approaches as a consequence of the assumption of homogeneity that lack provisions for individualization and differentiated instruction geared to both interindividual and intraindividual differences, and reflected (for mildly and moderately retarded students) curricula qualitatively different from that of general education.

For those children for whom educational programs were provided, the possible advantages were: (1) more favorable teacher-student ratio (that is, smaller class size), and (2) teachers specifically trained to understand and meet the educational needs of their pupils. However, neither of these advantages characterized services for children (and adults) labeled as severely and profoundly mentally retarded. For them, services were, at best, only custodial and were characterized by low staff-to-client ratios and untrained or poorly trained staff. In fact, even public school special classes for students classified as mildly and moderately mentally retarded were, in many instances, of less than optimal size; often, group instruction was the norm. (One special class instructor, asked to help in the field testing of a diagnostic teaching system, protested, stating, "I teach groups, not individuals!" He had 19 students in his class, all full-time, and no teaching assistant or aide.)

Restrictive educational practices for students classified as mentally retarded occurred within a broader context of societal attitudes. More damaging misconceptions, myths, and stereotypes are associated with the label mental retardation (and its predecessor labels, such as "feeble-mindedness") than any other label applied to exceptional individuals. That can be understood in part on the basis of the history of the field, as suggested in Part I. Contemporary effects are seen in the resistance of members of some communities to the creation of a group home within their neighborhood. They are also seen in the resistance that has been demonstrated by some educators to social and instructional integration of students who have been classified and labeled as mentally retarded or who have characteristics that have been associated with mental retardation (such as children with Down syndrome.)

Barriers to integration have been rationalized on the basis of three major concerns, first, that the child will not be able to experience success with the standard curriculum or learn as optimally as with a curriculum specifically geared to the learning characteristics, levels, and needs of mentally retarded students, resulting in the likelihood of teasing, social rejection, and even ostracism by peers and in both academic and personal/social failure; second, that learning opportunities for other students may be adversely affected because of the need to slow the pace of instruction and provide excessive help for the retarded student; and finally, that the very teachers who express receptive attitudes toward mainstreaming may question their own abilities to adapt and individualize curriculum and instruction to the extent presumed to be necessary (Keogh & Levitt, 1976). The most handicapping aspect of mental retardation, then, may be the label itself (Bogdan, 1986).

For some, the stigma attached to this essentially *educational* label may be removed by completing or leaving school and simply leaving behind their label (Mercer, 1973). That is increasingly less likely to occur, however, as Klein, Pasch, and Frew explain:

> Often the role expectations outside of school are more easily mastered. The academic expectations that presented a problem to the child while in school no longer apply. However, students who were not able to master basic reading and other basic skills, and who have either minimal or no job skills, may continue to be considered retarded. *This is increasingly true as our society becomes more technologically complex.* (p. 70, italics added)

Children labeled mentally retarded are not, of course, the only students at risk for school failure and subsequent limited opportunities; they do not even constitute a majority of that group, as school dropout and low literacy statistics evidence (Ysseldyke & Algozzine, 1982). There are many casualties of the educational system.

Such statistics are a major argument for the position that both regular and special education should be "restructured" (Reynolds, Wang, & Walberg, 1987), so that regular education would assume responsibility for serving all mildly and moderately educationally handicapped students. That would include the vast majority of students currently classified as mentally retarded (at least 70 percent), as well as those identified as learning disabled, and all students identified as behavior disordered except those with very severe emotional disturbance. This plan would eliminate the problem of eligibility criteria for special education that, for these three groups, has continued to be most perplexing and controversial, and it would be predicated upon a regular education structure equipped with the instructional resources to respond effectively and appropriately to differential student needs, rather than one oriented to a nonexistent homogeneous student population. Schools would not attempt to identify and refer out students who depart from the "norm." Students would not be assigned to one of several categorical programs, based upon frankly arbitrary and certainly inconsistent (Ysseldyke, Algozzine, Richey & Graden, 1982) criteria, since regular education would be expected to respond to student differences. Implementation of this kind of fundamental restructuring could be accomplished through:

1. More effective initial preparation and continuing staff development for regular education teachers to enhance their ability (as mandated under P.L. 94–142) to differentiate instruction.
2. More favorable teacher-student ratios.
3. Less categorically restricted allocation of resource services, including reading specialization, remedial and compensatory math instruction, speech and language services, and consultative services of such specially prepared personnel as school psychologists and school counselors.
4. Effective classroom use of microcomputers and other new technology.
5. More effective parent involvement and home-school cooperation, as well as incorporation of parent and other community volunteer assistance.
6. More flexible curricula, classroom organization, and time scheduling.

Young children demonstrating delayed development can thrive in early childhood settings characterized by *developmentally appropriate practices* with respect to goals and methods. They are at very high risk for failure in settings that follow practices that are *not* developmentally appropriate to the characteristics and needs of young children. That is because they, like all young children, require:

1. A great deal of experience with real, concrete materials and situations.
2. Opportunities to practice skills repetitively, as young children normally do in play, and to apply them to a wide variety of situations.
3. Peer models for play and social skill learning, speech and language development, understanding and practice of routines, and use of learning materials.
4. Provision for gradually and incrementally increasing performance demands, starting from a child-specific and task-specific base.
5. Flexible time requirements, geared to individual style, preference, and need of each child.
6. Structure that is supportive in helping the child to feel confident and secure, anticipate events, and understand relationships, including cause-effect relationships.
7. Support and stimulation for literacy behavior not limited to the printed or spoken word, but instead encouraging and allowing imaginative and representational play, concept acquisition independent of concept words, and other expressive modalities, such as use of art media and music.
8. Multisensory experiences.

DEVELOPMENTAL PROBLEMS PREDICTIVE OF SPECIFIC LEARNING DISABILITIES

There is a particular concern about labeling young children with the term *specific learning disability,* based in part on the lack of agreement as to the definition of SLD itself (Sutaria, 1985). One survey of 144 researchers, educators, and policy makers in the field of learning disabilities, conducted in 1981 (Tucker, Stevens, & Ysseldyke, 1983), revealed that most (82.6 percent) agreed that SLD was a viable classification, but 15.3 percent disagreed. Respondents were asked whether they believed that SLD could be identified in children on the basis of specific presenting symptoms or clusters of symptoms. Of those who responded to this question, an even larger majority (88 percent) agreed tht it could, although many expressed reservations concerning prevailing identification practices. Controversies continue as to whether the SDL classification identifies a category of students with common characteristics. Poplin (1984) has summarized the research evidence bearing on this central issue as follows:

> From over a decade of accumulated research findings perhaps only one undeniable "fact" has emerged—learning disabilities is not a single handicapping con-

dition with an easily defined set of characteristics. That is, learning disabled children are as different as they are from their normal peers. (p. 131)

The *individuality* of the characteristics and needs of children and youth in this classification is of fundamental importance, together with the implication for individual educational planning. If children identified as learning disabled are, by definition, very diverse, then no single form of education or instructional approach is appropriate for all. In an important sense, the field of learning disabilities, characterized by a very high degree of parent activism, helped set the stage for one of the key provisions of Public Law 94–142: the Individual Education Program (IEP).

As was noted earlier, SLD is currently the largest classification of students receiving special education, having dramatically increased in prevalence since the "cap" of 2 percent of school-age children was removed by the Congress. The U.S. Department of Education's *Seventh Annual Report to Congress on the Implementation of the Education of the Handicapped Act* (P.L. 94–142), submitted in 1985, revealed that the number of American school children classified as SLD had increased from 1.79 percent in 1976–77 to 4.57 percent in the 1983–84 school year.

Statistics such as these highlight the role of policy and its implementation in determining how students are identified and classified. Before the concept of learning disabilties existed, no children, of course, were so classified, although predecessor "categories" had been proposed since the late 1940s. Most of these (e.g., Clements, 1966; Cruickshank, Bentzen, Ratzeburg, & Tannhauser, 1961; Strauss & Lehtinen, 1947) had identified perceptual, perceptual-motor, and behavioral characteristics (notably "hyperactivity") believed likely to be associated with underlying neurological causes, and terms such as *minimal brain damage* or *neurologically handicapped* were suggested. An area of controversy yet raging concerns whether SLD should be defined in terms of intrinsic causes, and if it is possible to establish whether a child's learning difficulties are or are not due to underlying neurological problems. However this group of children is defined, children with such problems had existed prior to the creation of the category. Also, the increase in their numbers is undoubtedly due more to policy definitions than to epidemiology. As suggested in a succession of its annual reports, beginning in 1983, the U.S. Department of Education attributes the increase to several possible factors: (1) possible improvements in identification practices employed by schools; (2) more liberal eligibility criteria; (3) greater social acceptability of the LD label (perhaps accounting for parallel decreases in the numbers of children identified as mentally retarded); (4) lack of general education alternatives for students who experience problems in the standard academic program.

Such factors help to explain why sound arguments can be advanced for the kind of educational restructuring (e.g., Wang, Reynolds, & Walberg, 1987) discussed previously. Who are the real learning disabled students, and how many of them are there actually? That individual children and youth experience great difficulties in school, and that these difficulties and the instructional approaches they imply, are idiosyncratic is a reality. Whether classifying some—a growing number—of these students as learning disabled is of value or is an impediment to serving them effectively constitutes perhaps the basic controversy in this most controversial area.

The "official" definition of learning disabilities (*Federal Register*, 1977, p. 7) stresses impaired school performance in one or more of areas such as reading, writing, listening, speaking, spelling, mathematics, or thinking. Such problems are presumed to be attributable to disorders in one or more of the "basic psychological processes," a term used to ". . . refer to intrinsic prerequisite abilities such as memory, auditory perception, visual perception, and oral language." Janet Lerner (1985, p. 33) states that learning disabilities are associated with neurological dysfunction, attentional deficit disorders, uneven growth patterns, and difficulty in learning and with specific academic tasks. Cecil Mercer (1983) adds problems in intersensory integration, visual and auditory reception, selective attention, and impulsivity. The so-called "exclusionary clause" of the federal definition, which stipulates that an SLD child's learning problems are not primarily caused by sensory impairments, motor handicaps, mental retardation, emotional disturbance, or cultural, economic, or environmental disadvantage, adds to the definitional controversy.

It is the *discrepancy clause* that simultaneously best captures, for many, the essential aspect of SLD, results in differences in identification practices, and makes early identification of SLD children problematic, at best. According to the Federal Rules and Regulations for implementing P.L. 94–142 (Federal Register, 1977), a student may be determined learning disabled if:

1. The child does not achieve commensurate with his or her age and ability levels in one or more of the areas listed in paragraph (a)(2) of this section, when provided with learning experiences appropriate for the child's age and ability levels.
2. The team finds that a child has a severe discrepancy between achievement and intellectual ability in one or more of the following areas:
   i. Oral expression;
   ii. Listening comprehension;
   iii. Written expression;
   iv. Basic reading skill;
   v. Reading comprehension;
   vi. Mathematics calculation; or
   vii. Mathematics reasoning. (p. 65083)

What constitutes a "*severe* discrepancy" between a child's measured intellectual ability and measured achievement in any of these areas is not specified in federal policy; instead, that is determined by each state. Generally, a computational formula is prescribed, with a "discrepancy score" stipulated. However, recognizing problems such as (1) inherent shortcomings of the individual standardized tests of ability and achievement; (2) the possibility that a child's learning problems may depress his or her ability test score; and (3) the younger the child, the less probable is a criterial discrepancy score, standards followed in most states allow for an "override" decision by the team. That is, if the team concurs that a student is appropriately identified and served as SLD, although the discrepancy criterion may not have been met, the decision can be made accordingly. Thus, in many if not most instances, identification and placement decisions are based not on "objective" test data, but on collective professional (and parent) judgment (Ysseldyke et al., 1982).

Whereas early identification of children who may later be classified as learning disabled would seem desirable, in order to provide early intervention, the definitions of SLD obviously do no lend themselves well to this goal. Research has suggested (Leigh & Riley, 1982; Leigh, 1983) that the issue of early identification could be approached more productively. Rather than attempting to define the characteristics of preschool-age "learning disabled" children, we should attempt to identify indicators of the "predisposition to acquire" learning disabilities (Leigh, 1983, p.4). Such a predisposition would be associated with problems affecting a young child's present performance and with skills that the child presently lacks that will be needed in the primary grades. Thus, the recommended focus would be upon helping the young child learn to function effectively within present and also future environments. As Lerner (1985) notes, these problems may be observed in pre-academic skill areas, including attending, motor and perceptual skills, and language acquisition and use.

Among the difficulties associated with early identification of predicted learning disabilities are those involving the issue of developmentally appropriate vs. developmentally inappropriate practices (and expectations) in early childhood education programs. Is a child who has difficulty cutting with scissors, or drawing "within the lines," or consistently following left-to-right progression, or reading sight words, or constructing numerals and letters without reversing them demonstrating early indicators of a learning disability? Not necessarily, if these are nursery school or even kindergarten activities.

PROBLEMS IN EMOTIONAL DEVELOPMENT AND SOCIAL BEHAVIOR

As all parents know, each developmental period through which children pass has its own unique joys—and its own problems. Many rueful jokes suggest that another word for toddler is "a handful!" or that "disturbance" is a synonym for adolescence. All children experience actual stress in the course of growing up. Most from time to time experience acute loneliness, sadness, wounded self-esteem or recurring self-doubts, run-ins with adults, difficulties with peers, intense feelings of anger, alarming fantasies, paralyzing fears, or psychosomatic physical symptoms. Parents want their children to have a childhood free of conflict and pain. But conflict and pain are, to some degree, a part of virtually everyone's childhood, a part of "the human condition." It is a cliché that maturity, wisdom, competence in meeting life's challenges, and the ability to love self and others cannot be gained without them.

The successive periods of childhood and youth have been described as involving successive developmental tasks (Havighurst, 1972) to be accomplished, and Erik Erikson (1963) has applied the concept of developmental crisis to the successive stages of the life cycle. The difficulties and problems associated with growing as a person are, to some degree, universal and common to all of us. However, each of us experiences our own particular difficulties and problems as well. Also, we are all different in our ability to cope with both our own special circumstances and those we share with others. Many children must struggle with the series of difficult life events without the support and nurturance of a secure and loving home environment. Inconsistent and undependable love or discipline, parental preoccupations—whether with "success" or with sheer survival—or any of a multitude of possible family problems can make infinitely harder what is difficult enough when things go smoothly, the process of growing up.

Clearly, not all children who experience difficult, even abusive home situations become disturbed—nor are all children who apparently enjoy very positive home conditions free of risk for emotional and behavioral problems. Children's response to environmental stressors is highly individualistic. In addition, nearly all the behaviors commonly associated with disturbance are present in the repertoires of normally developing children and youth.

Children with serious problems of social-emotional development or behavior present a wide diversity of characteristics and needs. As with other areas of exceptionality, these children defy classification. As Peterson (1987) noted, variations in the behavior of young children may be attributable to momentary environmental influences or to physical factors. Young children's problem behaviors do not occur within a vacuum; there is always an *ecological context* that must be understood if we are to help a child behave more appropriately and constructively. Finally, there is the nature of childhood itself. Diagnostic classifications applied to adults are inappropriate for children, both because of the qualitative differences between children and adults and because children's development is in process, not already accomplished.

For purposes of education, however, we need to define clearly the manifestations of children's problems within the preschool or school context. Young children who experience unusual emotional stress, or who have acquired inappropriate or unacceptable ways of coping with conflict or stress, or in expressing feelings, may manifest any of three levels of behavior problem severity identified by Peterson (1987): disturbing behavior, behavior problems, or seriously disordered behaviors (pp. 231–232). In some young children, any of these levels may be associated with inconsistent, unpredictable, punitive, or absent parental discipline, guidance, and modeling. However, differences in temperament among children may both underly behavioral patterns and influence adult responses (Beckman-Bell, 1981; Thomas, Chess, & Birch, 1968;). Just as do "acting-out" behaviors, a child's troubling blandness, guardedness, difficulty in communicating or forming relationships with others, fearfulness, shy and withdrawn behavior, pervasive sadness and depression, or other manifestations may reflect a complex of learning and internal conflict.

We must first distinguish what is developmentally normal from problem behavior. Failure to do so can produce real problems needlessly and sometimes tragically. One children's services agency, for instance, received a mother's referral of her own child as a "fire-setter" at age two! The little boy had ignited curtains while playing with his mother's cigarette lighter, which had been left lying on a low table. Earlier, his exploration of a defective lamp cord had resulted in a small electrical fire. We might assume that "everyone knows" about a two-year-old's curiosity and the importance of adults anticipating and preventing accidents like these, but this young mother did not. She assumed there was something wrong with the toddler or that he was "bad." A caseworker's intervention, in this instance, prevented a tragic course of events that might have resulted in the mother "turning the child in." Information about child development, guidance in child management, and support in coping with her own problems not only helped the mother, they may have also prevented the making of a disturbed child from a perfectly normal, healthy, curious toddler.

Most teachers of young children would be concerned if told that a "behavior disordered" or "emotionally disturbed" child was going to be enrolled in their class. Of all the exceptionality labels these are among the most stigmatizing. Although it is extremely important to identify specific emotional and behavioral needs of the child, application of these labels to young children is seldom, if ever, warranted. The suggestions for practice described in the latter portion of this chapter do not differentiate techniques or methods based on category. Instead, we recognize that affective-social and behavioral principles are applicable without regard to classification or label.

PROBLEMS IN SPEECH AND LANGUAGE DEVELOPMENT

Clearly, not all young children experiencing difficulties in language development are mentally retarded or score within the range of retardation on measures of intellectual ability and adaptive behavior. However, virtually every young child so identified has difficulties relating to language development. Also, mainstream classroom activities emphasizing language are the major areas in which children with developmental delays may require special assistance, curricular and instructional accommodations, and specific targeting of objectives and monitoring of progress (Spodek et al., 1984). Therefore, although this chapter addresses a number of considerations for successful integration of children described as developmentally delayed, a major unifying theme is language-related accomodations and provisions for individual special needs within the early childhood classroom.

First we need to define the two closely related, yet distinct, concepts of speech and language and note the developmental problems relating to each. We will consider implications for the teacher concerning both individualized and group planning, in this chapter and in Chapters 10 and 11. Examples discussed include children with identified problems specific to speech or language development, as well as children whose speech or language problems coexist with other difficulties in the domains of motor, cognitive, sensory, or social-emotional development. These examples illustrate how difficult it is to categorize young children by "type" of disability.

Speech is an oral mode of expressing language. It is not synonomous with language; rather, it is dependent upon language. Yet speech is not the only mode through which people communicate meaningfully with others. What is required for communication to occur is a shared system of rules and symbols (Bloom & Lahey, 1978). That such communication is possible in the absence of speech has been increasingly recognized by the speech-using majority with the greater awareness of manual communication, or sign language, used by many deaf persons, as well as others. Most people rely primarily upon speech to communicate, but virtually all speakers, consciously or unconsciously, employ other communicative modes in conjunction with speech, including facial expression, "body language," non-speech utterances, and gesture.

Since language consists of symbols and rules for selecting and combining symbols, "Language exists even in moments of silence . . . [whereas] . . . speech exists only in moments of actual speaking or listening" (Lerner et al., 1987, p. 186). Some perspectives on children's language have emphasized the "internal" aspects, specifically the relationship between language and thought (Vygotsky, 1962). However, the focus of theoretical interest in children's language has shifted in recent times to the *social context* in which children use language (Bates, 1976; Bloom & Lahey, 1978).

A child's speech can be analyzed directly. Langauge, on the other hand, cannot be directly observed. Instead, language skills can only be inferred based upon speech, or other modes of communication, or based upon the child's behavior in response to language expressed by someone else (or a recording, computer voice, visible signals, etc.). Problems in *receptive language* may be revealed by a child's inability to respond, or inappropriate response, to messages intended to elicit a certain response. However, these must be distinguished from *sensory* problems. With any suspected difficulties in speech or language, the possibility of a hearing loss must first be considered.

Speech Problems

Speech problems have been defined (Van Riper, 1972) to include patterns of speech that either interfere with communication or call unfavorable attention to the speaker. The importance of the second aspect is reflected in the fact that our speech is a public expression of our selves; consequently, unfavorable reactions of others—or anticipation that others will react unfavorably—may be severely detrimental to self-esteem. Some young children with speech difficulties refrain from speaking to avoid embarrassment, or become shy and withdrawn. Consequently, helping young children with speech difficulties may have an impact upon many aspects of their social and emotional development.

Articulation. The most frequently encountered speech problems of children are problems of articulation. These include omissions of sounds, additions of sounds, substitution of one sound for another, or sound distortions. Young children progressively master the production of specific sounds in a fairly predictable sequence. Therefore, consideration of the child's age is obviously essential in determining whether a problem exists or whether young children of that age typically have not mastered a certain sound as yet. However, although developmental milestones in speech and language development have been identified, these do not rigidly define a fixed schedule of what is "normal" for five-year-olds, say, but not for four-year-olds. As in all areas of development, wide variations exist. Consideration of a range of what may be considered typical is necessary. Even delays or deviance beyond that range do not necessarily imply problems or presage more serious difficulties in learning or personal and social development. However, the belief that children will usually "outgrow" problems simply with the passage of time is quite erroneous. Individual or small-group speech therapy may be indicated to facilitate progress. The problem is how to identify early warning signs and institute appropriate interventions without unduly alarming parents or stigmatizing the child.

For the teacher of young children, there are four basic responsibilities specifically indicated: (1) identifying indications of possible difficulties and initiating a standard referral process through providing specific observation data on the child's speech pattern, leading to consultation with a speech and language pathologist; (2) working with the specialist to carry out a prescribed program within the classroom, if indicated, perhaps involving systematic reinforcement of specific speech behaviors to accomplish precise objectives; (3) providing a speech environment that is supportive, encouraging, and conducive to modeling and practice; and (4) ensuring that effective communication is maintained with the child's parents concerning needs and progress. For all young children, including those with specific expressive difficulties, the social context of the classroom or center should provide an appropriate setting for speech development and application of planned intervention:

> The classroom teacher is a speech teacher whether he is trained to be or not; indeed, whether he wants to be or not. Both as a speaker and as a listener, he creates an atmosphere either conducive to, or unfavorable to, the development of each child's speech. (Phillips, 1975, p. 13)

Fluency. The most common type of disfluency involves stuttering; however, actual stuttering problems are far less common than are problems involving articulation. The repetition of sounds characteristic of stuttering is very frequently observed in young children, and it does not necessarily signal a problem. Parents, teachers, siblings, and others should not call attention to such patterns by telling the child to slow down and start again. This can have exactly the opposite of the intended effect, because it can generate anxiety in the child. Instead, if the pattern persists, the child should be seen by a speech and language therapist (Lerner et al., 1987). Among older children or adults who stutter, effective treatment requires expert intervention by an appropriately trained and qualified person. In young children, occasional delays, blocks, and repetitions should be regarded as normal. They do not necessarily indicate that the child has a stuttering problem. Obviously, the teacher should note a child's repetitive or blocked speech as it occurs in order to determine frequency, antecedent events, and response of others and the child herself or himself. Other types of disfluency include a pattern referred to as cluttering, which again should not be considered problematic based on occasional occurrences. It is something that virtually everyone, including adults, experiences at some times, when the words "come out in a rush" and "run into each other." In some speakers, however, this becomes a chronic pattern, one that both impedes communication and elicits negative reactions in listeners.

Voice disorders. Voicing involves the sound quality of speech production, that is, whether it is pleasant or unpleasant to others, can be readily understood by listeners, and occurs comfortably for the speaker. Speech that is pitched too high or too low, based upon generally accepted social standards, implies a possible voice disorder, as does speech that is "too loud," "too soft," harsh, grating, gravelly, "whiny," etc. In some instances, differences in voicing reflect malformation of the speech production mechanism that might be correctable through surgical intervention. In those cases, as well as in situations where abnormal patterns of voicing have been acquired through modeling or otherwise learned, speech therapy can enable the individual to learn and practice more appropriate patterns of voicing.

Among children with cleft lip or cleft palate, or other *craniofacial* abnormalities, abnormal speech patterns have a physical basis. As surgical reconstruction proceeds, speech therapy is important in helping the child to learn to use speech more consonant with expected norms.

Some speech abnormalities are associated with certain other handicapping conditions. As was explained in Chapter 2, speech and language therapy is frequently identified as a critical *related service,* essential for handicapped children to benefit from special education. In addition to organic impairments of the mechanism involved in producing speech, including cleft palate and cleft lip, other conditions that sometimes impair speech include:

Hearing loss, where speech may reflect differences due both to the way the child hears the speech of others and to the feedback received from his or her own voice.

Neuromotor impairment, especially cerebral palsy, when the voluntary motor involvement includes muscles involved in speech production.

Down syndrome, where jaw formation results in tongue protrusion, affecting speech intelligibility and quality.

Significant emotional problems, manifest, among possible other ways, through deviations in speech quality or fluency, or sometimes articulation, or even *elective mutism* or unwillingness to use speech.

Significant vision loss, where speech may reflect mannerisms acquired through the inability to employ visual feedback to self-monitor and appropriately modify speech.

All of these speech problems may also involve language problems, which may be more significant and much harder to ameliorate. For any child who presents a speech problem, your role should include:

Helping the child feel comfortable about and have occasions for speech.
Helping the child use speech appropriately as a means of communicating thoughts, needs, feelings, intentions, and wishes to others.
Helping the child speak in such a way as to be understood by other children and in such a way as to encourage them to speak to the impaired child.
Helping the child practice skills learned in speech therapy and to generalize these skills in the natural social environment of the classroom.

Generally, children with any of the speech problems that have been described do not present particular needs for program modifications—physical, curriculum, materials, or schedule—within the regular preschool, kindergarten, or primary classroom.

You should, however, maintain ongoing and open communication with the child's parents, and also, if the child is being seen or has been seen by a specialist, with the speech and language pathologist. In some instances, the specialist may make specific recommendations for speech activities in the classroom. These are nearly always legitimate and motivating for all the children, as well as the child for whom they are specifically prescribed and may include, for example:

Blowing light objects, such as feathers or balloons, as an individual or team game.
Choral speaking or responding (e.g., Goldstein, 1986).
"Telephone," or other activity pairing children in speaker-listener dyads.
Games involving requesting, describing, questioning, or answering.
Using tape recorders, microcomputers, or other electronic language learning devices.
Singing.

The teacher and the speech and language therapist can plan "therapeutic" classroom activities to create a natural context for motivation and to capitalize on the social function of speech. As Spodek (1985) has stressed, "the unit of instruction in nursery school and kindergarten is the activity" (p. 217). Classroom activities can serve several purposes, enabling individual children to benefit in different ways. The natural social context of the classroom, as well as that of the home, is ideal for children to use and practice more effective speech patterns. We would not want children to practice ineffective or maladaptive speech patterns; guidance and monitoring are required. But generally the teacher guides and models, rather than corrects. For most children with significant speech problems, the efforts of the teacher and family members supplement and extend the work of the specialist.

Although language ability is innate and language potential develops according to a natural pattern of rule acquisition that is unique to humans (Chomsky, 1965), the way language is used in communication reflects learning. Children's acquisition of a specific vocabulary, for example, depends upon words the child hears. This explains differences among children in dialect and, to some degree, speech habits, involving rate, inflections, speech mannerisms, and even voicing. The specific patterns of a child's speech, although influenced by organic factors, are mainly learned through exposure to specific speech models. Another dimension of learning in acquisition of specific speech patterns is reflected in the differential reinforcements, especially by important others, of the words children use and the ways they use them.

These principles suggest the important role of teachers of young children in enhancing the communication skills of all children and in working with individual children experiencing mild delay or deviance in speech development. However, they also have implications for working with children experiencing more serious difficulties in speech.

A team of speech and language pathologists (Gottwald, Goldbach & Isack, 1985, p. 12) offer the following suggestions for working with young children with disfluency problems, such as stuttering, in the early childhood classroom:

1. Your own speaking style can be important. You should slow the pace of conversations, simplify grammar and vocabulary, reduce the use of direct questions, model appropriate speech courtesies (e.g., "please" and "thank you") instead of directing the child to use them, and attempt to respond to the meaning of what a child is saying rather than how it is said.

2. You should show patience and acceptance, and communicate through your actions that you are interested in and care about what the child is saying.

3. The classroom environment can be important in enhancing fluency. Gottwald et al. (1985, p. 13) suggest that the classroom environment should be one in which: interruptions are avoided; a nonjudgmental, nonevaluative climate regarding verbal performance is maintained; children are allowed to finish what they are saying; sufficient time is allowed for activities, especially those involving talking; group activities requiring individual verbal performance are avoided (such as roll call and certain circle time activities); a predictable schedule is followed; frustrating or frightening interactive situations (such as teasing) are eliminated; and many opportunities for success are allowed that enhance self-esteem.

4. Group oral activities, such as singing, choral speech, etc., enhance fluency.

CASE HISTORY 8.1:   BUDDY

Buddy, an eight-year-old boy with moderate delays in fine and gross motor skills and severe delays in speech and language development, had a diagnosis of moderate mental retardation. He was enrolled in a public school primary level (ages 5–8) classroom for children with moderate-to-severe handicapping conditions, including communication problems.

The primary difficulty involving a possible mainstream placement was Buddy's communication level. Although he had had speech/language therapy for five years, he continued to communicate mainly through pointing and uttering vocalizations unintelligible to others. His only intelligible words were home, Mom, and school. He apparently had no first or second grade level academic skills. On the positive side, however, Buddy was a very personable boy who always tried to please others. He took great pride in his accomplishments, and he had good self-help skills. Others found him pleasant and appealing.

The mainstream classroom situation being considered was a combination Grades 1–2 class. The 20 children in this class were all younger than Buddy but of comparable physical size. Many of the children already knew Buddy through Sunday school, which was viewed as a positive factor. Additionally, the teacher, Annette Brown, had experience in working with children who had significant communication delays.

Buddy's special education teacher met with Mrs. Brown to discuss the possibilities of mainstreaming Buddy for some activities. Mrs. Brown, already familiar with Buddy from seeing him in the halls, lunchroom, and on the playground, was eager to explore possibilities. She felt that mainstreaming would be desirable not only for Buddy but also for the other children in her class. Both her familiarity with

Buddy and her prior experiences working with other children with similar difficulties gave her confidence in her own ability to make it work. Buddy's mother was contacted and agreed to a conference with the special educator, Mrs. Brown, and the speech therapist who had been working with Buddy.

Together, the participants reviewed Buddy's strengths, analyzed the communication barrier posed by his limited expressive speech, and identified potential ways to circumvent that barrier. These included a Total Communication approach, use of a Picture Notebook, and other augmentative communication options. His mother was supportive of the use of either Total Communication (TC) or the Picture Notebook; however, with another young child at home, she did not have time available to enroll in a formal class in TC. Therefore, she agreed to work with a Picture Notebook, to support other communication programming that might be implemented. Both the special educator and speech therapist were fluent in TC. Although Mrs. Brown, the mainstream teacher, was not fluent in TC, she had previously used the approach in working with another child. Since Buddy presently lacked academic skills, it was determined that language arts and reading, mathematics, science, and social studies instruction would continue to be handled within the special class setting. The mainstreaming plan would initially involve:

Opening (pledge of allegiance, roll call, lunch count, social exchange with the children, and teacher reading to the class).
Art (once each week with the art teacher, and the other four days with the regular teacher).
Physical Education (with one session each week assisted by an adapted physical education teacher).

Library (once weekly with both the librarian and Mrs. Brown, in which children were usually first read a story, and then had an activity extending the story's theme, such as using puppets, planting a flower, going for a walk, etc.). Social Activities and Field Trips (as considered appropriate by Mrs. Brown).

Additionally, a Language Unit was implemented, consisting of sign language instruction three times each week for four weeks. Also, Buddy's mother and his special education teacher were provided with a Polaroid camera and film to use with Buddy in developing a Picture Communication book. Developing and using picture communication would be an ongoing process carried out with Buddy by the speech therapist, the special education teacher, and his mother. Teaching Buddy to use the Notebook effectively with various adults and children would be everyone's responsibility.

Language Problems

Disagreements exist concerning the definition and classification of language problems (Bloom & Lahey, 1978). Basically, language problems suggest a structure of symbols and rules that deviates from that which is typical among children because it is less sophisticated or complex or because it is qualitatively different in some way. Language delay or language deviance might reflect neurological, emotional, or experiential (that is, learning) differences. In many instances, the cause of a child's language problem may be unknown.

Children identified as mentally retarded typically manifest delayed language development. However, terms such as mental retardation or developmental delay do not explain language problems. In fact the reverse may be more accurate; for many children described as mentally retarded, language difficulties may "explain" low scores on measures of intellectual ability—and thus "explain" mental retardation or general developmental delay.

A language problem may be reflected in a child's difficulty in interpreting language within a specific context, or in using the context to interpret meaning. A problem may also be reflected in the child's difficulty in expressing meaningful thoughts within appropriate contexts. The meaning of words, in combination, in relation to other words, and in context is what is meant by the *semantic* dimension of language.

The ordering of words in the form of sentences, to express complete thoughts, following specific rules for the combination of words, is involved in the *syntactic* dimension of language. Meaningful communication is accomplished not only because of shared understanding of the meaning of specific words, but also through a shared (i.e., commonly understood and used) system for combining words, expressing sentence construction as statements or questions as the situation demands, or conveying concepts such as plurality or possession.

Both of these dimensions, as well as the *phonological* dimension, are employed in the context of communicating with others. This is referred to as the *pragmatic* dimension of language. Young children's learning of language occurs as a consequence of the mother-infant interaction, which involves non-speech as well as speech components (Owens, 1984). This social aspect of language development as a communication system is considered more important than that of syntactic structure analyzed in isolation. However, language is also private, internal, and important in enabling and amplifying thought, as well as essential for people to establish and maintain communication with each other. Children with language impairments may experience difficulties in either or both these critical areas.

An information-processing model can aid in understanding language process and function (e.g., Bell-Gredler, 1986). We must interpret incoming messages, and we must be able to send messages interpretable by others. Each of these requires the shared understanding of symbols and rules in order for meaningful communication to occur. Additionally, *inner language* (Myklebust, 1964) involves the "storage" of meaning units and a rule-based system for ordering and classifying them for retrieval. This is, in part, what we mean when we use the terms *memory* and *thought*.

Some children with language problems have a known or suspected neurologically based impairment. Children with cerebral palsy may have language processing difficulties associated with the brain damage that cerebral palsy implies. These may affect either expressive or receptive language, or both. For a great many children with cerebral palsy, however, no underlying language problem exists even though speech may be affected. It is estimated that approximately 50 percent of children with cerebral palsy have associated speech and/or language problems (Lerner et al., 1987). Some children with spina bifida may evidence some language abnormalities, frequently minor, consequent to hydrocephalus that may have occurred. Many more children with spina bifida, however, experience no language problem at all; linguistically, they are quite normal. Similarly, other neuromotor impairments may or may not, imply associated language impairment.

Neurological impairment may also be reflected in children whose expressive language, in the form of speech, is affected specifically. Specialists may use the terms *dyspraxia* and *apraxia* in describing children whose speech is significantly deviant or absent, respectively, with presumed neurological etiology.

Developmental aphasia is a term used to refer to assumed or hypothesized central nervous system dysfunction reflected in the way a child interprets communicative information (receptive aphasia), communicates linguistically (expressive aphasia), or generally uses language (central aphasia) (Lerner et al., 1987). Despite some similiarities to other conditions associated with language delay, specialists generally distinguish those situations where the child's ability to process linguistic symbols is significantly impaired (Eisenson, 1972).

It has long been recognized that a great many children have difficulties in learning that reflect probable minimal brain damage or neurological dysfunction, even though the cause cannot be positively or reliably identified. In some children, these learning difficulties tend to be more generalized, though they are apparent particularly in school learning tasks. Early indications of difficulty may be apparent specifically in developmental delays in language. Among these children are many who are likely to be identified, once they are in school, as having specific learning disabilities, while others may be classified in school as demonstrating mental retardation.

Although *childhood autism* is now classified as a chronic health problem (it had originally been viewed as an emotional disorder), it is language and communication that present the major focus for concern and intervention. Children identified as autistic often do not use language effectively and appropriately as typical children of the same age do. Sharon James (1982) suggests that the teacher create specific situations in order to teach the normal functions of children's language as identified by Bloom and Lahey (1978). These are: (1) to establish contact with other people; (2) to obtain desired objects; (3) to manipulate or regulate the behavior of others; and (4) to obtain or give information. In order to create teaching situations, she suggests taking advantage of normally occurring events, modeling the appropriate behavior, creating the need for language use (as for example to obtain a desired item), and ensuring that language use is reinforced appropriately (i.e., verbal response from another person, provision of item sought, appropriate compliance on the part of another person, provision of information requested or acknowledgment of information provided.)

Based upon a thorough review of research studies, as well as the experiences in the Jowonio/Syracuse Public Schools program for integrating and maintaining alternatives for children labeled autistic, Carroll J. Grant (1982) concluded that good teaching for these children is, basically, good teaching:

> A general statement about an effective teaching process for working with autistic children is that it is similar to the style of any good teacher. That is, there is little in the teacher's repertoire of behavior that is unique to working with autistic children. An effective teacher with a particular age group probably has the basic necessary skills for working with most children labeled *autistic* of the same age group. After all, a child labeled *autistic* is essentially a child who has a mixture of "normal" characteristics intertwined with characteristics that are atypical of most children of comparable age. It is these behaviors, characteristic of the syndrome of autism, that must be considered when working with an autistic child. (p. 283)

The special considerations identified by Grant (1982, pp. 283–288) as important for a teacher who has an autistic child in the classroom are, in most instances, applicable to accommodating many special needs children in the mainstream. They are also applicable to teaching children who have not been identified as exceptional:

1. *Flexibility* in teaching style, defined as, ". . . the ability to shift teaching behavior to appropriately meet a student's needs at a particular time" (p. 284). In Grant's words, "A flexible teaching style characterizes one who is sensitive to the child's thoughts and feelings and is able to accurately discern when to follow the child's initiative and when to impose his or her ideas on the child. Both responding to the child and directing the child are necessary and valid ways of

relating; however, it is an art to know when it is most effective to shift from one to the other" (p. 284).

2. A *nonthreatening manner,* characterized by calmness and patience, use of normal tone of voice, normal eye contact, smooth rather than quick body movement, and care to present tasks that are developmentally appropriate and manageable (that is, not overly novel or demanding) for the individual child.

3. Good *observation skills,* both to ascertain the feelings and needs of the child, and to assess the social and physical environment of the classroom.

4. Planned and child-appropriate use of *physical contact and physical prompts,* based upon awareness of the important role of one's own "body language," gauging proximity and touch on the basis of the child's response.

5. *Modified language,* including use of short and concise statements and questions, if indicated, in recognition of the likelihood of particular difficulties and delays autistic children may have in receptive, as well as expressive, language.

6. Initial use of *one-to-one teaching relationship,* to the extent that may be feasible, to avoid overwhelming the child with the complex stimuli involved in group activities immediately, but gradually introducing tasks that require independent effort and group involvement.

7. *Positive attitude and approach,* conveying expectancies for success and accomplishment.

The case description of Nick demonstrates the application of these principles in effecting the transition into a mainstream second grade class of a child diagnosed as autistic. Nick's story illustrates the importance of studying and considering both the strengths and the special needs of the individual child, rather than the implications of the diagnostic label.

CASE HISTORY 8.2: NICK

Nick, a seven-year-old boy who had been given a diagnosis of childhood autism, was placed in a public school primary-level classroom for children with multiple handicaps. The team considering his integration into a regular classroom looked at several behavioral areas expected to present problems: Nick's frequent loud outbursts of nonsense talk, which would not only call unfavorable attention to Nick but would disrupt the class; episodes of toe-walking (unrelated to orthopedic difficulties) and finger play; and difficulties in interacting with more than one child in close proximity. Nick also demonstrated difficulty in coping with change, no matter how minor.

The mainstream second grade classroom into which Nick was to be integrated had 19 children, none with identified disabilities (although two children received speech therapy for minor articulation problems). Nick's parents and his special education teacher, in considering mainstream placement for instructional purposes, first reviewed Nick's strengths and his current mainstream participation for recesses, lunch, social activities, art, physical education, and library. He functioned well, with few inappropriate behaviors in library and physical education, and he was outstanding in art. He experienced some difficulties, however, at lunchtime and in some social activities, where he appeared to be distracted by noise. During recess he typically played alone or with one child for short periods of time, often his sister or one of his sister's friends.

Nick's parents were enthusiastic about classroom mainstreaming; Nick was functioning academically at second grade level, so the regular curriculum seemed appropriate for him. His parents were also eager for him to have more opportunities to interact with his peers. They requested that Nick actually attend the conference with them, the second grade teacher, and the special education teacher. They felt it would be good for him to know what was being contemplated, why, and how, in order to facilitate his acceptance of, and adaptation to, the change.

The planning meetings were kept to thirty minutes—a manageable time for Nick. The participants, including Nick, met three times to discuss specific plans and then continued to meet periodically to review successes, problems, and possible solutions. Specific planning began in the preliminary meetings, where Nick's strengths were identified:

Nick was reading at second grade level and had been working in the same basal series as were children in the regular class.

Nick's mathematics skills were also at second grade level, and he had been working with the same series and materials.

In spelling, Nick demonstrated skills at a fourth grade level, and he was able to complete second grade workbook tasks independently.

Nick enjoyed writing and had good manuscript writing skills for his grade level.

In personal and self-help skills, he demonstrated age-appropriate skills, except that he had not learned to tie his shoes.

In the area of social interaction, Nick's ability to interact with one other child at a time was fair. He could interact well with adults who were familiar to him.

The preliminary meetings were also used to identify weaknesses:

Nick would become frustrated when involved with or in close proximity to more than two children.

Nick was very sensitive to noise, which typically would trigger loud outbursts of nonsense talking.

He would become very upset by any change in his physical surroundings (such as rearrangement of desks, pictures moved, etc.), as well as by changes in his personal routines (for example, having breakfast at 7:05 rather than 7:00, visiting an aunt's house rather than his grandmother's on Sunday, etc.).

When upset, Nick was difficult to calm, and the bizarre manneristic behaviors mentioned at the outset would be present.

The next step was to agree how mainstream participation would begin, at what times of day, and for what activities. Initial involvement in any morning activities (reading, mathematics, spelling or writing) seemed appropriate. In order to facilitate his coping with change, Nick himself was given the responsibility of choosing the subject in which he wanted to begin. First, however, he was asked to sit in on each subject. He selected spelling and writing. In order to reduce the number of classroom changes necessary, the teacher made a minor change in her schedule, putting writing and spelling one after the other, immediately followed by lunch and recess. This change created a big "natural reinforcer" for Nick.

The next step in the process of mainstreaming Nick was to effect a smooth and gradual transition. First, the second grade teacher placed a desk with Nick's name on it in her classroom a full week before his first day there. As an out-of-district special education student, Nick arrived at school every day twenty minutes before the other students. For that initial week, Nick went to his new classroom every morning for that twenty minutes and helped the teacher prepare, sat at his desk to draw, and was responsible for making one physical change of his choosing in the room each day. During this week, his parents and his special education teacher, as well as his new classroom teacher, continued to discuss with him what would occur. His sister was encouraged to talk more in family conversations about what happened in her own regular classroom.

Nick's behavior improved during the preparation week. His toe-walking, finger play, and loud talking occurred less frequently. Nick himself began to talk about Mrs. Cox, the second grade teacher, as his teacher. He responded well to other children who approached him to tell him that they had seen his name on his desk and were glad he would be joining their class. Mrs. Cox talked to the class about how many things Nick was good at doing. She explained that many people acted in many different ways when they were frustrated, encouraging each child to think about his or her own frustrations and ways of expressing them.

Nick's behavior early in the morning of the first day was somewhat erratic, with increased toe-walking and finger play. He did a great deal of talking about Mrs. Cox's class. Once there, he sat at his desk and followed all directions. However, he would loudly call out the time every five minutes. ("Mrs. Cox, it's 11:05, we have 25 more minutes of writing.") This continued throughout writing and spelling, and by the end of spelling, he was out of his seat frequently, running up to the clock and pointing when he called out the time. This disruptive behavior required discussion with the teacher to reassure her that it could work! Smaller steps were required, however. For a time, calming Nick and helping him simply to get through the day would need to be a priority.

A before-school meeting with Nick's parents was arranged on the second day. Both positive and negative aspects of the previous day were reviewed. Nick had followed directions for each task, but his talking out and leaving his seat were inappropriate and disruptive. His parents and teachers "made a deal" with Nick. He would start out by going only to spelling, which was scheduled just before lunch. He would be allowed to tell Mrs. Cox what time it was when he first came into the room and again remind her (quietly) of time to go to lunch. When he felt all right about that, and showed through his behavior that he did, he would also begin to participate in writing.

Two weeks were required before Nick seemed sufficiently comfortable. On only one day did he have a particularly difficult time, before a drill occurred during spelling time. However, he recovered quickly and both teacher and classmates understood and accepted the difficulties this event caused for Nick. The addition of writing went smoothly. Throughout the year, various small adaptations were made. Although mathematics was never added to his mainstreaming program, reading was successfully introduced.

Over the course of the year, Nick became an integral member of the second grade classroom. He became able to interact positively with eight other children playing with him on the playground, and he even began to initiate play with others occasionally. He also won the all-second grade Spelling Bee. His mainstream participation was continued in the third grade the following year, with science added.

Summary: Language Programming in the Classroom

A great many young children identified as developmentally delayed experience particular difficulties in the area of language and communication. Language is an area that both transcends classifications of handicapping conditions and implies the need for special emphasis within the early childhood program—all young children are in the process of development as language-users. The discussion in this chapter assumes that the reader, whether a student or a currently practicing early childhood educator, is familiar both with the process of language acquisition in the early childhood years and with teaching practices that are developmentally appropriate with respect to young children's language learning. Clearly, language development and intervention cannot be meaningfully understood in isolation from other areas—especially social, emotional, and cognitive. For some children with specific impairments, motor functioning and intervention must also receive important consideration.

In general, however, the language base for developmentally appropriate practices in early childhood education programs makes these programs uniquely conducive to developing the communicative competence of young children with special needs. As in other areas, most of the accommodations suggested for young children with delayed or impaired speech or language are congruent with good teaching principles for all young children. Few, if any, modifications of program content and organization are indicated that would not be desirable for typical children as well. Authors recommending language-related integration strategies in early childhood programs typically note the appropriateness for young children with special needs of activities that are traditionally included in early childhood programs. For example, Glenn and Cunningham (1985) suggested the value of nursery rhymes that, with their repetition of rhymes and words, provide an effective listening activity for young children with developmental delays.

For some children with special needs in the area of language and communication, it is especially important for the teacher to recognize her or his role as a team member, working together with one or more specially trained clinical specialists in implementing and monitoring an individually designed program. That topic is further illustrated in Chapter 10, in terms of individualized programming within the classroom, and in Chapter 13, in terms of working with consultative and resource persons.

The remainder of this chapter addresses what are, with language and communication, the major areas of special importance for integrating many young children with special needs effectively in the regular early childhood program: behavioral programming and curricular and instructional accommodations.

INTEGRATING BEHAVIORAL PROGRAMMING IN THE CLASSROOM

The most basic principle underlying behavioral approaches with children is that behavior is learned. *Applied behavior analysis* involves the systematic study of an individual's behavior in order to determine what consequences in the environment are functionally related to a specific behavior. The question is: when the person does something, what happens? To determine whether what is observed to "happen" is functionally related to the behavior, we can see whether the behavior changes when the thing that "happens" changes. If it does, we have an *empirical demonstration* (which is better than a belief or a guess) that offers the key to maintaining, increasing, or decreasing the behavior in question.

The key idea behind this approach to analyzing behavior is the concept of *reinforcement,* or *reinforcing consequence.* Whether a consequence (something that happens after the behavior occurs) is, or is not, reinforcing is determined by seeing what happens when either (1) the consequence is changed, or (2) the consequence is made to occur after a different behavior. A number of important questions parents or teachers may ask about young children may lend themselves to this kind of analysis. Applied behavior analysis offers a very practical approach.

Application of behavioral principles is mainly considered in terms of rewarding (reinforcing) desired behaviors and of not rewarding behaviors that are not desirable, appropriate, or in the child's own best interests. Advocates of behavioral programming rarely suggest the use of *aversive consequences* (punishment) of any kind. Rather, the emphasis is on helping the child to learn more effective, constructive, or socially acceptable skills, by systematically arranging the environment so that consequences observed to be reinforcing to the child are *contingent* upon the desired behavior occurring. The child is not reinforced for doing what he or she is not supposed to do (for example, having a tantrum, striking another child, using "bathroom" words, etc.) Instead, reinforcement is withheld until the child engages in behavior that is compatible with what has been agreed to be desirable. Clearly, in order to make this kind of intervention work, it is essential to do two things:

1. Identify the behaviors in question and define them in observable and measurable ways.
2. Know what consequences are reinforcing.

Applied behavior analysis (ABA) provides a scientifically grounded, systematic way of: (1) understanding a child's behavior and how that behavior is related to specific events in the environment; and (2) changing the behavior through modifying those environmental events. It represents a highly positive and optimistic approach: people can change! Applied behavior analysis provides the methodology, however, not the goal. Similarly, ABA provides a set of concepts, tools, and methods that are generally applicable. It remains for the early childhood educator to apply these in developmentally appropriate ways, that is, ways that are congruent with the philosophy and goals of early childhood education. As was discussed in Chapter 3, systematic behavioral procedures are stock-in-trade for special educators. However, this area may have represented the greatest single barrier to a shared philosophy between early childhood education and special education, hence a potential barrier to integration. Increasingly, this barrier has been broken down, and that is critical to the effective social and instructional goals of many young children with special needs in early childhood programs. A shared philosophy is possible to the extent that:

1. Recognition exists that some young children can progress developmentally if direct instruction and guidance are provided.
2. The uniqueness of the early childhood years is recognized and valued.
3. Behavioral practices are informed by the insights of cognitive psychology as these apply to young children (Anastasiow, 1981).
4. Teachers accept responsibility for gearing instruction to the differential needs of individual children, monitoring the progress of individual children, and modifying procedures based on data recorded for an individual child.
5. Behavioral procedures are employed to help the child move toward independence, self-initiative, choice, and autonomy.
6. Reinforcers are selected from those occurring in the natural environment, determined individually for each child based on observation of what is reinforcing for that child, and provided on a contingent rather than random basis.

These points are illustrated through discussion of a few selected concepts and techniques associated with applied behavior analysis practices (Alberto & Troutman, 1982; Cooper, Heron, & Heward, 1987; Meichenbaum, 1977); time out, the Premack Principle, contingency contracts, reinforcer sampling, fading, and self-management strategies.

The use of *time out procedures* is a standard part of any classroom management approach informed by behavioral concepts, but it is sometimes misunderstood and can be misused. Time out means time out from positive reinforcement, not punishment. In behavioral terms, the time out designates a period of time during which the child is not positively reinforced. Typically, a time out area is used, one that is not frightening, but also not rewarding, and within view of the teacher. The time out period should be short and specifically defined. Just as behavioral procedures in contemporary educational practice recognize and employ cognitive concepts, time out should be accompanied by procedures that help children understand the relationship between specific behaviors and their consequences. As Marion (1981) suggests, the teacher should explain that, when an unacceptable behavior occurs, the child will go to the time out area. This should be accomplished without stigma, embarrassment, moralizing, or other punitive consequences. Instead, it should be accompanied by effective child management procedures: following through consistently, social reinforcement for appropriate participation, and particularly ensuring that positive behavior is rewarded following the time out period. Again, time out does not mean sending children out of the room, making them "stand in the corner," or otherwise banishing them. It does mean taking measures to insure that (1) inappropriate behavior is not rewarded, and (2) children are helped to learn that it is their behavior that influences whether pleasant and satisfying things do or do not occur.

The *Premack Principle* is fully congruent with common sense and conventional wisdom. In fact, it is frequently identified as "Grandma's Law!" Technically, this principle ". . . states that any high-probability activity may serve as a positive reinforcer for any low-probability activity" (Alberto & Troutman, 1982, p. 356.) High-probability activities are those in which a child frequently engages; thus, these activities are inferred to be potentially reinforcing. Low-probability activities are those in which a child is unlikely to engage; that is, a child is observed infrequently to engage in them. Quite simply, the child is permitted to do the thing she enjoys as a consequence of first doing the thing she seems not to enjoy. In this way, an activity intitially found to be low-probability (e.g., sitting quietly during opening circle) is likely to increase if it is followed by an initial high-probability activity (e.g., playing with blocks.) The concept goes beyond mere common sense and conventional wisdom in that actual systematic measurement is involved and behavior is systematically consequated. That is, we do not assume that, since most young children enjoy playing with blocks, block-playing is a high-probability activity for a specific child. Instead, that is determined based on actual observation of what the child does, for example in free choice situations. Then the contingent relationship is established through consistent practice. Therefore, the early childhood teacher must determine that it is feasible to permit a specific activity in consequence of a desired one and to do so consistently.

Contingency contracts are specific agreements between the child and the adult. They help children recognize the relationship between their own actions and the consequences that occur and to accept the responsibility for their own behavior. The formats often used with older students—a clear statement of what the student will do, what will occur in consequence, with signatures of both student and teacher—can be adapted for use with younger children. Pictures, stickers, and single words or short phrases make more age-appropriate "legal language" than the somewhat more elaborate formats that may be highly motivating to older students.

Reinforcer sampling is a procedure by which children are brought in contact with potential reinforcers on a non-contingent basis so that their possible effectiveness can be ascertained. In the early childhood classroom, the most reasonable way of accomplishing this is through observation of what a particular child is drawn to, selects, and spends time with in the natural environment. Potentially reinforcing items and activities can be (and are) introduced into the classroom environment based on age-appropriate, setting-appropriate, and child-appropriate criteria. Watching cartoons on television may be something that most five-year-olds like to do, and something that Billy especially enjoys. However, that is an activity that is rarely, if ever, appropriate to the setting of a kindergarten classroom.

Fading is a technical procedure used to gradually reduce, and eventually remove, external *prompts* in order to transfer *stimulus control* to the naturally occuring stimulus. A *most-to-least* prompting procedure for helping a child acquire a skill might begin with total physical guidance through the entire procedure, with the adult gradually reducing physical guidance, then moving to visual prompts, and finally to verbal directions (Billingsley & Romer, 1983). Alternatively, *least-to-most* prompting presents the natural stimulus at each level of gradually increased assistance, and the student's behavior provides the indication of what level of prompting is needed. A resource person with special skills in the use of systematic instruction can develop, help to implement, and monitor a planned procedure for helping a child acquire a new skill with the level of special assistance that is actually needed, within a short period of time, leading to the child's ability to perform the skill as independently as possible.

Self-management strategies involve an individual's providing his or her own verbal prompts. With young children, applications involve moving from imitating an adult model to consciously monitoring their own actions with verbal mediation. Meichenbaum and Goodman (1971) described the procedure they used with hyperactive second-grade children to increase self-control and attention to the task while decreasing errors:

1. An adult model performed a task while talking to himself out loud *(cognitive modeling);*
2. The student performed the same task under the direction of the model's instructions *(overt, external guidance);*
3. The student performed the task while instructing himself aloud *(overt self-guidance);*
4. The student whispered the instructions to himself as he went through the task *(faded, overt self-guidance);* and finally,
5. The student performed the task while guiding his performance via private speech *(covert self-instruction).* (p. 32)

Although self-management strategies are widely and effectively used with students with learning disabilities and behavior problems, they have also been found to be valuable in working with severely handicapped students (Browder & Shapiro, 1985). Applicability with young children is evidenced in that helping children to cope with their environment and with their own feelings and impulses through using language is standard preschool practice. As in other areas, behavioral procedures often simply involve doing in a highly systematic and precise fashion, with certain children, what is normally done with all children, in a less carefully planned and systematically monitored way.

Case History 8.3:   Clint

Clint, a five-year-old, was diagnosed as severely behavior disordered, and demonstrated delays in speech and language development, as well as mild problems in visual perception. A valid assessment of his intellectual capability had not been obtained, and mild mental retardation was considered "questionable" in the report of the multifactored assessment. The potential mainstream placement situation available in Clint's school was a kindergarten classroom with 27 children—the only one in that building.

The analysis of Clint's strengths and difficulties revealed behavior as the primary difficulty in attempting to integrate him in a regular classroom. He was easily angered, especially when frustrated or overwhelmed by tasks that required perceptual and fine motor skills. When angered, he was very aggressive, both physically and verbally; typical behaviors included hitting, destroying his own and others' materials, spitting, screaming, and swearing. When reprimands or restraints were imposed, the behaviors would escalate, and such episodes might last an hour to 90 minutes. On the positive side, Clint actually appeared to acquire and retain new information well. He expressed awareness of differences between himself and the other children in his special education class, as well as his desire to be like the children who were not in special education.

When Clint's parents were contacted by phone to set up his IEP conference, his mother, Mrs. Malcolm, stated that they were not concerned with what Clint did in school, but that they did wish to have help in working with him at home. She was assured that the school team would provide home programming as well as school information, and that they were eager to have the parents' involvement and help. Mrs. Malcolm returned the form that waived her right to participate in the IEP planning, however. In a second telephone conversation during which she was audibly crying, she explained that her husband would not allow her to come to school, nor would he permit school personnel to come to their home, that she was sorry but the school personnel could not help her, and that she hoped Clint would "be good" at school.

Clint's special education teacher met with Ms. Short, the kindergarten teacher, to discuss possibilities of mainstreaming in her class and to obtain a copy of the kindergarten schedule. Ms. Short was hesitant, since she had never worked with a child with any type of identified handicap, but she was willing to try, provided that she would "have lots of support." The principal's endorsement and support were obtained.

At a preliminary meeting of the special educator, kindergarten teacher, and speech language therapist, three activity segments were agreed upon for possible kindergarten mainstreaming: Opening Circle (8:00–9:20), Recess (10:30–10:45), and Story Time (10:45–11:00). All three were structured more loosely than other periods of the session; all demanded little or no perceptual-motor coordination; and all offered the potential for Clint to have excellent opportunities for speech/language modeling. The morning was considered preferable to afternoon, both because it was his best time and because the morning class had two fewer children than the afternoon group.

Ms. Short visited the special education class in order to meet Clint and observe him. She told Clint about her class and invited him to come to meet the children and also, since she had watched him work, to watch her work.

The next morning, Clint visited the kindergarten class for about 15 minutes. On his return he made the following comments to his special class teacher: "They're all little, like me." "They can't write yet neither." "I think they have fun," "Ms. Short is a nice teacher." When asked if he would like to work in the kindergarten class every day for a while, he said "Yes!" and was very excited. For the rest of the day, he tried very hard at whatever he was doing, while talking to himself about being a "big boy" (something neither teacher had said) because he would be going to kindergarten. He exhibited no major acting-out behavior.

During the first week, Clint participated only in Opening Circle. He had to get used to raising his hand and waiting for Ms. Short to respond before he talked. This involved an expectation new to him: whereas he was always recognized in the special classroom for raising his hand, that was not always the case in the kindergarten class, since each of the children in the large group had to have opportunities to participate. Around the other children, he was quiet, and he had difficulty remembering their names. When his show-and-tell day arrived, he remembered, on his own, to bring something from home. He brought a toy car and showed it to everyone, but did not say a word. However, Ms. Short identified that as "normal" behavior. She seemed more comfortable with Clint every day during that week. On Friday, she met with the special educator and speech-language therapist to plan next steps, which would involve adding Recess and Story Time to his schedule.

During the second week, with his extent of participation increased, he continued to get along well during Opening Circle. He remembered the names of two children and each day sat with them. He both followed directions well and took cues from the other children. When a fire drill took place during Opening Circle on Thursday of that week, he watched the other children and did what they did. Ms. Short reported that during the week at least 10 other children had initiated conversation with Clint, and he initiated conversation with three other children.

Recess was outdoors each day that week, and the children lined up in their room to go to the playground. The first time, Clint stood in the girls' line, but before Ms. Short would explain the two lines for boys and girls, two of the boys pulled him over to their line and told him to stay with them. He followed playground rules, sometimes playing alone and at other times with small groups of boys. When the children had a large group game of Red Rover, he and another boy chose to stand with Ms. Short instead of participating in the game with the others.

Immediately after Recess was Story Time, and the children were expected to return to the classroom quietly and sit on the carpet to listen. On the first two days, Clint did not comply when he was told to sit down, instead first running around the room and then sitting at a table on the other side of the room until the end of the story. After consulting with the special education teacher, on the next two days Ms. Short, after asking him to sit on the carpet without his compliance, took his hand and led him to a spot on the carpet close to where she sat to read the story. Although he remained seated, he made loud noises throughout the story. Therefore, on Thursday, Ms. Short told Clint, privately, that although he could continue to come to kindergarten for Opening Circle and for Recess, he could not come for Story Time. Although she did not tell him why he could not participate in Story Time, when he returned, crying, to his special classroom he told the teacher he could not because he wouldn't sit down and be quiet. He and his teacher talked about how that made him feel "sad" and "mad" and how he could change his behavior in order to be allowed to participate in Story Time.

By the time he arrived in school on Friday, Clint was already in a bad mood after spitting on and even biting the bus driver. In kindergarten, he asked Ms. Short nine times if he could come to Story Time, but otherwise sat quietly and followed directions. After Recess, Ms. Short reminded him to return to his special class, since he could not remain for Story Time. Clint responded by spitting, kicking over a desk, and trying to tear up the day's story book. This sort of reaction had been anticipated, however, so the special educator was on hand to take him back. Clint spent the rest of the morning acting out and had to eat lunch alone. He was quiet and surly all afternoon, refusing to participate in any group activity and tearing up any individual work he was given to do.

When it was time for afternoon recess, while the other children were outdoors, Clint, his special education teacher, Ms. Short, and the principal had a meeting to talk over what had happened. Clint and Ms. Short did most of the talking, she focusing on how what Clint had done had made her feel. At first, Clint didn't connect his behavior with her feelings. And then he seemed surprised when she told him she felt the same when he acted that way ("sad" and "mad"). However, she had the other children, and herself, to make her feel happy again, while Clint was still sad and mad. She told him she would like to give him another chance to come to Story Time. However, he would have to follow the class rules.

During the third week, Opening Circle and Recess went well, as they had the previous week, but Story Time was harder. Clint seemed unable to control his energy after recess as quickly as the other children did. He would generally follow the directions Ms. Short gave the class, but he would continue to hum very quietly, drum his fingers, or tap his foot for the first five minutes or so of Story Time each day.

At the Friday afternoon meeting, the speech therapist shared her data, which showed significant improvement in Clint's language skills as well as improved conversational skills (such as more age-appropriate topics, better eye contact, longer sentences, and better turn-taking in conversation). Ms. Short and the special educator agreed on the benefits. However, Ms. Short expressed concerns about the other children's benefits because of Clint's persistent minor disruptiveness during Story Time. She felt that he was simply not as mature as the other children and therefore not as able to

settle down as quickly after recess. To address this, Ms. Short volunteered to change her schedule around, so that he would be able to go for recess, return to his special classroom while the other children had writing, and then return to the kindergarten for Story Time, which would be the last morning activity before the other children left for home. That would conflict with his scheduled speech therapy session, but the therapist found she could switch his session with that of another child.

This change was implemented in the fourth week. Although Clint was at first anxious about whether or not he was going back to the kindergarten class for Story Time, he was soon reassured. By the third day, he had adapted well to the changed schedule. His disruptive Story Time behavior stopped virtually immediately and totally.

Clint's mainstreaming schedule was maintained for the rest of the fall semester. In the spring semester, music, physical education, and art were added, each scheduled once weekly. Art presented some difficulties, due to the perceptual and motor requirements, but these were managed. Within his special education classroom he was given one-to-one instructions in standard kindergarten reading, mathematics, and writing materials. The next year, when Clint was six, he was again mainstreamed in kindergarten, but now for a full half-day. Also, his doctor had prescribed a mild dosage of Ritalin, and Clint was given eyeglasses. At the end of that year, he was moved out of special education placement entirely and into the regular first grade full-time. He also was given supplementary individual tutoring for three sessions of one-half hour each week, an arrangement that continued throughout the year.

CURRICULAR AND INSTRUCTIONAL ADAPTATIONS FOR THE CLASSROOM

Children identified as developmentally delayed, like those with physical or behavioral disabilities, are in fact more like "normal" children their age than they are like one another. Those features of the developmental early childhood program that emphasize active learning and discovery are made to order for the learning styles and special needs of many young children identified as developmentally delayed. Such features are a typical part of any developmentally appropriate early childhood classroom—preschool, kindergarten, or primary level. Teachers in such programs

1. Expect and tolerate differences in how long individual children will need to and want to engage in a particular activity.
2. Recognize, because of their Piagetian orientation, that thinking and overt language are not necessarily isometric, that young children's thoughts may be masked by a verbal facade (Almy, 1968).
3. Recognize the importance of direct experience with real materials and real situations in order for meaningful learning to occur.
4. Recognize the child's need for repetitive practice and active rehearsal through play.
5. Do not prematurely impose, as requirements, expectations involving writing skills, formal reading, and paper-pencil "seatwork" in the form of workbooks and worksheets, but rather capitalize on the literacy behaviors that are natural to young children (especially representational play in all its forms).
6. Increase children's awareness of and receptiveness to the sensory properties and other attributes of materials.

A teaching style that is characterized by these qualities also accommodates far greater diversity among young learners than does a teaching approach lacking these qualities. Such a style serves developmentally delayed children particularly well, since it provides precisely the "special education" approaches that have generally been believed appropriate for these children and reduces the discrepancy between them and their "normal" peers.

In summary, you should be aware that most young children described as developmentally delayed can be most optimally accommodated in early childhood classrooms that employ practices developmentally appropriate for all children. That does not mean that these children don't have special needs; it does mean that standard early education practices are in principle capable of addressing those needs.

Cook and Armbruster (1983) recommend the kinds of instructional accommodations that may be required for individual children:

1. *Concrete, multisensory tasks.* Preschool children naturally learn more easily when tasks are straightforward and concrete rather than abstract.

2. *Find the child's most efficient mode of learning.* Observe carefully to determine each child's strongest learning mode. If it is visual, then use visual cues to assist auditory directions; if it is auditory, then accompany visual tasks with auditory assists; if it is motoric, then use movement as much as possible to teach language and cognitive skills.

3. *Pacing.* Children who must work extra hard to concentrate or to process information usually tire easily. The amount of effort exerted should be varied to allow for occasional rest times, quiet activities, or soft music. Children who process information more slowly should receive less information or should receive it over a longer time.

4. *Repetition.* Some children need to try things again and again or need to have something repeated several times before it can be grasped. Intermittent practice helps children to remember skills they have learned.

5. *Plan for modeling and imitation.* Some children do not acquire information incidentally. If a specific response is desired, plan experiences where the behavior is demonstrated and positively reinforced. Once the child imitates the desired behavior, be certain to give the expected reinforcement.

6. *Task analysis.* Tasks must be broken into simple, short steps that can be sequenced from the easiest to the most difficult.

7. *Directions.* For some children it is necessary to give nearly all directions slowly and in small steps. One step can be completed before giving the next direction. (p. 201)

Mathematics and Science

Learning basic mathematics skills presents special problems for some handicapped children due to the required concept understanding and memorization (Turnbull & Schulz, 1983). Mastering basic facts in addition and substraction and, eventually, multiplication and division, can be highly valuable in establishing the foundation for later learning, however, and is also important in a motivational sense. "Facts" in arithmetic pose for the child concrete, definable, and potentially masterable tasks. Tying those facts to observable, and manipulable, phenomena can be accomplished through the use of concrete materials, concept blocks, abacus, coins, and entities to be measured. Thus, mathematical problems pose what are in many ways ideal learning experiences for young children, including those identified as developmentally delayed because:

They involve familiar situations in the "real world," that are meaningful to the child.

They lend themselves to both independent and cooperative learning activities.

They can involve the child in an active capacity.

They can involve multisensory experiences.

They lend themselves to repetitive practice.

They involve learning and performance not as dependent upon language
   proficiency as certain other types of tasks.
Math tasks can be self-correcting, or at least enable the child to monitor
   his or her own progress and successive accomplishments.

In mathematics and science activities in early childhood programs, materials
play an especially important role. The properties of materials, the way they are
arranged, and in what sequence they are introduced form important bases for key
concepts in early childhood. Strategies built around materials themselves formed
the very heart of the Montessori system (e.g., Montessori, 1912, 1949). However,
materials are also central to any early childhood program espousing a developmental philosophy informed by Piaget. Carol Seefeldt (1980) lists the following
types of activities involving concrete materials as congruent with concept learning
goals in mathematics appropriate to the preschool program:

1. Sorting and classifying collections of objects, leading to the comparison of
   groups of objects by matching, recognition of equal and unequal size of
   groups, and an understanding of sets and subsets.
2. Counting with cardinal numbers, promoting an understanding of one-to-one
   correspondence.
3. Measuring, first using arbitrary units, and observing such relationship as
   short/long, few/many, heavy/light, short/tall, and the like.
4. Explorations involving space and shapes in space. (p. 257)

Exploration with real materials and real problems, using manipulative as well
as visual and auditory modes, and "borrowing time" (McCoy & Prehm, 1987) from
other activities in order to allow for differential time needs do not mean that fact
memorization must be neglected. As Turnbull and Schultz (1983) state:

The probability that handicapped students will learn the basic facts increases
greatly when the instruction is geared to the student's level of achievement,
preferred learning styles, and rate of learning. The students' awareness of their
continuous and consistent progress often provides renewed impetus to master
math skills. These same principles of programming memorization of basic facts
apply to other aspects of the math curriculum requiring memory skills, such as
measurement tables and monetary relationships. (p. 259)

Tasks requiring memorization, even those involving short-term memory, may
be partially difficult for young children identified as developmentally delayed
(Spodek et al., 1984). Memorization is an important element in many aspects of
school learning, notably mathematics. Yet, good early childhood practice is predicated on the view that retention reflects the child's structuring of knowledge based
on active learning. Allowing sufficient time, direct involvement with concrete tasks
that are meaningful, and opportunity to generalize concepts across related situations can enable the child to master and retain math facts and concepts more
effectively and efficiently than instruction that is time-limited, removed from and

foreign to the child's direct experience (e.g., "problems," on worksheets), and isolated from other learning.

Materials and methods developed over the years by special education theorists and practitioners, especially in teaching mentally retarded students and those we now identify as learning disabled, are strikingly similar to those that are standard in early childhood education. The methods created by Itard, Seguin, and Montessori (e.g., Talbot, 1964) are probably the most familiar of pedagogical strategies created to enhance and exploit the sensory awareness of learners through the use of especially designed materials. In Montessori, a clear bridge was formed to general early childhood practice, at least from the standpoint of materials, their properties, and their potential role in children's learning. Although individual children present very different patterns of strengths and weaknesses, many children with developmental delays have difficulties in certain areas particularly important in math learning, as Turnbull and Schulz (1983) point out. These include attention, concept development, memory, generalization, delayed language, and fine motor problems. Good early childhood practices, as suggested in the foregoing discussion, are more likely to accommodate differences in these areas through:

> Using materials that invite focused attention because of their sensory properties, because they require direct involvement and activity, and are inherently interesting and motivating.
> Promoting concept learning through active exploration, repetitive practice dictated by the child's needs and inclinations, and application across situations.
> Regarding retention as requiring an active, rather than passive, role for the child.
> Using units that recognize and capitalize on interrelationships of curricular areas, phenomena, and situations.
> Permitting and encouraging problem-solving not dependent upon language skills.
> Using materials readily manipulable and controllable by young children (for example, the familiar cylinders, knobbed inlay puzzles, and other made-for-children materials developed not only by Montessori but others as well.

Science experiences in early childhood programs lend themselves particularly to active child involvement and to group participation. Thus, the young child with special needs can observe, listen, and experience directly the sights, sounds, smells, tastes, or tactile sensations associated with an experiment or other activity. With the other children, he or she can hypothesize "what will happen if . . ." and then find out directly if what was expected occurs. He or she can experience the sense of wonder and the satisfaction of discovery that make the early childhood years unique.

For most young children with special needs, few, if any, adaptations of science objectives, methods, and materials will be required. If a child has a sensory impairment, of course, certain measures can be facilitative, as Hadary (1976) has suggested. For example, for a hearing-impaired child, written labels, cards, and charts, prepared in advance, can be quite helpful. Materials used in an experiment can be labeled, and word cards can be used in discussion as appropriate. Cards or charts can also be prepared in advance with appropriate questions and directions, such as "Observe carefully," "What do you think will happen?" For a visually handicapped child, the principles of "talking the child through" the activity with verbal orientation and explanation apply, as well as preventive measures, such as securing equipment. The child needs to have the materials and their location described meaningfully. Arguably, these guidelines represent good practice in working with all young children.

Hadary (1976) also offers valuable suggestions for procedures in science experiments with emotionally disturbed children, as well as a rationale for the potential special value of science in working with many children with emotional problems. Science activities can help a child understand cause-effect relationships, distinguish feelings and facts, predict events, and contribute to the child's sense of autonomy and competence to deal with his or her world. They can also help the child to develop impulse control and to use discussion to facilitate understanding. Any or all of these may represent areas of special need for children experiencing difficulties in social and emotional development. The suggestions offered by Hadary involve proceeding in orderly and sequential fashion, yet capitalizing on the inherent excitement in the process of experimentation.

Language Arts and Reading

As has been suggested, young children described as developmentally delayed are very likely to manifest specific difficulties in language-related areas; the language arts components of the curriculum represent areas in which they may be most discrepant from their peers. At the same time, early childhood programs that are truly language-based can be accommodating of individual differences among children. If reading, writing, speaking, and listening skills are taught in isolation, unrelated to the child's language development, many young children—not just those already identified as delayed—experience unnecessary learning difficulties.

All young children are in their own way language users, even those whose language development is significantly delayed, those who do not use speech in order to communicate, and those experiencing difficulty in expressing feelings, wishes, and intents and otherwise communicating with other people. With every young child, language learning involves building upon the language base the child has already established.

In the early childhood classroom, Piagetian insights suggest that the teacher should observe the processes the individual child employs. Some of these lead the young child to a number of "wrong" ideas; yet, that is how learning occurs and how the child's intrinsic motivation for further learning is fostered. Willert and

Kamii (1985) observed that various young children demonstrated each of the following spontaneous strategies in their self-motivated desire to read: (1) focusing on the first letter of the word; (2) focusing on the word's configuration—that is, its length or shape; (3) obtaining semantic clues from pictures and situations; (4) looking for familiar letters and letter combinations; (5) repetitive practicing of spelling and copying words; and (6) inventing and applying their own phonological system. The absence of any of these observed in an individual child suggests to the responsive teacher possibilities for introducing reinforcing, supportive, and supplementary experiences, in contrast to emphasizing error correction.

Some young children with handicaps will manifest specific difficulties in learning to read that are associated with their disability, but teachers should not assume that the presence of a handicapped child in the group, in itself, signals the need to proceed slowly. Provision of more time may be essential for one child, while another is impatient to move ahead. Language-based early reading instruction builds upon each individual child's entering language base (Vacca et al., 1987).

The *Language Experience Approach* (Allen & Allen, 1970) lends itself well to accommodating a wide range of individual differences in readiness and skill levels among young children. Young children with specific or general developmental delays, as well as those who are quite advanced in their language skills and are both reading and writing, can participate in language-based communication activities that lead to reading and writing. Specific impairments imply some specific modifications in procedure, as with other activities. Since this general method involves shared vocal contributions by the group, which are then written on a chart, accommodations must be made for a child who is non-vocal or for whom individual recitation in a group setting is difficult. With such helps as a "buddy", gestural communication, and symbol-based augmentative communication, each child's ideas can be shared. In this approach, reading follows from the expression of children's own thoughts; thus, functional communication skill training is, for some children, tied directly to a key area of academic learning.

Logistically, the process requires certain provisions for children with either impaired vision or impaired hearing, and many young children identified as developmentally delayed experience accompanying vision and/or hearing impairment. In either instance, the child's placement in relationship to the chart and the location of the chart in the room are important. It should not, from the sensory-impaired child's perspective, have a window behind it. If a sign-using child works with an interpreter in the classroom, placement of the child, the interpreter, and the medium must be well planned. If the visually impaired child uses braille, that can become an exciting new tool, contributing not only to the child's sense of independence and control over his or her environment, but to all the children's understanding of the nature of communication itself (Curry, 1975; Spodek et. al., 1984).

In general, early exposure to oral expression, symbol interpretation, prewriting and writing activities, at least at the preschool and kindergarten level, need not place the child with developmental delays at a disadvantage. To the extent that formal reading instruction, writing requirements, spelling practice, and the like are a part of the expectations, delayed children are among those placed at risk for failure. The memory, perceptual-motor coordination, and language demands associated with academic tasks pose particular difficulties for those children likely to be identified ultimately as learning disabled or mildly mentally handicapped. For the teacher, that may imply the need to maintain a balance—for all pupils—of what children need and what "policies" dictate that they must have.

According to Cecil Mercer (1986, p. 137), at the preschool and kindergarten/ Grade 1 levels, learning disabilities are best approached from a preventive orientation, rather than a corrective/remedial one. Nonetheless, he recommends direct instruction, particularly in language-related activities. You may feel least certain of how to proceed in reconciling the needs of some young children with delays for direct instruction with a general classroom approach based on discovery and relying on incidental learning. Chapter 10 describes specific strategies for integrating individually planned programs of instruction, focusing upon specific targets, and employing systems for keeping data within the group classroom context. The guiding principle in approaching language-related and other areas of learning with children identified as developmentally delayed is that the child may need to be consciously taught to do certain things that other children seem to learn incidentally or on their own.

The general teaching approach for students with learning disabilities termed "direct instruction" does indeed emphasize error correction. The basic rationale is that behaviors that are practiced tend to be hard to change; therefore, it is better for the child to use the appropriate, desired, or correct response than one that is inadequate. As one master teacher of learning disabled students expresses it, "Practice doesn't make perfect; practice makes permanent!" Direct instruction in the specific skills required for academic learning clearly has more research support than the development of underlying processes to remediate problems in reading, writing, spelling, math and other areas with learning disabled students (e.g., Hammill, Goodman, & Wiederholt, 1974; Ysseldyke & Salvia, 1974.) There are also authorities (e.g., Engleman, 1966) who endorse specific skill training in pre-academic skill areas for young children at risk for school failure, as was discussed in Chapter 4. The general approaches described by the term direct instruction (Stephens, 1977) note the importance of specifying individually appropriate instructional objectives; pretesting, using a criterion-referenced approach; systematic instruction, incorporating reinforcement for correct responses; post-testing for the targeted objectives; and provision for generalization of specific responses across conditions. This implies a more individually structured method, involving systematic observation, maintenance of data for specific instructional targets, and criterion-referenced assessment than many teachers of young children may be accustomed to using in their general classroom approach. However, as was discussed in principle in Chapter 4, and is illustrated in practice both in Chapter 10 and through the various case examples presented throughout this text, the two are by no means incompatible.

Social Studies

Unit-based teaching in early childhood education recognizes that young children's learning is not compartmentalized, according to curricular "areas," but rather is integrated and holistic (Seefeldt, 1980; Bayless & Ramsey, 1987). Young children come to understand physical phenomena, social relationships, concepts, and feelings in an interrelated, rather than segmented, way. Thus, the separation of art, music, and social studies from language arts, math, and science activities in the early childhood years—primary as well as preschool and primary levels—is artificial and unnecessary. Expression through play, singing, movement, construction, and use of art media represent activities important and valuable in themselves and, at the same time ways of doing that make concept and skill acquisition meaningful. Experiences in the community, as well as in the classroom, that help children to understand and value social roles, relationships, and responsibilities also provide opportunities for young children to acquire, apply, and practice skills and concepts important in problem-solving, concept formation, obtaining information, and communicating with others.

Special education for students identified in the school years as mentally retarded has traditionally placed great emphasis on social studies curricula, especially those skills essential for maximally independent functioning in the community (e.g., Kolstoe, 1976; MacMillan, 1982). Instruction is both personalized and problem-focused, suggesting an experiential, real-world approach, rather than content-centered, abstract. Thus, standard and developmentally appropriate early childhood practice in the area of social studies is, by its nature, readily accomodating of special needs of young children with developmental delays. Further, the very diversity of a group of young learners provides a "natural laboratory" for social studies learning involving human relations, valuing of self and others, and ways in which people support and help each other in community life. Early childhood social studies learning typically requires few, if any, goal modifications or instructional adaptations specifically for young children with developmental delays.

Expressive Arts

The expressive arts have not generally been emphasized in special education approaches with mildly and moderately handicapped students of school age, nor have they been incorporated in early intervention programs to nearly the same degree as in typical early childhood programs (Bailey et al., 1982). **The important role of expressive arts in typical preschool, kindergarten, and primary classrooms represents one of the most important benefits of mainstream participation for young children with developmental delays.** By their nature, art, music, and movement activities invite and encourage spontaneous participation on the part of all children. They are sources of joy, rather than areas of potential failure (Bayless & Ramsey, 1987), and they provide for and value diversity rather than a common standard of performance.

Summary: Adapting the Instructional Program

The major concern expressed by teachers in providing for the special needs of exceptional children typically is how to accommodate diverse levels of readiness and learning styles within an instructional program that has been designed on the basis of what is typical for a particular educational level. What that basically requires is: (1) the expectation that individual students will differ from each other; (2) the ability to identify instructionally relevant individual characteristics of students; and (3) the willingness to provide individual learning experiences that represent a match to those characteristics. Although these three dimensions of teacher behavior indeed characterize special education, they by no means represent the distinction between "regular education" and special education. As McCoy and Prehm (1987) stated:

> With a minor adjustment of teaching strategy, an educational problem of a mildly handicapped child can easily be solved within the regular classroom. Not too surprisingly, the types of adjustments in teaching strategies that work well with mildly handicapped children work very well with learning problems that surface with normal children, too. (p. 34)

The types of "adjustments" recommended by McCoy and Prehm pertain not to the content of instruction but to the method. Basically, they involve establishing the expectancy for success, rather than failure; providing useful, or functional, feedback to the child concerning his or her efforts; helping the child learn to organize information; providing opportunities for useful practice; and providing reinforcement. Their recommendations are based on an assumption that different students will achieve at different rates and in different ways.

Applying these principles to the early childhood classroom requires one basic proviso: that the intended learning outcomes are developmentally appropriate to the characteristics and needs of young children. If the curriculum and the instructional context of the early childhood classroom do indeed represent developmentally appropriate practices, provisions for variation among children in readiness and learning styles will be made as a matter of course.

Guidelines for Adapting Instruction for Young Children with Developmental Delays

1. Expect and provide for differences in time required for individual children to complete tasks.
2. Help the child to attend to the task through such strategies as:
   Visually highlighting the task.
   Reducing or eliminating distractions in the environment.

Providing visual cues and signals, accompanied by verbal cues.

Using appropriate levels and types of prompts.

Establishing regular and predictable routines.

Identifying certain types of activities, and behavior appropriate for those activities, with specific areas of the classroom

Using eye contact and encouraging the child to maintain eye contact with you when you are speaking.

3. Encourage and provide direct experience with actual materials.

4. Use direct instruction techniques selectively when they are appropriate for individual children in specific situations, especially when introducing new and unfamiliar tasks, including such strategies as:

Using task analysis to determine the specific skill components required for the task and the sequence with which they need to be performed.

Assessing the child's current level of skill mastery in the hierarchy required for the task.

Focusing on discrete, observable behavior.

Providing appropriate reinforcement, determined through observation of the individual child, contingent upon correct response.

Maintaining continuous data collection.

Using error correction procedures to prevent practicing of incorrect responses.

5. Employ a multisensory approach, using visual, auditory, tactile, kinesthetic, and, where possible and appropriate, even taste and smell modalities.

6. Model and demonstrate, rather than relying entirely on verbal directions, and arrange and group children so that peer modeling and demonstration can occur.

7. Introduce tasks of manageable scope, building gradually through consistent success.

8. Provide opportunities for repetition and practice.

9. Use general case programming principles in teaching concepts and skills for generalization, by using examples and enabling practice across various:

Object exemplars and materials (e.g., many different types, colors, sizes, and shapes of cup; various ways of opening and closing, etc.

Settings and times.

Social contexts.

10. Select these based on the present and future environments in which the child will need to apply the concept or perform the skill.

11. Recognize and reward appropriate behavior and good work.

12. Help the child learn to use language to gain mastery over his environment, identify and understand his feelings, and regulate his own behavior.

13. Encourage choice and help the child move toward increasing self-selection and independence.

14. Select activities when possible based upon the child's current functioning, rather than always needing to help the child adapt to the activity.

15. Recognize and exploit the potential in academic areas to help the child acquire and strengthen more basic readiness skills, such as attending, self-control, listening, sequencing, discriminating, and fine motor control and coordination.

SUMMARY

The vast majority of students identified as handicapped have "invisible" handi-caps. Many of these children have not been identified as potentially in need of special education until they enter school, at which time their problems become apparent. The difficulties they experience are directly related to the social and academic learning demands of the school. Although they are frequently described as "mildly handicapped." their problems in school learning may actually be quite severe and debilitating. Also, although there are compelling arguments for provid-ing nearly all of the instruction for nearly all of these students within the context of "regular education," rather than "special education," the demands that places on the mainstream teacher are frequently greater than would be the case for a student with severely impaired mobility, vision, or hearing. However, mainstreaming stu-dents with "high incidence" handicaps for instructional as well as social purposes is nearly always preferable, is generally feasible, and is occurring in schools everywhere.

These children are not likely to be identified in early childhood as mildly mentally retarded, learning disabled, or behavior disordered. That is partly be-cause such distinctions would usually be difficult to make, but mainly because these distinctions and labels, when applied to young children, are really not very helpful and in fact may be potentially harmful. The broad term *developmentally delayed* may be applied in order to establish children's eligibility and need for special assistance, with the goals of preventing later academic failure and second-ary personal-social problems; promoting optimal development through helping the child learn compensatory, self-regulatory, and corrective strategies, as well as develop confidence, independence, and a positive sense of self; and supporting and strengthening family resources and bonds.

Meeting these goals within the mainstream early childhood classroom may require certain adaptations in some very basic areas. Those that were specifically considered in this chapter involved: language and communication needs, sys-tematic behavior management and direct instruction, and adapting the curriculum and instructional program. As is the case with young children with special needs of other kinds, however, these adaptations are both possible to implement with minimal modification of the classroom program and potentially valuable for other children, "normal" as well as those identified as exceptional.

CHAPTER 9

Integrating Young Gifted and Talented Children

Some children are exceptional in ways that do not involve risk for educational handicaps. They stand out because of the unusual abilities they demonstrate. These children have special educational needs, just as their peers with handicapping or disabling conditions do. In fact, when educators fail to respond to the unique needs of gifted and talented children, these children become handicapped.

As with all exceptional children, this "group"—gifted and talented—is not really a group at all; gifted and talented children are extremely heterogeneous. Various areas or forms of giftedness are increasingly being recognized in school programs.

WHICH CHILDREN ARE GIFTED?

Specialists, general educators, lay persons—and especially parents—are likely to have a variety of answers to this question. Some argue that all children have their own special gifts. Most would agree, however, that some are exceptional with regard to abilities that they demonstrate or potential for accomplishment that they seem to possess. Most teachers have felt concern about a certain child's opportunities in the school setting to demonstrate full potential, to be intellectually challenged, to progress in learning at a more rapid rate.

The 1980s have witnessed growing societal concerns about excellence in education, with attention focused upon needed school reforms through a series of major and highly publicized reports, (Adler, 1982; Boyer, 1983; Carnegie Commission on Excellence, 1985; Goodlad, 1984.) One particularly memorable phrase from the first of these reports was "a rising tide of mediocrity" in American education.

Although the focus of the school reform movement has been broad, encompassing all aspects of the educational process, the perceived failure of American education to identify, stimulate, and provide appropriately for children and youth with very high intellectual and academic potential was an important aspect that was specifically addressed.

This would seem to suggest a fairly straightforward proposition: there are children with exceptional achievement potential, and these children ought to be encouraged to exploit that potential. However, the simplicity is misleading, for several reasons: (1) different children may excel in different ways; (2) it is not always easy to identify those children with potential to excel in one area or another; and (3) it is not always apparent how best to enable a child to exploit his or her potential for excellence in a particular area while developing optimally in those areas in which he or she is more similar to peers than different. These problems are compounded in young children. Perhaps that is why few public school special programs are provided for gifted and talented children until about Grade 3, if then (Hollinger & Kosek, 1985; Roedell, Jackson, & Robinson, 1980).

Young children who are very bright, even precocious, present a paradox. Parents and teachers may expect a young child identified as gifted to excel in everything, although a gifted child, like any other, will have specific strengths and weaknesses (Roedell, 1986). More importantly, adults may assume a level of sophistication equal to the level of apparent intellect and may expose children to ideas and information with which they are not emotionally equipped to deal. We all need to be sensitive to the impact of information that is readily available but, even for a bright and sensitive child (or perhaps particularly so), not easily processed. Examples would include news events such as bombings, kidnappings, natural disasters, famines, and the like. Even religious materials may be frightening, especially to the young child with a vivid imagination and the ability and interest to follow the narrative, understand the words, and construct images suggested by the stories (Roedell, 1986).

Despite their apparent sophistication, gifted and talented children are still first and foremost young children. As Wendy Roedell (1986) notes, a parent's aggressive concern for more "academic rigor" in a young child's preschool experience should signal you as teacher to the need for a thorough explanation of the learning process that is common to both more and less advanced children. You need to point out that paper-and-pencil instruction is developmentally inappropriate for all young children, since all (including the intellectually gifted) learn through direct experiences with concrete materials. **The child's own interests and motivations must be encouraged, not the parents' expectations.**

CHARACTERISTICS AND EARLY IDENTIFICATION

The following are among the characteristics frequently observed quite early in life in young children later identified as gifted (Silverman, 1986):

Unusual alertness
Long attention span
High activity level
Less need for sleep
Smiling or recognizing caretakers early
Advanced progression through developmental milestones
Keen sense of observation
Extreme curiosity
Excellent memory
Early and extensive vocabulary development
Intense interest in books
Rapid learning ability
Abstract reasoning ability
High degrees of sensitivity
Perfectionism
Excellent sense of humor
Preference for older companions
Advanced ability to play with puzzles, mazes, or numbers. (p. 75)

It should be unnecessary to add that these are based upon subjective impressions of parents, rather than any well-defined and measurable criteria. It is also important to note that not all these signs may be exhibited.

Creative or productive thinking, one of the areas of giftedness included in Marland's (1972) frequently cited definition, does not necessarily coexist with intellectual giftedness.[1] According to E. Paul Torrance (1983), a pioneer and leader in the study of creativity in children, young children with high creative potential may demonstrate characteristics such as the following: (1) long attention span; (2) capacity for organization; (3) ability to see things in different perspectives; (4) tendency to take a closer look at things; (5) use of fantasy to solve developmental problems; (6) use of storytelling and song making; (7) ability to produce new combinations through manipulation.

Policy definitions of giftedness in children have been criticized (Renzulli, 1978) because of their tendency to combine processes (intellectual, creative, and leadership functioning) with performance (academic and artistic accomplishment) while failing to take into account motivation. In Renzulli's view, giftedness results

---

[1]Marland defined gifted and talented children as ". . . those identified by professionally qualified persons who by virtue of outstanding abilities are capable of high performance. These are children who require differentiated educational programs and services beyond those normally provided by the regular school program in order to realize their contribution to self and society. Children capable of high performance include those with demonstrated achievement and/or potential ability in any of the following areas:

1) General intellectual ability; 2) Specific academic aptitude; 3) Creative or productive thinking; 4) Leadership ability; 5) Visual & performing arts" (p. 10)

from the interaction of above average intelligence, creativity, and task commitment. Because the relationship among these characteristics in young children and future accomplishment has not been investigated, the usefulness of this definition in identifying young children with gifted potential is not known.

Despite difficulties in identification of preschool-age gifted children, there have been attempts to identify such children during the first few months of life. Specific behavioral patterns, such as visual attention, crying, and interest shifts in relation to auditory stimuli have been studied, as have biological and socio-familial variables (Abroms, 1983).

While early identification has proved problematic in the past, especially identification by teachers (e.g., Kirk, 1966; Jacobs, 1971) the expertise that is potentially available is rarely used. There is no national "child find" effort in this area paralleling that mandated under P.L. 94–142 and P.L. 99–457 for handicapped, developmentally delayed, and at-risk infants and young children. In the view of Karnes and Johnson (1986), professionals have been reluctant to stress early identification of eligible children if no programming is available for them. Such an effort not only would be considered wasteful of financial resources, but might also be viewed as a disservice to both child and family (Bagnato & Neisworth, 1980).

Public schools provide very few special programs for young gifted children. One national survey (Jenkins, 1979) identified only 113 such programs at the preschool or primary level. Of these, only 20 kindergarten-level and just five preschool-level programs were provided by school districts. The lack of programs for very young children no doubt reflects limitations in the schools' ability, in most states, to use public funds for the education of children younger than mandated school age. We should note also that private programs available would not have been identified in survey responses provided by public education officials (Karnes & Johnson, 1986).

Whatever the funding limitations, however, the lack of programs for young children of legal school age is puzzling. Karnes and Johnson (1986) cited two possible reasons for the tendency for public schools to delay introduction of "gifted programs" until the intermediate (post-primary) grades: (1) recognition of the difficulty in accurately identifying younger children, coupled with the belief that abilities will have stabilized sufficiently by, but not before, about age 9; (2) perhaps surprisingly, and contrary to stereotypes of "pushy parents," their observation that parents generally have not expressed major concerns for the needs of their children for special provisions until they reach about this level.

Difficulties that adults have in recognizing unusual potential in children, especially young children, are problems not only in determining eligibility for special programs if they are available, but also in providing optimally for children within typical environments. Stereotypes, expectations, and personal values all may influence a teacher, or other adult, to err in either, or both, of two ways when attempting to determine which children may be gifted. Some "misleading behaviors" (Ehrlich, 1986) may prompt us to believe erroneously that young children are gifted, including being very verbal, very conforming or well behaved, or unusually able to demonstrate advanced performance in certain academic areas as a result of inordinate home pressure. On the other hand, young children who seem shy or withdrawn, inattentive, low achieving, uninterested in reading, erratic in attendance or punctuality, defiant, reserved, or inclined to misbehave, demand attention, or clown may be gifted but not recognized as such (Ehrlich, 1986).

The very characteristics that suggest high potential may not be consonant with the expectations of adults or the requirements of the classroom setting. Thus, some unusually capable children may be identified, but as "problems," rather than as gifted children, while many others no doubt learn early to suppress the very qualities that make them unique. Dr. Joanne Rand Whitmore has effectively described the dilemma experienced by many children:

> The gifted child is vulnerable to social discomfort and difficulty in the classroom because of several specific requirements of that social setting. Teachers expect children to dependably follow directions, not to give them; to participate cooperately in group activities, not function independently in isolated activity; and to exhibit reasonable levels of self-control, not impulsive behavior. Furthermore, despite academic rhetoric about classroom climates that affirm diversity in our society, there still is a powerful press on highly creative and gifted children to not be so different, to adapt to the social setting, to blend in. All of these factors make the gifted child very vulnerable to social conflict in school. (p. 124)

ESPECIALLY HARD-TO-IDENTIFY GIFTED CHILDREN

Young gifted children who have a handicapping condition and those of ethnic minority or low socioeconomic background are most likely to have their gifted potential go unrecognized and unnurtured (Ehrlich, 1986).

> It is likely that the largest number of overlooked gifted children will be found among the handicapped. There is a tendency on the part of both parents and professionals to focus on the negative aspects of being handicapped rather than on the positive qualities of potential giftedness. (p. 65)

Ehrlich notes further that stereotypes and generalizations about handicapping conditions compound the problem, for many people erroneously assume impaired learning ability in children with a physical disability. Although some physical disabilities are often associated with impaired cognitive functioning, that is not always the case. The full range of intellectual potential is represented among children with impaired mobility, vision, or hearing or with chronic health problems, for example. To illustrate the point Ehrlich (1986) reports an instance of a family's complete surprise to learn that their young daughter, who had cerebral palsy, achieved an IQ score of more than 175.

Frequently, a disability or health problem may mask gifted potential. One example especially pertinent to teachers of young children is *otitis media,* or middle ear infection. As noted in Chapter 6, children who have had histories of chronic middle ear infection are at risk for both hearing impairment and difficulties with specific types of learning tasks. Middle ear problems also make identification of high potential difficult, but awareness of associated hearing and processing difficulties can enable teachers more effectively to differentiate learning opportunities based upon both strengths and weaknesses. Ironically, neither the child's learning difficulties nor the child's learning aptitudes may be recognized among gifted children who have experienced chronic or recurrent ear infections early in life. As one author (Silverman, 1986) notes in discussing her own work with this special group of gifted children, ". . . their gifts are hidden by their auditory disabilities, and their disabilities are masked by their giftedness. The net result is that they appear 'average' in intellectual ability" (p. 79). She explains that these children are likely to have genuine difficulties with certain simple and rote memorization tasks, but may have superior vocabulary, conceptual, and reasoning skills. Paradoxically, these children fail in the simpler tasks while excelling in the more complex ones!

As was discussed in Chapter 2, assessing the intellectual abilities of children with a sensory, motor, or speech impairment poses special problems, because of the performance requirements of the formal, standardized tests typically used, and also because these measures do not have norms for individuals with these disabilities since they were not included in the standardization process. Some tests have been especially designed, and appropriately normed, for use with individuals with disabilities, although each has its own limitations in terms of tapping the person's "true" intellectual potential. As Jerome Sattler (1988) has cautioned, even when the assessment procedures are appropriate, the psychological examiner's interpretations may be colored by the same sort of personal beliefs, expectations, and stereotypes that limit the ability of others to find high potential where it was not expected. Just as in the diagnostic assessment of all handicapped children, only a multifactored approach, drawing upon diverse data sources, rather than test results alone, is appropriate.

Whitmore (1985) suggests other obstacles to the identification of gifted children who are handicapped, including the problem in communication often involved among the various professionals who may see these children. If information is not shared, educators may be unaware of relevant medical information, physicians may not have access to school performance data, and psychologists may lack sufficient information about the child's behavior in school or other settings. Parents may not be tapped, or their reports not accorded appropriate credibility. The result is a necessarily incomplete, and potentially highly misleading, diagnostic picture.

Another problem occurs once the focus upon the child's disability has led to special class placement, for that setting may not provide opportunities to demonstrate superior intellectual abilities or high potential in the visual or performing arts, creativity, or critical thinking. Whereas science and social studies provide opportunities to stimulate higher level cognitive abilities, the special curriculum is more likely to emphasize basic skills in reading, writing, and math, and self-help. Thus, **special class placement is more likely to lead to fulfillment of the self-fulfilling prophecy than to the discovery that the prophecy was in error.**

Finally, according to Whitmore (1985), handicapped children fall victim to the "Terman Myth" that gifted children excel in all areas: that they are well-motivated high achievers, linguistically fluent, independent, and tend to be accorded, or to assume, leadership roles. Therefore, demonstrating the "spread phenomenon" (Sattler, 1988, p. 73), adults, including well-trained professionals, may assume erroneously that a child with a disability that limits verbal ability, high achievement in all academic areas, independence, or social leadership cannot be bright, highly creative, or artistically gifted. Significantly the criteria most frequently employed to identify gifted children potentially discriminate against the handicapped student: teacher nomination, scores on standardized ability and achievement tests, and evidence of prior accomplishment.

Clearly, with very young children, the issue involves our ability to recognize "exceptional potential for learning" (Whitmore, 1985) through a variety of sources of evidence, rather than test scores or evidence of past accomplishment alone. June Maker (1977) has noted the importance of a focus upon potential in identifying gifted children who are handicapped. She also recommends comparing the student with other similarly handicapped peers, rather than with those who are not handicapped, and observing the skills a handicapped child demonstrates in compensating for a disability.

PERSONAL AND SOCIAL DEVELOPMENT OF YOUNG GIFTED CHILDREN

The issue of acceptance by peers and maintaining friendships reflects yet another paradox. According to extensive research (Terman & Odom, 1959), gifted individuals, as a group, are generally better "adjusted" than the general population. Most studies (e.g., Kelly & Colangelo, 1984; Lehman & Erdwins, 1981) indicate that gifted children are more likely to have positive self-concepts than typical children. Yet, gifted children (and adults) may be especially vulnerable, as well, and many report feelings of unhappiness, self-doubt, and loneliness.

As far as social relationships and friendships are concerned, gifted children are found typically to be popular with peers (Gallagher, 1985). Yet gifted children themselves, especially the highly gifted, often report dissatisfaction with their ability to make friends. They also report that friendships are more typically formed with older children than with peers their same age (Janos, Marwood, & Robinson, 1985). Friendships are developed and maintained around common interests, after all. Not surprisingly, young gifted children share certain interests with children who are older, including preferences for certain games, scientific pursuits, and hobbies. That does not necessarily imply that young children who are intellectually gifted have nothing in common with typical children their own age. It does imply the need for some flexibility in grouping children to provide peer group contexts based upon common interests, sometimes crossing age and grade lines.

Far from being overly serious, many young gifted children are seen by their typical peers as fun to play with. Fiscella and Barnett (1985) investigated the play styles of a group of gifted and nongifted preschool children and found that the gifted children demonstrated higher degrees of physical, social, and cognitive play styles, but were equivalent with their peers in the degrees of humor and general affect they demonstrated. Boys showed more active physical play patterns, as well as more teasing and joking than did girls, while girls changed activities more frequently. Generally, the play styles of gifted boys and girls both reflected a more imaginative quality than those of the typical peers.

The gender-related differences found in Fiscella's study, in both gifted and nongifted children, suggest an area of general concern that may affect adversely the assertiveness, inquiry, and exploratory inclinations of girls. Research documents that different societal role expectations for boys and for girls are reinforced in a great many ways, some obvious and some more subtle, through toys, literature, role models portrayed in the entertainment media, and at home. Regrettably, similar patterns of differential reinforcement are observed in school, beginning in preschool programs. For example, a study of preschool children conducted by Serbin, O'Leary, Kent, & Tonick (1973) revealed that teachers tended to reinforce girls for remaining physically near them, while aggressive behavior in boys was more likely to elicit teacher response than when girls engaged in such behavior. Teachers were found to provide more verbal guidance in response to requests from boys as compared to girls. Although school factors may threaten to suppress giftedness and creativity in children of both sexes, there may well be reason for special concern in this regard for girls.

The social behavior and social skills of many gifted young children may be more like those of their same-age peers than of their intellectual peers, although adults may expect social maturity commensurate with the child's intellectual development. Consequently, a bright child engaging in age-appropriate behavior may be seen as presenting "behavior problems."

Similarly, differences in self-esteem are found among gifted children. Although many studies (e.g., Kelly & Colangelo, 1984; Lehman & Erdwins, 1981) have reported that gifted children who are homogeneously grouped have more positive self-esteem than nongifted children, some have found children to view themselves less favorably in comparison to peers of equal or greater ability (e.g., Coleman & Fults, 1982, 1985). These studies imply the need to take into account the individual child's apparent level of self-esteem in considering what type of educational placement might be more appropriate.

Peer acceptance and popularity are influenced by many possible factors, as with all children, but there is some evidence that extent of giftedness may be one of them for many children. Moderately gifted children tend to be more popular with peers than those who have extremely high levels of ability (Gallagher, 1985.) Concerns have been expressed in the literature for many years (e.g., Hollingworth,

1942; O'Shea, 1960) that highly gifted children may be unable to communicate with peers of their same age and that these difficulties are apparent in the preschool years.

It is difficult to summarize research findings relating to personal and social development of young gifted children, because the diversity among these children is so evident. The old stereotype of the bookish, socially awkward or aloof child, whose interests are restricted to intellectual pursuits, like all stereotypes, has clearly been proved wrong. Some gifted children experience extreme self-doubt and feelings of inadequacy, while others have realistic positive self-concepts. There is a danger that adults may expect more social maturity than is warranted, based on children's advanced performance cognitively. Such expectations, along with other forms of inordinate pressure to think about adult subjects, and to think about them as adults do, to take on responsibilities for looking out for themselves, and to hurry through childhood have been identified as great problems today for many children in our culture. (The best statement of these concerns is no doubt Dr. David Elkind's book, *The Hurried Child*.) It seems reasonable to assume that very capable children are at especially great risk of being deprived of the experience of childhood.

EDUCATIONAL ALTERNATIVES FOR YOUNG GIFTED CHILDREN

Traditionally, the three major approaches that have been developed for students identified as gifted and talented have been: (1) special classes and special schools; (2) acceleration in completing the standard educational program; and (3) enriched learning opportunities within the regular program. Schools have employed variations or combinations of these approaches in order to provide "differentiated educational programs and services beyond those normally provided by the regular school program" (Marland, 1972, p. 10). In very recent years, however, one such variation has gained such widespread use that it has acquired its own designation and special character. That is the "pull-out" program, which might be more formally designated as a special resource program approach. Although this strategy is discussed here, it needs to be reiterated that formalized special programs of any type are very rarely offered for young children. For that reason, as well as because the focus of this entire book is on providing effectively for diversity among children within the regular classroom, most of the following discussion involves strategies for enrichment.

Special Class and Resource Programs

As in other areas of special education, the special class or special school model was based on the premise that more advantages could be provided to students in homogeneous groupings than was feasible within the regular school situation. "Segregation" of the most capable is in fact the oldest form of special education: in past centuries, only those assumed to be most capable were formally educated at all. Youth believed worthy of education were typically those of most privileged circumstance. An additional consideration, of course, was often gender. Perhaps concerns about "elitism" that have been raised about special education for gifted students have their origins in these traditions.

The special class and special school approaches implemented in American public education since the 1920s have generally attempted to include all those eligible by virtue of ability. Such programs generally have focused upon intellectual giftedness and academic aptitude; consequently, measures of ability (IQ test scores) and academic achievement (achievement test scores, together with performance records and teacher referral) have most commonly defined eligibility criteria. When specific criteria are stipulated for eligibility, programs vary, although one criterion typically has been an IQ score at or above a specific point, frequently 130. Public education has tended to employ the special school model for students with specific areas of talent or special aptitude, for example, in the arts.

The possibility of a special "track" for gifted students raises the question of the relative merits of homogeneous vs. heterogeneous grouping. The concept of the Least Restrictive Environment refers specifically to maximum involvment of handicapped students in regular classroom situations that are necessarily heterogeneous. However, in the view of some authorities (e.g., Hershey, 1981), that term ". . . takes on an inverse connotation when applied to the gifted exceptional student" (p. 27). That view suggests that learning environments for gifted students are less restrictive when such students are grouped with others who have interests and abilities similar to their own. It does not necessarily imply, however, that a small group of exceptionally capable students should be placed in a program that is totally separate for all facets of their schooling.

The model that can accommodate partial separation and partial integration for a gifted student is, in a sense, the resource room/program concept employed with many handicapped students in reverse. "Pull-out" programs can potentially provide for many gifted students "the best of both worlds." In the heterogeneous, mainstream classroom setting, the gifted child has the opportunity to interact with same-age peers in areas of possible common interest as well as the opportunity to excel. The special provisions enable high ability children to participate together regularly in areas that can challenge and stretch them intellectually. The focus of programs for which students are "pulled out" might include certain projects, shared special interest areas, community-based learning activities, or advanced academic work.

The wide range of possible areas of focus that might be made available implies that diversity among unusually capable students might be more readily accommodated than is the case when the question is an either-or proposition of regular class vs. special class. One well-known design for accommodating more students through more options, termed the *Revolving Door Model,* was proposed by Dr. Joseph Renzulli (1978) in order to accomplish several objectives for programming he considered critical. These included making special provisions available to a greater number of students; providing for students' intraindividual differences, including special strengths, aptitudes, and interests; providing for individual students' changing special needs; and de-emphasizing label and placement distinctions between those identified as "gifted" and "not gifted."

Another design with some features similar to those of Renzulli's model was proposed by Hershey (1981). She recommended first that a pool of potential participants be created through the use of screening and nomination procedures. Next, more specific, intensive study, emphasizing personal interviews, would be conducted in order to ensure that those gifted children for whom special programming with "full staffing" would constitute the "least restrictive alternative" would receive such programming, and that the number of those identified in this group would be of reasonable, manageable size. A second and third "stream" would be identified, so that all nominees would be provided for; no "rejections" would be required. The especially trained gifted education personnel would work closely with regular class teachers in implementing such options as ". . . seminars [to allow peer interaction], mentorship provisions, flexible 'pull-out' alternatives, and cluster grouping" (p. 28). Flexibility and adaptability to a wide diversity of student needs would seem to constitute the hallmark of such designs as Hershey's and Renzulli's.

The fact that these or other models that involve special program components outside the regular class have been implemented very rarely at the primary grade level does not imply that such will be the case always. If major reasons for deferring special programming include uncertainty about positive identification and the fact that young children's abilities have not stabilized yet, flexible and multifaceted designs would appear especially appropriate in the first years of schooling. Such designs involve teamwork between regular classroom teachers and specialists, as well as between both and parents.

Acceleration

Acceleration refers to any of a variety of means by which children may be enabled to complete any phase of schooling within a shorter period of time. It encompasses early school entrance, grade or part-of-grade skipping, and enrollment in advanced-level courses. The last is frequently done at the high school level, with some students taking courses designated as advanced placement sections or taking work for specific college credit prior to high school graduation. For young children, acceleration practices involve early kindergarten enrollment or enrolling directly in Grade 1.

The relative merits of both grade skipping and grade retention, as well as possible problems they might entail, continue to be argued. It is probably safe to say that, at least beyond kindergarten, full-grade skipping is not practiced widely. Similarly, both early kindergarten entry and kindergarten retention remain somewhat controversial, as was discussed in Chapter 3. Acceleration for gifted children has generally been found to be effective for many or most gifted children for whom it was provided, not only intellectually and academically but in terms of personal and social development as well (Paulus, 1984). Concerns that have been expressed about the latter would not seem to be justified, based upon the research data. The challenge provided, and minimization of boredom and frustration, as well as children's flexibility in accepting individual differences among their peers, offset the momentary inconveniences for most children of very high ability. However, rather than simply providing a one-time grade-skipping alternative, continuity in planning for the individual child is essential so that the momentary advantages are not lost (Kitano, 1986).

Clearly, any form of acceleration requires consideration of the individual child and all dimensions of her development. That is certainly true in the case of selective early school entry, which can be very appropriate and beneficial when decisions are based upon comprehensive child study (Wallis, 1984).

Part-time rather than full-time acceleration may be appropriate for some children, particularly those with uneven patterns of high ability in academic or pre-academic areas, or those whose social or physical development is significantly less advanced than their cognitive ability or academic performance (Kitano, 1986). Needless to say, an ungraded primary program lends itself ideally to such differentiation. However, part-time acceleration can be beneficial for some children within a more rigidly age-graded structure. Again, it is the individual child and a complete analysis of all his or her abilities and needs that should guide a placement decision.

Enrichment

As noted earlier, enrichment strategies are both more generally compatible with standard early childhood education practices and more congruent with the focus of this book than the other broad options. Since we have noted that special placement options are not widely provided for young gifted children, enrichment within the regular classroom would appear to be the most promising area to pursue. However, implementation of enrichment strategies by no means precludes the concurrent use of both acceleration and "pull-out" or resource program alternatives.

The idea of providing appropriately for children of high ability in the regular classroom through enrichment appears appropriate and reasonable. Genuine enrichment, appropriate to the intellectual and motivational needs of young gifted children, is difficult to provide, however, certainly no less than providing for children demonstrating delayed cognitive development. Kitano (1986) has expressed this effectively:

> Although conceptually sound, appropriate enrichment is difficult to implement given large heterogeneous classrooms with one teacher. Assurance of teacher effectiveness with gifted children and individualization to meet the special needs of individuals are critical factors in selecting the enrichment option. (p. 94)

This section will more specifically address these two "critical factors."

Kitano (1982) offers six general recommendations for an enrichment program to consider in fostering the gifted child's thinking processes within the context of the standard curriculum: (1) provide activities that enhance creativity; (2) enhance higher cognitive processes; (3) enhance executive operations; (4) promote inquiry and problem solving; (5) promote affective development; and (6) incorporate process and content objectives into units. Implications of these recommendations for young children are suggested in specific curricular and activity areas in this section.

An important consideration is the extent to which curricular goals and instructional planning in the regular classroom are compatible with the curriculum and instruction features specifically recommended in the literature for young gifted children. According to Whitmore (1986), there are four major attributes of curricular programming appropriate to the needs of young gifted children:

1. Provisions are made for the assessed strengths and weaknesses of the individual students.
2. Provisions are made to insure ample opportunities for higher level thinking and problem solving, inquiry and discovery learning, and creativity and self-expression, balanced against skill development, and across all instructional areas.
3. Provisions are made for systematic and comprehensive *affective education,* across all curricular areas, to enhance motivation, self-esteem, and social competence.
4. Provisions are made to insure that children acquire and practice self-regulatory strategies, impulse control, and alternative adaptive modes of expressing emotions and coping with frustration or stress. (pp. 129–131)

In addition to the recommendations and attributes suggested by Kitano and Whitmore, respectively, Swassing (1985) suggests that the following principles need to be addressed in providing a program for young gifted children:

The program should be holistic, addressing both cognitive and affective aspects of development.

The approach should be individualized to provide an optimal match between the learning environment and the children's unique characteristics and abilities, previous learning and experiences, and needs as preschoolers and gifted children (and, in some cases, their handicapping condition).

Academic skills should be integrated into the program, but only to provide children with necessary tools.

A parental component is necessary for both parental support and parent education or training, to help parents facilitate their child's development.

The identification model must relate to the type of differentiated program provided.

The teacher should have certain characteristics and skills and should model the behavior that is the goal for the children. (p. 106)

These three sets of recommendations reflect some differences in emphasis, but taken together they imply a set of guidelines that are applicable in integrating gifted and talented children within the "mainstream" preschool, kindergarten, or primary classroom. The guidelines that follow have evolved from these analyses of effective special programs for young gifted children, from consideration of other related research on young gifted children, and from analysis of effective practices for young children generally.

Enrichment Guidelines for Teachers of Integrated Early Childhood Programs

1. *Model the idea that diversity is valued.* The problem associated with attempting to provide for the young child who is intellectually gifted with a typical classroom environment is, in part, the fact that all children want to be like their peers. These children not uncommonly hide their abilities, and "act average" (Whitmore, 1980).

2. *Model the idea that originality and divergent thinking are valued.* As Dorothy Sisk (1979, p. 528) has stressed, "Teachers should value creative thinking and be flexible in their instruction. Good teachers of the gifted are comfortable with different ways of doing things."

3. *Encourage children to engage in higher-order thinking processes and problem-solving strategies, even within the constraints of a prescribed curriculum.* Barbara Clark (1986), among others, has stressed the critical importance for all children, but especially children who are intellectually gifted, of using their intelligence. This involves assigning more complex, rather than simple, redundant, repetitive tasks; providing challenge and novelty; requiring students to anticipate and plan for future consequences; and presenting real problems for which multiple solutions might be considered.

4. *Relate practices that are standard in good early childhood education to the learning needs of young gifted children.* Two closely related examples are practices implied by a Piagetian orientation, discussed in Chapter 3, which are predicated on recognition of the active role of the child in constructing his or her own learning, and the "open framework" approach associated with the British Primary School. Karnes and Johnson (1986), for example, have reported that their University Primary School program for gifted children ranging in age from three to eight has as its philosophy principles directly derived from the open framework model of the English Infant School. These principles are summarized (Karnes & Johnson, 1986, p. 52) as follows: (a) learning involves acting on the environment, (b) learning is developmental, (c) learning is facilitated by participation in decision making, (d) learning integrates knowledge, and (e) learning is based on dialogue.

5. *Consult resource persons and, where appropriate, plan with those persons so that a child can have supplementary and/or partially specialized learning experiences.* Again, the issue of placement for any exceptional student is not an

"either-or" matter. The idea is to optimize learning opportunities for gifted and talented children both through providing special education resources and through providing differentiated teaching to accommodate the individual needs of these children within the regular curriculum and the regular classroom program structure. There are few, if any, advocates for children who would endorse total segregation, in special education classes, for all children who demonstrate superior abilities in specific areas of learning.

6. *Be especially aware of the possibility for sex-role stereotyping in all aspects of the early childhood program, the possibility for restricting the development of all young children, boys and girls, gifted handicapped and "typical, through early childhood experiences that unduly stress differentiated sex roles, and the special concerns indicated for young girls who may be unintentionally limited.* One important area for examination is the arrangement of play areas and learning centers. For example, attention can be given to the integration of the housekeeping corner, as Callahan (1986) suggests. Callahan also suggests that teachers should be conscious of even apparently innocuous nursery rhymes and the unintended "messages" they may communicate. As she reminds us, for example, Little Bo Peep sits passively waiting for the sheep to come home, while Little Jack Horner, even though he has ruined a pie, states "What a good boy am I!"

7. *Provide encouragement without pressuring the child.* As Roedell (1986) points out, it is important to encourage optimal effort, yet pressure can be detrimental. How to encourage and foster the young child's intellectual development, making available stimulating and intellectually challenging tasks without imposing external pressure and interfering with the child's natural, intrinsic motivation? That is the dilemma for both parent and teacher. Yet, it is a manageable one. The solution, Roedell suggests, lies in observing and listening to the child, in responding to the child's actions and questions, whether or not they are verbalized, rather than in attempting to impose external pressures or incentives.

8. *Be judicious in the use of praise or other extrinsic rewards.* For some teachers, the "reward system" that is part of classroom routine poses yet another dilemma with regard to motivation of young gifted children. It has often been observed (e.g., Glasser, 1969) that when children enter school they are intrinsically motivated to learn and to behave constructively. But an external system of controls, rewards, and punishments is imposed upon children in school. This takes the responsibility away from the child. It may also detract from the naturally reinforcing processes of discovering and learning, motivated by curiosity and the need young children have to use their intellectual resources (Bruner, 1966). Presumably, this presents special concerns for young gifted children, who are naturally highly motivated, yet find themselves in a situation in which both incentives and constraints are externally, rather than internally, provided.

As children progress in school their intellectual achievements are rewarded through grades, and a whole range of other symbolic means: smiling faces, stickers, check marks, teacher smiles, words of praise, and touch. This creates a double-edged sword. If good performance is always praised (or otherwise re-warded) for the child who "always" performs well, it becomes meaningless. At the same time, if it is not provided (or is for some children, who seem to need more of it, more than others) that can be confusing. Also, as Roedell (1986, p. 28) notes, "Constant praise also can en-gender the suspicion that parents or teachers are constantly evaluating the child, and that if the child ever falls short, love will be withdrawn. The fear that a parent only loves a child because of the child's accomplishments can be a real problem for gifted children." Although the nature of the relationship is different, the principle also applies to teachers. Fi-nally, Roedell (1986, p. 28) makes this significant observation: "Feelings of in-adequacy or of being an 'imposter' can result from overdoses of praise or crit-icism."

The general principles of good early childhood education practice that are ap-plicable to this problem (which is more acute with many gifted children, but po-tentially present in all children) include: (1) respect for the child's intrinsic motivation, (2) awareness of the child's sensitivity to unintended adult messages, and (3) valuing of all children as individu-als, not on the basis of how they perform or behave.

9. *Personalize instruction through consider-ing the child's needs and interests and incorporating these in planning learning activities.* Knowledge of each child's spe-cial interests can enable a teacher to maximize motivation, involvement, and investment in learning activities. This principle is applicable to all children, but is especially important in attempting to stimulate the creativity of a gifted child.

10. *Personalize competition, so that the child competes only against his or her own past performance*. In this way, disparities among the accomplishments of children within a group are less obvious, for each child's standard of performance is a per-sonalized one. Also, errors, often seen by perfectionistic gifted children as failures, are more likely to come to be regarded as a natural part of the learning process.

11. *Recognize the need not to neglect basic academic skill areas, but avoid making this a tedious area.* Swassing (1985) has recommended ensuring that basic skills are acquired as tools, rather than ends in themselves, and that basic mathematics, reading, and other areas be seen as po-tential areas for concept development, rather than merely for skill practice. An important point, as Whitmore (1986) noted, is that basic skills cannot be ne-glected, but must be balanced against op-portunities for exploration, inquiry, creativity, and problem-solving.

12. *Adapt advanced materials so that they can be managed and remain motivating to younger children who have age-appro-priate attention spans despite their more mature interests and more advanced cognitive levels.* In addition to modifying the time requirements, where indicated, the teacher can also incorporate appro-priate activity components matched to the individual child's needs in the areas of motor and social skills. Thus, it is rea-sonable that a given activity may be geared, not just to the child's "level," but to the child's "levels" in different areas of functioning, some of which may be ex-pectable based on his or her chronologi-cal age, others more or less advanced.

13. *Introduce a wide variety of topics, ac-tivities, and materials in the regular classroom program.* Teaching units, field trips in the community, and a wide vari-

ety of other activities can capitalize on the inherent curiosity and intrinsic motivation that all young children, including especially capable children, bring to learning.

14. *Provide opportunities for independent and even solitary work, as well for pursuing self-selected activities and organizing one's own time.* Again, balanced against needs to help the child develop socially and to interact constructively with peers in shared responsibilities, as well as to follow adult direction and to conform to necessary (not arbitrary) classroom rules and routines, the natural inclination he or she may have to function autonomously can be recognized, valued, and encouraged. The task commitment dimension of giftedness implies that these children may often be able to persist for extended periods of time; provision can be made for time flexibility to permit this, as well as for the child, when appropriate, to set his or her own objectives, approach, and time frame.

INTEGRATING YOUNG CHILDREN WHO ARE BOTH GIFTED AND HANDICAPPED

As was discussed earlier in this chapter, some young gifted children are more difficult to identify, not because they are not "out there" but because they are children of disadvantaged or culturally different background who may or may not come from homes in which English is the primary language. Special efforts have been invested in improving the schools' ability both to identify gifted children of culturally diverse backgrounds and to provide appropriate instructional programs. However, public schools have not yet had great success in developing identification tools sufficiently free of bias to permit effective identification. Once identified, children reflecting cultural differences are likely to be provided for within the standard program of services for gifted students, often without special consideration of needs they may have that are unique. Special efforts at the early childhood level, at least under the public schools' auspices, have been very rare. However, there have been reports of effective demonstration projects, such as the Pippi Program in New York, which serves gifted culturally diverse and bilingual three- and four-year-olds. This program, based on Piaget's and Erikson's theories, attempts to develop critical, creative, and logical thinking abilities in young children of high potential (Swassing, 1985).

We noted previously that young gifted children with handicapping conditions are also particularly difficult to identify and that one reason for this is professionals' and parents' tendency to focus upon the disability. Whitmore (1985) has urged professionals who work with handicapped children both to be aware of this special concern in their work and to improve their skills in responding effectively to those special needs of their students that may be associated with special abilities. These involve:

(a) recognizing and nurturing attributes of intellectual giftedness, (b) capitalizing on those strengths to facilitate overall growth and to mitigate the effects of the disability, and (c) guiding the individual to cope effectively with the negative consequences of the interaction between the giftedness and the disability. (p. 288)

These same skills would be important for the regular classroom teacher whose integrated group includes young children with handicaps, some of whom may have gifted potential.

Educational planning for young children who are both gifted and handicapped is most closely identified with the work of Dr. Merle Karnes and her associates at the University of Illinois. Through federal funding to develop, evaluate, and disseminate a model for identifying and serving young gifted/handicapped children, Dr. Karnes and her co-workers undertook a project that they called *Retrieval and Acceleration of Promising Young Handicapped and Talented* (RAPYHT). With funding awarded through the Handicapped Children's Early Education Program (HCEEP), this project was initiated in 1980 and has been replicated in numerous other locations. Karnes and Johnson (1986) have reported replication in 77 sites in 18 states. The RAPYHT approach includes preparing both an Individual Education Plan (IEP), identifying needs and strategies associated with a child's specific weaknesses, and a Talent Education Plan (TAP), providing for individualization appropriate to the child's specific areas of strength. These two plans are integrated to ensure that improved functioning in the child's area of disability results, as well as generalized positive effects on the child's self-esteem through increasing the likelihood of successful performance.

Eligible children range from three through five in age and have diagnosed mild and moderate disabilities in one or more of the following areas: sensory, physical, social and emotional, or behaviors associated with learning deficits. They are also identified as potentially or functionally gifted in one or more of the five areas included in Marland's (1972) definition, with the addition of giftedness in the psychomotor domain.

Program goals are to increase creative thinking abilities in all areas, to increase basic skills within the identified area of special talent, and to increase problem-solving abilities such as analysis, synthesis, and evaluation. Supplemental goals are to increase willingness to persist at tasks, to increase willingness to try new and different tasks, and to augment the child's positive self-concept. Although core goals are taught directly, discovery learning is fostered, since programming is based on both J. P. Guilford's Structure of Intellect model and the open classroom concept, associated with the English Primary School. The highly individualized approach to planning is based on a comprehensive individualized assessment approach called The Talent Assessment for Program Planning (TAPP) (Karnes, Steinberg, Brown, & Schwedel, 1982).

Another program, with similar design and purpose, also funded under the Handicapped Children's Early Education Program, is the Chapel Hill Training Outreach Project, in North Carolina. This program provides both enrichment and remediation for children who have been identified as both gifted and handicapped (Leonard & Cansler, 1980; Mauser, 1981). Individualized plans, based upon comprehensive assessment to pinpoint both strengths and weaknesses demonstrated by individual preschool-age children, form the basis of the instructional program.

CASE HISTORY 9.1:   FRED AND KAREN—TWO YOUNG GIFTED CHILDREN

Fred and Karen have several things in common, including the fact that they have both been identified as intellectually gifted. In addition, both of these children have severely impaired motor functioning, with limited mobility and impaired use of hands and arms. Karen is eight years old, and Fred is nine. Both have been enrolled in specialized early intervention programs, but now they both attend a regular elementary school. Each of them has attained an IQ score on an appropriately adapted individual measure of learning ability of more than 130; thus, both have demonstrated levels of intellectual functioning within the highest percentile, suggesting superior intelligence. Both are fortunate to live in communities that have well-developed special education programs that include services for gifted, as well as handicapped, students. Both are even more fortunate to have parents, teachers, and building principals who are sensitive to their unique needs as gifted children, as well as handicapped children. The plans that have been developed for each reflect that awareness of the dual nature of their special needs, as well as a great deal of open and frank communication between home and school. In both cases their parents are, for the time being, satisfied with the program, but continue to be closely involved with their child's school planning. They anticipate the likelihood that modifications in the program may prove to be desirable in the future, and they are aware of their right, and responsibility, to advocate changes.

Karen's physical impairment limits her voluntary control of large muscles in both arms and legs, on both sides of the body. She uses a motorized wheelchair, with which she is capable of totally independent movement from the moment the hydraulic lift lowers her in her chair from the bus in the morning to the moment, at the end of the day, when she again boards her bus. Her elementary school is fully accessible, and so, although she has a serious motor impairment, she is not "handicapped" when at school in terms of mobility and access. That is, she requires no assistance to enter the building, or to go to her own "homebase" classroom or two other classrooms to which she needs access, the all-purpose room, the office, or anywhere else.

Home base for Karen is a resource room for orthopedically handicapped students, one of two housed in this school that also has a third "low-incidence" class for students whose severe and multiple impairments include severe language delay and associated cognitive impairment. Language is not a problem for Karen; in fact, her vocabulary and the complexity of the sentences she uses reveal a great deal of language sophistication, as one might expect in an eight-year-old with a 130-plus IQ. However, her speech is somewhat unclear, both because the nerves that provide feedback from the movement of the mouth are not sensitive and because foamy saliva is continuously present in her mouth. As she has in other areas, though, Karen has learned to compensate for these difficulties to the extent that her speech, although unusual, is quite intelligible to others.

Her sensory impairment also makes her incapable of receiving feedback from objects she touches with her hands, but her ability to see the book and page number, for example, enables her to hold it open and turn the pages as she reads—although her fingers cannot feel the page as she turns it. Her hand dexterity is adequate to enable her to keep pace with her rapid silent reading.

Eating is more complicated than reading a book, or even completing exercises in a workbook. Since she would have no way of knowing when the fork was in her mouth, her tongue was in position, and she was chewing and swallowing, she uses a mirror that someone must fasten onto her chair or table. As with other areas of daily living, and also school activities, as long as she can see herself in relationship to other things, she readily learns to use visual information to compensate for the tactile and kinesthetic information she has no way of receiving. Knowing that she has a chronic nasal discharge, Karen has learned to carry tissues and use them regularly, although she senses no discomfort or awareness of when their use might be necessary.

Karen works in the OH resources room for a short time each morning, mainly to catch up on written work, which, for her, requires much more time than for her "mainstream" classmates. Once the assignment has been presented, she knows immediately what to do, but her resource teacher is also available for help should she need any. Her assignments are difficult, for she is mainstreamed in a third grade class for math and science and a fourth grade class for reading and language arts, as well as social studies. This does not make her an "oddity," for other accelerated students participate in that aspect of the school district's program for gifted and talented students.

Each Thursday, Karen and about 20 other children take a bus to another elementary building in the district to participate in the special program for gifted elementary students provided there. Participating in this "pull-out" program is one of Karen's great joys; her parents had had initial reservations, however, about the greater physical, social, and intellectual demands it seemed to entail. After talking it over fully with Karen herself, they agreed, and Karen has formed friendships there because of the opportunity to get to know other children who share her abilities. Her best friend, however, is Susan, one of her third grade classmates.

Unlike Karen's parents, Fred's parents had requested that he be allowed to participate in the special program for gifted and talented students in his district. At the urging of the principal of the school he had been attending for Grades 1 and 2, however, they agreed to allow him to remain in that building to be fully mainstreamed in a third grade classroom. Mr. and Mrs. Cain are not easily influenced; quite the contrary. Throughout their son's "educational career", which began just before his second birthday, they had been firm in stating what they wanted for their son, sometimes in opposition to the counsel of professionals. That was how Fred had come to attend a regular community nursery school, rather than the special preschool for children with physical handicaps, although at that time Fred had more limited strength and motor skills than nearly all the children in the special program.

In this case, the principal's major argument was the excellent enrichment provisions made by Mrs. Bloom, who would be his third grade teacher. The principal, John Swain, showed the Cains school district printouts of the ability and achievement test data, demonstrating that this school, overall, led the district—a point of considerable pride to Mr. Swain. A matter of even greater pride, however, was the commitment among the teaching staff to providing as effectively as possible for all the children in their classes, and to promoting social integration among the typical and the substantial number of handicapped children who attended, and learned together, in this school. Mr. Swain knew that Fred's elementary school experiences at Maplegrove Elementary School would be beneficial socially as well as academically. He was convinced that Fred would be challenged in a regular classroom, with peers of his same age, although he would be the brightest in the group. He had yielded on other points to the Cains; the adaptive device that had been acquired to help Fred and two other disabled children manage the stairs, for example, turned out to be a less normalizing alternative than one Mrs. Cain had suggested, and therefore he had requisitioned the alternative. However, he held firm in his position that Fred's dual special needs could be most appropriately served within a regular classroom at Maplegrove.

This school placement decision was not made on the basis of physical access, although Fred uses a wheel chair. Maplegrove School does have an elevator shaft—but at present, no elevator. (The elevator, together with other access-related modifications Mr. Swain and a faculty committee have worked out with an architect, will be "in place" next year.) During his three years at Maplegrove, Fred has been helped—by a roving special aide, classmates, and nearly daily by Mr. Swain himself—with the business of entering the building, accessing certain tricky parts of the building and playground, using the device to ascend and descend stairs, and using the bathroom.

Fred has a disorder of his muscle system that is rare to the extent that doctors are hesitant to suggest a prognosis for the future. Unlike most children with muscular dystrophy,

Fred seems to have a nonprogressive form, and in recent years he seems even to have gained some strength. In the classroom, he is helped from his wheel chair into a chair that is situated strategically: he works at his desk or joins his reading, math, and social studies groups simply by having a classmate turn his chair. In either situation—working at his desk or participating (actively, as he always does) in small-group discussion, Fred looks, and is, exactly like everyone else, except for one thing: that is, the especially insightful nature of the comments or answers he contributes to discussion, reflective of the generally high cognitive and creative level of his schoolwork. His teacher states that he is a leader, for the quality of his work and the level of his motivation set a standard and provide a challenge for others. At the same time, many of his classmates suggest ideas in discussion periods that challenge his wits. Topics range—literally, at least in social studies and science—all over the world and all over the universe.

Fred has a special friend in the class, another boy who shares some of the many hobbies that Fred enjoys. These activities, pursued after school and on weekends, require creativity and imagination, or discussion, shared problem-solving, shared collections, or music, but make few physical demands. However, Fred has many interests, and many other friends. At school, he takes part in all of his class's physical education activities, though in his wheelchair. Many of these activities are done by pairs, or sometimes groups of three or four, and no one ever needs to be "assigned" to Fred. Everyone seems to know what the limits of his "partial participation" will be and accepts them.

Handicapped children who are gifted and talented, like Karen and Fred, place the issue of *appropriate education,* as mandated by P.L. 94–142, into a particularly sharp focus. In both their situations, educational planners have attempted to provide for their special abilities as well as their disabilities. Although Fred is not involved in a special program for gifted children, the classroom approach, for Fred and other students, represents optimal use of the concept of educational enrichment. Karen, however, receives special out-of-class services while her mainstream placement is accelerated. In both their situations, the efforts have been to provide education that is appropriate to the special abilities they demonstrate, and meets the special needs associated with their disabilities.

Does appropriate education, then, necessarily mean optimal education for a handicapped student? To some extent, that question has been addressed by the courts. The most widely publicized court case was that of *Rowley v. Hendrick Hudson Board of Education,* the first case related to P.L. 94–142 that was heard by the U.S. Supreme Court. At issue was whether or not Amy Rowley's school district should be required to provide a sign language interpreter for Amy when she was in school, as a *related service* defined under P.L. 94–142. Amy was fully mainstreamed in her third grade classroom and was a good student. Due to her hearing loss, however, she was able to comprehend only about 60 percent of the language content in her classroom. In other words, she was missing nearly half of what her classmates heard. In spite of this disadvantage, Amy was achieving above the median (midpoint) level of her class. This meant that her achievement exceeded that of more than half her classmates. On this basis, the Court ruled that the school was not required to provide an interpreter, since the evidence indicated that Amy was already receiving an appropriate education.

Presumably, a student performing better than at least half the other students in the class, despite what she missed within the communicative context of school, would be able to achieve far more (and experience less frustration) if she could understand everything that was being said. But, according to this precedent, *appropriate* is not interpreted by the courts to mean best, that is, the educational program through which a handicapped student's achievement can be maximized. The evidence that she could succeed as well as she did within a mainstream classroom was determined by the Court to imply that she was receiving an appropriate education. The ruling does not suggest that interpreter services for hearing impaired children do not have to be provided if they are needed. Instead, the position reflected concerning the definition of *appropriate education* is a more conservative one than many advocates for handicapped children would like. It is entirely possible that future cases could alter this conservative position in the direction of defining appropriate as optimal, rather than as adequate. Clearly, advocates for children of superior learning potential (as Amy would seem to be) would not be satisfied with the position that these children are being appropriately educated as long as their achievement levels rank them above the midpoint when compared to their peers. However, Amy's case was not considered on the basis of the question: what is an appropriate education for a gifted and talented student? The due process provisions of P.L. 94–142 do not yet provide for that consideration.

PARENTS OF YOUNG CHILDREN WHO
ARE GIFTED AND TALENTED

The Rowley case may inspire parents of gifted and talented children to advocate more strenuously for public policies that mandate a definition of appropriate education more congruent with the position of the field of gifted education, as well as with the recommendations for school reform such as those of the Carnegie Commission. Clearly, parents of children who are both gifted and handicapped can be expected to advocate for education responsive to their child's special abilities, as well as his or her disabilities. As has been noted, however, despite stereotypes to the contrary, most parents of young gifted children have typically not been aggressive or militant in the policy arena, in contrast to parents of young children with handicaps.

Nevertheless, parents have played a most important role in stimulating and fostering the development of young children of unusual ability. Parental support and nurturance of special gifts during the early childhood years appear to be critically important in influencing the extent to which gifted children develop their special abilities and achieve to a degree commensurate with their potential (Bloom, 1985). A child's parents are always, potentially, his or her best resources; that is certainly the case with young children of unusual potential. No school program can provide the ongoing encouragement, discovery opportunities, sharing, modeling, and reinforcement that parents can provide. Programs for young gifted and talented children can help by:

> Enabling parents to better understand their gifted child.
> Encouraging parents to stimulate their child's development in the areas in which he or she demonstrates special potential while providing support in all other areas as well.
> Providing information and counsel concerning child management and motivation to support parents in enabling their child both to contribute optimally and to have positive feelings about herself or himself.
> Enabling parents to be effective advocates for their child.

In special programs such as RAPYHT (Karnes et al., 1982), family involvement and parent-educator partnership are central, emphasizing an approach that is individualized, based on the needs of families as well as children, and responsive to family needs. The fact that RAPYHT serves young children who are both gifted and handicapped does not imply that family involvement and partnership are important only if the young gifted child also has a disability. Additionally, parent involvement and parent-professional teamwork are just as important for young gifted children participating in typical mainstream programs as opposed to special programs. As noted previously, by far the majority of young gifted children are in the "mainstream," rather than in special programs.

For teacher and parent to communicate effectively is, of course, always important. However, it is not as easy as one might imagine to maintain shared perceptions of the child, as well as of the child within each of the two contexts, home and school. There is an old story about the teacher who established instant rapport with parents by beginning her open house greeting by making the following promise: she would believe just half of what their child said happened at home if the parents agreed to believe only half of what their child described as happening at school.

The point of this story is not that children are either liars or inherently cunning manipulators. Rather, it is to underscore two very important realities:

1. The concerned teacher, like the child's own parents, cares very much about the child.
2. Both teachers and parents necessarily have a perspective that is based upon the unique context of their own interactions with the child.

These concerns, and the importance of effective and open communication, may be even greater when gifted children are involved. From the parents' perspective, there is real, and frequently warranted, fear that their child's special abilities will not be recognized and nurtured in school. From the teacher's perspective, there may be the suspicion that parents just want to push the child inordinately and inappropriately, sacrificing his or her "child-ness" (Elkind, 1981), possibly exploiting the child to enhance their own self-esteem and meet their own status needs. Both of these views imply stereotypes: the "pushy parent" and the "mediocre teacher," who is both unchallenged and unchallenging. Like all stereotypes, they are dangerous. They can interfere with the process of individual persons coming to know each other as such, in order to create a relationship and establish the quality of communication that can enable both to help the child optimally. Wendy Roedell (1986) has effectively described the problem and emphasized the importance of preventing or correcting it:

> . . . frequently, parents and teachers end up in a concommunication standoff. The parent wants to be sure the teacher knows about the child's abilities, and begins to tell the teacher all the wonderful things that the child can do. Defensively, the teacher thinks that the parent has an unrealistic view of the child, and proceeds to explain all of the child's flaws. The parent, thinking that the teacher has overlooked the child's real strengths, continues to explain while the teacher continues to describe how the child's handwriting, social skills, and perhaps particular academic abilities are not up to par. The teacher may not have seen the extent of the child's real abilities in the classroom. Parents, on the other hand, may not have a good understanding of how their child responds in a group learning situation. Both parent and teacher have a great deal to learn from each other, and this learning can only benefit the child. (p. 26)

SUMMARY

The diversity among young children in early childhood programs is attributable in part to the wide range of abilities, in various areas, that is typically represented. The term gifted and talented is used with reference to those children of unusually high potential, and/or of unusually high level of accomplishment, in general intellectual ability, specific academic area, social and leadership abilities, creativity, or areas of artistic endeavor. Although the importance of recognizing and encouraging unusual "gifts" in children has been stressed throughout history, efforts to do so in the schools have tended to wax and wane. The notion that gifted children will "make it" and even excel under any circumstances is erroneous. The belief that gifted students usually tend to be odd, eccentric, not adept socially, and physically awkward is equally mistaken. However, we cannot assume that all gifted students are well adjusted, at peace with themselves, socially confident, and good at everything they do. This so-called "Terman myth" may be nearly as inaccurate, unfair, and potentially dangerous as those myths that involve the opposite stereotypes. In fact, gifted children are unique individuals with unique characteristics and needs, strengths and weaknesses. Collectively, they represent a group "at risk" to the extent that their individuality is not respected and their personal and social needs, as well as their special abilities, are not recognized and provided for appropriately.

In the early childhood years, the vast majority of this group of exceptional children are in the educational mainstream. Whether for them that represents the least restrictive environment, however, depends upon the appropriateness of what is provided for their unique needs. Programs and approaches that provide challenge, nurture diversity and divergent ways of thinking, and enable children to learn at their own pace are more congruent with the needs of these children—indeed, of all children—than those that require lockstep progression, stifle originality and creativity, and impose constraints on individual initiative. For many young gifted children, complementary or in some instances alternative programs may be critical to the full development of their abilities.

Identification of gifted children in the early years is generally especially difficult; however, certain groups of children are especially "under-identified." These include minority children, those of low-income families, and those with handicapping conditions. For the last of these, provisions may be made in school based on their disability but often not based on their ability. Even children who have severe disabilities may be gifted in one or more of the areas that need to be nurtured in school. Like all other children with disabilities, however—and like all gifted children who do not have disabilities—they need to experience social situations and opportunities appropriate to their age.

Like parents of young children with handicaps, parents of gifted children have often been misunderstood, underestimated, and even feared by professionals. Effective communication and teamwork between home and school can be maintained, and "stand-offs" and mutual distrust avoided, if teachers recognize and respect the fundamental need, right, and prerogative of parents to advocate what is best for their child.

PART III

Teaching in an Integrated Early Childhood Classroom: Issues in the Mainstream

CHAPTER 10

Teaching the Individual Child

A philosophy of integrated teaching primarily stresses respect for the individuality of each child, and the practice of integrated teaching is successful to the degree that it accommodates diversity among children. Children with diverse characteristics and needs can be effectively socially integrated within a classroom to the extent that favorable and receptive attitudes exist and that the social behavior of individual members can be accommodated within a range of acceptability expected by peers and adults. That implies the need for planning, preparation, and effective communication. These areas have been addressed in previous chapters and are summarized in specific application strategies in Chapter 11: *Working with the Group*. The focus of this chapter is *instructional integration,* through which differentiated learning objectives and teaching methods (that is, instruction geared to the specific needs of individual children) can be achieved.

There is no question that instructional integration of handicapped students within the mainstream situation is most feasible if there is a reasonable *cognitive match* between the handicapped student and the group. However, that does not imply that a child described as "severely handicapped" would not be considered for mainstream participation for instruction. For many children with severely impaired vision, hearing, mobility, or communication the regular classroom is not only the *least restrictive* environment, it is clearly the environment that is most appropriate to their learning abilities. In addition, for some of these children, additional options appropriate to the interests and abilities of gifted learners need to be found, as discussed in Chapter 9.

However, a child with severe mental retardation is far less likely to be served appropriately within a mainstream situation for instructional purposes. For this child, integrated experiences are essential, but the regular academic curriculum is less likely to be appropriate. Generally, self-contained classes *that are located within typical schools,* permitting contact, communication, and social integration with nonhandicapped peers, represent the least restrictive environment for children with significantly impaired cognitive functioning (Snell & Renzaglia, 1986). For other young handicapped children, indeed for the vast majority, the issue involves integration of teaching strategies that are responsive to individual differences in skill level, learning style, emotional needs, and social behavior.

We must not confuse diagnostic classification with educational functioning. Probably the best example that can be noted in this context is Down syndrome. In the past, Down syndrome was associated with severe mental retardation; when the classification "trainable mental retardation" was used in schools, children with Down syndrome were typically described as constituting the largest diagnostic classification within this group (e.g., Gearhart & Litton, 1975). However, we now know that many children and adults with Down syndrome are capable of much higher levels of cognitive functioning than had been previously assumed (e.g., Hanson, 1981; Hayden & Haring, 1977; Snell & Renzaglia, 1986). Children with Down syndrome are often excellent candidates for mainstreaming, especially in early childhood programs. These beginnings often lead to continued mainstream participation. Needs for additional resource assistance may continue, but these can be addressed even for children in the regular classroom.

CASE HISTORY 10.1:   SALLY

Sally, a girl with Down syndrome, was enrolled in an early intervention program when she was about 18 months old. Over the next year or so, she responded very well both to staff members and to the other children. She had some motor delay, and particular needs were apparent in language and communication skills; she showed excellent progress in both areas, as well as in the group classroom activities. She appeared to be an excellent candidate for transition to a nursery classroom in the same building that, up to that time, had not enrolled a child with Down syndrome. A gradual transition process was implemented. Since Sally was one of two preschoolers with handicaps making the transition, a resource teacher provided

initial assistance in the classroom. However, it was soon apparent that Sally was able to participate in all classroom activities without special assistance from the resource teacher. Also, she was readily accepted by the other children.

Sally's mother, Mrs. Faye, went directly to their neighborhood elementary school during the spring preceding Sally's kindergarten year. She met with the principal and discussed Sally's abilities, as well as Down syndrome with him. She told him about Sally's successful experiences in the regular preschool and conveyed her teacher's belief that Sally should and could be placed in a regular half-day kindergarten class with her typical peers. The principal agreed, and he asked Mrs. Faye to observe each of the two kindergarten classes and request the teacher for Sally that she thought would be better able to provide for her needs within the regular kindergarten classroom. Mrs. Faye observed and talked with both teachers and, before leaving the building that same day, had requested that Sally be enrolled in Ms. Stiles' class.

However, the following week, Mrs. Faye received a call from the district's school psychologist, who told her that the principal had been in error. He explained that "kids like Sally" were bused to a nearby school district that provided a very good program for children with severe and multiple handicaps. Mrs. Faye indicated that she was quite familiar with that program, but that she and her husband had decided that Sally should continue her schooling with nonhandicapped peers, as she had done for the past three years. She also stated that they would be interested in any support services the psychologist could arrange, such as speech and language therapy and occupational therapy, during the half-day that Sally would not be in kindergarten. At that point, the psychologist suggested that the best thing to do was to test Sally and proceed from there. Although he indicated that the district would provide the multifactored assessment prescribed by law, at no cost to the Fayes, Mrs. Faye expressed a preference to arrange for the testing to be provided by a multidisciplinary team in a community agency that had been involved previously. The agency team was presented with the reason for the referral and agreed to provide the multifactored assessment. Sally was quite cooperative and scored well in most areas. The results were forwarded to the district, and a placement meeting was arranged. An agency representative, Sally's preschool teacher, the kindergarten teacher, the psychologist, and a school administrator,

as well as Mr. and Mrs. Faye were present. The group decided that Sally would attend half-day regular kindergarten, a plan strongly endorsed by both teachers, and would ride the school bus with the other children as well. However, speech and language services and occupational therapy would be provided by the agency during the afternoons.

In the fall, when Sally began kindergarten, Mrs. Faye volunteered in the classroom twice a week and worked in the school library one day each week. Initially, everything went very well. However, in March, the kindergarten teacher became ill and missed two months of school. During that time, the Fayes approached the school psychologist, suggesting that they saw the need for a full-time aide for the substitute teacher. They offered to hire the aide themselves for the remainder of the year, or until Ms. Stiles returned, both in order to help Sally and to emphasize to the school administration that they were cooperative and helpful parents who were concerned about the other children as well as their own child.

Due to Ms. Stiles' extended absence, Sally's experience was not everything that either the Fayes or the school personnel thought it could have been. However, they all did learn to work together for Sally, and the provision of the aide did ensure that Sally's classroom participation was facilitated more effectively.

Prior to the beginning of the next year, the Fayes attended a placement meeting. With the strong support of the school psychologist and three agency staff members, they prepared a set of goals for the year. The Fayes requested that Sally repeat half-day kindergarten in the morning and that she attend a resource room program for additional help, as well as speech and language services, in the afternoon. The recommendation was acceptable to all, and Sally made good progress under this plan.

INTEGRATED TEACHING AND THE CRITERION
OF DEVELOPMENTAL APPROPRIATENESS

Clearly, the teacher is the key to successful integration of young handicapped and nonhandicapped children. A review of research on early mainstreaming published under the auspices of the Federal government in 1975 (the year in which P.L. 94–142 was signed into law) concluded that ". . . the ability and attitude of the teacher appears to be the most important factor in the success of an integrated program" (Wynne, Ulfelder, & Dakof, 1975, p. 75). It is the *teacher* who must structure the environment, adapt the materials, determine the child's optimal mode of learning, initiate desired responses from the children, and reinforce responses that should be encouraged. This may seem to imply a great deal of responsibility for the teacher, but in fact it simply represents recognition of the central role *always* played by the teacher in early childhood programs.

Providing individualized, structured, and carefully planned learning experiences is essential to the successful integration of children with special needs into early childhood programs (Tawney, 1981). For teachers with a developmental orientation, however, such individualization is only natural. Such an approach enables you as teacher to identify and appropriately provide for every child's unique strengths and needs. In good quality early childhood programs, children are not expected to move from level to level as a group; instead, progress is based on individual accomplishment. Provision is made to ensure opportunities for success geared to each child's specific strengths, and areas of difficulty and challenge for each child are identified and appropriately addressed.

As we have suggested throughout this book, the individuality of needs for both handicapped and nonhandicapped children is based on the uniqueness of each child and the uniqueness of the early childhood period itself. This has not been adequately recognized in the preparation of teachers for both regular and special education, as evidenced in the very fact of the distinction made between these two areas. "School personnel think and operate in terms of regular personnel and programs for 'regular needs' students and special personnel and programs for 'special needs' students" (Stainback & Stainback, 1984, p. 66).

The distinction between regular and special education is an artificial one, especially (although not exclusively) in the early childhood years. The reality is that most early childhood programs expect children to mature at varying rates during these years of rapid, and uneven, physical, mental, and social development. These differences, and the resulting differences in children's skills, are accommodated within the curriculum (Moyer, Egertson, & Isenberg, 1987). In fact, because of the rapid development associated with the early childhood period, the "normal" range is much broader than at upper grade levels (Cook & Armbruster, 1983). In addition, the methods and materials usually found in preschoool or kindergarten classrooms are conducive to the development of all young children. Exploration, manipulation, expression, repetitive and self-regulated practice, sharing, and active involvement provide opportunities for teachers to ensure that meaningful interaction occurs between handicapped and nonhandicapped children, to a greater degree than may be possible at upper levels.

Chronological age-appropriateness has been increasingly stressed as a key element in placements and activities for students with handicaps. It has been necessary to highlight this criterion especially for older students and adults because, in the past, many had been provided instruction and leisure activities inappropriate to their age. As explained in Chapter 3, that was a major limitation of a developmental model as a framework for teaching students with handicaps, for it implied that many of these students should be viewed as functioning at a level that was equated with that of significantly younger typical students. There is a logic in integrating handicapped children in early childhood programs based on similiarities in developmental levels in order to minimize discrepancies between children with handicaps and their classmates, and enhance social, as well as instructional, integration (Peck et al. 1978). Children more readily tend to imitate those who are only somewhat more advanced, rather than much more advanced, in their cognitive, communication and social play skills (Guralnick & Paul-Brown, 1977). Thus, it may be reasonable in specific instances for a child with developmental delays to represent the upper end of a chronological age continuum typically found in a preschool, kindergarten, or primary class. However, for the child to be substantially older would not usually represent developmentally appropriate placement.

The typical presence of an age continuum, rather than rigid age homogeneity, in early childhood programs and the expectation of child diversity rather than sameness are two key factors that make age-appropriate integration especially feasible in early childhood. Stainback and Stainback (1985) contrasted two sets of assumptions about learners which, on the one hand, interfere with mainstreaming and, on the other hand, facilitate mainstreaming:

> 'All students of the same chronological age are ready to be taught the same objectives,' vs. 'Students vary from one another in regard to the age at which they are ready to learn specified objectives.'
>
> 'All students require the same amount of time (i.e., an academic year) to master the predesignated objectives,' vs. 'Students vary from one another in regard to the rate at which they learn given objectives.'
>
> 'All students can master the predesignated objectives for the grade level across all curriculum areas during the same years,' vs. 'Students vary within themselves in regard to how fast they progress through the objectives in different curriculum areas' (p. 147)

Remember that the presence of a handicapping condition does not, in itself, imply developmental delay. And certainly not all handicapped children experience difficulty in meeting the cognitive and personal-social demands of the preschool, kindergarten, or primary program. Similarly, children who do have difficulty vary widely in their needs. This is also true among children who have the same type of handicapping condition, such as Down syndrome, cerebral palsy, or hearing impairment. At one time, special education teaching methodology reflected the assumption that certain instructional approaches were indicated for specific "types" or "categories" of exceptionality (Safford, 1983). We now recognize the wide variability within all categories. Knowing the handicap "label" in no way dictates the teaching approach. In general, young children with special needs are appropriately taught to the degree that: (1) developmentally appropriate practices for young children characterize the program, and (2) their individual characteristics, rather than the "type" of exceptionality they present, influence any special provisions that are made.

WHAT IS REQUIRED OF THE TEACHER?

As with any teacher, the most important requisite is a positive attitude toward the child. Certainly teaching disabled children can elicit particular kinds of emotional stress, just as teaching any young children can. Being aware of potential negative feelings—and of how to turn them in a constructive direction—is the first step in learning how to cope. White and Phair (1986) have identified some of the emotional traps we may find in working with handicapped children.

1. *Denying the child's problem helps neither teacher nor child.* Instead, identify the specific problem area and work to find specific solutions.
2. *Feelings of sadness are not productive.* Instead, identify the positive aspects of the situation, especially what the child can do and what progress has been made.
3. *Anger is nonproductive,* if sometimes understandable. Instead, seek out the joy in the child's accomplishments.
4. *Guilt is not productive.* Instead, take pride in the help you can provide the child.
5. *Fear for the child reflects our own insecurities.* Instead, improve your competence by acquiring more relevant knowledge, planning carefully, and implementing and monitoring the effects of your planned interventions systematically.
6. *Overprotection.* This limits the child's opportunities to participate in learning activities, to gain competence, and to enhance self-esteem. Instead, identify what the child can do and provide assistance only when and where needed.
7. *Defensiveness is nonproductive.* Rather than regarding the suggestions of parents or fellow professionals as implied criticisms, be open to suggestions and alternative ideas.
8. *Jealousy and feelings of competition result from defensiveness.* These tendencies can be effectively counteracted by a team ap-

proach characterized by sharing of insights, mutual observation, and mutual respect.

9. *Frustration is natural and understandable.* It can be productively dealt with by maintaining a focus of attention on the children, rather than ourselves: "By reaffirming our commitment to the handicapped child we can put other problems in perspective" (White & Phair, 1986, p. 47).

10. *Exhaustion.* This indicates that we all have the need for opportunities to relax and to have other interests.

11. *Fatalism.* This sometimes results if we concentrate on things that are beyond our control, such as "home conditions," or biological limitations imposed upon the child. Instead, maintain hope and identify and strive for those things that we can do.

Knowing what actual knowledge and skills are required for "regular" teachers to work effectively with special needs students in mainstream classes involves identifying knowledge and skills that are different from those needed to be effective with all students. In early childhood education, authors (e.g., Allen, 1980; Safford, 1978) have suggested that teachers of handicapped children demonstrate certain competencies that are *generic*. That is, they represent skills that all early childhood educators need and can reasonably be expected to demonstrate, and they are not associated specifically with handicapping conditions. This does not mean that individuals who have specific expertise do not need to be involved. Instead, the role of the teacher needs to be defined based on two fundamental assumptions: (1) all children have individual characteristics to which early childhood classroom programs must be responsive, and (2) teachers work as key team members, and some young children's special needs imply consultative, supportive, or complementary contributions from other team members.

Guidelines for Regular Early Childhood Teachers

Generally, teachers should:

1. Possess knowledge of both processes and sequence of children's development in all domains (physical and motor development, cognitive development, language development, and social and emotional development), and be aware of atypical, as well as typical, patterns of development.

2. Be able to recognize symptoms and indicators of possible developmental and learning problems in young children.

3. Be able to apply specific procedures for observing and recording behavior of individual children.

4. Be able to apply informal procedures in diagnosing educational problems within the classroom setting.

5. Be able to identify specific requirements for children's effective social and instructional participation, both in the present

classroom environment and the anticipated next educational environment.

6. Be able to prepare long-term goals and short-term objectives that are developmentally appropriate and also consistent with an individual child's style of learning and observed strengths and weaknesses.

7. Be able to structure the classroom environment to adapt to specific needs of individual children.

8. Understand the philosophy that underlies the curriculum model in use.

9. Be able to develop a trusting relationship with children through effective communication and positive expectations.

10. Be able to enhance positive interactions between children of varying levels of skills and abilities.

11. Be familiar with and able to access and use effectively appropriate resource persons in the school and community.

12. Be able to recruit, train, and work cooperatively with paraprofessionals, such as teaching assistants, and classroom volunteers, including parents or community persons.

13. Be able to listen reflectively to and communicate effectively with parents and to develop and implement strategies for parent involvement that are responsive to the individual needs of parents.

14. Be able to facilitate children's learning of those social skills necessary for optimal integration, such as initiating and responding appropriately in conversations with peers; participating in group activities; following directions and classroom routines; and adjusting to delayed feedback and reinforcement.

15. Be able to initiate a formal referral process when indicated.

16. Be able to synthesize and apply child study information based on assessments conducted by other professionals and classroom procedures identified on a child's IEP or recommended by other professionals or parents.

Specific applications of these principles have been illustrated through discussion and examples throughout Part II. Two key areas, working with parents and using resources, are addressed more comprehensively in Chapters 12 and 13. The following portion of this chapter summarizes certain principles and practices that are critical to an individualized approach. The chapter concludes with examples illustrating technical skills that are frequently essential in implementing an individualized plan for teaching: systematic observation and use of classroom data. This is preceded by a discussion of social-emotional development problems that are encountered often in early childhood classrooms.

PRINCIPLES OF INSTRUCTIONAL INTEGRATION

We can summarize the general principles of instructional integration in four major areas: philosophy and goals of the program; the physical environment of the classroom; the social environment of the classroom; and the development and implementation of planning for individualized teaching.

Program Philosophy and Goals

Well-articulated goals and objectives are important attributes of quality early childhood programs, whether they have been designed primarily as intervention-oriented or as programs for typical children in which children with special needs are also served (Guralnick, 1982). According to Guralnick, in a program implementing a mainstreaming plan: (1) the fundamental structure and philosophy of the program should remain basically the same; (2) the developmental needs of all children, handicapped and nonhandicapped, should be met; and (3) the program must be compatible with the values of integration. These include promoting awareness of and respect for the rights and contributions of others and the valuing of human diversity.

Physical Environment and Instructional Materials

Examples of "physical and cognitive adaptations in the classroom" (Blacher-Dixon, Leonard, & Turnbull, 1981, p. 236) that may be indicated based on the needs of children with certain handicapping conditions were presented in Part II. However, handicapped and nonhandicapped children typically will use the same instructional and play materials. You will seldom find it necessary or appropriate to introduce materials into the classroom specifically for the use of the handicapped child alone, other than prosthetic items he or she might use, and even those should be used no more than is necessary, so that the child's "differentness" is not highlighted (Hart, 1981). Rather than special materials, what may be required is modifying and adapting certain items, based on the specific needs and functioning characteristics of individual children (Ross, 1982). Most adaptations of the physical environment indicated to insure safety, access, and maximum participation for children with handicapping conditions are also appropriate and beneficial for nonhandicapped children. The types of materials, how they are arranged, and how they are to be used should be developmentally appropriate for young children in order to follow two integration guidelines suggested by Blacher-Dixon et al. (1981): "provision of multisensory learning stimuli and experiences" and "focus on independence and exploration of the environment" (p. 236).

Social Environment of the Classroom

Although the group and social integration are the focus of the following chapter, they cannot be separated from consideration of effective instructional integration of the individual child. In fact, specific strategies involving peers to support individualized instructional programming for handicapped children are described in Chapter 11. Two of the guidelines suggested by Blacher-Dixon et al. (1981, p. 236) to support successful integration in early childhood programs directly involve the social climate of the classroom. They are: *promotion of peer tolerance for and acceptance of all children* and *promotion of social interaction*.

Among the instructional practices specifically involving peer interaction described in greater detail in Chapter 11 is the use of *cooperative activities* (Johnson & Johnson, 1981), which involve shared activity in pursuit of a common goal. Stainback, Stainback, Courtnage, & Jaben (1985) note that these activities, by their nature, promote interaction and require students to coordinate efforts if the goal is to be reached. They also note an important point with regard to individual differences made by other authors (Slavin, Madden, & Leavey, 1984): "Cooperative learning can be used as a method to bring students of various achievement and intellectual levels together in a positive way, while at the same time allowing each student to work at his/her own individual level and pace" (Stainback et al., 1985, p. 146). Thus, paradoxically, group activities can be effective strategies for individualization.

Instructional Plan

Individualization requires the integration of individual plans developed for specific children with the overall plan for the classroom group. The latter represents a key area with which all teachers are familiar: unit plans that are translated into daily lesson plans. Such plans are most appropriate and effective when they are responsive to the differential needs of individual children, rather than following a pre-established curriculum guide. In any case, classroom activities provide the *context* within which individualized experiences are possible and individual children's behavior is guided and monitored. The classroom instructional plan identifies the *why* (i.e., general instructional objectives, as well as the *what* (what activity and with what materials), *when* (schedule and sequence), *where* (e.g., specific centers), and *how* (mode of presentation, etc.) The additional important consideration is, of course, *who* will engage in what activity, with what materials, specific adaptations or special instructional procedures.

Examples of specific instructional procedures might include certain pre-planned cues or prompts to be used with a specific child, specification in advance of a desired response identified as an instructional target for the child, and provision of a specific reinforcing consequence. This suggests an individual plan that is implemented in various classroom contexts, to be reviewed regularly and, if appropriate, revised, based on systematic recording of the child's response to instructional intervention. Such a plan might be developed to address initially just one of the numerous areas of learning considered important for the child in the classroom (Halle & Sindelar, 1982).

An IEP, legally required for a handicapped student, has two fundamental limitations for the regular classroom:

1. It specifies goals and objectives in those areas in which the child is to be provided special education and therefore may not include areas for which instruction is provided in the regular classroom. (Some children who are fully mainstreamed may not have an IEP.)

2. The goals and objectives on the IEP are stated much more generally than the objectives teachers need to establish for daily classroom instruction. The educational plan has to be translated into a day-to-day instructional plan.

Individual plans may be developed in order to address concerns in the area of social behavior. The use of such plans is most effective if target behaviors are identified specifically so that data can be recorded systematically. This is particularly true when specific behavioral targets can be defined objectively, directly observed within natural settings, translated into specific intervention plans, and recorded across multiple data points (Hayden & Edgar, 1977, p. 84). Such targets are identified to be maintained, accelerated, or decelerated (Alberto & Troutman, 1982). Further discussion and examples illustrative of such plans are provided later in this chapter.

PROBLEM AREAS FREQUENTLY ENCOUNTERED IN YOUNG CHILDREN

Young children frequently exhibit certain kinds of behavior that, especially if it is intense in form, may lead observers to infer that there is a "behavior problem." In fact, these kinds of behaviors are typical of all young children. They do not necessarily lend themselves to intervention or supportive guidance; each child is unique and working with any child in the classroom or center requires individual study and problem-solving. We cannot emphasize enough the importance of effective communication, cooperation, and, optimally, consistency among parents, teachers, and other professionals.

Separation Difficulty

Separating from a parent or other familiar caregiver is difficult for all young children. In fact, we should be concerned about the child who moves from the care of one adult to another without protest, worry, or hesitation. Initial insecurity in new surroundings, with one or more new adults, may indicate the child's security in the love and care of those who are familiar.

When separation difficulties move into separation problems, the parent's or caregiver's role is often important. Especially in this era of widespread outside-the-home child care, we should not undervalue the relationship of child and parent by assuming that separation is routine. Be willing to suggest and support a parent's gradual withdrawal and to provide reassurance to the child. A number of things can help: verbal assurance, a reminder to the child of the routines of the day, presentation of a familiar doll or toy, providing a "buddy" for the child, even letting the child "cry it out" if that plan is mutually agreed upon between parent and teacher in an effort not to reinforce undesirable behaviors.

Extreme Fearfulness

Worries, fears, and anxieties are universal in early childhood. Growing up involves the constant struggle to gain mastery over frightening feelings, to develop confidence and trust, to venture into new and challenging situations, and to work toward the accomplishment of goals at home, at school, with peers or alone, at work or at play. Fears are inevitable and in fact essential to the development of a child's coping abilities; this is as true for children with disabilities or handicaps as it is for "normal" children. For some children, however, managing such feelings is particularly difficult—either at specific times and under specific circumstances, or most of the time. Indications that a child is having such difficulties include sleep disturbances, clinging behavior, extreme timidity, speech reticence, and even, paradoxically, aggressive behavior, noncompliance, and tantrums. Such behaviors are not necessarily indications of more severe behavioral disabilities; in fact, they affect virtually all children at some point.

Generally, children's fears are mastered through internal, not external resources. Whatever the circumstances, close communication between parent and teacher is, of course, essential. Significant adults can help a child to use his or her own coping resources effectively. The first requirement is to respect the reality of the child's feeling and convey that respect to the child through words and actions.

Shyness and Reticence

Virtually every classroom contains children who do not join freely in the group; their behaviors may range from simple timidity or shyness to serious withdrawal. In our frustration in dealing with such behavior, we may attempt counterproductive strategies: forcing or embarrassing the child, ignoring the child, asking why he or she won't take part. Instead, the child might be allowed a "safe place" from which to observe and gradually move closer. Increasing the child's social participation is a matter of building trust and self-confidence, in order to enhance self-esteem (Cook & Armbruster, 1983).

Children identified as handicapped are often provided specific training and practice in initiating social contact with their peers and interacting with them (Strain, 1987). Children not so identified can also benefit from guidance in this area. Dr. Alice Honig (1987) has offered a number of suggestions, including: (1) observing how the child approaches peers, then teaching "door openers;" (2) using stories with which the child can identify; (3) promoting security through predictable routines; (4) encouraging a sense of humor; (5) not forcing children to perform for others; (6) deemphasizing competition; and (7) listening attentively when the child is speaking.

Noncompliance and Self-Control Problems

Young children need to explore, assert autonomy, and make choices. At the same time, in the interests of both child and group, structure and compliance with the instructions of teachers or caregivers are essential. The conflict between autonomy and compliance is a major issue for all toddlers but, as Alice Honig points out (1985b), the conflict is resolvable. "More harmonious and compliant behaviors will result if adults realize how important a sense of choice and control may be in smoothing the way for a toddler's cooperation" (p. 44). Those children having difficulty with self-regulation present special challenges within the child care setting (Howes & Olenick, 1984).

Noncompliance with adult direction can be addressed more productively if compliance is viewed not as an end in itself but as a means to the goal of self-control and self-regulation. Episodes of difficult, "acting out" behavior then represent opportunities for helping young children accomplish key developmental tasks—not simply sources of frustration. Honig (1985b) suggests the following strategies for helping children learn prosocial behaviors: (1) socially reinforcing appropriate behaviors; (2) modeling appropriate behaviors; (3) modifying or restructuring the classroom environment; (4) using language in helping the child to understand and mediate emotions; (5) using sociodramatic games; (6) encouraging the child to consider the consequences of alternative actions.

Speculating about whether a child's acting out is "caused" by biological or environmental factors is generally not particularly productive; what is important to remember is that the teacher's response to inappropriate behavior can be critically important in helping the child learn to regulate his or her own behavior. Physical punishment for hostile or aggressive behavior simply serves to model the very kinds of actions we want to reduce. Ignoring hostility or acting out implies acceptance. Clearly, any behavior that might cause injury to anyone should not be tolerated and should be prevented.

Frequently a teacher can prevent acting out epidodes by flexibly modifying routines, groupings of children, or other aspects of the classroom environment in response to "cues" from a child who is having difficulty managing. Modeling, explaining, and reinforcing appropriate behaviors all suggest to the child alternative methods of coping. Recognizing that some children have particular difficulties with self-regulation, Dr. Bettye Caldwell (1977) recommends calm intervention before the behavior escalates; she advises adult calmness, a nonjudgmental approach, and a positive emphasis as most effective in preventing situations from getting out of hand. As Dr. Lillian Katz notes (1984), critical incidents in the classroom that require teacher intervention should prompt you to ask: "What can I be teaching the children in this situation?" Situations in which a child's desires are thwarted or frustrated can provide occasions for helping students learn turn-taking, negotiating, and coping skills, using language as an effective means of resolving differences and of asserting one's rights, and growing in the understanding of principles of justice. Dr. Katz differentiates between "nonprofessional responses," which concentrate on what is happening and "professional responses" which concentrate on what is being learned.

Children's temperaments are likely to influence how others respond to and interact with them. Much research on temperamental differences has grown from the pioneering work of Thomas, Chess, & Birch (1968), which identified three basic temperament "clusters:"

"Easy" children (approachable, predictable, positive in mood).
"Difficult" children (unapproachable, unpredictable, more intense).
"Slow to warm up" children (lower activity and intensity levels, require more time to adapt).

These basic patterns occur in children with and without disabilities; they are not necessarily cues that a child is or is not having behavioral problems.

For some children who present particularly difficult classroom behavior, the kinds of responses suggested above are applicable, but special attention may need to be given to implementing a systematic approach to guide the child's learning of appropriate behavior. Specifically, some system of maintaining a record of behavioral data may be critically important in maintaining an objective focus, specifically defining a behavior problem and an attainable goal, accurately identifying antecedent events and situations likely to trigger inappropriate behavior, determining what interventions and alternative forms of reinforcement elicit desired behavior changes, and providing concrete evidence of progress.

CASE HISTORY 10.2:   JON

Jon was a seven-year-old boy of average stature and pleasant appearance whose communication, self-help, fine motor, and social skills were significantly delayed. He had been diagnosed as autistic. Although nonverbal, Jon would occasionally vocalize loudly. He had begun to use rudimentary signs—mostly one-word, but some word combinations—to label objects and to express his needs, both to his mother and to his special education teacher. He had difficulty remaining seated for more than two or three minutes and was easily distracted, especially when involved in group activity with a few children. He also manifested stereotypic and self-stimulating behavior, such as rubbing his hands together, flapping his arms, and sometimes galloping. Jon displayed advanced gross motor skills. Specific activities he seemed especially to enjoy included: lining objects up in straight lines, playing with balls, running, listening to music, spinning objects, and watching other children, which he would do intently.

His special education class included six children, all with severe communication delays, as well as delays in other areas. All were socially integrated with typical kindergarten, first grade, or second grade groups for recess, lunch, and social activities such as parties or movies. In addition, each was selectively mainstreamed into other activities as individually appropriate.

Jon typically exhibited age-appropriate social behavior at recess and lunch. At other times he vocalized loudly, watched the projector instead of the movie, sat backwards in his chair, and flapped his arms. However, when he was seated with a small group of children (less than five) who were familiar to him, who modeled appropriate behavior and occasionally redirected him (e.g., "Jon, turn around and watch the movie like us") his behavior was observed to improve quickly. Wishing to build upon this evidence of potential, the special education teacher, Jon's parents, the school psychologist, and the teacher of combination

Grade 1–2 class in which he was socially integrated met to consider possible next steps. They reviewed: (1) the present schedule in the Grade 1–2 classroom; (2) Jon's typical "behavior schedule," which indicated that he was usually more interested and participatory in the mornings than in the afternoons; (3) Jon's strengths and sources of enjoyment, as well as his weaknesses and apparent dislikes; and (4) Jon's existing social situation in the Grade 1–2 classroom.

Jon seemed to be generally accepted by the other children, but his loud vocalizations sometimes frightened them. Two younger boys appeared to like him genuinely and would seek him out on the playground and in the lunchroom. For his part, Jon seemed vaguely interested in and responsive to them. The entire class, as well as the teacher, were learning sign language in twice-weekly sessions conducted by the special education teacher and were attempting to communicate with Jon in this manner. There were 21 children in the group, not including Jon, 9 first graders and 12 second graders.

It was decided to place Jon in the mainstream classroom each morning for math, initially for 10 minutes each day, but to be gradually increased to the full 35-minute math period. The morning schedule included reading, math, writing, and one "special" (that is, gym, music, art, etc.) for which Jon was already included. Writing was ruled out since Jon was presently unable to hold a pencil, unable to do work independently in a workbook, and had no concept of letters. In addition, writing was taught in a large group mode for two different levels, so that one group was always working independently. Similarly, Jon had no use for reading as yet, not having a sufficient language base for personal communication, and reading was considered to present situations that would elicit negative behavior.

In math, however, it was age-appropriate to use objects in activities instead of just paper-pencil tasks. He could do something he specifically liked (i.e., lining things up), which would promote positive classroom behaviors (remaining quiet, staying in his seat, attending to tasks.) Also, activities could be made appropriate and enjoyable, both for Jon and for the other children. Jon's parents felt that he showed interest in money, and they were eager to promote that interest at school as well as at home, through counting and learning beginning math concepts for which coins could be used.

Several classroom changes were made in order to accommodate Jon's learning style without restricting the teacher's time or infringing upon other children's learning. The class was divided into small groups, three with six children and four in Jon's group. Each group rotated to different stations, some changed each day, while others were altered each week, for activities such as practicing number writing skills, counting objects, learning one-to-one correspondence, practicing beginning addition or subtraction, etc. In this way, all children moved through the year at a pace equivalent to that achieved through the previous math instructional approach. Activity time at each station was approximately 5–7 minutes. Initially, Jon stayed for two stations, and then gradually increased his time to include five minutes of introductory time, to orient all groups, all station sessions, and 5–10 minutes for general closure. The teacher was free to move about the room, helping and answering questions, and the children were encouraged to talk softly with each other and help each other, as well as to ask the teacher for help. This provided excellent social skills modeling for Jon, as well as helping him to acquire math skills. It did not require him to remain seated, but it did require him to increase on-task behavior.

The work stations consisted of a table, with the work materials in a basket under the table, or of clusters of desks with work materials, or an open area where children could work on the floor or employ gross motor activity, such as counting by walking sequentially to numbers or sets taped to the floor. The teacher and the other children so enjoyed this station arrangement that it was continued long after Jon had advanced to the next grade.

THE ROLE OF ASSESSMENT

Inextricably associated with educational provisions for exceptional children is the concept of assessment. Mandated practices for ensuring that a handicapped child receives a free appropriate public education involve a sequence of assessment processes:

> Screening, to identify children who may possibly be eligible.
> Diagnostic evaluation, to determine an individual child's eligibility, as well as the type of program and related services that are indicated.
> Ongoing instructional assessment.
> Evaluation of the child's progress in achieving goals and objectives written in the IEP.

Screening, as discussed in Chapter 2, is implemented in various ways, by various individuals, and for various purposes. Some screening procedures involve the use of formal, standardized screening tests. Although such tests may be useful, we need to remember that their uses are limited to identifying possible cases. In themselves, screening tests cannot be relied upon for purposes of individual diagnosis or as bases for making decisions about individual children (Meisels, 1985a). The teacher of young children may play a role in screening activities that lead to the identification of special needs. However, screening is a first step toward identification, and ideally involves information concerning diverse areas of children's functioning, obtained through the use of diverse measures and diverse sources.

As was explained in Chapter 2, once a "suspected" handicap has been identified, PL 94–142 is quite explicit that assessment must be: (1) conducted only with informed parental consent; (2) nonbiased and nondiscriminatory; (3) multi-factored; and (4) conducted by professionals with appropriate training and expertise in the respective areas in which assessment data may be needed (i.e., interdisciplinary).

The primary purpose of this phase of the assessment process is to determine a child's eligibility for special services. The assessment data form the basis for specific elements of a child's IEP, including the description of the child's current levels of educational functioning. This description suggests: (1) annual goals and short-term instructional objectives; (2) procedures by which the child's progress will be evaluated in terms of each of the goals and objectives; (3) the related services that will be required; and (4) the extent of the child's participation in regular education.

The teacher may have specific responsibilities for the evaluation of the child's progress which are stipulated in the IEP. However, phase #3 in the assessment sequence listed at the opening of this section, ongoing instructional assessment, is not explicitly prescribed in the IEP. This phase is the responsibility of the teacher to develop, just as any specialists working directly with the child need to maintain their own system for ongoing assessment.

Whereas screening and diagnostic evaluation are likely to involve both norm-referenced and criterion-referenced procedures, ongoing instructional evaluation generally relies exclusively on the latter. Norm-referenced assessment procedures take the form of standardized tests and scales that allow an individual's performance to be compared with other children the same age or at the same grade level. They yield scores in the form of developmental age equivalents or grade equivalents, percentiles, stanines, or quotients. Criterion-referenced procedures may be formal or informal, published or teacher-generated, and are intended to assess an individual's performance in terms of some criterion task or goal. The tests that teachers of older students administer at the end of a unit are examples of criterion-referenced assessment procedures. Many teachers also use a variety of other means for this purpose, including class recitation and discussion, homework assignments, class exercises, science laboratory activities, compositions, and others.

Unlike screening and diagnostic evaluation, ongoing instructional assessment is directly related to teaching. That is, assessment and instruction are interdependent: we identify specific skills to be taught through assessment and then test to determine that the skills have been learned. One way of viewing this process is in terms of a *test-teach* model (Bricker, 1976), in which assessment generates hypotheses for instruction that can be systematically tested in an experimental fashion.

Recently, much interest in the field of special education has focused upon the concept of curriculum-based assessment (Tucker, 1985), a criterion-referenced approach in which the criteria are based explicitly upon the existing curriculum of a school. As defined by Gickling and Thompson (1985),

> Curriculum-based assessment is a methodology used to determine the instructional needs of students based upon their performance within existing course content. As a direct classroom assessment approach, it provides the most readily available and useful source of information. The CBA title, however, is misleading unless one realizes that it is oriented toward instruction as much as assessment. It focuses on how to collect, interpret, and use data in order to impact directly upon instruction. (p. 217)

Criterion-referenced procedures specify some desired "end point," that is, a criterion to be achieved. Nearly always, however, these approaches provide a means for determining the student's present functioning in relation to that criterion, or, alternatively, they allow for the identification of the criterion once the student's present skill level is ascertained. An informal diagnostic approach widely used in early childhood classrooms, variations of Piaget's "clinical method" (Ginsburg & Opper, 1969) is an excellent illustration of the latter strategy. The method that Piaget ultimately developed for use in studying children's thinking ". . . involves posing questions concerning concrete materials, allowing the child to 'answer' by manipulating the materials, if this is at all possible, and. . . . stating questions and pursuing answers in a flexible and unstandardized way" (Ginsburg & Opper, 1969, p. 119).

TASK ANALYSIS

An aspect of criterion-referenced assessment that is very basic to special education practice is *task analysis*. This involves analyzing the component skills of a task that is to be learned, identifying the sequence in which those skills are required, identifying the steps that have already been mastered by an individual student, and then proceeding to teach the remaining skills until, ultimately, the goal is reached. Task analysis may be tailored to fit the learning needs of any child. If a child shows difficulty in learning a task even if it has already been analyzed, the specific step where breakdown in learning occurs can be pinpointed. That step can be reanalyzed, broken into yet smaller steps, and retaught. Applications of task analysis are useful at more independent levels as well. For example, steps in a sequence can be portrayed through photographic slides, or presented through interactive videodisc technology, so that children can be guided by models and also monitor and self-correct successive mastery of steps in a learning sequence. Some typical examples of the application of task analysis with young children follow.

A. Finger Painting

PREPARATION:
    Teacher has sheet of fingerpainting paper and plastic tub of fingerpaint laid out on table in front of seated child. If specific handedness has been determined or is being encouraged, the tub of paint would be placed on the appropriate side (right or left) and toward the top edge of the paper. If handedness has not been determined, the tub of paint might be placed on the right side for half the activity and on the left for half the activity, with the child encouraged to use both hands.

TASK SEQUENCE:
    1. Child reaches forward toward paint with open hand.
    2. Child places fingers in paint.

3. Child lifts hand out of paint tub.
4. Bending at elbow, child pulls hand back to paper.
5. Child moves arm/hand/fingers randomly over paper (or according to teacher directions.)
6. Child repeats steps 1–5 as desired.

B. Snack: Peanut Butter on Bread

PREPARATION:
Child is seated or standing at table. Teacher lays out 1 slice of bread, peanut butter jar (lid off), and table knife.

TASK SEQUENCE:
1. Using right hand (if appropriate) child picks up knife.
2. Using left hand (if appropriate) child holds peanut butter jar steady.
3. Child scoops peanut butter onto knife.
4. Child releases jar with left hand.
5. Child moves left hand down to hold edges of bread slice.
6. Child spreads peanut butter onto bread.
7. Child lays knife down on table.
8. Child picks up bread slice and eats!

C. Zipping a Coat

PREPARATION:
Child (or teacher) puts coat onto child correctly.

TASK SEQUENCE:
1. Child's head is guided (if/as necessary) to watch activity.
2. Left hand holds same side bottom of coat with fingers slightly bent grasping lining and thumb straight on outside of coat pointing toward zipper.
3. With thumb and forefinger of right hand, child grasps zipper pull.
4. Child curls other fingers of right hand along bottom of coat, grasping firmly.
5. Child moves right and left hands, holding coat toward midline of body.
6. Child uses left hand to place zipper bottom into zipper pull.
7. Child slides zipper bottom down into zipper pull.
8. Child maintains firm grasp with left hand.
9. Child maintains thumb/forefinger grasp on zipper pull.
10. Child releases right hand curled fingers from bottom of coat.
11. Child simultaneously gently pulls down bottom of coat with left hand while sliding zipper pull up with right hand.
12. When zipper is pulled all the way up, child releases both hands.

All three of these examples illustrate classroom activities involving fairly complex motor skill sequences. For a young child with significant motor delay or one who experiences difficulty with fine motor coordination, they illustrate assessment-based strategies for teaching complex skills. It is certainly preferable, when other children in the class are participating in these or other activities, for children with significant motor (or other) disabilities, to be enabled to perform the same tasks independently, instead of having someone else do it for them.

Task analysis is one strategy for assessment-based teaching. Although it may be reflected in many aspects of teaching in the early childhood classroom, obviously a "fine-tuned," highly specific analysis is not needed in working with most young children—including most young children with delays or disabilities. Continuous assessment of young children's learning, social behavior, and emotional needs represents a major element of the role of all teachers of young children (Bredekamp, 1987). Much of this assessment is done informally and naturalistically. That is, insights can be obtained based upon ongoing direct observations of children, talking with the child, learning from parents about the child's behavior and accomplishments at home and in the community, and frequently providing specific learning activities that serve as vehicles for assessing and monitoring progress and determining next steps. Each of these can be done in a highly systematic fashion, as needs dictate, in addition to the methods teachers may generally use for observing children in the classroom and maintaining written records of their progress. That is particularly true of observations focused upon individual children in specific learning contexts, among the most critical means of assessment as a guide to planning.

METHODS FOR OBSERVING AND RECORDING IN THE CLASSROOM

Teachers use a variety of methods of observing important events and incidents, ranging from making a mental note of an occurrence involving an individual child, a transaction between children, or a group response to conducting a highly systematic observation of some predetermined action sequence. Methods of recording range from descriptive statements written when time permits to notations of specific behavioral events at the time they occur. It is sometimes possible, and may be important, to capture an activity or activity sequence as it occurs by means of videotape recording for later analysis. That has the obvious advantage of allowing the observer to stop the action to note what is occurring, to replay a sequence of specific actions, to take all the time that might be needed to produce a detailed record of events, or to observe a sequence together with a parent, a teaching colleague, or a resource specialist in order to share insights. The value of such technology in identifying problems and suggesting solutions is well known to football coaches. Videotape recording in classrooms has been a valuable resource in the field of education in three major areas: (1) research, (2) clinical experiences in teacher training, and (3) classroom observation.

Most often, however, classroom observation is done "live"—that is, by someone observing the action as it occurs. That "someone" may be the teacher or it may be another person whose classroom role, at that particular time, is that of observer. The latter has clear advantages and is perhaps more likely to be practicable than we might think. The possibilities for enlisting the assistance of someone to observe include:

A fellow teacher or co-teacher.
A teaching assistant or aide.
A classroom volunteer, such as a community person or an older student.
A child in the classroom itself.
A parent, observing his or her own child.
A college student, preservice teacher, or other field experience participant or volunteer.
A resource specialist or other interdisciplinary team member.
A program supervisor.

Who might represent the most appropriate observer depends first of all on the purpose of the observation. For purposes of this chapter, we are concerned with observation of an individual child, acting within the classroom context. We might be specifically concerned with any of a wide variety of behaviors, including:

The child's response to certain tasks or materials.
Behavior patterns associated with time of day or activity sequence.
How the child approaches or initiates interaction with others.
How the child responds to interactions initiated by others.
Conditions that seem to be related to the child's attention to tasks, attention to and compliance with adult direction, conformity with classroom procedures, rules, and expectations.

Possibly, and sometimes necessarily, the teacher may be the observer, combining that role with the role of arranger, facilitator, guide, questioner, and provider of reinforcement or corrective feedback if needed. Observation procedures must then be physically feasible; that is, done fairly mechanically without diverting other children's or teacher's attention. Some aids have been developed for just this purpose, including a counter that can be worn like a wristwatch or carried in your hand, so that each time the behavior is observed, you can easily push the counter button. Times of observation, time periods, activity contexts, etc., can be predetermined or noted later. If a counter is not available, use other strategies, short of keeping count on full-page data sheets. For example, carry an index card or tape one to a handy surface, even your own clothing.

A *behavior* must be defined so that it can be clearly recognized when it occurs. It is best to focus on a single, specific behavior, at least initially, and to observe during specific, consistent time intervals.

Observation data form the basis for the intervention plan. First, record *base-line* data (that is, behavior as it occurs with no intervention), and then record its frequency once an intervention has been introduced. For example, a child may appear to be out of his seat excessively during the time period for math. In this instance, you would count out-of-seat occurrences during math instruction over several (e.g., three or four) days, until the rate of such behavior appears to be fairly stable. Then, you would initiate whatever intervention seems to be indicated. Selection of the intervention might be based on other observation data, especially observation of the child's response to certain consequences and/or observation of what occurs prior to this problem behavior. As the intervention is introduced, you would count out-of-seat behavior to see whether it decreases in frequency. This information can then be graphed, and the result may be a vivid piece of evidence and indication of positive change that can be shared with others, including parents and even the child herself or himself.

An observation system can be developed for recording a child's social interaction with other children in settings that tend to encourage social interaction with peers and adults, such as on the playground, in large-group discussion, and in small-group activities. The technique involves recording what occurs during an observation, so observation periods (e.g., one minute) are alternated with non-observation periods of the same length. Use of a stopwatch is best to insure time consistency, but that may not be essential if accuracy can be achieved with a digital watch or one with a sweep second hand. Observations might be carried out during ten-minute intervals, so that each observation period would include five data points.

As with other observation procedures, coding can be used to record all important information efficiently. For this purpose, you should note (1) who initiates the interaction, (2) who responds, (3) how interaction is initiated, and (4) whether a response is elicited and, if so, what form it takes. Therefore, each observation might involve the following type of code system:

INITIATOR	RESPONDENT	HOW INITIATED	TYPE OF RESPONSE
S = Subject	S = Subject	V = Verbal	V = Verbal
C = Another child	C = Another child	P = Physical	P = Physical
	T = Teacher	G = Gestural	O = Observational
T = Teacher	#C = More than one child		G = Gestural
	G = Group		NR = No response

To illustrate, in a situation in which the child who is the focus of observation ("Subject") runs over to a small group of children and pushes one of them, and two of those children push the child and ask him what he wants, the observation would be coded: *S   2C   P   VP*. (Subject initiates through a physical act and two children respond both verbally and physically.)

Conducting this type of observation requires:

1. An individual who is available to observe and record on a specific schedule.
2. Clear definitions for each notation (e.g., specifically distinguishing between physical and gestural behaviors initiated, and between physical, gestural, and observational responses).
3. Sufficient practice as well as prior comparison of different observers' codings to insure an acceptable level of agreement, or reliability (e.g., 80 percent agreement).

Data collection procedures can be most readily and effectively carried out in the classroom if they are carefully planned and sufficiently simple so as to be manageable. Use of simple forms for recording data, keeping the forms accessible, using mechanical aids such as counters when feasible, and conducting data collection at feasible time periods enable the teacher to manage a data system without interrupting the normal flow of classroom activity (Strain, McConnell, & Cordisco, 1983). Many teachers may find data keeping awkward and somewhat unwieldy at first; however, with practice, it becomes routine and almost second nature.

For certain purposes, someone other than the teacher may need to be the individual responsible for taking data. That is particularly the case when many different behaviors involving many different individuals are to be coded.

A simpler type of data system can be used to pinpoint specific difficulties with certain learning tasks. For example, if the child is using worksheets, whenever individual help is needed in the classroom, the teacher (or assistant) can simply note with an *X* the specific place on the worksheet (math problem, word, etc.) where assistance was provided. Accumulated worksheets thus provide a running record from which number of times help was provided and type of help required can be charted. These can be used to discuss with a resource teacher the problem areas that are indicated and the remedial approach that might be instituted.

EXAMPLE 1: NED

Ned is a seven-year-old boy who has been diagnosed as autistic, but is verbal and has an IQ within the average range, based on testing. He was mainstreamed into a second grade classroom for math and handwriting. A problem presented was associated with Ned's excessive concern about keeping to a rigid schedule and preoccupation with clocks and time. In class, he would yell out the time every five minutes. Since the class was very large, with 29 pupils, the teacher could not either acknowledge or correct Ned each time this occurred. Therefore, she decided that Ned would keep his own data! The teacher and the other pupils would ignore his behavior. Ned also designed his own data sheet and agreed that, each time he shouted out in class, he would mark an X in a box on the sheet:

Oops! I yelled out.

☐ ☐ ☐ ☐ ☐

☐ ☐ ☐ ☐ ☐

☐ ☐ ☐ ☐ ☐

Initially, if Ned shouted out the time less than five times during math and writing, he was allowed to announce the time, as well as what was next on the schedule, at the end of each class period. The number of times yelling out occurred gradually was reduced to zero.

EXAMPLE 2: PATTY

Patty's situation illustrates how a peer can help with an intervention program by keeping data. Patty, a six-year-old with moderate retardation and corrected vision problems, was mainstreamed into a first grade classroom for language and handwriting, as well as for the "specials" (gym, music, art, and library). Patty had difficulty attending to a task. She seemed to need almost constant redirection in order to complete simple assignments that were well within her capability. Obviously, the teacher could not redirect Patty continuously, and also record data, while working with the rest of the class. The system that was developed solved this logistical problem, and an effective program evolved for Patty to maintain longer periods of attention, so that eventually she required only occasional redirection. For language and handwriting, she was seated at a table with another girl assigned as her "tutor," who was trained by the teacher both to redirect Patty and to use a data sheet to indicate each time she had to intervene:

Subject:
Date:
Time:
    I helped Patty pay attention (tutor tallies below, using / / / marks, each time she redirects student)

EXAMPLE 3: CHARLES

Charles, age five, was fully mainstreamed in a half-day kindergarten program although he was described as presenting severe emotional and behavioral problems, as well as severe language delay, and was considered mildly mentally retarded. Of major concern in the mainstreaming situation was Charles' tendency to be destructive of other children's possessions or play materials. In order to initiate an effective behavioral intervention program, accurate data concerning what the behavior actually was, and where, when, and with whom it occurred were needed. The kindergarten teacher taped an index card at each work or play station in the classroom. She marked the card at the station where Charles was working each time he attempted to destroy another child's work or play materials. The data were used to evaluate the locations and the specific children most frequently targeted. These data were combined with narrative information concerning what happened immediately before and immediately after each incident when those could be observed. It was then possible to attack the problem by focusing on critical situations and modifying antecedent conditions and consequences systematically. The frequency of these incidents was immediately reduced and eventually they were virtually eliminated.

EXAMPLE 4: JANIE

Janie, a seven-year-old girl with cerebral palsy and associated visual impairment, severe language delay, and probably significant mental retardation, was mainstreamed into a regular first grade classroom to participate in story time. Initially, however, problems were presented because of her excitement that led to disruptive behavior. When excited, she would shake her head, wave her arms, and squeal. This was disruptive for the other children, and the teacher could not hold the book to read and show pictures to the children, while providing a physical prompt for Janie and keeping data on the sheet provided for that purpose. It was important to keep regular data so that the resource teacher could carry out a behavior management program within this activity context. The system that was developed solved the problem. The teacher made tallies each day on a piece of wide masking tape stuck on her skirt or pantleg, which could be managed while holding and displaying the story book. What was important to record was not only whether the behavior occurred, but also whether the teacher intervened or Janie herself controlled it as she was being taught to do. The teacher simply noted either of the following:

+ (behavior occurred, teacher intervened)
⊕ (behavior occurred, student controlled without teacher intervention)

Consistent patterns requiring teacher intervention indicated that a change of intervention conditions was needed. Incidents suggesting self-control were related to specific intervention variables, and within a short time, the disruptive responses had virtually ceased.

EXAMPLE 5: GINA

Gina, a six-year-old girl with mild retardation and language delay and multiple forms of seizure disorder, needed observation in order to provide precise information to her doctors for monitoring her medication, and also to help her teachers realize when mild seizure activity actually was occurring. Gina's primary school placement was in a special classroom for children with multiple handicaps, but she was mainstreamed in a regular first grade classroom for language, social studies, music, art, library, recess, and lunch. Her seizure-related behavior was considered the main problem with her mainstreaming placement and the principal obstacle to fulltime participation in the regular classroom. Seizure episodes and behavior suggestive of mild seizure activity occurred as frequently as 26 times daily in school, with a minimum of five recognizable seizures. Similar activity was observed by her foster parents at home.

A system was developed for monitoring Gina's behavior both at school and at home. *Behaviors* rather than seizures were identified, and they were intentionally listed on the data sheet in random order to insure objectivity in observation. In this way, the observer's opinion about the type of seizure that might be occurring would not affect the observation; behaviors that actually occurred would be noted, rather than those thought to be associated with a particular level of seizure. Frequency of observed behaviors was graphed daily and compiled for Gina's doctors on a weekly basis (Figure 10.1).

SUMMARY

Educational practices that are developmentally appropriate in early childhood are those that recognize and respond to the unique characteristics and needs of the individual child within a context of goals and activities responsive to the uniqueness of this developmental period (Bredekamp, 1987). An individualized focus is shared by early childhood educators and by special educators; individualizing the program is not something that is required only for young children who are exceptional. Providing appropriately for children's individual needs requires the use of procedures for determining what those needs are and how they can most

Figure 10.1

DATA SHEET FOR RECORDING GINA'S
SEIZURE-RELATED BEHAVIOR

Student: _____   Observer: _____

Observable Behaviors

1. Check all behaviors observed during each episode.
2. Note time beginning and time ending for each episode.
3. Comments: A) Note what occurred just prior to the episode.
                       B) Note how the child behaved immediately following the episode.
                       C) Any other relative comments and behaviors not listed.

Time Begins:	Time Begins:
Time Ends:	Time Ends:

☐ Staring, does not respond to name.	☐ Staring, does not respond to name.
☐ Eyelids flutter or eyes roll.	☐ Eyelids flutter or eyes roll.
☐ Does not respond to touch.	☐ Does not respond to touch.
☐ Bluish color skin.	☐ Bluish color skin.
☐ Wets or soils pants.	☐ Wets or soils pants.
☐ Labored breathing.	☐ Labored breathing.
☐ Stumbles.	☐ Stumbles.
☐ Jerking of legs.	☐ Jerking of legs.
☐ Chewing movements.	☐ Chewing movements.
☐ Body stiffens briefly.	☐ Body stiffens briefly.
☐ Says she feels sick or "freezing."	☐ Says she feels sick or "freezing."
☐ Shallow breathing.	☐ Shallow breathing.
☐ Walks around as if in a daze.	☐ Walks around as if in a daze.
☐ Frothy saliva around mouth.	☐ Frothy saliva around mouth.
☐ Repeated aimless movement (pulling clothes).	☐ Repeated aimless movement (pulling clothes).
☐ Hoarse cry	☐ Hoarse cry
☐ Trembling of RIGHT arm.	☐ Trembling of RIGHT arm.
☐ Trembling of RIGHT leg.	☐ Trembling of RIGHT leg.
☐ Falls.	☐ Falls.
☐ Whole body convulsions.	☐ Whole body convulsions.
☐ Jerking of arms.	☐ Jerking of arms.
☐ Trembling of LEFT arm.	☐ Trembling of LEFT arm.
☐ Trembling of LEFT leg.	☐ Trembling of LEFT leg.

Comments: Comments:

effectively be addressed. That is the role of assessment. However, this does not imply necessarily that formal tests be used. Especially for young children, assessment methods that are more directly useful than tests as guides for determining children's accomplishments, interests, preferences, and needs are available. Especially important sources of assessment information, in addition to the child's parents (discussed in Chapter 12), are observations of what the child actually does under specific circumstances or within specific activity contexts.

The general structure of developmentally appropriate early childhood programs provides for individualized learning experiences in a number of ways. That is essential, for each child structures his or her own learning in unique ways; in fact, learning itself is determined by the individual child. Young children need opportunities to exercise choice of activities, to spend varying amounts of time interacting with materials, and to formulate and test their own hypotheses, ask their own questions, and to arrive at their own tentative conclusions. Good early childhood programs reflect recognition and respect for individuality, diversity, and the fundamental principle that, although adults and materials facilitate, it is the individual child who learns. Far from being a passive recipient, the young child is the principal *actor*.

However, that implies neither that the teacher's role must be a passive one nor that activities and materials should be provided in a casual or unplanned manner. The teacher indeed does structure the learning environment, and decisions about time, space, and materials made by the teacher, as well as provisions for individual, small group, and large group activities, should be made on the basis of knowledge of specific children's needs. For some young children with handicapping conditions, this individualized planning may require a more systematic approach. However, the basic principle in integrating specialized methods is but an extension of the philosophy and basic pedagogy that undergird developmentally appropriate early childhood education.

CHAPTER 11

Working with the Group

. . . a radical alteration of the educational environment of a handicapped child may create new interaction patterns that could significantly affect the course of development. One such potentially dramatic change for handicapped children which occurred quite recently is the setting in which educational and therapeutic services are provided. More and more, such services are being provided in classroom settings containing non-handicapped children. The impact of mainstreaming and integrating handicapped and nonhandicapped children is a core issue in the early education of handicapped children (Guralnick, 1982, pp. 457–458).

The relationship between any individual child in the classroom or center and group is reciprocal: the group affects each individual member, and each individual impacts upon the group. An *ecological perspective* (Hobbs, 1980) reminds us that an individual, including a handicapped child, can never be meaningfully considered in a vacuum.

Applying these realities to early childhood education, and specifically working with young children with special needs within typical, mainstream early education settings, suggests two important considerations:

1. The behavior of the young child with special needs can be expected to be different from what it would be in another type of educational setting.

2. The presence of the young child with special needs can be expected
    to have some effect upon the group, its social dynamics, and the
    behavior of its individual members.

Neither of these principles is true only for handicapped children. They are
true of the relationship between any individual child and the classroom group.
Nevertheless, they do indeed become critically important principles where young
children who are handicapped or developmentally delayed are concerned.

In part, this is true, as Dr. Michael Guralnick's statement indicates, because of
the *intervention* goals of early education for young children who are handicapped
or at risk. The impact upon the development and learning of the young handicapped child may be enhanced, or not, to some extent because of basic characteristics of a program, such as the composition and character of the peer group, the
skills and sensitivities of the teacher and other adults, and the ways in which these
interact.

Mainstream placement of young handicapped children is indicated where the
group can contribute positively to the child's development, and the child can
contribute positively to the group (Meisels, 1979). This chapter addresses principles, techniques, and strategies for: (1) optimizing the impact of the group upon
the young child with special needs who is enrolled in a mainstream early childhood
setting; and (2) optimizing the impact of the young child with special needs upon
the group.

SOCIAL ACCEPTANCE BY PEERS

One of the most significant concerns expressed by both parents and teachers in
considering mainstream placement for a young handicapped child is: how will the
child be accepted socially by other children? Will the child have friends? Will
others approach him or her as readily as they will any other child? Will the child be
avoided, shunned, or even actively teased or scapegoated?

What determines how readily a handicapped child is accepted by other children? Are young children oblivious to characteristics that may seem problematic
from an adult's point of view, such as use of special aids, inability to move about
unassisted, or differences in speech or appearance? Will peers be more likely to
"accept" a child whose disability is regarded as mild than one whose disability is
considered severe?

But first, what do we mean by *social acceptance* in the context of an early
childhood program? Some people might define social acceptance as *tolerance*.
Others might feel that "tolerance" is not enough. Who wants just to be tolerated
by others, and what parents want only this for their child? Clearly, we mean that
we do not want the handicapped child to experience rejection by others or to be
made to feel isolated, unwanted, *different*. More than that, however, we are likely
to want other children to relate to the handicapped child in a positive way:

We hope that other children will approach and initiate interaction with the handicapped child in play situations and also in other classroom situations that present opportunities for verbal interaction, physical proximity, and shared activity.

We hope that other children will respond to overtures made by the handicapped child in conversational and play situations.

We hope that other children will identify the handicapped child as a friend, describe him or her in positive terms, and identify as important attributes of the child that are unrelated to his or her disability.

Adult logic might suggest that the more severe a child's disability, the less likely it is that these manifestations of social acceptance will occur. No doubt, adult logic would consider such factors as these:

Discrepancy, how similar to or discrepant from the "norm" of the particular group the child is or may appear to be (for example, in stature, pitch of voice, ability to complete tasks other children are expected to complete, mannerisms, etc.).

Unfamiliarity, how likely or unlikely it may be that the other children have previously encountered individuals with characteristics like those of the handicapped child.

Visibility of the handicapping condition, assuming that more severe problems are generally more likely to be visibly apparent if adaptive equipment is required, or if the disability is manifest in other highly visible ways, such as facial expression or structure.

Attribute valence, the relative perceived importance of such attributes as physical attractiveness, independence in eating, dressing, and toileting, motoric skill, physical grace, verbal proficiency, prosocial behavior, etc.

Tendency to evoke emotional response, since young children are assumed to entertain many fantasies, based on fear of loss or fear of punishment, inaccurate or incomplete knowledge, egocentric thought, etc., that might be evoked by association with a child with absent limbs or facial features, malformed body parts, or other apparent disabilities.

Again, the above reflects *adult* logic. It is based upon the adult conception of attitudes, social awareness, beliefs, thinking styles, fantasies, and fears of young children. In many respects, such logic is superficially sound and informed by theoretical insights concerning the thought and emotional life of young children, provided by Freud, Piaget, and other theorists. However, it represents inappropriate oversimplification, because it is based upon stereotypes, not only about certain handicapping conditions, but also about young children generally. Following this logic could lead us to a conclusion that is simply wrong. Specifically, we might conclude that many children should not be integrated in mainstream settings, because we grossly underestimate the abilities and the sensitivities of young children, as well as the abilities and skills of many who have severe disabilities.

The following anecdote provides an example of the fascinating and delightful ability of young children to surprise us, no matter how knowledgeable we might be about child development. An eight-year-old was asked by his aunt, a social worker, whether any of his classmates were handicapped. He answered, "Well, there's this kid in a wheelchair." Further conversation conveyed convincingly that the child was seen by classmates as "a pretty good guy," with interests in sports and hobbies, who did "pretty good, I guess" in his schoolwork. Did he have any problems in school? Well, not really. However, the child finally noted, this boy held his pencil in his teeth, when drawing or writing, since he could not use his hands.

According to our "adult logic" criteria, the boy's problems would be considered severe and of a sort that might not suggest a high probability of social acceptance by other second graders. If "adult logic" had been our criteria, the child might not have been mainstreamed. In terms of social acceptance, he might have been considered a "poor candidate." Yet he was not only able to meet the academic and other demands of the regular class setting, he was also apparently quite well accepted by the other students. He was considered "a good kid." What was important about him, from his classmate's point of view, was that he liked sports and shared interests in certain hobbies important to eight-year-old boys. That he used his mouth for writing and other activities, instead of his hands, was an afterthought.

WHAT DETERMINES PEER ACCEPTANCE?

> Contrary to the myths that nonhandicapped children will make scapegoats of handicapped children, we have found a great deal of caring and responsiveness. Children have initial curiosity about unusual appearance or behavior. With young children, this curiosity may be expressed very directly. . . . Our teachers try to respond directly, to provide both reassurance and information. Children have concerns about frightening or aggressive behavior and how to deal with it; one child who pinches others without warning was avoided by many of his peers, although now they seem to know how to deal with him. For example, he was hugging one little girl very tightly and an adult headed toward them, fearful of a possible "attack." Sue (age 5) looked up at the adult and said, "No, I'm all right. I just tell him not to do it so hard and he stops." (Knoblock, 1982, p. 19)

This anecdote involves a program for mainstreaming autistic children at *Jowonio: The Learning Place,* in cooperation with the public schools of Syracuse, New York. A diagnosis of *childhood autism* might seem to imply limited potential for a child's integration with nonhandicapped peers in school. However, the Jowonio experiences convincingly illustrate that that is not the case. Professionals need to get beyond the label and focus instead on the child.

There has been much concern about the extent to which handicap labels contribute to attitudes of others toward someone who is so labeled. The issues relating to identification and labeling, social roles, stigma and other social phenomena were discussed in Part I. They will not be specifically addressed again here except to note the probable importance of what teachers and other important adults say about a handicapped child influencing, directly and (through parents) indirectly how the child is accepted by peers.

If children hear labels applied to specific classmates by their parents, teachers, or other significant adults—such as bad boy or bad girl, little lady or little gentleman, bully, tease, clown, leader—they are likely to accept those labels in some sense as true. Feelings about the child so labeled are affected, and children will be likely to respond to that child in a different manner. The effects might be either positive or negative, depending in part on the label itself, but especially on what the label signifies to the child who hears it. Teachers need to be very careful about references made to another child when speaking to children or to their parents.

Apart from the descriptive references normally made in conversation, we need also to be concerned about the more or less "official" labels that adults use to refer to children with disabilities. A partial list of such labels would include blind, deaf, crippled, brain-damaged, retarded, autistic, special ed kid, special, handicapped, Down syndrome child, delayed, spastic, epileptic, slow learner, hyperactive, and so on. Some of these labels are clearly inappropriate at any time. However, we do not know to what extent even an "appropriate" label (that is, a label that is generally accepted and officially "correct") might influence negatively the responses of other children.

This has been the subject of research, since the continued use of some forms of labeling is probably a reality that needs to be addressed (Hobbs, 1975). Also, although we may strive to minimize it, children will probably have some awareness of their peers' labels. Studies have attempted to investigate how, or whether, awareness of labels may affect children's attitudes and behavior toward handicapped peers.

In one study (Van Bourgondien, 1987) some girls were shown a videotape of a handicapped child behaving "appropriately," and others saw the same child behaving "inappropriately." Some of the girls were told that the child was "in a special class for the retarded" and others were not. Expressions of their attitude toward the child were recorded, and then their subsequent behavior in interaction with the same child they had seen on the videotape were observed. Neither their expressed attitudes nor their behavior were found to be influenced by the label ("in a special class for the retarded"). However, both expressed attitudes and observed behavior were significantly influenced by the behavior they had seen. Those who had observed appropriate social behavior viewed the girl in a positive manner and actually interacted with her more positively. Those who had observed the child behaving inappropriately in the videotape expressed negative attitudes and actually interacted with her in a less positive manner. The investigator also found that both groups were receptive to assuming and effectively carrying out helping roles, however, even those who had an unfavorable initial impression based on the videotape.

We should not conclude from this study that children are not susceptible to the problem of labeling. Labels can influence social acceptance, at least initially, and can add significantly to the burden a handicapped child bears. However, the Van Bourgondien study is an example of many, referenced in Chapter 4, that underscore the critical importance of appropriate social behavior in influencing the extent to which a handicapped child is accepted socially by peers, and the extent to which peers interact positively and helpfully with the child. One researcher (Simpson, 1980, p. 10) summarizes that positive peer attitudes toward, and constructive interaction with, a handicapped child are ". . . based at least partially on patterns of acceptable behavior by exceptional children, [implying] . . . an approximation of normality, especially in the area of social responsiveness."

Interestingly, and perhaps not surprisingly, **teachers and parents often observe that children are more accepting of a peer's norm-discrepant behavior if they are aware that the child has a handicap, one they can see and understand, than when this is not the case.** Inappropriate responses on the part of a child with a "hidden handicap" (as learning disability has often been described) may not be as readily accepted and understood as those of a child whose impairment is visually apparent. Ironically, however, it may be the former who is more likely to misread social "signals," or otherwise depart from expected norms for peer interaction.

Learning to interact with others in ways that will foster acceptance and friendship is important for all young children. Every teacher has observed that certain children seem to be more "popular" with peers than others, while some may frequently be rejected, or at least not selected, by peers in play situations. This problem is certainly not specific either to handicapped or to nonhandicapped children; it is one of the many situations common to both. For some children with disabilities, even severe ones, social acceptance by peers and acquiring and maintaining friendships is simply not a problem at all. For handicapped children in a mainstream setting, however, being accepted by classmates is of critical importance, and for some handicapped children, this is a particularly difficult area. It is no less important, however, to the typical child.

Certainly, the teacher must ensure that a handicapped child does not experience rejection or teasing. That is the greatest concern of parents considering mainstreaming (e.g., Bailey & Winton, 1987), and understandably so. Although peer avoidance or other adverse reaction to children with facial deformities is unlikely in early childhood settings and can be prevented from occurring through effective teacher modeling and guidance, these children may be at particular risk in terms of long-range impact:

> Children appearing even slightly different from their peers are potential candidates for serious psychological and emotional problems. These children often evoke reactions that affect their interactions with others throughout their life. Severe facial abnormalities set in motion an entire series of subtle and overt

rejections that must be handled carefully and properly by those who interact with these children. (Moncada, 1987, pp. 112–113)

Again, **it is the teacher's example that is most influential in determining the children's response.** Curiosity, perhaps reflected in direct questions, is appropriate and should be respected. The child's self-esteem and social confidence cannot be enhanced without incurring some risk. Starting early to involve the child in normal learning situations with typical peers offers the best assurance that she or he will be accepted as a child and thus enabled to gain socially and emotionally. Young children will be aware of pronounced differences. That awareness and attendant curiosity should not be viewed as negative, undesirable, or inappropriate. With effective adult response, young children get past that point very rapidly. What is important to them is far more likely to be how well the child can play.

With some children, reasons for being "rejected" or not approached or selected seem obvious. However, the teacher needs to determine accurately what is occurring and to assess the child's social acceptance based on precise observations of the child's skills, preferences, and specific difficulties in specific situations. Some questions a teacher might ask to be assessed through observation, have been suggested by Hazen, Black, and Fleming-Johnson (1984).

1. Does the child's success in social interactions seem to deteriorate when she or he interacts with more than one child at a time? Does the child become less responsive to others, or use less adaptive interaction strategies?
2. Does the child seem intimidated about entering ongoing social interaction, and withdraw from groups that are already at play?
3. Does the child tend to use stereotyped routines to initiate social interaction, rather than flexibly adapting to individual children and situations?
4. Does the child have a repertoire of play themes that are meaningful to other children, or are they highly idiosyncratic?
5. Does the child clearly indicate to whom she or he is speaking?
6. Does the child focus heavily on just one other child and ignore others?
7. Does the child attend to the initiations of others by at least acknowledging them?
8. When rejecting the ideas of others, does the child offer reasons or alternatives? (p. 32)

Implied in the above list of questions for observational child study is a set of social skills that, depending upon age level of the social group, may be important for the teacher to consciously teach a child. The topic of social skills training is addressed more fully in a subsequent section of this chapter.

For some children, maintaining appropriate social behavior may be difficult because the child cannot readily "read" and correctly interpret the cues that other people provide in social situations. These difficulties in social perception have been described as a problem experienced by many children with learning disabilities (Lerner, 1985). Consequently, a child may not be liked by others, and the difficulties experienced in being accepted can contribute to emotional problems as well (Bryan, Pearl, Donahue, Bryan, & Pflaum, 1983). The child may need to be taught directly the skills she or he needs. With young children, adult modeling, role-playing, and peer-mediated assistance can be effective (Lerner et al., 1987).

THE ROLE OF OTHER CHILDREN IN PROMOTING SOCIAL SKILLS

Research conducted by Strain and his co-workers (e.g., Shores, Hester & Strain, 1976; Strain & Weigerink, 1976) suggests that opportunities for spontaneous interactions with peers (facilitated and arranged by the teacher) may be more effective than direct teacher intervention in bringing about social interaction among handicapped and nonhandicapped preschool-age children. Creating situations in the classroom in which positive peer interaction can occur, such as opportunities for sociodramatic play, may be more effective than direct strategies, such as systematically reinforcing social behaviors.

This does not imply an inactive, "bystander" role for the teacher, nor does it imply that "mere exposure" will lead automatically to constructive interaction and social acceptance. The research literature suggesting that the teacher needs to plan and to structure social interaction situations was summarized in Chapter 4. One team of researchers who had studied preschoolers' social interaction in integrated classrooms, summarized the most important general principle for the teacher to bear in mind:

> . . . more advanced interactional behaviors . . . will not occur at optimal levels between nonhandicapped preschool children and their handicapped peers unless they are systematically guided and encouraged through active programs. (Faught, Balleweg, Crow, & Van Den Pol, 1983, p. 214)

A teacher can structure classroom interaction in many different ways to maximize the teaching role of typical children in regard to their peers who are delayed or less competent in social development. Snyder, Apolloni, and Cooke (1977) summarized many of these. Perhaps the most basic and obvious strategy is simply to structure situations so that children with delayed development have ample opportunities to observe their peers, and to provide reinforcement when desired behaviors are imitated. Specific reinforcements should be selected from available alternatives within the natural classroom setting and should include those activities and/or materials that have been observed to have reinforcing properties for that particular child.

A second strategy outlined by Snyder et al. (1977) is the *generalized imitation approach,* in which developmentally delayed children are taught to imitate their peers; such training can result in the imitation spilling over into situations in which imitation training has not been specifically provided. The "teaching" role of the normal child is simply to do whatever he or she would normally do; the delayed child is taught through a sequence of cueing, prompting, and reinforcing to attend to and imitate the peer.

A third method requires a more direct version of the concept of *peer confederates*. Here, typical children are taught to distinguish the behaviors that are desired and to reinforce them on a contingent basis. Again, typical children are basically "doing what comes naturally;" the difference is that special care has been taken to ensure that their teaching will be systematic and not random. If the behavior-consequence relationship is clarified and maintained, appropriate behavior is much more probable. (We should emphasize that this helping behavior is extremely rewarding—and reinforcing—for the typical child as well!)

Another application of reinforcement principles involving the peer group suggested by Snyder and his colleagues is to associate the delayed children themselves with rewards generally found within the early childhood classroom, so that interaction with their handicapped peers is associated with desirable events experienced by the typical children. In one study (Cooke & Apolloni, 1976), this concept was taken even a step farther, so that the delayed children themselves provided the reinforcement. The delayed children were taught behaviors such as smiling, verbal complimenting, positive ways of physically contacting, etc. These prosocial behaviors made interacting with them reinforcing to their nonhandicapped, primary-age peers. In general, that strategy illustrates that the principal value of social skills training is that it results in mutually rewarding experiences.

The LEAP program at the University of Pittsburgh (Learning Experiences . . . An Alternative Program for Preschoolers and Parents) (Strain, 1987) integrates typical and autistic preschoolers, relying extensively on large-group instruction that incorporates individualized planning. The nonhandicapped peers in this model program are trained to provide specific forms of social initiation in interacting with the autistic children. These include verbal invitation to engage in play, or acknowledgment of such engagement; offering or giving play material to another child; helping a child; asking another child for help; making complimentary statements; and physically demonstrating affection.

In Chapter 4 we noted that agreement exists about the importance of training in social skills for many young children with developmental delays in order for experiences in the mainstream to be maximally effective and to lead to more likely future mainstream participation. Snyder et al. (1977) emphasized the long-term value to children with mental retardation of acquiring behavioral patterns that are socially desirable and acceptable, and not associated with cultural stereotypes of "retarded behavior." They also stressed the importance for these children of learning to imitate behavior appropriate to specific contexts selectively, enabling the child more readily to adapt to novel and unfamiliar situations.

Do children need to acquire the requisite social skills before being placed in a mainstream classroom situation (Gresham, 1982), or can those skills more readily be acquired within a typical classroom situation (Strain & Shores, 1983). The research of Snyder et al. (1977), Cooke & Apolloni, (1976), Michael Guralnick, and

Philip Strain and their associates, and others makes a convincing case in support of the proposition, expressed by Guralnick, with which this chapter began: the social setting itself exerts potentially great, positive impact upon the behavior of young children.

We cannot assess accurately a child's "social competence for mainstreaming" or teach such competence effectively in classroom settings that are markedly different from the mainstream classroom environment. Strain and Shores (1983) express this fundamental principle as follows:

> The basic message from naturalistic and intervention research is quite clear. If maximum skill performance is to be portrayed, children must have the basic opportunities to respond. It seems doubtful whether the opportunities (e.g., presence of socially responsive partners) can be made available in developmentally segregated classes; therefore, it is questionable to us whether handicapped children will ever be judged as "ready" for mainstreaming. (p. 272)

Simply assessing a child's "readiness" for mainstreaming when the child is in a segregated special program is difficult, if not impossible for similar reasons. Because of the interdependent quality of children's social behavior, observing handicapped children in segregated settings will always result in *underestimating* their performance, potential, and "readiness" with respect to social skills (Strain & Fox, 1981).

Specialized early intervention programs, provided that they integrate typical children, can contribute to preparing the child for more effective social skill development, as part of a transitional process. An important consideration, however, is provision for *generalization* of the skills that are acquired. Basically, teaching for generalization involves *varying* task elements so that the child will perform what is learned under different conditions. Programming for generalization of social skills in early intervention programs involves several instructional elements that can be systematically varied. Powell and Lindeman (1983) describe the following elements:

> *Prompts* (the words that are used in instructions).
> *Praise* (verbally reinforcing the desired behavior in different ways).
> *Training area* (using different locations where children are likely to be playing).
> *Time of day* (provide opportunities at different times during the day and at different points in the classroom schedule).
> *Teacher* (have different adults prompt and reward the behavior).
> *Student grouping* (periodically change the composition of the group setting in which the skill is performed, especially gradually exposing the child to a greater number of different children).
> *Activities* (the actual activities and the materials used should be varied often). (p. 74)

These same suggestions are applicable equally within the mainstream early childhood classroom setting. Because of the nature of early childhood programs, and in particular the recognized contributions of the children themselves to each other's learning in good early childhood programs, a more accommodating environment for acquiring and practicing social skills in such a way as to foster generalization exists than in most specialized early intervention programs. What is required for many young children with special needs is that the teacher integrate a systematic learning process, targeted upon specific skills, within a teaching-learning situation that normally emphasizes the role of self-guided discovery and incidental learning. Since what is of major concern in the area of social skills is positive interaction with typical peers, most effective teaching approaches build upon the principal resource that is already present: the peer group itself.

Maximizing the contributions of peers does not necessarily require either integrating special instructional strategies or training typical children as "peer confederates." Usually, teaching strategies that are indicated are considerably less intrusive and more congruent with the general approach employed by the teacher with all young children in the classroom.

For example, Rogers and Ross (1986) suggest that the teacher's role primarily involves setting the stage, monitoring, and providing ongoing guidance, as needed, in providing opportunities for interaction and communication. Based on their review of research in this area, they suggested that teachers of young children

> Provide activities in which children interact with minimal adult supervision, such as blocks, water, sand, and dramatic play.
>
> Observe, assess, and group children so that those who are effective "social negotiators" can interact with children whose skills are less refined.
>
> Help children learn to ask questions, observe a group before entering, improve their communication skills, and talk about their feelings and desires. Pointing out effective behaviors or suggesting ideas may be needed by some children. (p. 17)

THE ROLE OF PLAY IN LEARNING SOCIAL SKILLS

In settings for young children, all the children are acquiring and practicing social skills. To a great extent, the most important way in which young children learn social skills is through play. As Rudolph and Cohen (1984) have asserted, children's play, despite its important role in child development theory and research—and traditionally in the early childhood curriculum itself—is still not well understood even by some of its advocates. A discussion of why play is so centrally important in the development of all young children is beyond the scope of this text, but we hope that you, as a student of young children, possess genuine respect for children's play.

If the importance of effective play skills can be assumed, let us consider the implications for a child who does not naturally acquire some of those skills in the course of early development and who *must be taught to play*. Actually, once again, teachers of young children should be aware of the extent to which they are are presently engaged in teaching young children to play, even children who are not handicapped or significantly delayed. Especially with increasing numbers of very young children—infants and toddlers—being provided care outside their own home, in group programs (whether center-based or in family day care situations) caregivers need to guide young children in their learning to play.

Eheart and Leavitt (1985) suggest activities for adults that support play for both special needs children and typical children in this age group:

> *Observe* to gain insight for selecting individual children's activities and materials and guiding their participation.
> Take advantage of opportunities to *expand* play.
> Encourage exploration and experimentation with materials.
> Encourage independence.
> Avoid interrupting play.
> Let children know you're interested by encouraging them to talk about their play.
> Be available when needed for assistance.
> Either be observing children or involved with them—not talking with other adults.

Various types of play and play situations are appropriate to the early childhood program, and all represent important modes of learning for young children. Beers and Wehman (1985) have differentiated four categories of play that are important for the young child with special needs to experience in order to progress cognitively as well as socially: exploratory play, toy play, social play, and structured game play. Each requires certain skills, ranging from basic physical manipulation, to interacting cooperatively with others, to understanding "the rules of the game." They correspond generally to the developmental sequence described by theorists such as Piaget and Bruner.

Since play has such an important role in the mental and social development of young children, it is in itself a legitimate curriculum area, especially for young children who have difficulty in developing play skills. (We should remember that by no means all handicapped children experience difficulty in learning to play, and also that other typical children may not have acquired play skills or internalized play as a style of learning.)

According to Rudolph and Cohen (1984, p. 109), there are at least two major explanations for the ". . . children who wander aimlessly or get into one aggressive episode after another, who can't or won't, or don't settle down to play." These are: (1) limited life experiences due primarily to the need for their families to focus upon day-to-day survival, and (2) the impact of technology, particularly television, that may affect the play dispositions and habits of young children of any socioeconomic level. Although play indeed "comes naturally" to young children, there are clearly factors that may interfere with its natural development. If play is the primary means by which young children develop through interaction with the environment, following Piaget's description of development, this interaction depends upon the sensory and motor activity of the child, and it depends also upon the nature and quality of the environment to which the child is exposed.

The role of the teacher with respect to the teaching of play skills and, more importantly, the attitude toward play, can involve many facets. Clearly, it involves creation of an environment conducive to play, as well as the provision of opportunities for play to occur. However, for some children it involves more than simply providing the time, the place, and the materials; it requires focused and purposeful instruction, using techniques ranging from modeling and demonstration, prompts, verbal guidance, and systematic reinforcement that will ultimately lead to play itself becoming reinforcing. For some children with handicapping conditions, difficulties in play situations are not due to lack of understanding of what play is or a desire to engage in play, or to the inability to relate effectively to peers in social play situations. They may instead be due to the sheer difficulty a child may have in moving about, extending an arm, grasping an object, and controlling its movement. As in areas of self-care, formal skill learning, use of art media, or other activities, what is then needed is some form of adaptive physical management that enables children to learn through play. Conversely, play can be an effective medium for working therapeutically with a child as well (Musselwhite, 1986).

SOCIAL INTEGRATION IN DAY CARE

Day care represents a common area of need for families of both typical and handicapped children. Increasingly, a child's participation in a day care program supplements his or her participation in another setting. For school-age children, before-school and after-school care is increasingly perceived as a need. For younger children, day care involvement may take place during times when the child is not served by another program. These needs prevail whether a child is handicapped or nonhandicapped, developmentally typical, advanced, or delayed.

The participation of young children with special needs in day care may require specific attention to certain medical needs. For children with delayed development who do not present specific concerns relative to health care, mobility, or other areas the major focus may be upon social and emotional development.

Levine and McColum (1983) emphasize the value of integrating handicapped and nonhandicapped infants within child-care settings, based upon accumulating evidence of social responsiveness and peer interaction even within the very first year of life. They suggest that the values of *imitative learning* associated with integration and mainstreaming for preschool-age and school-age children are present for very young children as well and that earliest possible exploitation of imitative learning opportunities can be beneficial. For infants, they suggest the following considerations regarding mainstreaming infants in developmental child care programs:

1. Repeated nearby placement of handicapped and nonhandicapped infant peers can serve to sensitize children to their peers as social beings. However, nearby placement alone is not sufficient to stimulate the emergence of social behaviors between handicapped and nonhandicapped peers.
2. Peers of varying developmental levels can increase the frequency of accommodation and modeling situations, thus supporting emerging social behaviors. Younger nonhandicapped infants may more closely match older handicapped peers in some developmental abilities. Older nonhandicapped infants may be more skilled and persevering in their behavioral repertoires and thus be able to maintain social interactions with less skilled peers.
3. Toys play a special role in enhancing the interactions between handicapped and nonhandicapped infant peers. As a focus of mutual interest and engagement, the features of toys can set the stage for an expanded learning environment. (p. 25)

Klein and Sheehan (1987) advocate mainstream day care provisions for children with moderate and severe handicaps that *complement* their participation in early intervention programs, specifically in terms of social integration goals. However, a study conducted by Bagnato, Kontos, and Neisworth (1987) revealed that handicapped children served in day care components of 13 federally funded early intervention programs were perceived by staff to have more difficulty in the area of social skills than in any other area. This would appear to indicate the need to set realistic and appropriate goals for social skill development, determine effective methods for promoting social development in the day care setting, and provide resource assistance to help day care staff implement effective social skills training.

There have been reports (e.g., Smith & Greenberg, 1981) that, even when the process of integrating significantly delayed children into a typical, mainstream day care program was characterized by careful planning and a step-by-step approach, problems may be experienced. Concerns have arisen more about the impact of the experiences upon the handicapped child involved, however, than upon the typical children. Problems occur to the extent that the specific needs of the young handicapped child are not addressed adequately in the process. At the same time, day care participation for the young child with special needs is intended to accomplish basically the same purposes as for the typical child. Day care, in itself, is not expected to be able to provide interventive programming, but rather to provide quality care and further opportunities for positive general personal and social development, goals for all young children. Good day care experiences should be viewed as potentially supplementing, though not supplanting, specialized, individualized early intervention experiences that many young handicapped children will continue to require (Klein, 1981; Klein & Sheehan, 1987).

Quality day care experiences can contribute significantly to promoting developmental progress even of children with severe impairments (Fredericks, Baldwin, Grove, Moore, Riggs, & Lyons, 1978). Fredericks and his co-workers found that moderately and severely handicapped children could be integrated effectively within a typical day care setting. They also found that participating children demonstrated increased social interactions and language skills.

Four basic elements appear to be critical in achieving effective integration of young handicapped and nonhandicapped children in day care:

1. Communication, cooperation, and collaboration both with parents and with others involved in working with the child.
2. Physical environment, materials, and program of activities conducive to positive social interaction, communication, and imitative learning.
3. Teachers and caregivers who consciously and planfully structure situations and activities involving peer interaction.
4. Availability and use of supportive and resource assistance.

The use of facilitating social situations and provision of appropriate materials go hand in hand. Teachers and caregivers can promote opportunities for constructive interactions between young handicapped and and nonhandicapped children through (1) planning the way the physical environment is organized; (2) appropriate selection of toys and other materials; (3) providing for pairings, small groups, and parallel play situations.

As Hanline (1985) suggests, certain materials such as dolls, blocks, and housekeeping materials encourage socially interactive play. Also, the teacher or caregiver can select games that encourage imitation and then actively encourage imitation in the course of children's play.

A great many questions remain unanswered about the potential in family day care for integrating young handicapped children and the relative merits for children with specific types and degrees of impairments of family vs. center-based day care (Jones & Meisels, 1987). However, we should not assume that only center-based programs provide viable mainstreaming options. In fact, community programs like the Technical Assistance Program (TAP), advising the Cleveland, Ohio, area, discussed in this chapter and in Chapter 13, have been successful in assisting both types of programs to integrate children with handicaps.

TEACHING SOCIAL SKILLS: USING THE NATURAL GROUP CONTEXT

The group context can be used to maximize peer acceptance of the child with special needs and to promote positive psychosocial learning of all children. It is also often important in achieving specific instructional goals for the young handicapped child. For some handicapped children, especially those with more severe handicaps, IEP objectives will specifically include enhancing the child's interactive functioning within present and future environments (Snell & Grigg, 1987;

Snell & Renzaglia, 1986). Severely handicapped children often have particular difficulty in initiating social interactions or in reciprocating and responding appropriately when others do. Consequently, peers may tend to avoid the child (Strain, 1982). Lacking reinforcement, the social skill repertoire of the child weakens even more (Renzaglia & Bates, 1983). It is critically important, therefore, for the child to experience situations with peers that are *mutually reinforcing.*

According to Odom and Strain (1984), this area has not received specific attention commensurate with its importance. This may be due in part to the difficulty in defining the specific skill areas involved in social interaction so that they can be systematically measured and remediated. Renzaglia and Bates (1983) identified the following key dimensions of social skill competence:

1. *Social decoding,* effectively discriminating among social cues while extracting relevant information.
2. *Social communication content,* including specific behaviors such as giving and acknowledging greeting, praise, positive information, neutral information, criticism, demands, requests, and questions.
3. *Nonverbal behaviors,* communicating qualitiatively, for example through smiling.
4. *Independent social skills,* being able to function alone within a social context without attracting undue attention.

Social skills are thus seen as skills involved in social communication, or engaging in ". . . any behavior that conveys a social message" (Rogers-Warren & Warren, 1984, p. 58). Such behaviors may be of many types, nonverbal as well as verbal, but communicative behaviors are necessarily always interactive (Wilcox & Campbell, 1986). Enhancing the child's ability to engage in communication with others, using whatever communicative modes are available to that particular child, then becomes the major priority in teaching social skills. That can only be effectively accomplished within a natural, social context, such as the classroom. Thus, it is important to provide opportuntiies for social skills to be applied naturally (Odom & Strain, 1984). To some extent, prior training to prepare the child who is handicapped to respond appropriately to the subtle social cues in the interactive environment of a regular classroom may be important (e.g., Alden & Lipson, 1983; Gresham, 1982). However, the situation itself provides a more appropriate and effective context for acquiring these behaviors (Strain & Shores, 1983).

Children with less severe impairments may also experience particular difficulty in the area of social skills. The teacher can employ a variety of techniques—prior simulation and practice, modeling, verbal prompts, and exposure to peer models—to help children acquire such "amenities" as using a situationally appropriate facial expression, establishing eye contact, modulating tone of voice, pausing for a response, requesting more information when appropriate, saying "please," "thank you," "excuse me," etc., when appropriate, and adopting a pleasant manner.

Social participation is essential for children to acquire and learn to use social skills. For many young children with special needs, that co-involvement with nonhandicapped peers may occur quite naturally. For others, however, it will occur only with some degree of planning and structuring. With severely handicapped children, highly individualized adaptations may be required in order for the child to be socially and instructionally involved with peers to whatever degree is feasible. For students with severe handicaps, the *principle of partial participation* (Baumgart, Brown, Pumpian, Nisbet, Ford, Sweet, Messina, & Schroeder, 1982) is based on the following assumptions:

1. Partial participation in chronological age-appropriate environments and activities is educationally more advantageous than exclusion from such environments and activities.
2. Severely handicapped students, regardless of their degree of dependence or level of functioning, should be allowed to participate at least partially in a wide range of school and nonschool environments and activities.
3. The kinds and degrees of partial participation in school and nonschool environments and activities should be increased through direct and systematic instruction.
4. Partial participation in school and nonschool environments and activities should result in a student being perceived by others as a more valuable, contributing, striving, and productive member of society.
5. Systematic, coordinated, and longitudinal efforts must be initiated at a young age in order to prepare for at least partial participation in as many environments and activities with nonhandicapped chronological age-appropriate peers and other persons as possible. (p. 19)

This concept underscores the principle that every handicapped child, no matter what the nature or degree of severity of the handicap may be, can participate with typical children of the same age in activities that involve interaction and communication. For even the most severely handicapped child these opportunities are of critical importance. They can be arranged in any setting in which severely handicapped children are served in the same building, even though in separate special classes, to the extent that communication and cooperation of the respective staffs is present; physical and temporal proximity exists; naturally occurring contact is exploited; and additional interactive contact is specifically planned.

For children with less severe impairments, the importance of opportunities for peer interaction as social learning situations also needs to be recognized. The skills young children learn to use are critical not only for their immediate acceptance by peers but also in terms of long-range goals for future normalized educational and social functioning.

CHILDREN HELP EACH OTHER

Young children are willing and eager to help a classmate who may need assistance. In fact, the problem may be that some children are too helpful, not that they are not helpful enough. Autonomy and maximum independence are goals for the child with special needs, and over-solicitousness or providing assistance when it is not needed interfere with attaining those goals. Also, some young children may have come to be overly reliant on the assistance of others. Again, this is of course true of both handicapped and nonhandicapped children. Some young children with disabilities may be manipulative of peers or adults. Usually, peers will be able to deal with this effectively so that the child with a disability is not allowed to boss or otherwise control. However, both handicapped and typical children may need adult guidance in their social interactions, should things not be proceeding well. A "bossy" child may seem amusing, but only for a brief time. The teacher's own example can be effective in communicating what forms of help are appropriate for a specific child in certain circumstances.

Another side of the issue of seeking and providing help when needed is the difficulty some children may have in learning how, when, and whom to ask for help. Clearly, there are times when a child may need help that would not be needed were it not for the disability. There are also times when any young child may need help; it is not an issue that sets young children with handicapping conditions apart from their peers. Learning to help someone else is an important opportunity for young children to have in school. For all children, dealing appropriately with helping, being helped, or indicating that no help is needed is an important element of their social learning. That fact may be accentuated by the presence of a child who is handicapped, but in this respect the handicapped child is certainly not unique. Mara Sapon-Shevin (1983) summarizes the elements in helping and being helped:

1. *Asking for help appropriately* (e.g., "Can you please reach my coat for me," rather than "Give me my coat.")
2. *Offering help appropriately* (e.g., "Do you want me to help you?" rather than "You're too short—I'll get the ball," or simply doing something for another individual without asking whether help is needed.)
3. *Accepting help appropriately* (e.g., "Thanks for getting my coat.")
4. *Refusing help appropriately* (e.g., "No thanks—I can do it myself," rather than "Leave me alone, stupid, I'm not a baby—I can do it myself."). (p. 30)

Helping is a concept central to early childhood practice, not only in promoting socialization goals but also in specific curriculum areas. Young children come to understand cooperation, interdependence, sharing, teamwork, and group membership mainly through experiencing those concepts at home and at school. Specific curricula and types of learning based on these concepts, such as those described by Johnson and Johnson (1981), both bring children of varying ability and skill levels together in pursuit of a common learning goal and simultaneously provide for differences in time requirements and level of difficulty (Slavin et al.,

1984). These *cooperative learning activities* elicit coordinated effort, modeling, mutual assistance, and the enhanced motivation associated with group identity and collaboration.

THE CLASSROOM ENVIRONMENT

Both the physical environment of the classroom and the provision for activities within it are important in promoting both social and instructional integration. A number of considerations important for accommodating young children with sensory or motoric disabilities were discussed in Chapters 5, 6, and 7, and environmental and program adaptations to enable individualized provisions for specific children were suggested in Chapter 10. However, the way in which teachers plan and use time and space can be an important determinant in how effectively the group program is orchestrated as well.

Some design principles for learning environments to promote and enhance integration have been suggested by Cohen, Beer, Kidera, and Golden (1979). They recommend:

1. *Settings that are not noticeably different.* When it is necessary to make changes in school environments to accommodate handicapped children, the modified spaces and equipment should be usable by and attractive to all people.
2. *Common entry and circulation.* A common entry for all students that is part of a circulation system should be usable by all children and connect the entire school building.
3. *Linked activity areas.* Cluster regular and exceptional activity zones to link them conceptually as well as physically. Eliminate the necessity for children to move through long, undistinguished corridors.
4. *Orderliness and consistency.* School environments should be orderly and consistent. However, environments should neither confuse exceptional children nor be too subdued for nonhandicapped children.
5. *Repetition and multiple coding.* Develop a learning environment rich with information for all the senses. Multiply code spaces and objects by color, shape, and texture; use repetition of cues and elements to help children grasp concepts and ideas and learn to generalize.
6. *Public display of accomplishments.* Provide places and times where good work and other accomplishments can be displayed.
7. *Individual work areas.* Places appropriate in scale for use by one child or a child and a teacher should be created within the regular classroom.

8.   *Manipulable settings.* Allow children to manipulate and make decisions about their own environment.

9.   *Retreat areas.* Small sheltered places should be provided adjacent to activity areas so that children may separate themselves from the larger group when they are feeling overwhelmed or overstimulated.

10. *Places for informal socialization.* Provide "informal" territories for spontaneous interactions among children.

11. *Range of environmental stimuli.* A rich, stimulating environment can benefit the basic abilities of all children, especially if such stimuli are direct and meaningful and used to express the nature of the environment. Ensure a range of stimuli from simple, bold forms with a limited message to a place with sounds, smells, and textures.

12. *Barrier-free design.* All children should be able to move easily from one area to another.

Access, visual impact, traffic patterns, light, and sound factors all need to be considered from the perspective of the children. Where materials are located and which ones are displayed and which stored are also important considerations, for the group as a whole as well as for the individual child. The various social groupings that occur in play contexts in early childhood classrooms have been identified by Adcock and Segal (1983) as: (1) a *dyad* (two or three children); (2) a *play group* (formed around an activity center, such as a sand box or water table) comprising up to about eight children; and (3) a *family group* (which focuses upon pretend play). All provide valuable social contexts for handicapped children to interact with their typical peers, all can be enabled by the way in which the classroom is physically arranged.

The use of learning centers in organizing the physical environment represents a way of building in opportunities for social interaction as well as an individualized teaching approach. Learning centers make possible both self-directed and self-motivated discovery within a context defined by the center and its contents and cooperative and interactive learning shared by pairs or small groups of children. The concept of a learning center is based on the need to impose some organizing system upon the learning environment, while still permitting learning to be open-ended and child-directed, rather than teacher-directed or prescribed. However, the *contents* of a specific center can vary from materials that are usable in innumerable ways to materials the use of which is specifically prescribed and that are self-correcting. Learning centers provide opportunities for children to observe and imitate each other, to cooperate in a shared activity, and to work together in pursuit of a common goal.

In addition to the use of space, time and its management are important considerations in effectively working with the group, as well as for individual children. The duration of activity segments and provisions for transitions from one activity to another may be especially important for some young children with developmental delays, but they also must be considered for all young children. In early childhood programs, attention span and time tolerance, as well as shifting behavioral modes appropriately to shifts in activities are areas of potential difficulty for many young children. Consequently, the sequence of activities can significantly impact upon group behavior and motivation. For example, in one study (Krantz & Risley, 1977), the percentage of time preschool children listened to a story was greater when story time was preceded by a quiet activity than when it was preceded by an active session.

CURRICULUM RESOURCES

Curriculum materials are available that contribute in at least two major areas: (1) encouraging positive attitudes toward human diversity and about individual differences, and (2) helping children to acquire effective social skills. Both types of materials are potentially very helpful in enhancing integrated education.

Teaching children about differences among people is important not only concerning disabilities, but also concerning *all* the ways in which people differ from each other, including differences in race, manner of dress, language, or dialect, or customs. Some of the curriculum materials that have been developed specifically to foster awareness and understanding of people who are handicapped are applicable to all other areas of individual differences. Conversely, general human relations education materials, or materials that focus upon a specific area of human relations, can be valuable in helping young children to deal with feelings, express questions, and gain information and understanding relating to handicapping conditions.

Young children can internalize through their participation in activities and discussions relating to differences among people and human relationships the ". . . principle that to be different is not to be inferior, that one may be different and equal at the same time" (Gold, Grant, & Rivlin, 1977, p. vii). Gold et al. have prepared an excellent resource for educators titled *In Praise of Diversity: A Resource Book for Multicultural Education* (available through the Teacher Corps and the Association of Teacher Educators, both based in Washington, D.C.).

A valuable resource on multicultural educations geared specifically to early childhood is *Diversity in the Classroom: A Multicultural Approach to the Education of Young Children,* by E. F. Kendall (1983). It provides guidelines for applying a multicultural approach and philosophy in teaching young children, whatever the specific competence of one's classroom might be. Kendall stresses the importance of recognizing and understanding one's own attitudes in order to work effectively with children concerning attitudes toward diversity.

In emphasizing the applicability of curriculum materials concerning disability and human exceptionality to other areas, Dr. Mara Sapon-Shevin (1983) illustrates by discussing the curriculum developed by Shirley Cohen (1977) titled *Accepting Individual Differences* (available from Developmental Learning Materials, P.O. Box 4000, Allen, TX 75002). Included are suggested problem-solving situations that actively involve young children. The curriculum emphasizes the ideas that disabilities are extensions of the differences in individual characteristics found among all people, and what disabled and nondisabled people have in common. Four themes are developed: (1) people are different, and people are the same; (2) people learn in different ways; (3) even though we are different, we like each other; and (4) a person's appearance seems significant only when we don't know him or her.

Such materials can be valuable in fulfilling what Guralnick (1982) states is a fundamental intent of Public Law 94–142: ". . . to create circumstances in which mutual understanding, tolerance for diversity, and ultimately the recognition of the value of diversity by both handicapped and nonhandicapped children would flourish" (p. 464). Curriculum can contribute effectively toward fostering positive integration experiences for young children, while the presence of disabled children can contribute toward learning in a curricular area important in its own right.

Curriculum approaches that focus directly upon children's learning to be aware of and to use social skills have recently received great emphasis in special education because of the importance of these skills to social acceptance, self-esteem, and school and vocational success (e.g., Cartledge & Milburn, 1980). Even children who are believed academically "ready" for mainstream participation may experience difficulties because they have not acquired the ability to interpret and act upon subtle social cues, such as facial expressions, tone of voice, and body language. Some researchers (e.g., Alden & Lipson, 1983) have recommended that special educators should include these among the regular classroom conditions included in an ecological inventory implying the "survival skills" to be taught directly to handicapped children who are to be mainstreamed. However, the mainstream early childhood educator can continue to encourage the child's success through conscious awareness of the skill areas that are important, both within the present classroom environment and in future environments.

One of the best-known social skills teaching programs for elementary-age students (kindergarten through sixth grade) is called ACCEPTS: A Curriculum for Children's Effective Peer and Teacher Skills (Walker, McConnell, Walker, Clarke, Todis, Cohen, & Rankin, 1983). Five major skill areas are emphasized: (1) classroom skills, (2) basic interaction skills, (3) getting along, (4) making friends, and (5) coping skills. Included among the classroom skills are those that teachers regard as essential, such as listening and following directions, while the other areas emphasize skills that are important in interacting with other children or adults in an effective manner. Like other approaches, direct instruction of the specific skills involved is utilized by means of examples, practice activities, and error correction.

PREPARATION OF NONHANDICAPPED CHILDREN

Anticipation of a new child who happens to be handicapped entering the class should not be seen as a "crisis" that requires some form of "intervention" with the children, for their benefit and for that of the handicapped child. Head Start teachers, who have been involved for many years in successfully integrating handicapped children, do not "make a big production" of preparing the other children (Klein, 1975). Preparation activities are counterproductive if they imply staff concerns and insecurities and communicate these to the children, rather than feelings of confidence and security. Talks with individual children, rather than a general class discussion, may be more appropriate in some situations. However, determining what kinds of preparations should be made depends primarily on the procedures normally followed any time a new child is about to join the group.

It is better for preparation to be ongoing than for specific activities to be scheduled in anticipation of a specific new arrival. Ideally, the classroom environment will already be one in which children understand and value diversity. Beyond the general mode of interaction among children and between children and adults, that can be facilitated by certain learning activities.

One of the best-known and most widely-used such activities is a program involving puppets called "Kids on the Block" (Aiello, 1977). Resource persons who have been trained to present "Kids on the Block" to classes and groups of children are available in every state and they can be brought in to schools and programs in virtually every community. Like all puppet shows that children love, this one enables children to interact with the puppets and thus actively relate to them. The puppets portray children who happen to have specific characteristics associated with disabilities, but mainly have personalities to which children can relate and with which they can identify. The puppets tell about themselves, interact with each other, and respond to questions raised by the children.

In some communities, similar programs have been developed that are specifically intended for preschool-age children. The Technical Assistance Program (TAP) in Cleveland, Ohio, has prepared a presentation called "We're More Alike Than Different" for preschool and day care programs:

> The program begins with a brief discussion of the ways we are all alike and different. Small hand puppets talk about their disabilities with the preschoolers, and the children are invited to ask them questions. They are introduced to Jonathan, who has cerebral palsy, and who is playing at school with his new friend, Robin. He explains to her that "No, you can't catch cerebral palsy, like a cold or the flu—it's something that you're born with!" Walter, who is visually impaired, "can do anything anybody else can!" He plays his favorite game, baseball, with a beeper ball. Patrick doesn't need to turn the television up as loudly as he once did, thanks to his new hearing aid, and Susan, whose developmental delay isn't easily noticed, learns things much slower than most people.
>
> Ample time is then provided for "hands-on" experiences by the preschoolers. The children use the puppets, and also equipment used by people with disabilities. Wheelchairs, walkers, crutches, canes, braces, beeper balls, and braille books are available. This is also a valuable time for teachers to observe and answer questions.
>
> Follow-up activities are suggested to the teacher. Equipment can occasionally be left with the class, and resource teachers can respond to any further needs. ("We're More Alike Than Different," Technical Assistance Program (TAP) Society for Crippled Children, 11001 Buckeye Road, Cleveland, Ohio 44104, (216) 795-7100.)

SAMPLE FROM "WE'RE MORE ALIKE THAN DIFFERENT": TALKING TO CHILDREN ABOUT HANDICAPS[1]

—FAMILIARIZE YOURSELF WITH THE HANDICAP. Ask questions, read, and get all the information you need to understand the handicap and how it affects the child. When you are knowledgeable, and feel comfortable that you know all you need to know about a specific disability, you will be able to translate that information to children.

—TALK TO THE CHILDREN ABOUT INDIVIDUAL DIFFERENCES. Talk about the ways we are all alike and different. Let them know that each person is different and special, with their own likes, dislikes, and capabilities. Explain that all people are good at some things and need help with others. Although we are all different, we are the same in many ways, and we all have many of the same feelings. There are many excellent books available in your public library that you can read to the children to help you with this discussion.

—EXPLAIN A CHILD'S HANDICAP TO CHILDREN IN LANGUAGE THAT THEY CAN UNDERSTAND. Use correct terms, but explain what they mean and how a disability affects a child in words a child can understand. Keep it simple. If a child was born with a handicap, explain that to the children. Let them know a handicap is not something they can catch. When explaining a handicap to a child, don't use the word "sick". They may fear that when they get sick, the same thing may happen to them.

If the handicapped child will look different to the other children, explain that to them. If he/she will be using any special equipment, such as hearing aid, walker, wheelchair, prosthesis, etc., explain the reason for it and how it works. If appropriate, encourage the children to try the equipment to see how it works. Let them know it is not something to fear. REPEAT INFORMATION SEVERAL TIMES.

—ENCOURAGE THE CHILDREN TO ASK YOU ANY QUESTIONS THEY MIGHT HAVE, AND LET THEM KNOW YOU ARE AVAILABLE TO TALK TO THEM ABOUT THE HANDICAP.

—ENCOURAGE THE CHILDREN TO WELCOME THE CHILD WITH THE DISABILITY INTO THEIR GROUP. Let them know that the child with the handicap needs and wants friends, just as they do. Encourage them to get to know the child.

—REMEMBER THAT YOUR ATTITUDE AND ACCEPTANCE OF A CHILD WITH A HANDICAP IS THE BEST MODEL FOR THE CHILDREN TO FOLLOW.

---

[1] For further information contact:
The Technical Assistance Project
Society for Crippled Children
11001 Buckeye Road
Cleveland, OH 44104
(216) 795-7100

Visiting is another good strategy. There is potential value in mutual visiting by children, parents, and teachers, not only in anticipation of an impending transition of a child from specialized to mainstream program but as part of the ongoing awareness and human relations emphasis in early childhood education. Teachers and parents of handicapped children need to know the requirements of the regular program, that is, what a child needs to be able to do to function successfully within the classroom.

An example of a mutual visitation program involving prekindergarten, kindergarten, and primary grade mainstream and special program children is one that teachers in Cleveland and Shaker Heights, Ohio, public schools initiated several years ago. First, the teachers themselves meet, observe each others' classrooms, and exchange information on programs and children. Activities follow that are oriented toward enabling both groups of children to know who their new friends will be. Slides portraying the individual children are shown to the respective groups, each child is identified by name, and each child's special interests and "likes" are mentioned. Eventually, exchange visits occur, with special activities including games in which children are paired with buddies to whom they had already been "introduced" through slides, photos, and exchanged letters. Parents participate also. In the spring teachers and parents plan a social event.

The young handicapped children have a variety of physical impairments and associated difficulties in communication, movement, and self-help skills. For them, these experiences are part of a process of transition into more typical, mainstream school programs. That process continues for some with visits and partial involvement in the actual classroom in which they will be integrated. For others, it may precede a total placement change to be implemented the following year. However, the visits are regarded primarily as a learning opportunity, as inherently enjoyable, and, in some instances, as a source of continuing friendships, rather than as trials to assess "readiness" for mainstreaming.

For the typical children, these particular visits are not isolated experiences in meeting new friends at other schools. Disabilities are discussed and adaptive equipment is described and explained, but these awareness activities are ongoing and integrated within general discussions of what people have in common. Once the children actually meet, there is a good deal of interest in and curiosity about wheelchairs, walkers, and other equipment, but the disabled children themselves are of far more interest than the equipment. The children learn songs that they sing together, and children spontaneously hold hands as they accompany each other when the visitors arrive and prepare to depart.

ORGANIZING THE CLASSROOM PROGRAM

Teaching young children inevitably involves two parallel levels of ongoing planning: planning that is done for individual children, and planning of the overall program. The latter involves varying time periods: (1) units may be planned to which several days or even weeks may be wholly or partially devoted; (2) traditionally, weekly plans take into account both regularly scheduled and variably scheduled "special" activities and events; and (3) a daily plan typically specifies time periods, how activities will be sequenced, large group and small group activity times, and where provision will be made for teacher-directed and for child-initiated and child-selected activity. All three forms of group planning need to be done in consideration of the individual needs of all children. And as in nearly all things, careful planning is the key to effective integration of young children with special needs in the mainstream program.

Guidelines for Enhancing Disability Awareness

1. Awareness activities with young children need to be ongoing since children's time concepts are uncertain, specific information may be forgotten or even distorted with the passage of time, and special activities precipitated by an impending new pupil tend to highlight the "special" characteristics of the child.

2. People with disabilities should be described and handicapping conditions presented in a realistic manner. It is misleading and even potentially harmful to portray people with disabilities as uniformly possessing extraordinary courage, motivation, and other virtues. Such a view of people with disabilities would surely make them seem very different from ordinary people.

3. Discussions with young children should focus on issues and use examples that are meaningful to them, that is, close to their own experiential world in time and space. That does not mean that children cannot identify with other children portrayed in a different historical or geographic/cultural context, however.

4. Children can understand the difference between empathy and sympathy, if adults help them to clarify this distinction, and why empathy is a more helpful and supportive response than feeling sorry for someone.

5. Children need to understand the concept of *independent functioning* and why that is such an important goal for a child with a disability, in the same way it is important for themselves.

6. Discussion and examples should stress and clarify the distinction between "helpful behavior" and "doing behavior." Young children need to know, for themselves as well as for other children who have disabilities, that everyone sometimes makes mistakes, needs assistance, and takes longer to learn some things than others.

7. Young children can understand the concept of the *uniqueness* of each individual, although there are many factors that are common to all: *we are all different, and we are all alike!*

8. Young children can both acquire empathy and grow in self-understanding through discussing and role-playing situations involving feelings that they experience and so do others, including children with disabilities: happiness and sadness; anger; curiosity; feelings of jealousy; being frightened; being embarrassed; feeling lazy; feeling proud, glad, upset, silly, frustrated, or grouchy.

9. Awareness activities should, at some point and in some manner, include and involve parents of the nonhandicapped

children. Young children's understanding and acceptance are mainly influenced by what they sense their parents', as well as their teacher's, attitudes to be. A teacher who makes a practice of communicating effectively with the parents and who invites parents to participate is both likely to have parents' confidence and support generally and to gain parental reinforcement in the area of disability awareness and acceptance.

10. The above presupposes the teacher's own understanding, both of children with disabilities and of the purposes and goals of mainstreaming.

11. The teacher's positive approach needs to include encouraging and reinforcing social interactions of nonhandicapped children with their handicapped peers.

12. The *physical environment and instructional arrangement* within the classroom should be planned so that social interaction is possible and is encouraged normally; thus, children are accustomed to working together, sharing, helping each other, and learning from each other.

13. In anticipating situations for imitation and modeling, the teacher can provide duplicate toys or other materials, so that children are accustomed to working and playing in parallel situations.

14. The teacher should avoid being judgmental, moralistic, or overly directive, both in preparatory awareness discussions and in actually implementing the integration process. Facilitating, guiding, and reinforcing typical children's positive initiation of interaction and appropriate helpfulness work better than coercing, punishing, or playing upon guilt, all of which are likely to be counterproductive.

15. A variety of activities can be effectively used, such as open-ended stories, class discussion, role play, and classroom guests such as people with disabilities or who know a lot about certain problems that they can share effectively with the children (Miller, 1988).

Guidelines for Organizing the Classroom Program

1. *Each child needs a "place"* where her things are kept, coat is hung, and papers are placed to be taken home, labeled with the child's name and, preferably, identified with the child's picture.

2. Circle Time may begin or end the day, or both, but it is a time for children to share, to be made especially aware of other children in the group, and to experience the attention and awareness of peers. Every child can participate! A child who requires adapted seating should be positioned to approximate the position of others in the group—in a wheelchair or adapted chair if others are seated in chairs, but an appropriate lying position may be needed if others are seated on a rug or on carpet squares. Adapted or augmentative communication procedures should be used if they are needed by some children. Children who have difficulty remaining seated during this highly important period of the day need to be specifically and systematically helped to do so through implementation of a data-based contingency management program.

3. *Transitions* from one type of activity to another are important to manage effectively. Teachers need to ensure that such

transitions are accomplished smoothly, rather than chaotically, without undue loss of time, and without some children being disoriented, at loose ends, or having to wait with nothing to do while other children's movements are coordinated. For some children, transitions may be especially difficult, and others may present logistical problems of locking and unlocking braces, etc.; however, for all young children they provide potentially valuable opportunities for teaching and learning. Young children learn to anticipate transitions, and routines that are familiar and clear need to be established. Effective transitions encourage children to learn to listen to specific directions and attend to cues.

4. Times for *self-selected activity or free play* provide ideal opportunities for observing children's individual preferences as potential reinforcers. They also may present, for some children, especially difficult times due to the lack of externally imposed structure. Thus, they present opportunities for instruction as well. However, since many children with developmental delays may not have extensive experience in situations requiring that they make choices, it is precisely *that* ability that can be fostered.

5. Attention should be given to the *placement and storage of materials* to ensure that unnecessary distraction is minimized, while access to needed/intended materials is enhanced. The items placed on low shelves, in learning centers or areas, or otherwise readily accessible should reflect pre-planning and careful selection. Items not intended to be used should be stored out of sight.

6. *Learning centers* provide ideal vehicles for peer-mediated learning and modeling cooperative learning, multisensory and concrete experiences, accommodating differences in learning style and time requirements, and involvement with self-directed and self-correcting materials that increase children's ability to work independently and enhance motivation to do so.

7. Varying *large-group and small-group activities* and varying group compositions provide children opportunities to apply, practice, and generalize skills in different social contexts, while also adapting the instructional mode to fit the instructional objectives. Some activities (e.g., creative movement activities, listening to/watching a dramatized story presented by teacher or peers) can better be accomplished if the entire group is involved, while others are more suited to dyads or small groups of three to five children. Alternating these can enhance all children's interest and involvement, while varied small-group compositions provide opportunities to apply and practice social skills while simultaneously addressing other skill areas.

8. *Time schedules* should be set but should be sufficiently flexible to allow continuation of especially productive activities, for individual children or groups, as well as differences in time requirements of individual children. *Transitions* can be structured so that children can move as individual needs dictate, and some activity sequences can involve a flow, rather than discrete beginning and ending points for all children.

9. *Bathroom use* can be accomplished based on individual rhythms to the extent feasible so that special needs of some children can be more readily accommodated and less group learning time is lost.

10. *A buddy system* can enable individual

children who require special help in orienting or moving to be assisted without reliance on the teacher and in a manner supportive of helpfulness and cooperation values.

SUMMARY

Accommodating and providing for individual children within the context of a group program *so that the learning of all group members is enhanced* is the core issue in integrated teaching in early childhood programs. Teaching young children in groups is surely more economically feasible than providing each child his or her own teacher. However, the group context of the classroom is far more than merely an economic necessity. Developmentally appropriate practices in early childhood education are in large measure predicated on a belief in the inherent value for young children of interacting with peers. Such practices do not reflect the assumption that all young children in a group have identical learning needs, styles, and characteristics. The challenge for the teacher is twofold: (1) to respond appropriately to the uniqueness of each child, and (2) to exploit the potential presented by the group situation for socialization, peer-mediated learning, and development of positive attitudes toward self and others.

CHAPTER 12

Working with Parents as Partners

The tradition of parent involvement in early childhood education is a long and a strong one. A great many nursery schools, day care centers, and special programs for handicapped children came into existence primarily or entirely because of the efforts of determined parents. During the ferment of the late 1960s and early 1970s, there was a burgeoning of "alternative schools," often generated by parents who were dissatisfied with what public education was providing for their youngsters. In this area, as in the case of community programs for children with special needs, the resourcefulness, diligence in fund-raising, and sheer hard work was a truly amazing example of the determination of parents to provide for their children the very best learning opportunities possible. One effect, in both alternative schools and special programs, was to stimulate public policy makers—federal and state agencies, as well as local community agencies and boards of education—to progress much more rapidly in developing public-supported programs and services.

The story of parent involvement in educational programs is too extensive to be fully recounted here. However, teachers and other professionals need to be cognizant of the fact that many of the services provided for children today, including services for children with special needs, came into being because of parent activism. Consequently, it is truly unfortunate that many professionals have been slow in learning to work effectively with parents as full partners, co-members of a team devoted to serving the best interests of the child. The preparation of teachers has typically stressed working with students but neglected working with parents and families. Content concerning families may be relegated to a single course, and some early childhood educators enter the profession without having had field experience with the parents of the children in the practicum settings in which they have worked.

Indeed, parents have been a potent political force but like all groups, parents designates a group made up of individuals, each with individual characteristics needs, strengths, and aspirations. The single unifying characteristic of all parents is the critical role they play in the lives of their children.

SPECIAL NEEDS OF FAMILIES

The ideal of a normal childhood is cherished by all parents. When parents learn that their new baby has a handicapping condition, or when they are told that the baby is at risk, their greatest fear is likely to be that that expectation will not be realized—that the dreams they had for this new son or daughter will be dashed. The very words that may be used by a doctor, nurse, social worker or other professional—words like birth defect, impairment, delay, or retardation—arouse the worst possible fear: the child will not be normal.

For most parents of handicapped newborns, the first reaction is shock. Despite whatever thoughts they might have entertained that their child might be among those with handicapping conditions, few have actually considered the realities of such a possibility. Some parents who have participated in genetic counseling and undergone preliminary medical tests may know from early in the mother's pregnancy that the child whose birth they await will have a condition termed Down syndrome, cerebral palsy, or spina bifida. Some may know only that the probability is high that their child will have a problem, but not how severe that problem will be, or what form it will take. Such advance knowledge does not soften the blow very much.

Not all children who are handicapped are impaired at birth, of course. For some children, the cause of a handicapping condition is not genetic or related to damage during pregnancy or the birth process. In many instances pregnancy, birth, and even early development are normal, but illness or accident results in permanent impairment of hearing, speech, vision, or cognitive motor or social behavior. For other children, the condition that results in developmental problems is present at birth but is of such a nature that the problems do not appear until later in life.

At whatever point the parents learn that their child is handicapped, a process of coping begins that, although experienced differently by different families, typically proceeds in stages leading to some degree of acceptance and adjustment (Bromwich, 1981; Gargiulo, 1985). Particularly illuminating accounts have been provided by professionals who are also parents of handicapped children (Turnbull & Turnbull, 1985). As these individual stories illustrate, parents must cope with many factors in addition to the emotional impact of having a child with a handicapping condition. These accounts by parents of children with handicaps also make clear that each family's experience is unique, just as each child is unique.

The effect on a family of having a handicapped child depends greatly on how the family defines the problem (Grossman, 1972). Although parents' adjustment to the child's handicapping condition is influenced by the severity of the disability, as well as the external support system (Schell, 1981), the parent's own values and perceptions are more critically important than the specific problems of the child (Bradshaw & Lawton, 1978). But for many parents, knowing where to turn for help, or what types of assistance might be available and how these can be accessed, are major concerns (Featherstone, 1980).

A number of potential sources of stress on parents and other family members may arise in the course of the child's development. Caregiving demands upon mothers are reported as major sources of stress (e.g., Beckman-Bell, 1981). In one study involving parents of preschool-age handicapped children (Winton & Turnbull, 1981), approximately two-thirds of the parents surveyed felt that a major value of early intervention was to provide a break from their continuous responsibilities for caring for their child. Also, opportunities for social interaction may be limited, both because of a child's needs for care and the difficulty in obtaining assistance to provide for those needs and because taking the child on visits, for recreational activities, shopping, or to church may itself be stressful (Bailey & Wolery, 1984). School placement issues constitute yet another major source of stress. The desire for a maximally normal educational placement is weighed against concerns about potential teasing and rejection, as well as the constant awareness of discrepancies between the handicapped child and typical peers. This dilemma is not necessarily resolved during the school years; for some parents, similar conflicts surround work and living arrangements associated with the transition to adult life (Blacher-Dixon & Turnbull, 1979).

Early childhood educators need to be aware of the continuing nature of the parents' involvement with this child, not only for the majority of the time she or he may participate in a preschool program or be a member of a kindergarten or primary-grade class but also throughout the years to follow. Teachers and other professionals will come and go, moving into and out of the child's life, but it is the parents who both provide continuity and must negotiate anew each year as their child's advocate (Association for the Care of Children's Health, 1987).

Fathers

Parents' involvement in early childhood programs is not limited to the involvement of mothers. The past assumptions and practices relating to mothers' role during the early years and as the parent most involved with the schools are familiar to everyone, as are some of the changes that have altered the situation for a great many mothers of young children.

One phenomenon that increased greatly during the 1970s and 1980s was single parenting of young children. Usually, in this situation we assume that it is the mother who is principal family support and principal nurturer, as well as the one who must strive to locate, and work to afford, quality child care for the young child. Increasingly, however, there is a possibility that the "single parent" of a child in day care or nursery school may be the father (Briggs & Walters, 1985). The scheduling of child care service presents difficulties for single fathers just as for single mothers—perhaps no more, but certainly no less (Orthner, Brown, & Ferguson, 1976).

In families of young children with special needs, school personnel and other professionals often assume that it is the mother who needs to be more involved, since (1) mothers have typically been given significant responsibilities for carrying out early intervention programming at home, especially in self-care activities such as eating, dressing, bathing, and toileting (e.g., Gallagher, Scharfman, & Bristol, 1984; Murray, 1984); and (2) a higher prevalence of father absence, divorce, and never-married mothers has been assumed with special needs children, although research results in this area are inconclusive (Darling & Darling, 1982). In fact, the incidence of divorce among parents of children with disabilities does not appear to be greater than that of parents of normally developing children when social class is held constant (Wikler, Haack, & Intagliata, 1984).

Many mothers' response to the question of whether an early intervention program had encouraged fathers' involvement is negative, or at least not strongly positive. When interviewed, mothers often state that they wished it would have been possible for their husbands to have been more involved. Programs designed for young children with handicaps and developmental delays have attempted to address this problem directly and creatively. Programs and materials specially designed for fathers have been developed (e.g., Meyer, Vadasy, Fewell, & Schell, 1986). Program elements intended to involve fathers more directly have been reported by a number of authors, based on their efforts to address what has posed a genuine dilemma and to enhance the beneficial impact of early intervention programs on the family as a whole, as well as on the child (e.g., Linder & Chitwood, 1984; Meyer et al., 1986; Markowitz, 1984). Lerner et al. (1987) have summarized these as including such provisions as: making videotape recordings of sessions available for home viewing; planning Saturday activities specifically for fathers and their children; specifically contacting the father; and having more male staff members involved in these programs.

Brothers and Sisters of Young Handicapped Children

In addition to the child with a handicap, parents' concerns may be shared among several siblings. A sister or brother of a handicapped child, whether younger or older, will frequently be affected by the fact of the sibling's disability. Her or his own role in the family will be influenced, to some degree, by the needs of the child with a disability. But siblings of disabled children are also individuals whose characteristics and needs are determined by the same complexity of influences that affect children who do not have a disabled sibling. We cannot generalize meaningfully, since each child, and each family, is unique.

Yet, there has long been concern that siblings of children with disabilities may be at risk for problems in social and emotional adjustment (e.g., Hannah &

Midlarsky, 1985; Powell & Ogle, 1985). There is some evidence (e.g., Breslau, 1982) that boys experience more psychological stress associated with having a handicapped sibling than girls; however, there is no evidence that a disproportionate number of emotionally disturbed children have siblings who are handicapped. This suggests that, although stress may be present, children—like their parents—manage to cope effectively with it, and may often be strengthened in the process.

Formal involvement of siblings in special programs serving young handicapped children and their families has taken at least two distinct forms. On the one hand, "reverse mainstreaming" in integrated preschools for handicapped children has been accomplished sometimes through the participation of typical siblings in the same programs. The siblings are not necessarily enrolled in the same actual classroom groups, but participate in age-appropriate groups in which their own specific social and cognitive needs can be addressed.

Some programs also provide opportunities for support groups for siblings themselves. Most often, professionals who work with parents stress the importance of including typical siblings in family discussions concerning the disabled child. Open discussion among nonhandicapped siblings, involving them in family decisions, and enlisting their help in integrating the handicapped child into the community, can diminish distress and elicit positive coping (Garland, Swanson, Stone, & Woodruff, 1981).

Specific programs and curricula have been developed for use with groups of siblings of handicapped children (e.g., Chinitz, 1981). Some have been specifically geared to working with nonhandicapped siblings of preschool age (e.g., Lobato, 1985). In general, these group approaches have been found effective in helping siblings both to understand disabilities and to understand themselves better, resulting in more effective coping skills and more positive attitudes relating to their situation and relationships.

Two forms of assistance that early childhood educators may apprise families of are *Sibshops* and the Sibling Information Network. *Sibshops* (Meyer, Vadasy, & Fewell, 1985) is a handbook for implementing workshops for siblings of handicapped children and focuses on ways to provide siblings with an opportunity to

> Meet other siblings in a relaxed recreational setting;
> Discuss common joys and concerns with other siblings;
> Learn how others handle situations commonly experienced by siblings of handicapped children;
> Learn more about the implications of their brother's or sister's handicap;
> To provide parents with an opportunity to learn about common sibling concerns. (p. 11–13)

The Sibling Information Network (Powell, 1986) publishes a quarterly newsletter for an international sibling readership. It is affiliated with the University of Connecticut in Storrs, Connecticut.

Extended Family Members

Extended family members, especially grandparents, may both pose additional difficulties and represent a potential, often ineffectively used, resource (Gabel & Kotsch, 1981). Some mothers report (Safford, Harvey, Krutilla, Safford, & Thompson, 1988) that lack of understanding and support from their husbands' parents has represented a major source of stress. Early intervention assistance has been reported by parents to be helpful in enabling parents to discuss and explain their child's disability to relatives (Safford & Arbitman, 1975). A grandparent can provide the most constant and effective support. In some families, a grandmother may in fact be the child's principal caregiver—the person with whom the teacher primarily communicates and who participates in the program components intended to involve parents. Grandparents frequently experience many of the same emotions as parents on learning of the child's handicap (Vadasy, Fewell, & Meyer, 1986). They need the same information and support but do not have the same access to it that parents do.

Most grandparents who are primary caregivers of young children will prove cooperative with the school, preschool, or daycare staff, helpful in carrying out recommendations at home and in following consistent approaches with the child at home and in school. They, like the professionals, are concerned primarily with the best interests of the child. Their unique insights and far more intimate knowledge about the child prove indispensable.

PARENT INVOLVEMENT IN EARLY INTERVENTION PROGRAMS

Although parent involvement is traditional in all areas of early childhood education, it has been especially emphasized in programs designed especially for young children with special needs (Peterson, 1987). The basis for the especially strong emphasis in these programs derives from research, legal mandates, and common sense (Cartwright, 1981). Parent involvement may take many forms, ranging from passive, "audience" roles, through increasingly greater levels of more active involvement with professionals, to "parents as decision makers, policy makers, and advisers" (Cartwright, 1981, p. 4).

The forms of parent involvement in early intervention programs include those typical of many nursery school programs, and others, as well. Welsh and Odum (1981) identified six general forms of parent involvement in programs serving young children with special needs:

1. Providing social and emotional support for parents, through counseling and through parent group participation.
2. Parent education, in the form of individualized training in working with their child, parent education groups, or both.
3. Parents carrying out programming with their child, using techniques and

strategies demonstrated by professionals, in the school or center setting, at home, or both.
4. Parents participating in the classroom, as observers or as teaching assistants.
5. Parents and professionals communicating with each other to exchange information about the child's strengths, interests, needs, progress, etc.
6. Parent involvement in program planning, management, administration, and evaluation. (p. 16)

Based on the experience of the Portage Project, one of the best-known pioneering early intervention programs emphasizing parent-professional collaboration, Shearer and Shearer (1977) summarized the following important principles:

1. Parents of handicapped children need parenting and teaching skills that parents of typical children do not necessarily need to have.
2. Since they know their own child best, parents can provide a valuable resource to professionals in developing functional objectives for the child.
3. Optimally, there is planned consistency between the educational program and the experiences provided by the parents.
4. Siblings of the handicapped child can benefit from the parent education, training, and guidance parents receive through their involvement in their handicapped child's program.
5. Parents can acquire skills both to teach new skills and to modify inappropriate and interfering behaviors.
6. Parent involvement can greatly accelerate the child's rate of learning. (p. 78)

Some of the specific areas of focus in parent training include: physical management, managing self-care and daily living activities, guidance and behavior management, and communication. Obviously, needs differ depending upon both child and family. In general, Honig (1978) has suggested that parents' ability to cope effectively with the demands of having a handicapped child can be enhanced if they are helped to develop certain characteristics and behaviors, especially flexibility, observation skills, ability to challenge the child, nurturing skills, and teaching skills.

Some early intervention programs especially designed for young children with significant delays or impairments in social skills and/or who manifest behavioral problems—such as the LEAP Program at the University of Pittsburgh (Strain, 1987), and the Early Intervention Centers of the Positive Education Program (PEP) serving the Greater Cleveland, Ohio, areas (Maxwell & Pallotta, 1979)—have specific requirements for parent participation with their children.

For parents of children with physical disabilities or motor delays, specific demonstration and guidance are provided for parents to be able to help their child manage dressing, eating, bathing, and other self-care areas, as well as enhancing mobility and play skills (e.g., Finnie, 1975; Hanson & Harris, 1986).

The nature of children's language development suggests the need for working directly with, and through, parents in the early years. Recognizing that young children's language development proceeds from prelinguistic communicative inter- actions between infant and caregiver, Stremel-Campbell and Rowland (1987) state that professionals must have specific skills based on our understanding of the communicative basis of language, including

> . . . the ability to (a) identify effective and ineffective parent interaction patterns, (b) identify and then point out the infant's competences to the parent, (c) demon- strate strategies that promote infant responsiveness and mutual engagement, and (d) provide contingent feedback to the parent for effective exchanges. (p. 54)

Parent programs can be home-based, center-based, media-based, or a com- bination of these (Cartwright, 1981). Although much needs to be done in terms of evaluating the effectiveness of various forms of parent involvement, there are indications (e.g., DeBerry, Ristau, & Galland, 1984) that participation rates are highest in programs that provide both training and information.

CHANGING VIEWS ON PARENT INVOLVEMENT IN EARLY INTERVENTION

Of particular interest to the mainstream early childhood educator should be the changes in perspective that have recently occurred among professionals who provide special services, especially through early intervention programs. While the important role of parents has always been recognized, there is a new recogni- tion of and respect for the needs of families and for the differences among families (Gallagher, Beckman, & Cross, 1983).

Typically, early childhood special education programs have designed specific "components" relating to parents of the children served. Decisions about these components have been based primarily upon the professionals' understanding of parents' needs and of their potential contributions toward the achievement of program goals. Increasingly, however, professionals have come to recognize, and respond to, the diversity of needs that parents themselves have, as well as those of their children. Whereas the original "model" for parent involvement in early childhood special education programs derived from programs for children at environmental risk, especially because of poverty, parents of handicapped children span the full spectrum of family income and environmental circumstance. That fact, together with the increased recognition of the dynamic, changing nature of families and their needs, led Foster, Berger, and McLean (1981) to state:

> The time has come to stop thinking of parent involvement as implying a specific set of activities (e.g., parent groups, observations, meetings, or political action). Rather, a concern for parent involvement is best shown through a point of view that continually takes into account the needs and skills of the entire family. Such a point of view does not rule out any of the current types of parent services (each of

which is appropriate for many families) but rather requires that services be selected on the basis of a comprehensive understanding of a family's unique situation. Professionals need to learn to think as well about family development as they do about child development. (p. 63)

It has become increasingly clear that families have different needs and that parent education and support efforts need to provide for this individuality on the part of families as well as children. For example, Winton and Turnbull (1981) found that mothers of preschool handicapped children indicated preferences for different areas of activity and involvement in their children's program. They also found that the needs and preferences of individual mothers changed over time.

These observations imply the need for professionals to learn more about relationships between parent characteristics and needs, on the one hand, and the elements of effective programs, on the other. That is, parents could be matched with services and, where indicated, the services could be adapted or modified to fit the needs of specific parents at any point in their development as parents.

One well-known early intervention program for handicapped infants and their families (Hanson, 1981), noting the diversity and dynamic quality of parents' needs, provided services of four general types:

1. *Demonstration and teaching* of parenting and facilitative skills by teachers and therapists.
2. *Assistance provided in the home.*
3. *Parent support activities,* including advocacy and guidance, parent support groups, and full parent involvement in the regular review of children's programs.
4. *Parent workshops,* for presenting information opportunity for social interaction among parents and for family members who are unable to attend daytime activities to be present and involved.

The very diversity of forms of parent involvement in programs for young children with special needs has made it difficult to evaluate its effectiveness as a component of early intervention. Research results are inconclusive (e.g., Casto & Mastropieri, 1986). However, some authors (e.g, Deberry et al., 1984) conclude that individual programs with effective parent involvement components are those which, although structured in terms of explicit objectives, are also individualized and responsive to the individual needs of parents. Further, seemingly anticipating the intent of PL 99–457, Welsh and Odum (1981) concluded from their review of research that successful early intervention programs appeared to be those that support parents in their role as the child's primary teacher and work toward strengthening the parent-child relationship. Increasingly, those who provide services for young children think in terms of *program involvement with families,* rather than family involvement with programs (Association for the Care of Children's Health, 1987).

The current emphasis on focusing services on the family unit rather than solely on the child reflects recognition of the legitimacy of the needs of parents and other family members, as well as of the critical role of the family in influencing the course of the child's development. That concept characterized programs developed to serve the complex needs of low-income families, such as Parent and Child Centers, Child and Family Mental Health projects, Homestart, and Child and Family Resource Programs. As E. Zigler and V. Seitz (1980) observed, the Child and Family Resource Programs (CFRP) were based on the premise that children's development cannot be optimal as long as serious family problems remain unresolved.

Even prior to the enactment of PL 99–457, formalizing the concept of an Individual Family Services Plan (IFSP), programs for young handicapped children that provided family-focused intervention had been developed. An example is the Family Intervention Project (Berger & Fowlkes, 1980), which attempted to address needs of all family members, including those of the handicapped child. Using a family network approach, this program develops linkages for families with community agencies and services. Issues deemed most important by family members provide the focus for intervention and assistance.

Although families of handicapped children have in common with most families a number of basic characteristics, concerns, and needs, many such families experience difficulties specifically related to the needs of the handicapped child. Moroney (1981, cited in Mallory, 1981) summarized the types of "private troubles" to which families of handicapped children are so especially susceptible that they warrant public concern, addressed through public policy:

1. additional financial burdens
2. actual or perceived stigma
3. extraordinary demands on time for personal care of the child
4. difficulty with feeding, washing, and dressing
5. decreased time for sleep
6. social isolation from friends, relative, and neighbors
7. decreased time for leisure activities
8. behavior management difficulties
9. difficulty in performing routine domestic activities
10. general feelings of pessimism about the future. (p. 83)

Like persons with disabilities themselves, parents and other family members neither need nor want pity because of the difficulties and special stresses they may experience. Many parents recognize and accept the special responsibilities they may have, while also valuing the positive aspects of family life. Professionals should recognize parents' legitimate rights to relate to the child as a child, rather than as a "client," and to pursue their own interests, separate from those relating specifically to the handicapped child.

Stressing the importance of parent involvement to enhance children's development, professionals often have failed to recognize the legitimate needs of parents to have others assume responsibility for working with their child (Winton & Turnbull, 1981). This, for a brief time, relieves the parent of responsibilities that otherwise must be borne for most of the child's care and guidance. Parents, like teachers and other professionals who work with children, perhaps especially those with disabilities, may experience "burnout" (Hagen, 1981). Special educators involved in providing early intervention services have not, until recently, shown recognition of either differential stress upon parents associated with the child's temperamental characteristics or the consequent differences in the needs of parents during this period in their child's development (Beckman-Bell, 1981). Indeed, parents would presumably be even more susceptible to "burnout" than professionals—particularly if their child's characteristics and needs are especially stressing. Their emotional involvement is infinitely greater, as parents, and the scope of their involvement is far more comprehensive and continuous (Schell, 1981).

There is no doubt that "parent involvement" is viewed as important by parents of young handicapped children as it is by professionals. But that involvement does not necessarily imply that parents think they can, or should, do the job of professionals—as well as their own, already demanding job. In their study of perspectives on parent involvement of parents of preschool-age handicapped children, Winton and Turnbull (1981) found that, "Parents valued competent and sensitive professionals being involved with their children's education so that they could have a break from these responsibilities for a part of the day." (p. 18). About two-thirds of these parents felt that a major benefit of an early intervention program was to give them a break from the continual responsibility of caring for their child. However, they also valued opportunities for regular, informal contact with their child's teacher. Although these parents wanted to maintain regular and frequent contact with the teacher, most did want to act as teachers themselves.

PARENTS' NEED FOR CHILD CARE

Day care represents an important need for parents of handicapped children, as well as for other parents. In fact, financial stress experienced by families of young handicapped children increases their need for employment, which is generally the primary reason parents of young children have for seeking child care outside the home (Klein, 1981). Winton and Turnbull (1981) reported that 35 percent of the mothers of preschool-age handicapped children they surveyed worked and stressed the availability of quality day care as a highly important concern. Day care programs are regarded by parents as family support systems (Belsky & Sternberg, 1978). For parents of young handicapped children, they provide opportunities for their child to interact with nondisabled peers and to have experiences congruent with the principle of normalization (Klein, 1981).

Teachers in half-day preschool programs can anticipate being asked for suggestions from parents of handicapped children about possible child care options complementary to participation in the half-day program. Such needs are realistic considering work requirements, and they are peculiar neither to parents of handicapped children nor to parents of typical children.

Resources that may be of value for parents include *A Parent's Guide to Day Care* (Publication OHDS 80–30254, Superintendent of Documents, U. S. Government Printing Office, Washington, D. C. 20402, $3.50), and *Choosing Child Care: A Guide for Parents* (Auerbach & Freedman, 1976, available from Parent and Child Care Resources, 1169 Howard Street, San Francisco, CA 94103, $3.00).

Dittman (1986) suggests important guidelines for parents seeking good child care for both typical and special needs infants and toddlers. She notes the importance of safety considerations, a stimulating environment, and caregiver qualities of responsiveness to the individuality of babies and toddlers, their tendency to talk with and respond to each, and their encouragement of parental involvement with their child.

PARENTS' BELIEFS ABOUT INTEGRATION AND MAINSTREAMING

Do parents of young children with disabilities want their children to be integrated in regular, mainstream programs? How do parents of nondisabled children feel about it? Aren't many of the former fearful that their child may be teased because of his or her differences or rejected or scapegoated by peers? Or aren't they concerned that the child's special needs cannot be addressed as effectively as in a special setting? Aren't many of the latter concerned that a child with a disability may require so much of the teacher's time and attention that their own child may be neglected?

These questions merit both attention within an individual class or program and research studies designed to identify beliefs and possible concerns. Dr. Ann Turnbull and her associates (Turnbull, Winton, Blacher, & Salkind, 1982) summarized their research findings concerning the perspectives of parents of kindergarten-age children, noting that parents of both handicapped and nonhandicapped children shared very similar viewpoints. They agreed both on the benefits of mainstreaming and on the potential drawbacks for handicapped children if their special needs were to be insufficiently addressed. They shared the view that important social benefits can result for both groups. Very importantly, parents of the typical children saw their own children's development of more sensitivity as the greatest benefit of mainstreaming. The researchers suggested that, based on this finding, concerns about "backlash" did not seem to be warranted. The only disagreement reported was that parents of the handicapped children agreed more strongly with the statement "mainstreaming makes handicapped children want to try harder." That is, parents of children with special needs attributed greater potential motivational benefits for their children in mainstream situations.

The perceived potential drawbacks pertained to instruction, rather than social aspects, and focused on the special needs of children with handicaps, rather than their typical peers. Both groups of parents indicated that it was essential that handicapped children receive whatever special help and individualized instruction they might need within the regular kindergarten. This they believed, depended greatly on the ability and preparation of the teacher. The researchers concluded that parents believe that educators must develop strategies through which interventions sufficiently intensive and individualized can be provided within the mainstream kindergarten environment. This parental concern that teachers need to be able to meet special needs of young handicapped children in the mainstream classroom environment has been found especially important in other studies as well (e.g., Bailey & Winton, 1987).

Initially, some parents of nonhandicapped children may be concerned about the prospects of children with handicapping conditions participating in a program with their own children. First, they may have had some exposure to people with disabilities in a society where segregation, myths, and stereotypes existed, and they may have preconceptions about disabilities and emotional reactions to a disability label. Second, any parent's initial concern about any change from past practice (a new teacher, moving to a new school location, a different schedule, etc.) will be, "How will it affect my child?" But virtually all nursery and day care, kindergarten, and primary grade teachers and administrators discover that concerns, or even fears, that parents have quickly dissipate once parents can see the handicapped child and interact with his or her parents.

As with the children, parents' expectations are greatly influenced by the attitude communicated by the teacher. Parents of both typical and disabled children are reassured by a teacher who:

Respects the individual needs of all children.

Conveys uniformly positive attitudes toward each child in the group, not singling out one or two as sources of potential concern.

Conveys a sense of self-confidence in his or her ability to work with all children in the group.

Refrains from speaking negatively to any parent about the characteristics or behavior of another child.

Responds directly and factually to questions raised by a parent, whether of a handicapped or a typical child.

Bailey and Winton (1987) reported that initial concerns expressed by parents of nonhandicaped children participating in an integrated day care program were substantially reduced after a nine-month period. Parents of both handicapped and nonhandicapped children agreed on their perceptions of the major benefits of mainstreaming: enhanced experience for the handicapped child and enhanced acceptance by others. Nonetheless, parents of the children with disabilities in this study continued to express concern that their child might experience teasing or rejection. The researchers suggested that such persisting concerns imply the need for teachers to be particularly sensitive to subtle indications that might otherwise go unnoticed.

A good principle to remember is that, whereas every parent is concerned primarily about her or his own child, a commonality exists among all parents in that very concern; therefore, parents readily relate to the concerns and aspirations of other parents once they have the opportunity to know and interact with them as individuals. "Mainstreaming" and "integration" are abstractions, principles to which individuals who happen to be parents may, or may not, be committed. General attitudes and values of individual parents, and also commitment to a program's philosophy that espouses integration and mainstreaming, are surely very important considerations. Yet more important are the relationships among parents of young children in a given program.

WHAT DO PARENTS WANT FROM THEIR CHILD'S SCHOOL EXPERIENCE?

It may seem an oversimplification to state that parents of a young child with a disability want for their child what all parents want for their children. Disappointments occur and sometimes expectations may have to be modified. Yet most parents' expectations and hopes are both realistic and appropriate. Special concerns that the child have the assistance and support he or she needs, and is entitled to, are balanced against the desire for the child to be treated like all other children, to become maximally independent, and to be accepted and respected on the basis of her or his own merits and accomplishments.

One mother reported that her son, a child with a physical disability who had been mainstreamed since kindergarten, began to manifest some behavior problems when in school:

> There was a lot of behavioral acting-out, clowning around, mouthing off: 'Here I am, somebody pay attention to me!' There has been some of that 'poor little crippled kid' attitude underlying a lot of things that happen. It's easier for them [school personnel] sometimes to go overboard than to treat him like a normal student who has difficulty getting around. They put his disability first, and act upon that, rather than act in response to him as a student. That's probably what contributed to some of those little behavior problems, the fact that he's sensitive enough to understand that, and so now he's trying to use it. But the school system is now aware of that problem and they have told him that they will not cater to him.
>
> They had hired an attendant, who helped him with catheterization. He's been self-cathing since he entered school, but the aide assisted him in that area and getting up and downstairs and that sort of thing. And although she was a very nice person, she was perhaps too helpful. For instance, I remember walking into the classroom one day and he was just standing there so she could take off his mittens and hat, which she did without even thinking, and stuffed them in his pockets.

What we've always done is, whatever he can do himself, he does for himself. So there were some mixed messages. At home nobody did anything for him, and at school this aide did everything for him. She had the idea that, if she really wanted to earn her pay, she should help him even with things he didn't need her for. She's gotten better.

Although communication between school personnel and parents has always been considered of utmost importance, though not always ideally effected, parent involvement in the education of exceptional children is especially emphasized, both in policy and in practice. The parent is one of the three persons who must sign an IEP and, at minimum, informed parental consent to specialized diagnostic assessment of the child and to the resultant educational plan is mandated.

Some reports (e.g., Baker & Brightman, 1984; Cone, Delawyer, & Wolfe, 1985) reflect that parent involvement in the school planning process for their handicapped students is far from uniformly present and effective. Schools sometimes fail to fulfill their responsibilities to ensure parent input and participation in the decision-making process. Following the letter of the law can occur without maintaining the spirit of the law. It is still frequently reported that the extent of a parent's involvement is to approve a pre-prepared IEP and acknowledge and approve the recommendations presented at the time for annual review. In some instances, even that minimal level of involvement may not be present.

The idea of a partnership between parents and professionals, however, is reflected in the way many parents involve themselves in school planning and the way many professionals recognize and respect the role of parents. Such mutual respect, communication, cooperation, and collaborative team effort is not an unachievable ideal, but something that is realized in school-parent teamwork in schools throughout the nation. Among the numerous examples of evidence of this was a study reported by Meyers and Blacher (1987), indicating that the parents of the severely handicapped children studied, overall, were both highly involved in their child's school program and very satisfied with it.

As noted previously, more intensive levels of parent involvement have characterized programs serving young handicapped children. Increasingly, these programs have attempted not only to maximize parent participation in order to facilitate the child's developmental progress, but also to address the needs of parents and families themselves. In fact, the primary reasons for early intervention have been stated to be, ". . . to enhance the child's development, to provide support and assistance to the family, to enhance the child's and the family's benefit to society, and to avoid some or all of the costly difficulties that can accrue for both the child and family when intervention is delayed" (Joint Statement of the Division for Early Childhood and Interact, 1986).

If enhancing the quality of life for the child and the family is the major goal of early education for young children with special needs (Fewell & Vadasy, 1987), the perceptions of parents must be considered. As Wolery (1987) has observed, parents and professionals do not always agree on goals and priorities. He recommends a negotiation process based on mutual respect, through which parents recognize that their own values and opinions are considered leading to collaborative goal-setting.

Past difficulties in achieving and maintaining such relationships have been in part due to professionals' lack of understanding of the realities of parents' responsibilities and needs (Turnbull & Turnbull, 1985). Professionals may have emotional responses to the parents and their situation that can interfere with communication. Even over-concern or over-identification with parents can impede the relationship. Understanding, openness, and mutual respect are essential to a productive parent-teacher relationship. Beyond that, what parents expect of the teacher is to teach their child. They also expect that the teacher will have specific priorities and goals in mind. However, it is not only in the interest of building rapport, but also to determine what are indeed the most appropriate and meaningful objectives, that the teacher should ask, "What do you want your child to learn? What do you want me to help your child be able to do?"

INTEGRATING PARENTS

Effective communication with parents is critical to the success of integrated teaching. Just as the interrelationships among typical and handicapped children on a child-to-child level are important, similar relationships among parents both enhance children's mutual acceptance and friendship formation and build a common sense of ownership of and identification with their children's program. Parents, too, will recognize the many things they have in common, even though all of their children are unique individuals. For parents of young handicapped children, their own and their child's participation in a "mainstream" preschool, kindergarten, or primary experience constitutes an appropriate and a needed area of normalization.

Early childhood centers that already have a high degree of parent involvement—a very active parent group, parent contributions to the classroom program, as in a co-op preschool, participation in social or fund-raising projects, etc.—have available the best ways of involving parents of handicapped children. That principle also applies to the school setting, where room projects, officers, committees, and other mechanisms represent effective ways of "integrating" parents of young children with special needs. In an important sense, the effectiveness of the integration that young handicapped children experience is greatly enhanced by the degree to which their parents and those of nonhandicapped class members interact, know and respect each other as individuals, and work together in pursuit of common goals. And, as in the case with the child's integration in the classroom, full and meaningful parent integration is in large measure dependent upon the quality of ongoing parent communication and involvement.

SUMMARY

As public schools become increasingly involved in serving young children through prekindergarten instructional programs, extended kindergarten programs, and day care, they will become increasingly involved with families, in a manner qualitatively different from that that has become traditional with families of older students. The typical style in early chilldhood programs has emphasized mutual communication and awareness. It has replaced the *in loco parentis* "contract" with an understanding that parents do not turn over their responsibilities to school personnel, that educators cannot assume parental prerogatives. With young children a different level of shared responsibility is required than can be achieved through a simple downward extension of present practice in maintaining home–school communications. That is well understood by most teachers of young children, whether in public school or preschool settings. Teachers are well aware of their shared responsibilities for nurturing the early learning and development of the young child, but they approach their task with a sense of humility, recognizing the profoundly important, and continuing, role of parents.

Parents of young children with handicapping conditions share the concerns that all parents have about their child during these critically important early years, but their anxieties are multiplied. Nevertheless, like all parents, they too have other concerns: other children to be cared for, concerns about relationships with spouses or others, work, and simply time for themselves. It is a disservice to people with disabilities to expect all to have an extra measure of courage or to be uniformly pleasant, courteous, agreeable, and eager to please. Similarly, it is a disservice to parents of children with disabilities to expect these and other virtues of them, more, that is, than of other parents. Many parents of young children with disabilities have already learned, often through hard experience, that if they do not advocate for—perhaps even demand!—what is right for their child, no one else will. But parents are generally likely to see their child's teacher as their ally, as their partner, and as the single person most likely to share their feeling for their child as a very special, unique individual.

CHAPTER 13

Using Supportive and Supplemental Resources

Providing for children with disabilities within mainstream early education class-rooms requires basically the same skills in teaching children and in working cooperatively with parents that a teacher needs in any classroom situation. The key additional abilities that are required are those that enable you to access and use resources that may be beneficial or even essential for a specific child. Such resources can make the difference between reasonable and unreasonable expectations for the teacher, and between a truly optimal experience for the handicapped child and one that is less than positive.

For handicapped children served in special education settings, a team approach is considered essential. Several professionals, each with a particular expertise, contribute to the planning and implementation of appropriate programs. Providing for the handicapped child within the mainstream does not suggest that there is no further need for supportive or supplementary assistance or for a team approach. On the contrary, such an approach continues to be essential.

As is true of other areas, however—planning the classroom environment, selecting activities and materials, talking with children, and working with parents—accessing and using school and community resources to facilitate mainstreaming simply involves extending what is desirable for all children. *Learning Opportunities Beyond the School,* a publication of the Association for Childhood Education International (1987) is devoted to discussions of numerous potential resources in the community and in the home that can be drawn on to enrich their lives and learning. Every school provides a wealth of potential resources on which creative teachers can draw, in order to bring into the classroom the special knowledge of fellow teachers and other staff, as well as a wide variety of instructional media.

You may be reassured by the discussions in this chaper of the kinds of assistance likely to be provided, how teachers and other personnel have worked together in other communities, and to whom you might bring specific types of questions. In presenting this information, we will pull together concepts and guidelines that have been discussed and illustrated through examples throughout previous chapters.

Topics addressed in this chapter fall into three main categories: *transition* from one educational setting to another; *coordination of services* provided for children and families by various personnel and agencies; and *consultation and support* for working with the child in the classroom setting. We will spend the most time on the last, since this is likely to require the most effective and creative problem-solving on your part. Remember, however, that here too you are a member of a team. Mainstreaming does not mean that either you or the disabled child are left "on your own."

Much is expected of teachers today. The roles of those who provide care outside the home and who teach young children have changed substantially in recent years, and continue to change. Before we describe the variety of ways in which professional specialists and other potential sources of assistance can contribute to integrated teaching, some observations about the status of and expectations for teachers in the early childhood field are in order.

TEACHING YOUNG CHILDREN: A ROLE IN TRANSITION

The role of teachers of young children may be more complex and multifaceted even than that of other teachers. The complexity and diversity of teaching and caregiving roles may account for the difficulty sometimes reported (e.g., Feeney & Chun, 1985) in identifying what personal and professional qualities contribute most to making an effective teacher of young children. Concerns about the professional status of early childhood educators (e.g., Bredekamp, 1987) have led to a heightened focus upon the knowledge base of the field, and the relationship between theory and research in child development and practice in early childhood programs. Knowledge of the learning process, appropriate applications of alternative instructional techniques, and of "content" in the various curricular areas for which teachers are responsible are all expected. The last of these includes more than a little learning in the sciences, mathematics, the social sciences, literature, art, and music. Increasingly, elementary teachers are required to have a *content area specialization* as well as a *comprehensive liberal education* prior to or in addition to their specific professional training. Teaching young children appropriately is informed by philosophical considerations and personal values inherent in the concept of a liberal education. Although teachers of young children need to be well trained, they also need to be well educated.

Because of the expansion of day care and nursery programs in recent years, standards of preparation, competence, status, and reimbursement in these fields have emerged as major national issues (Bredekamp, 1987). Whitebook (1986) has reported persistent problems in the day care field, all interrelated, including a serious shortage of well-qualified personnel, low morale, low pay, and high turnover. We cannot expect well-trained professionals with baccalaureate or even graduate degrees to work long hours, enjoy few fringe benefits, have little or no job security, and receive an hourly wage that is substantially subprofessional.

Professional status, wages, and benefits for individuals who provide child care represent the extreme form of a more general problem that this country has been attempting to address since the first of the major educational reform reports appeared in the early 1980s. The teaching profession has been strengthened as a result of these attempts, but the vital importance of the work that teachers do continues to be insufficiently recognized, and the contributions of teachers at all levels continue to be insufficiently rewarded.

Teachers are regarded as *professionals,* as experts or specialists who have been prepared professionally to fill an extremely important role. However, the teacher is not assumed to be a special educator or a therapist. The presence of children with disabilities does not require a different style of teaching than that which is appropriate for all young children. But that presence may enable teachers to become more effective in using general teaching practices.

That principle applies both in school and in day care situations. For example, Carole Ellison (in personal communication with the author) reported that teachers in centers participating in a Special Needs Day Care Consortium were both receptive to handicapped children placed in their programs and quick to adapt to the special needs they presented. She reported that three role dimensions, in particular, appeared to be significantly strengthened in these situations: (1) teachers' informal, ongoing observation and recording of children's behavior; (2) mutual support and assistance among teaching staff members; and (3) teachers' adaptations of materials in the centers for individual use by children.

In summary, early childhood educators are *expected* to accommodate a wide range of abilities, developmental levels, emotional needs, and personal-social characteristics within the group program (Bredekamp, 1987; Moyer et al., 1987). Diversity among children in every early childhood classroom is a central reality that the person who intends to teach must recognize. What is good early childhood practice for typical children is good, in most instances, for those who have special needs.

However, with some children, the teacher may be one of several professionals—and the school or center may be one of several agencies—involved with the child or family. Where that is the case, communication, cooperation, and consistency are important. The teacher's work with the child can be greatly enhanced, "mixed messages" to child and family will be less likely, and the efforts of others can be enhanced by the teacher's observations and insights. At the core, of course, is the family itself. Families of children with handicaps have all too frequently experienced fragmentation of services and difficulties due to the lack of communication among professionals and agencies. A special monograph of the Association for the Care of Children's Health, *Family-Centered Care for Children With Special Health Needs* (1987, 2nd edition) describes this problem most effectively and suggests policies and practices for professionals and agencies to adopt in order to correct it. In addition, for a specific child in the classroom or center, supportive and consultative assistance of others can be readily accessed and used.

WHAT KINDS OF HELP DO MAINSTREAM TEACHERS WANT?

Generally, expressed needs for resource assistance for childhood teachers and caregivers fall into the following groups:

1. *Background information* about the child, the nature of the handicapping condition, and relevant guidelines based on the nature of the disability (e.g., seizure potential, medical or dietary precautions, etc.);
2. *Direct assistance,* if needed, for as long as needed, in the person of a resource teacher, special therapist, classroom aide, or other individual, as appropriate;
3. *Indirect assistance,* in the form of consultation, suggested strategies, and guidance in response to specific questions;
4. *Special instructional or adaptive materials* that might be helpful in working with a specific child.

Many teachers and day care staff are outspoken about the necessity for these forms of support. Some have experienced frustration when, from their perspective, little or no outside aid was provided to support their work with a young child who had special needs. The other side of the coin is suggested by several points previously addressed in this book: (1) a normalized, rather than "special" approach is desirable, so that the role of the disability is minimized; (2) effective teaching of young children with disabilities is not qualitatively different from good teaching for all young children; (3) highly specialized instructional materials are not only undesirable (from the standpoint of normalization), they are seldom necessary; (4) many specialists may regard young children with mild and moderate disabilities as, quite simply, "no problem!"

Mainstream teachers must understand these points, but therapists, special educators, and parents must attempt to view mainstreaming situations from the perspective of the mainstream early childhood educator as well. There is one basic reason why the latter is important: *to maximize the likelihood of successful experiences for the children involved.* In some instances, the regular teacher may quickly come to see that initial fears, concerns, and felt needs were unwarranted. The concerns of those seeking help are real to them, however. We must provide help. For a resource person, a request like, "Tell me what children with cerebral palsy are like" is problematic. But the best response is simply to answer the question. In the course of hearing a brief, introductory, descriptive discussion of cerebral palsy, the questioner may form more pertinent and appropriate questions.

However, resource assistance focuses most frequently on specific children. There are particular kinds of information about any disabled child that must be communicated at the outset, including:

> *Medical and health-related information,* such as specific allergies (including food allergies and allergies to certain medications); medical precautions; whether the child may experience seizures; other information relevant to a specific health-related concern, such as chronic cardiac or respiratory problems, hemophilia, osteogenesis imperfecta (brittle bone disease); medications the child is taking; history of otitis media.
>
> *Information concerning vision and hearing,* including whether the child has specific difficulties in either area, nature of difficulty, implications for classroom participation, correction measures and limitations, and related services and/or specific instructional adaptations indicated.
>
> *Information concerning motor functioning and self-care skills and needs,* relating to mobility, prosthetic or orthotic equipment, positioning guidelines and adaptive equipment, or special considerations concerning eating (adaptations, food textures, etc.) or elimination (e.g., catherization, schedule, etc.).
>
> *Information concerning communication skills, needs, and adaptations,* if any are required.

As is the case for all children, parents of children with handicaps are the primary source of information concerning health-related information. Specific medical data and physicians' recommendations are accessed by the school contingent upon parent release, and state laws require that certain kinds of information (such as immunization records) be forwarded to the school. The school nurse is generally the key professional resource for the teacher in this area. Other areas listed above have been illustrated through discussions in the appropriate chapters in Part II, and these are summarized in subsequent sections of this chapter. First, however, we should look at the potential role of a professional likely to be a key resource person for the mainstream teacher.

THE SPECIAL EDUCATION TEACHER AS RESOURCE

Increasingly, special educators recognize that an important aspect of their role (in some cases, the most important aspect) is serving as a resource to the teacher in the regular classroom. If a handicapped student receives some of her or his instruction in a resource room program, in an elementary school, for example, the "consultative" process is two-way: (1) the special educator must know where the student needs help in order to succeed in certain areas, including those areas, if any, in which all instruction is to be done in the resource room; (2) the teacher in the regular classroom can be apprised of the student's progress in remediation, compensatory approaches that are being used and that might be employed in the regular classroom, motivational strategies that seem to be "working," etc. Significantly, this involves a *co-equal* consultative relationship, not one in which advice and assistance are supposed to flow from the "specialist" to the "nonspecialist." The success of each is dependent in some measure upon the other.

The attitudes of the special educator and the mainstream teacher toward each other and toward each other's roles are critically important. Mutual respect, nondefensiveness, openness to ideas, and a shared focus on helping the child are necessary. In addition to the special educator's attitude toward mainstream colleagues, individually and collectively, her or his attitude toward integration itself influences the receptiveness of regular classroom teachers. In one study intended to identify the best predictors of teachers' attitudes toward mainstreaming, the attitude of the special educator was found to the most important influence (Thomas, 1985). A resource person who views mainstreaming negatively is not likely to enhance the confidence of the regular teacher.

Conversely, if the regular teacher is less than enthusiastic, a special educator's positive and genuinely helpful approach can affect the attitude of a mainstream colleague, not only about integrating a specific child but toward the principle of integration itself. Salend and Johns (1983) concluded from their study that the most effective way to bring about a positive attitude change is to assist teachers in having a successful teaching experience with a handicapped child. Other reports (e.g., Safford & Rosen, 1981) have demonstrated that, as measurable behavior change for a child occurs through classroom-based intervention provided with the help of a special educator, a teacher's initial concerns or even resistance can readily dissipate. Obviously, two conditions are necessary: (1) the teacher must be willing to accept assistance and (2) the specialist must be willing, and able, to provide it.

Resource teachers can contribute substantially to successful mainstreaming experiences in a variety of ways. First, there is evidence (e.g., Safran & Safran, 1987) that the way in which information about a child is presented can influence positively or negatively the regular teacher's attitude and belief that the child can be successfully mainstreamed. That does not imply, of course, that the child's difficulties should be glossed over. It does mean that the child's *strengths,* as well as problems, should be emphasized, as was illustrated through the case examples presented in the preceding chapters.

Another area in which special education teachers work with regular classroom colleagues prior to effecting a transition for a child is visitation. As has been repeatedly emphasized, the special educator needs to be thoroughly familiar with the regular classroom environment, curriculum, expectations for children's participation, and classroom schedule and routines. The mainstream teacher should also have observed the specific child prior to effecting a full mainstream transition. However, **the group context will have considerable influence upon the child's functioning and behavior.** Teachers must consider the ecological context in which the child is observed; regular education teachers have been able to view young children with developmental delays as appropriate mainstreaming candidates more confidently if they have been observed in integrated situations (McEvoy, Nordquist, & Cunningham, 1984). Thus, the special educator might arrange for observation in a trial integration situation. Under P.L. 99–457, the likelihood of such observation opportunities is significantly enhanced for *integrated,* rather than segregated, preschool programs constitute the acceptable alternative to full mainstream placement. Although situations in which as many as half the children do not have disabilities (integrated preschool programs) are still ecologically quite different from the mainstream classroom, which might include one to four children with disabilities (Family Child Learning Center, 1987), they represent approximations of the norm.

The special educator can also work with the classroom teacher in analyzing classroom structure, including use of time, space, and materials, in order to accommodate more effectively children representing a diversity of needs, characteristics, and learning styles (Madden & Slavin, 1983). Especially trained support teachers can provide classroom-based interventions, directly or through the teacher, that specifically address problem situations posed by individual children (Cantrell & Cantrell, 1976).

Special education teachers who function as resource persons to facilitate mainstreaming are part of the public school structure. However, those who work in early intervention programs outside the schools have increasingly served in comparable roles, especially since the enactment of P.L. 99–457. Some programs have served in this capacity for a number of years.

The Technical Assistance Program (TAP) provided by the Society for Crippled Children of Cuyahoga County in Cleveland, Ohio, is representative of programs available in other communities. TAP has experienced considerable success in finding child care placements for handicapped children and in maintaining children in those placements through training and resource assistance for their staffs. The approach represents a blend of developmental and intervention philosophies and an integration of day care and special education.

TAP's staff generally has experience in day care and educational backgrounds in early childhood; their specialized familiarity with special needs is acquired through training. That is important because **an understanding of day care programs is critical to the credibility of staff members who work with day care providers in home and centers.** Familiarity with the realities of day care aids in determining when workshops might best be scheduled—for example, mid-to-late afternoon, when most school personnel are used to having meetings and workshops, is generally a particularly busy and inconvenient time for day care workers.

TAP resource teachers are available to help parents of handicapped children

(1) locate day care centers/homes that are acceptable to the parent and geographically accessible; (2) understand day care and be prepared for both the problems and the successes their child might encounter in the mainstream; and (3) feel secure, by providing and maintaining contact, in person and by telephone, as long as the child is enrolled in day care. TAP resource teachers are available to help teachers/staff in day care placements by (1) identifying and discussing initial apprehensions that may block understanding; (2) coordinating meetings between any community agencies with whom the child has been involved who can help with the education of the staff and the planning of integration; (3) substituting in child care centers, to free teachers to visit special needs agencies and learn firsthand about a handicap; (4) helping a staff plan for the inclusion of a child with a handicap, by consulting with the parents, preparing the other children, preparing the other parents, and educating any peripheral adults who have contact with the center; (5) working in the classroom beside the teacher through the first few weeks of integration and developing a plan for the care and education of the child; and (6) maintaining contact on a regular basis as long as the child is enrolled.

In addition, TAP provides workshops in the community, listings of community resources and of books, filmstrips, and other media that are available for professionals in the area.

TAP SERVICES FOR CHILD CARE PROVIDERS[1]

TAP will prepare a staff or provider for enrollment of a child with special needs by

explaining the handicapping condition and the child's specific needs
responding to staff/provider questions and concerns
helping providers learn how to explain a child's special needs to the other children
    in the center or home
securing pertinent information from agencies serving the child

TAP will provide on-site assistance and support while a child with special needs is integrated into the program by

helping in the classroom or in the home during the first days of placement
observing and consulting with staff/provider regarding adaptations to program,
    space, and equipment
substituting in a class to free the teacher to visit a special needs program serving
    the child

TAP will provide resources for staff-provider as they integrate a child with special needs through

staff inservice on relevant topics—can include films and filmstrips

---

[1]Technical Assistance Program (TAP)
Society for Crippled Children
11001 Buckeye Road
Cleveland, Ohio 44104
795-7100

TAP library loans—materials and books for children and adults about main-streaming and handicapping conditions

equipment loan—to be used by the child in the center or home, or as a "hands-on" preparation material for use by the other children

presenting a program for children about handicaps—presentation includes handi-capped puppets who explain the ways they are like everyone else, as well as different, and "hands-on" experiences with equipment used by people with handicaps

TAP will help with questions from other parents about the integration of a handicapped child

at a parent meeting
in a newsletter article

TAP will remain in contact with parents, staff, and providers throughout a child's enrollment

Guidelines for Resource Teachers in Promoting Successful Integration of Handicapped Children into Day Care Settings

1. The resource teacher should step out of the picture as soon as possible, since the primary relationship needs to be between the parent and the day care staff member.

2. All staff members in a program should be oriented about an incoming child, not simply the one who will be primarily responsible (who will occasionally be absent).

3. If a child is also participating in a special program, the resource teacher should substitute to enable the day care teacher to visit that program.

4. Parents should be invited to participate every step of the way.

5. The children should know that there is an adult who knows what's going on, how to operate any adaptive equipment that might be used, and what to do in situa-tions (e.g., seizures) that might occur.

6. The resource teacher should stay at the center for the first few days; even experienced teachers may regress after a satisfactory start.

7. Parents of a handicapped child who has been in an early intervention program may be used to constant feedback and can misinterpret when nothing is told them. The resource teacher and the regular teacher should both be sensitive to this and should provide regular feedback to parents about things that are going well, as well as problems.

8. The resource teacher should take care to be nonthreatening to both staff and parents.

9. Parents of handicapped children are generally eager to answer questions from other parents, especially if the alter-

native is fear or misapprehension on the part of those other parents. Resource teachers and staff members should be ready to facilitate this.

10. Preparation activities for children should

recognize the needs of young children to touch, hold, and be physically involved with the materials used, including puppets, dolls, and other toys.

TRANSITION FROM SPECIAL TO MAINSTREAM SETTINGS

Many handicapped children have been served from the time they were preschoolers in typical, mainstream programs. For these, the concern is maintenance of optimal functioning in the mainstream. Others, however, and especially young handicapped children, are likely to move to a regular setting from a more specialized setting. For these, the goal is to enable the child to move to educational settings that are progressively closer to the mainstream, until full mainstream participation, if feasible, is achieved. Planning for any handicapped child should be based on that principle from the beginning (Strain & Kerr, 1981).

Since enactment of P.L. 99–457, the likelihood has increased that from birth to age two, developmentally delayed children (including those with identified handicaps and those considered at risk for handicaps) will receive services as part of a plan based upon the needs of the family as well as the child. Any number of community agencies may be involved in helping the family, and some form of direct intervention may be provided either at home or in a special habilitative setting.

In many states, such services are coordinated at the state level by the same agency responsible for overseeing and regulating the public schools. In other states, the coordinating agency may be a separate department of health, children's services, or the like. Beginning at age three, however, the handicapped child's educational needs in all states are the responsibility of the state education agency.

Regardless of what service structures exist in a given state, reaching the age of three suggests the need for effective transitional planning for any handicapped or disabled child, a process that will continue as long as the child proceeds through school. In the words of Noonan and Kilgo (1987), transition for young children is "(a) a longitudinal *plan*, (b) a *goal* of smooth/efficient movement from one program to the next, (c) a *process* including preparation, implementation, and follow-up, and (d) a *philosophy* that movement to the next program implies movement to a program that is less restrictive than the previous program" (p. 26).

Transitional planning is increasingly an area of responsibility for both the "sending" and the "receiving" program personnel. Hutinger (1981) has defined transition practices for young handicapped children as "strategies and procedures that are planned and employed to insure the smooth placement and subsequent adjustment of the child as he or she moves from one program into another" (p. 8).

One teacher in a special education preschool program noted that she and her colleagues experience a dilemma when their children are being moved into a regular preschool. On the one hand, there is the expressed need for resource assistance to support the child's placement; preschool teachers need and request information about the child's functioning and special needs. On the other hand, those teachers have their own plan and curriculum, and the new teacher will need to establish a relationship and way of communicating with the child. The specialist needs to recognize the legitimacy of the regular program. However, in our eagerness to ensure that the child's individual needs are appropriately addressed, we may also be somewhat overprotective. The specialist's relationship with the regular program is that of a supportive resource and source of information concerning the child within another context. It cannot be a consultative relationship, in the sense of the expert advising the less-informed. Rather, it is a relationship of peers, each of whom has legitimate expertise and an "agenda" appropriate to his or her own particular role.

Even after a child has made an effective transition into a regular preschool or regular kindergarten, the anticipation of change is an important dimension of continued planning. A child doing well in kindergarten, in large measure as the result of careful prior planning, including analysis of what is required in the kindergarten setting, may continue to need help with change. Dettre (1983) has recommended extending the strategies suggested by Vincent and her colleagues (Vincent et al., 1981) to the first grade. This implies studying the skill requirements of "life in the first grade" and practicing the use of these skills in order to build "bridges" to success. This would include actually simulating first grade, following visits to a first grade class—that is, "playing first grade" (Dettre, 1983, p. 58). She also suggests specific experiences in oral expression, listening skills, a form of reading modeling that she terms "Almost Reading," writing experiences, and math learning, as well as computer skills. In the face of concerns that kindergarten has become too much like the first grade as it is (Moyer et al., 1987), that may seem incompatible with principles of developmentally appropriate practice. However, it is possible to integrate individually needed specific preparation experiences within a context that recognizes the superiority of an environment that nurtures play over one built upon skill training as the primary mode of instruction for young children. Piaget's distinction between social knowledge and logico-mathematical knowledge (Kamii & DeVries, 1978) may provide perspective: the former is legitimate, even essential, but it is the latter that underlies development in children.

The special education teacher may be a very helpful resource to regular classroom personnel in analyzing and planning for the continuing series of transitions that characterize going to school in our society, for each of these, from the standpoint of handicapped child and family, may constitute a crisis point. But it is the mainstream teacher who must *integrate* specific strategies suggested for a particular child within the framework of a developmental philosophy and curriculum.

The teacher who has been prepared specifically to work with children with handicapping conditions presents a perspective complementary to that of the regular early childhood educator. Both are specialists. Some special educators have specific expertise in working with young children, by virtue of their academic training, professional experience, and possibly certification. Depending upon training and certification practices in individual states, some special educators have even more specific specializations. Some have been trained specifically as teachers of children with hearing impairments, visual impairments, learning disabilities, etc; some may have more generic credentials, as teachers of children with severe and/or multiple impairments vs. children with mild/moderate learning and behavior problems. Special educators with specific early childhood expertise are less likely to have strictly "categorical" specializations to work only, for instance, with learning disabilities; their preparation may have emphasized children's learning needs across developmental domains (e.g., cognitive, communication and language, motor, personal-social). However, in certain areas of disability such as hearing impairment, teachers may have specific early childhood expertise. Clearly, not all special education teachers are equally expert in all matters pertaining to teaching handicapped students.

In addition to special education teachers (and in connection with medical and health needs, the school nurse), several other specialists provide specific forms of supportive and resource assistance. For children participating in special education programs, such specialists should be key members of the team that assesses the current functioning and needs of the child, contributes to the child's IEP, implements the program of special education and related services, and periodically reviews the program. Their roles and unique contributions have been described previously. In the following section, we will consider potential contributions of especially trained therapists as resource persons who provide assistance in support of teaching handicapped children within the mainstream.

SUPPORTIVE SERVICES PERSONNEL

A variety of specialists are qualified to provide specific kinds of services, either directly to the child, parents, or both, or indirectly, through consultation with the teacher. For children who are identified as handicapped and whose educational planning is based on an IEP, one or more such specialist may be specifically responsible to provide a *related service,* that is, a service needed for a handicapped student to benefit from special education. Among the more frequently included forms of related services for school-age handicapped students are (1) transportation; (2) speech and language therapy; (3) physical therapy; (4) occupational therapy; (5) adapted physical education; (6) provision of an aide; (7) sign language interpreter; and (7) counseling for child and/or parent.

Whether any of these services is to be provided depends upon the IEP that has been prepared for an individual student. Questions frequently arise about whether such services must be provided by a school for a student who is fully mainstreamed. If no IEP is required for the student, then the provisions a state is required to make under Public Law 94–142 do not apply; the above or other services do not have to be provided. That does not mean, however, that, if certain forms of special assistance are needed by a child, a school should not or would not provide them. For example, many children who are not enrolled in special education receive speech and language services, provided by a qualified speech and language therapist. More children with speech and language difficulties as their primary problem are mainstreamed than any other classification of exceptional children (McCormick, 1986).

Since virtually all classifications of handicapped children are likely to involve special needs in the area of speech and language, and since language programming is one of the major aspects of early intervention, the speech and language therapist is likely to be one of the most valuable resource persons for the early childhood mainstream educator. Although specifically trained to diagnose and treat communication problems in individuals, this professional is likely to be able to assist the teacher through:

Observing the child's language behavior within the social, interactive context of the classroom.

Suggesting language training activities appropriate to the needs of an individual child that can be incorporated into normal classroom routines.

Working individually with a specific child within the classroom.

Leading and demonstrating language training activities with small groups or with the whole group within the classroom.

Providing guidance to the teacher concerning problems presented by individual children, such as reticence or hesitance to interact verbally with others; disfluency; dialectal differences; or functional articulation problems.

Speech and language specialists are likely to be available in every school, in Head Start programs, in preschool programs intended to serve young handicapped children as well as nonhandicapped children, and at least accessible to staffs of other preschool and day care programs. They may have assigned "caseloads" that include young children who are mainstreamed. In addition, a portion of their role assignment may include providing direct or indirect (consultative) assistance for other children. If that is not the case, you may want to seek out this professional on your own.

Physical therapists and occupational therapists also may have very important roles to play as sources of direct or indirect assistance to the mainstream teacher. Their respective roles were discussed in detail in Chapter 7, and we noted that they represent complementary areas of expertise that are critically important in meeting special needs of many children with impaired motor functioning or delays in motor development. Increasingly, not only are specialized therapy goals integrated with educational goals in planning a child's program, but the services themselves may be integrated within the classroom program. An Integrated Services approach (Sternat, Messina, Nietupski, Lyon, & Brown, 1977), or, more recently, an Integrated Team approach (Campbell, 1987) has been recommended for students of any age with severe handicapping conditions. Specialists provide ongoing consultation to teachers and caregivers, as well as working with the child directly in all relevant environments (i.e., classroom, home, community and recreational settings, vocational settings, etc.)

A child in a mainstream classroom placement may need direct physical or occupational therapy services. Generally these will be provided on a supplementary basis, that is, outside the classroom and in some instances outside the school, but regular communication is still needed among therapist, parents, and teacher. Rather than integrating therapy services inside the classroom, teachers may be able to integrate the suggestions and recommendations of the therapist. Specialists often need to observe the child in the classroom, and one or more specialists may work with the teacher in developing a problem-solving approach. Other specialists may be involved as well, especially in considering possible applications of technology for a child within the classroom.

CASE HISTORY 13.1: MARY BROWN

FOLLOW-UP REPORT
NAME: Mary Brown
DATE: January 5, 1987

SUMMARY OF OBSERVATIONS

Mary was observed in her classroom, during language tutoring, in gym class, in the library, and in a variety of unstructured school situations as well as during transitions to and from these activities. She was observed on 11/18/86, 11/25/86, 12/3/86, and 12/9/86 by the resource coordinator and she was also observed on 12/16/86 by the occupational therapist and rehabilitation engineer. Ecological inventories and time samples were initiated in an attempt to identify potential problems and solutions that would expedite improved programming for Mary and provide an opportunity to assess the appropriateness of several high/low tech adaptations.

Three areas of concern emerged during the observations: a) Staff instructional inconsist-

encies; b) Mary's motor complications; and c) Mary's interfering behavior.

INSTRUCTIONAL INCONSISTENCIES

All of the teachers and assistants at Elm have done a commendable job of adapting classroom programming for Mary. They have integrated Mary successfully into nearly all activities, investigating alternative teaching methods in a positive manner. Due in part to the newness of integrating a handicapped child into daily routines, inconsistencies among teachers in dealing with issues such as: a) Mary's requests/demands for attention; b) "w" sitting; c) amount, type, and frequency of assistance provided for Mary in various situations; d) teacher expectations; and e) amount of time allotted/permitted for Mary to complete a task were observed. Additionally, teacher cues and prompts directed to Mary occurred between 5 and 7 times more frequently than teacher cues and prompts directed to peers in the same classroom setting.

MOTOR COMPLICATIONS

Mary's motor complications involve two distinct areas that impact on her classroom performance, specifically: 1) positioning and 2) fine motor skills. During the course of these observations, Mary was alternated between three basic positions, adaptive wheelchair, prone standing board, and free-form floor lying or sitting. With the exception of the floor position, these positions preclude the possibility of "normal" peer interaction due to the nature and size of the adaptive equipment involved. This can potentially be a key factor in developing social interactions, especially during the elementary school years where a large part of the day is devoted to seatwork and floor activities.

Mary's fine motor skills make it extremely difficult, if not impossible, for her to perform many of the daily activities involved in early childhood education. Writing, coloring, cutting, and pasting often seem to increase Mary's frustration level and as a consequence appear to lead to an increased amount of off-task behavior. One method of attempting to guide students back to the activity at hand is to increase the number of verbal or physical prompts provided during the activity. The amount of time that Mary may require to *complete* any of these tasks satisfactorily, even with some adaptation, will be significantly longer than the time required by her classmates.

INTERFERING BEHAVIOR

During these observations, Mary demonstrated numerous behaviors that might be viewed as "interfering behavior." Interfering behavior involves particular behavior that is counterproductive to educational purposes and/or creates a situation where instruction is very difficult. The time that Mary actually spends "on task" (actively involved in the learning experience at hand) averaged only 42% of the time across 5 separate observations in a variety of settings. During the remaining 48% of the time, she was engaged in activities such as: a) Actively seeking adult attention; b) actively seeking peer attention; c) looking around the room at both teachers and other students; d) participating in activities not related to the activity at hand. Possibly due to confusion as to appropriate means of dealing with Mary, many teachers inadvertently reinforced both inappropriate demands for attention or assistance and inappropriate behavior such as "W" sitting. In some instances, Mary was physically guided through activities in one area that she had successfully completed unassisted in another. Mary has clearly identified those individuals with whom she can "get away" with things and those with whom she cannot and attempts to use this to her advantage in a variety of ways.

RECOMMENDATIONS

1. Identify with the teacher consistent forms of adult behavior that will be carried out in *all* school and home settings.
2. Identify everyday situations where Mary will clearly need assistance. Define what type of assistance will be provided, how the assistance will occur, and assure that all parties involved with Mary are carrying out the procedure in a like manner.
3. Identify a set of "rules" for Mary so that she is clear as to what type of behavior is considered appropriate. Decide on a particular consequence that will occur if Mary is not compliant with these "rules." Assure that all parties involved with Mary adhere to the procedure.
4. Increase the amount of time for Mary to complete certain tasks.
5. Investigate alternatives to coloring, cut-

ting, and pasting that may be more appropriate and functional for Mary.

6. Investigate the use of keyboard access to an IBM PC Jr. computer with the use of an adaptive keyguard as an alternative to writing.

7. Discuss and employ alternate positioning that will allow Mary to experience more normalized interaction with peers (floor sitting position, elementary school chair with special insert, etc.)

8. Increase Mary's time on task by providing activities that she can complete with minimal assistance.

9. Decrease cues and prompts so that Mary may begin to experience more of a sense of independence.

10. Investigate other forms of adaptive/technical assistance as the need arises.

Other resource persons who may be consulted concerning specific needs represent a wide array of specializations, including school psychologists, audiologists, adapted physical education teachers, braille instructors, orientation and mobility trainers, music therapists, art therapists, and school social workers.

As schools, Head Start programs, community nursery schools, and day care programs increasingly develop collaborative approaches with a variety of other community agencies, especially in implementing P.L. 99–457, which calls for such collaboration, resources within these agencies are increasingly available to the classroom teacher. But the need for coordination and communication among community agencies and between these agencies and the school continues to be critical. In many communities that are relatively "service-rich," there are numerous sources of assistance for schools and centers. Making use of these community resources is an important part of the responsibilities of those who work directly with young children.

At another level, however, the needs of many families suggest that only a coordinated plan, developed by agencies in collaboration, can ensure that needed services are provided, without duplication, and that families know how to access the specific kinds of help they need (Elder & Megrab, 1980). Although problems have been encountered by those attempting to orchestrate coordinated service delivery for children and families (Pollard, Hall, & Keeran, 1979), these problems are not insurmountable and indeed must be overcome. Clearly, young children and their families are most effectively served when all agencies involved collaborate and coordinate their efforts (Nordyke, 1982; Association for the Care of Children's Health, 1987).

CASE HISTORY 13.2

A three-year-old came to the day care center through regular employment/training referral for the mother who did not come during the child's orientation; a relative did. Very quickly the staff discovered this to be a special child with little impulse control and prone to aggression (such as deep biting). When the mother came in at the center's request, she was found to be very young, immature, and impulsive. Her life, as well as the child's, was filled with crises such as accidents, financial upheavals, changes of residence with different relatives, and departures of friends she'd just started to count on.

After two months the mother began to appear very depressed and confided to the Center director her fear of abusing the child or commiting suicide. The director immediately got a case worker from the counseling service in a sister agency to come to the day care center. This started a long-term counseling relationship that the mother gradually became more able to use. The mother also began to trust the director and one teacher.

The staff in this center had had previous experience and consultation on emotionally disturbed children. They taught the child how he could touch other children gently by demonstrating to him and arranged quiet times for him away from the group. They taught the other children how to defend themselves from his aggression by stretching out their arms, etc. The staff's encouragement helped older children to see this child as especially needy and to nurture him, too.

The staff feels that especially in such cases all adults working in the center need to be enough in tune with the case to be able to step in and support and assist the special child's teacher. After six months they know that there will continue to be much more that he and his mother need from them.

PARAPROFESSIONALS AND VOLUNTEERS: OTHER VALUABLE HUMAN RESOURCES

"Twenty-eight children in my class, and I don't even have an aide!" Although counter to what most early childhood specialists regard as appropriate, many kindergarten and primary classrooms, and even some nursery programs, have very large groups. In many cases, local district policies, specific preschool policies, or states' standards for day care regulate and specifically limit enrollment. However, that is not always the case. Even when it is we can ask on what basis 20 is considered an appropriate enrollment, or 18. **A group of young children of almost any size can be more effectively taught if others are present to help.** That, of course, assumes that the "others" are carefully selected, oriented to the roles they will fill, and effectively supervised. Some inexperienced teachers may find it very difficult to use other helpers in the classroom effectively; often, their preparation has not included training in procedures for supervising volunteers and paraprofessionals.

Probably the most striking difference between typical special education classes and typical regular classes is the size of the group. In most states, enrollment in special classes and resource room programs is specifically limited. Although some states also provide such guidelines for regular classes, these policies are more typically made at the local level. Often, they reflect economic pressures at the community level, rather than educational considerations. A second pronounced difference, especially in special education programs for young children, is the likelihood that there will be two or even more adults in the classroom. As was discussed in Part I, early intervention programs have been changing in that regard, intentionally to approximate more closely the regular classroom environments in which young children are prepared to function in the future. Nevertheless, the adult-to-child ratio is typically much higher than in the mainstream early childhood classroom or center. The issue of class size is very likely to be raised (as it has been raised by teacher organizations, sometimes in the context of collective bargaining) when mainstream placement for a handicapped child is considered.

We should again emphasize that many children with handicaps require no special adult assistance beyond that required by other children. Nonetheless, there are certainly children with handicaps for whom mainstream placement depends, for maximum appropriateness and effectiveness, upon the presence in the classroom of someone to assist the teacher. In regular preschool and day care situations in which a classroom team approach is used, that need may be met by the sharing of responsibilities for working with individual children and the group by two teachers, who agree between themselves how they will work together. Clearly, however, that usually requires not only a good working relationship but also careful advance planning.

More typically, if there is a "second adult" in the classroom, that individual is in an assisting role, rather than a co-teaching one. That means that the teacher must assign tasks and supervise performance, while the assisting adult seeks guidance and direction from the teacher. Three levels of assistance have been distinguished (e.g., Cook & Armbruster, 1983): teacher assistants, teacher aides, and volunteers. For purposes of the present discussion, volunteers are discussed separately, and the term *paraprofessionals* is used to refer to the first two.

Teacher assistants are usually individuals who have had, or are currently having, some preparation through formal training for their roles, or they intend, upon completing their training, to become fully qualified teachers. Performing in an assisting capacity in classrooms for young children is an important component of their professional preparation to be teachers (Bredekamp, 1987). Sometimes persons who have completed their preparation and are qualified to be teachers serve in an assisting capacity, either through choice or until a vacancy (especially in public school programs) occurs. Teacher assistants are expected to assume specified decision-making responsibilities as determined by, and agreed upon with, the teacher who supervises their work. The availability of a teacher assistant can be particularly desirable if one or more children require an unusual degree of individual assistance, because of either physical or behavior management needs. As a general rule, two such children is probably the maximum desirable in a mainstreaming situation for a single classroom (Family Child Learning Center, 1987).

Teaching aides are generally differentiated on the basis of level of specific preparation and training and in the extent of responsibility for independent decision making. In some early childhood classrooms, an aide may already be present. In other situations, an aide may be provided specifically in order to assist with one or more children with special needs. An IEP may require an aide as a related service that must be provided, although an aide for a specific child is less likely to be required if the child is mainstreamed, since the mainstreaming program often will provide that service. The assignment of an aide may result from discussion, and sometimes negotiation, with parents. If the aide's role pertains specifically to services for one or more handicapped children, critical considerations are: (1) selection of an appropriately qualified individual; (2) specific orientation and training of the individual concerning the needs of the child, or children, and how they are to be met; (3) ongoing supervision; and (4) avoiding interacting with the child in a manner that sets him or her apart as "different" or "special," by ensuring that the aide provides only the help that is required.

There are many sources of potential *volunteer* (i.e., non-paid) assistance. Many community and school programs make extensive use of volunteers in a wide variety of ways, and volunteers constitute a valuable resource in assisting with young children who have special needs as well. It goes without saying that volunteers, like paid paraprofessionals, want and need effective supervision by the teacher in order to optimize their helpfulness. We should remember that, unlike paid staff members, volunteers are not likely to be available every day, throughout the day, and also that their "contract" is an informal one, involving mutual agreement. Recognizing the altruistic motives of volunteers does not imply that supervision is not required or that inappropriate forms of help should be tolerated. Teachers generally find that the majority of individuals who want to volunteer their services can make valuable contributions and are responsive to guidance.

Potential sources of volunteer assistance include:

1. Individual parents and parent organizations
2. Service organizations in the community
3. Youth organizations
4. Colleges and universities (including specific programs preparing students for careers as regular or special education teachers, child care providers, psychologists, and other fields, for which the voluntary services may fulfill specified field experience requirements)
5. Older elementary school or high school students
6. Retired persons, as individuals or as members of organizations.

These and other sources can be tapped in order to recruit potential volunteers. The presence in a classroom or center of young children with special needs serves as a special attraction for many potential helpers, especially for young people (school or college age) considering or preparing for careers. Many individuals in the community want to help someone, perhaps a young child, who has a disability. We need to respect and value altruistic motives but we also need to ensure that adults—like the other children in the classroom—understand that *empathy,* rather than sympathy, is appropriate, and that the child should not be regarded as an object of pity. Rather, it is in the child's interest to become maximally independent and to have a sense of personal competence.

The Community Care Center in Lakewood Ohio, has made successful use of retired persons, and the Program's director has described the careful work necessary to identify, assign, and supervise the participating seniors. Both generations find that the opportunities created through this program for them to interact and learn to know each other are richly rewarding (Church, 1987). This is also a program that has for many years successfully integrated handicapped preschoolers, and the retired volunteer helpers provide a valuable source of resource assistance for these children. The growing numbers of older persons in American society and the wish of many to continue to be active and to provide a service suggest that this is an area of great potential for supporting the growing commitment to young children, including those with special needs.

Guidelines for Using Paraprofessionals and Volunteers Effectively

---

1. Assign tasks that are appropriate to a specific individual's competence, taking into account that individual's specific interests, wishes, and scheduled availability.
2. Give specific assignments and provide structure for the paraprofessional or volunteer.
3. Provide sufficient and appropriate initial orientation.
4. Provide ongoing supervision, including specific feedback concerning the person's activities and performance.
5. Provide recognition and reward.
6. Show sincere respect for the individual.
7. Conduct regular meetings for planning and for feedback.
8. Provide recognition to individuals and also to groups, both expressing appreciation for their services, and rewarding their accomplishments.
9. Use written, as well as oral, communication, to recruit potential volunteers, describe responsibilities, and provide positive feedback and constructive guidance.
10. Remember that the teacher is a *role model* for the other adults who may be involved in the classroom or center, and practice the behavior, as well as demonstrating the attitudes, that others should emulate.

SUMMARY

Potential resources exist in many forms, and providing effectively for the diverse needs of individual children—both those who have disabilities or delays and those who do not—is infinitely enhanced when the teacher is able to identify and to access resources, both people and things, that enrich the total classroom program or that respond to specific situations and needs. In addition to the children themselves, their parents, and other family members, a wide variety of sources of help are available to support integrated teaching in early childhood programs. Much is required of today's teacher of young children; however, it is neither expected nor appropriate for a teacher to attempt to be "all things to all children." Just as parents of young children with disabilities are reassured by the knowledge that they are not alone or left with the sole responsibility for meeting all the child's special needs, so teachers should recognize that assistance is available to support their work.

Services for handicapped children and for their families are provided based upon a *team* model that recognizes the importance of each team member's contribution as well as the need to *integrate* the special knowledge, insights, and expertise of all members of the team in a unified plan. When children with disabilities are integrated within the educational mainstream, it is with the expectation that any special needs that continue to be present may require an extension of the team approach within the typical environment. That often implies the continuing involvement of one or more specialists in providing direct or indirect assistance. Where that is the case, the professionals, and the parents, must have a very clearly defined and mutually agreed-upon plan, including provisions for continuing communication and monitoring of progress.

Not all important resources and resource persons are "special," however, in the sense of being required specifically for children with handicapping conditions. Resources presently available in the school or center, in the children's homes, and in the community are helpful for all children. Their effective use requires thoughtfulness, skill, and effort on the part of the teacher, and will be richly rewarded because of the enhanced opportunities for all children's learning.

Many of the preceding chapters have noted specific sources of resource material or information. The Appendix includes a listing of agencies, organizations, and other sources of help that may be of value to teachers in obtaining information they can use themselves and for sharing with parents.

Appendix: Resources for Teachers and Families

GENERAL

Directory of National Information Sources on Handicapping Conditions and Related Services (2nd ed., 1980)
Clearinghouse on the Handicapped
Office of Human Development Services
U.S. Government Printing Office
Washington, D.C. 20401

A Training Resource Directory for Teachers Serving Handicapped Students, K–12 (1977)
Office of Civil Rights
Department of Health and Human Services
Room 5146
330 Independence Ave. SW
Washington, D.C. 20201

Special Education Programs for Severely Handicapped Students: A Directory of State Education Agency Services
National Association of State Departments of Education
1202 16th St. NW
Washington, D.C. 20036

Directory of Services and Facilities for Handicapped Children
Council for Exceptional Children
1920 Association Drive
Reston, VA 22091

Other information can be obtained from:

The American Humane Association
Children's Division
PO Box 1266
Denver, CO 80201

Association for the Care of Children's Health
3615 Wisconsin Ave.
Washington, D.C. 20016

Association for Childhood Education International
11141 Georgia Ave., Suite 200
Wheaton, MD 20902

Association for Persons with Severe Handicaps
7010 Roosevelt Way NE
Seattle, WA 98115

Child Welfare League of America
67 Irving Place
New York, NY 10003

Children's Defense Fund
122 C Street NW
Washington, D.C. 20001

Council for Exceptional Children
1920 Association Drive
Reston, VA 22091

National Association for the Education of Young
  Children
1834 Connecticut Ave. NW
Washington, D.C. 20009

National Information Center for Handicapped
  Children and Youth (NICHCY)
PO Box 1492
Washington, D.C. 20013

National Rehabilitation Association
1522 K St. NW, Suite 1120
Washington, D.C. 20005

Special Olympics, Inc.
1701 K St. NW, Suite 203
Washington, D.C. 20006

Toll-free numbers:

Center for Special Education Technology
800-345-TECH

Children's Defense Fund
800-424-9602

ERIC Clearinghouse on Adult Career and
  Vocational Education
800-848-4815

Higher Education and the Handicapped (HEATH)
800-54-HEATH

National Health Information Clearinghouse
800-336-4797

National Organization on Disability
800-248-ABLE

National Rehabilitation Information Center
800-34-NARIC

National Special Needs Center
800-233-1222
800-833-3232

FOR TEACHERS AND PARENTS OF THE VISION IMPAIRED

American Council for the Blind
1211 Connecticut Ave. NW, Suite 506
Washington, D.C. 20036

American Foundation for the Blind
15 West 16th St.
New York, NY 10011

American Printing House for the Blind
1839 Frankfort Ave.
Louisville, KY 40206

Association for Education of the Visually
  Handicapped
919 Walnut St.
San Francisco, CA 94121

Blind Children's Center, Inc.
4120 Marathon St.
Los Angeles, CA 90029

Hadley School for the Blind
700 Elm St., PO Box 299
Winnetka, IL 60093

National Association for the Deaf-Blind
2703 Forest Oak Circle
Norman, OK 73071

National Association for the Visually Handicapped
3201 Balboa St.
San Francisco, CA 94121

National Society for the Prevention of Blindness,
  Inc.
79 Madison Ave.
New York, NY 10016

Canadian National Institute for the Blind
1929 Bayview Ave.
Toronto, 350, CANADA

World Council for the Welfare of the Blind
56 Avenue Bosquet
75007 Paris, FRANCE

Materials of particular interest:

*Reach Out and Teach: Meeting the Training Needs
of Parents of Visually and Multiply Handicapped
Young Children* (Ferrell, 1985). Available from
the American Foundation for the Blind. A highly
useful and readable set of materials including a
Parent Handbook and Reachbook, in which
parents apply specific activities and record their
progress. Other related resources include an
introductory slide presentation and a Teacher's
Manual, which enable teachers to use all the
Reach Out materials in early education
programs.

Move It and *Get a Wiggle On* (Drouillard and
Raynor); *Learning to Play* (Recchia); and *Take
Charge* (Nousanen and Robinson). These and
other pamphlets are available from the Hadley
School for the Blind.

*Talk to Me: A Language Guide for Parents of Blind
Children; Talk to Me II;* and *Move With Me*.
These brief booklets are available from the Blind
Children's Center.

Toll-free numbers:

American Council for the Blind
800-424-8666

Hadley School for the Blind
800-323-4238

Job Opportunities for the Blind
800-638-7518

RP Foundation for Fighting Blindness
800-638-2300

FOR PARENTS AND TEACHERS OF HEARING-IMPAIRED CHILDREN

Alexander Graham Bell Association for the Deaf
3417 Volta Place NW
Washington, D.C. 20007

American Speech, Language, and Hearing
  Association
9030 Old Georgetown Rd.
Washington, D.C. 20014

National Association of the Deaf
814 Thayer Ave.
Silver Springs, MD 20910

National Association for the Deaf-Blind
2703 Forest Oak Circle
Norman, OK 73071

Toll-free numbers:

Better Hearing Institute Hearing Helpline
800-424-8576

National Association for Hearing and Speech
  Action
800-638-TALK (voice or TDD)

National Crisis Center for the Deaf
800-446-9876

National Hearing Aid Society
800-521-5247

Occupational Hearing Services (O.H.S.)
800-222-EARS

Tripod Service for the Hearing Impaired
800-352-8888

FOR TEACHERS AND PARENTS OF MOTOR- AND PHYSICALLY IMPAIRED CHILDREN

American Physical Therapy Association
1156 15th St. NW, Suite 500
Washington, D.C. 20005

Epilepsy Foundation of America
4351 Garden City Drive
Landover, MD 20785

March of Dimes Birth Defects Foundation
1275 Mamaroneck Ave.
White Plains, NY 10605

Muscular Dystrophy Association
810 7th Ave.
New York, NY 10019

National Easter Seal Society for Crippled Children
  and Adults
2023 West Ogden Ave.
Chicago, IL 60612

Spina Bifida Association of America
343 S. Dearborn St., Suite 319
Chicago, IL 60604

United Cerebral Palsy Association
666 East 34th St.
New York, NY 10016

Resource Materials of Particular Interest:

Anderson, R. D., Bale, J. F., Blackman, J. A., & Murph, J. R. *Infections in Children: A Sourcebook for Educators and Child Care Providers.* Rockville, MD: Aspen, 1986.

Batshaw, M. L., & Perret, Y. M. *Children with Handicaps: A Medical Primer.* Baltimore: Brookes Publishing Co., 1986.

Blackman, J. A. (Ed.) *Medical Aspects of Developmental Disabilities in Children Birth to Three.* Rockville, MD: Aspen, 1984.

Bleck, E. E., & Nagel, D. A. (Eds.) *Physically Handicapped Children: A Medical Atlas for Teachers.* New York: Gruce & Stratton, 1982.

Finnie, N. *Handling the Young Cerebral Palsied Child at Home.* New York: E. P. Dutton, & Co., 1975.

Williamson, G. G., *Children with Spina Bifida: Early Intervention and Preschool Programming.* Baltimore: Brookes Publishing Co., 1987.

Toll-free numbers:

American Kidney Foundation
800-638-8299

Epilepsy Information Line
800-426-0660

Lung Line (Lung Disorders, Allergies)
800-222-LUNG

National Cystic Fibrosis Foundation
800-344-4823

National Down's Syndrome Society
800-221-4602

National Easter Seals Society
800-221-6827

National Spinal Cord Injury Hotline
800-526-3456

Spina Bifida Hotline
800-621-3141

For Teachers and Parents of Developmentally-Delayed or Behaviorally-Impaired Children

American Association on Mental Deficiency
5101 Wisconsin Ave., NW
Washington, D.C. 20007

American Association of Psychiatric Services for Children
1701 18th St. NW
Washington, D.C. 20009

American Psychological Association
9030 Old Georgetown Rd.
Washington, D.C. 20014

Association for Children and Adults with Learning Disabilities
4156 Library Rd.
Pittsburgh, PA 15234

International Directory of Mental Retardation Sources (ed. R.F. Dybwad).
President's Committee on Mental Retardation
Washington, D.C. 20006

National Association for Retarded Citizens
P.O. Box 6109
2501 Avenue J
Arlington, TX 76011

National Association of School Psychologists
1511 K St. NW
Washington, D.C. 20005

National Society for Children and Adults with Autism
1234 Massachusetts Ave. NW, Suite 1017
Washington, D.C. 20005

President's Committee on Mental Retardation
U.S. Dept. of Health and Human Services
Office of Human Services
Washington, D.C. 20006

For Teachers and Parents of Gifted and Talented Children

Gifted Child Society, Inc.
59 Glen Gray Road
Oakland, NJ 07436

Gifted, Creative and Talented Magazine
G/C/T Publishing Co.
Box 66654
Mobile, AL 36606

Journal of the Education of the Gifted
School of Education
University of Virginia
Charlottesville, VA 22903

National Association for Gifted Children
217 Gregory Drive
Hot Springs, AR 71901

National/State Leadership Training Institute on the Gifted and Talented
Ventura County Superintendent of Schools
535 East Main St.
Ventura, CA 93009

Selected Resources for Teachers in Integrated Classrooms

"Special Delivery"
Lauren Productions, Inc.
PO Box 666
Mendocino, CA 95460
707-937-0536

Five 30-minute videocassettes with accompanying teachers' guide. For children ages seven to ten. Intended to help children accept and welcome handicapped peers, have positive attitudes toward people with disabilities, understand handicapping conditions, and develop realistic expectations. Can be readily integrated into regular curriculum, requires no special knowledge from teacher, designed to solicit free and open questioning.

"Different From You . . . and Like You, Too"
Lauren Productions, Inc.
PO Box 666
Mendocino, CA 95460

Filmstrip for grades K–3. Accompanying activity guide in six sections; what is prejudice; correcting misconceptions; nature and origins of handicaps; eliminating social and environmental barriers; visit for first-hand awareness; summing up.

"Kids come in Special Flavors: Understanding
   Handicaps"
Cashdollar and Martin: The Kids Come in Special
   Flavors Co.
PO Box 562
Dayton, OH 45405
   Guide and accompanying activity materials,
developed by parents of handicapped children, to
provide "doing" opportunities for children to learn
about handicaps.

"My Friends and Me"
Duane E. Davis: American Guidance Service, Inc.
PO Box 99
Circle Pines, MN 55014-1796
   Kit including 190 activities and lesson plans
(activity manuals, dolls, magnetic shapes,
recorded songs, etc.) intended to help children
develop positive, confident, and realistic personal
identity and essential social skills and
understandings.

"Hal's Pals"
Mattel: Therapy Skill Builders
3830 E. Bellevue, PO Box 42050-A
Tucson, AZ 85733
   Five sets of materials dealing with amputation;
hearing impairment; leg braces; blindness; and
wheelchairs.

DUSO I (Revised)
Dinkmeyer and Dinkmeyer: American Guidance
   Services, Inc.
PO Box 99
Circle Pines, MN 55014-1796
   For grades K–2. Set of materials intended to
help children gain appreciation of individual
strengths and acceptance of limitations; beginning
social skills; and awareness of feelings, priorities,
and choices.

"Hello, Everybody . . ."
SFA: James Stanfield Film Associates
PO Box 1983
Santa Monica, CA 90406
   Six color/sound filmstrips with accompanying
Teacher's Resource Book, which identifies both
cognitive and affective objectives and provides
suggestions for introducing and following up
filmstrips. Films focus on hearing and speech
impairments; orthopedic handicaps; developmental
disabilities; learning disabilities; behavior
disorders; visual impairments.

The Bookfinder
American Guidance Service, Inc.
PO Box 99
Circle Pines, MN 55014-1796
   Excellent for locating appropriate books for
children to help learn about handicapping
conditions, identify children with specific
problems, and explore attitudes and feelings.

Some specific books of potential value to teachers
of young children include the following:

Baslin, B., & Harris, K. (1984). *More Notes From A
Different Drummer: A Guide to Juvenile Fiction
Portraying the Disabled.* Ann Arbor, MI: Bowher.

Buchbinder, D. (1984). *Special Kids Make Special
Friends.* Association for Children with Down's
Syndrome. 2616 Martin Ave., Bellmore, NY
11710.

Feshback, N., Feshback, S., Fauvre, M., & Ballard-
Campbell, M., (1984). *Learning to Care.* Glenview, IL: Goodyear Books

Field, T., Roopnarine, J., & Segal, M. (1984).
Friendships in Normal and Handicapped Children.
Norwood, NJ: Ablex.

Krause, Bob (Ed.). (1977).
An Exceptional View of Life: The Easter Seal Story
Norfolk Island, Australia: Island Heritage Limited.

McElmurry, M. (1983) *Belonging.* Good Apple, Inc.
Box 299, Carthage, IL 62321-0299.

Schuncke, G., & Krough, S. (1983) *Helping Children Choose.* Glenview, IL: Goodyear Books.

References

Abelson, M. A., & Woodman, R. W. (1983). Review of research on team effectiveness. Implication for teams in schools. *School Psychology Review, 12,* 125–138.

Abrams, K. I. (1983). Affective development. In M. B. Karnes (Ed.), *The underserved: Our young gifted children* (pp. 118–143). Reston, VA: Council for Exceptional Children.

Adcock, P., & Segal, M. (1983). *Making friends: Ways of encouraging social development in young children.* Englewood Cliffs, NJ: Prentice-Hall.

Adler, M. (1982). *The Paidea proposal: An educational manifesto.* New York: Macmillan.

Aiello, B. (1977). *Kids on the block.* Reston, VA: Council for Exceptional Children.

Alberto, P. A., & Troutman, A. C. (1982). *Applied behavior analysis for teachers: Influencing student performance.* Columbus, OH: Charles E. Merrill.

Alden, L., & Lipson, A. M. (1983). Mainstreaming: Unwanted side effects. *Academic Therapy, 15,* 167–273.

Algozzine, B., Mercer, C., & Countermine, T. (1977, October). The effects of labels and behavior on teacher expectations. *Exceptional Children,* 131–132.

Allen, K. E. (1980). *Mainstreaming in early childhood education.* New York: Delmar.

Allen, R., & Allen, C. (1970). *Language experiences in reading.* Chicago: Encyclopedia Brittanica.

Almy, M. (1968). Introduction to the 1968 edition of *The nursery years: The mind of the child from birth to six years* by Susan Isaacs. New York: Schocken Books. (First published in England by Routledge & Kegan Paul., 1929).

Almy, M., Chittenden, E., & Miller, P. (1966). *Young children's thinking: Studies of some aspects of Piaget's theory.* New York: Teachers College Press.

Als, H. (1981). Assessing infant individuality. In C. C. Brown & T. B. Brazelton (Eds.), *Infants at risk: Assessment and intervention* Boston: Johnson and Johnson.

Anastasi, A. (1958). Heredity, environment, and the question: "How"? *Psychological Review, 65,* 197–208.

Anastasiow, N. J. (1978). Strategies and models in early childhood intervention programs in integrated settings. In M. J. Guralnick (Ed.), *Early intervention and the integration of handicapped and nonhandicapped children.* Baltimore: University Park Press.

Anastasiow, N. J. (1981). Early childhood education for the handicapped in the 1980s: Recommendations. *Exceptional Children, 47*(5), 276–282.

Anastasiow, N. J. (1986). The research base for early intervention. *Journal of the Division for Early Childhood, 10,* 99–105.

Antia, S. D. (1982). Social interaction of partially mainstreamed hearing-impaired children. *American Annals of the Deaf,* February, 18–25.

Apolloni, T., & Cooke, T. P. (1978). Integrated programming at the infant, toddler, and preschool levels. In M. Guralnick (Ed.), *Early intervention and the integration of handicapped and nonhandicapped children.* Baltimore: University Park Press.

Arnold, W., & Tremblay, A. (1979). Interaction of deaf and hearing preschool children. *Journal of Communication Disorders, 12,* 245–251.

Association for the Care of Children's Health (1987). *Family-centered care for children with special health care needs.* Washington, DC: Association for the Care of Children's Health.

Auerback, S., & Freedman, L. (1976). *Choosing child care: A guide for parents.* San Francisco: Parent and Child Care Resources.

Ayres, J. (1972). *Sensory integration and learning disorders.* Los Angeles: Western Psychological Services.

Bagnato, S. J., Kontos, S., & Neisworth, J. T. (1987). Integrated day care as special education: Profiles of programs and children. *Topics in Early Childhood Special Education, 7,* 28–47.

Bagnato, S. J., & Neisworth, J. T. (1980). *Linking development assessment and curricula.* Rockville, MD: Aspen.

Bailey, D. B., Clifford, R. M., & Harms, T. (1982). Comparison of preschool environments for handicapped and nonhandicapped children. *Topics in Early Childhood Special Education, 2,* 9–20.

Bailey, D. B., Jr., & Winton, P. J. (1987). Stability and change in parents' expectations about mainstreaming. *Topics in Early Childhood Special Education, 7,* 73–88.

Bailey, D. B., & Wolery, M. (1984). *Teaching infants and preschoolers with handicaps.* Columbus, OH: Charles E. Merrill.

Baker, B. L., & Brightman, R. P. (1984). Access of handicapped children to education services. In N. D. Repucci, L. A. Withorn, E. P. Mulvey & J. Monahan (Eds.), *Children, mental health, and the law,* pp. 289–307. Beverly Hills, CA: Sage Publications.

Ballenger, M. (1983). Reading in kindergarten. *Childhood Education, 59,* 186–187.

Bandura, A. (1969). *Principles of behavior modification.* New York: Holt, Rinehart, & Winston.

Bandura, A. (1971). Vicarious and self-reinforcement processes. In R. Glaser (Ed.), *The nature of reinforcement.* New York: Academic Press.

Bandura, A. (1977) *Social learning theory.* Englewood Cliffs, NJ: Prentice-Hall.

Barker, J., & Bermatz, H. (1975). Eye function. In W. Frankenburg & B. Camp (Eds.), *Pediatric screening tests.* Springfield, IL: Charles C. Thomas.

Barraga, N., (1976). *Visual handicaps and learning.* Belmont, CA: Wadsworth.

Barraga, N., & Collins, M. E. (1979). Development of visual efficiency in visual functioning—Rationale for a comprehensive program. *Journal of Visual Impairment and Blindness, 73,* 121–126.

Barry, M. A., (1973). How to play with your partially sighted preschool child: Suggestions for early sensory and educational activities. *New Outlook for the Blind,* December, 457–467.

Bates, E. (1976). *Language and context: The acquisition of pragmatics.* New York: Academic Press.

Batshaw, M. L., & Perret, Y. M. (1981). *Children with handicaps: A medical primer.* Baltimore: Paul H. Brookes.

Baumgart, D., Brown, L., Pumpian, I., Nisbet, J., Ford, A., Sweet, M., Messina, R., & Schroeder, J. (1982). Principle of partial participation and individualized adaptations in education programs for severely handicapped students. *Journal of the Association for the Severely Handicapped, 7,* 17–27.

Bayless, K., & Ramsey, M. E., (1987). *Music: A way of life for the young child* (2nd ed.). Columbus, OH: Charles E. Merrill.

Becker, J. M. T. (1977). A learning analysis of the development of peer-oriented behavior in nine-month-old infants. *Developmental Psychology, 13,* 481–491.

Beckman-Bell, P. (1981). Child-related stress in families of handicapped children. *Topics in Early Childhood Special Education, 1,* 45–53.

Beers, C., & Wehman, P. (1985). Play skill development. In M. Fallen & W. Umansky (Eds.), *Young children with special needs* (pp. 403–440). Columbus, OH: Charles E. Merrill.

Behr, S., & Gallagher, J. J. (1981). Alternative administrative strategies for young handicapped children: A policy analysis. *Journal of the Division for Early Childhood, 2,* 113–122.

Bell-Gredler, M. E. (1986). *Learning and instruc-*

tion: Theory into practice. New York: Macmillan.

Belsky, J., & Sternberg, L. (1978). The effects of day care: A critical review. *Child Development, 51*, 1163–1178.

Bereiter, C. (1986). Does direct instruction cause delinquency? Response to Schweinhart and Weikart. *Educational Leadership, 44*, 20–21.

Berger, M., & Fowlkes, M. A. (1980). Family intervention project: A family network model for serving young handicapped children. *Young Children,* May.

Berreuta-Clement, J. R., Schweinhart, L. J., Barnett, W. S., Epstein, A. S., & Weikart, D. P. (1984). *Changed lives: The effects of the Perry preschool program on youths through age 19.* (Monographs of the High/Scope Educational Research Foundation, 8). Ypsilanti, MI: High/Scope Press.

Best, G. A. (1977). Mainstreaming characteristics of orthopedically handicapped students in California. *Rehabilitation Literature, 38*, 205–209.

Best, G. A. (1978). *Individuals with physical disabilities: An introduction for educators.* St. Louis.: C. V. Mosby.

Bigge, J. L. (1982). *Teaching individuals with physical and multiple disabilities* (2nd ed.). Columbus, OH: Charles E. Merrill.

Biklen, D. (1985). *The complete school: Integrating special and regular education.* New York: Columbia University Press.

Billingsley, F. F., & Romer, L. T. (1983). Response prompting and the transfer of stimulus control: Methods, research and a conceptual framework. *Journal of the Association for Persons with Severe Handicaps, 8*, 3–12.

Blacher-Dixon, J., Leonard, J., & Turnbull, A. P. (1979, April). Preschool mainstreaming: Definitions, rationale, and implementation. *Education Unlimited,* 16–22.

Blacher-Dixon, J., Leonard, J., & Turnbull, A. P. (1981). Mainstreaming at the early childhood level: Current and future perspectives. *Mental Retardation, 19*, 235–241.

Blackie, J. (1967). *Inside the primary school.* London: Her Majesty's Stationery Office.

Blankenship, C., & Lilly, S. (1981). *Mainstreaming students with learning and behavior problems.* New York: Holt, Rinehart & Winston.

Blatt, B. (1977). Issues and values. In B. Blatt, D. Biklen, & R. Bogdan (Eds.). *An alternative textbook in special education.* Denver: Love.

Blatt, B., & Kaplan, F. (1966). *Christmas in purgatory: A photographic essay on mental retardation.* Boston: Allyn & Bacon.

Bliton, G., & Schroeder, H. J. (1986). *The new future for children with substantive handicaps: The second wave of least restrictive environment.* Bloomington: Indiana University, Division of Special Education, Indiana Department of Education and Developmental Training Center.

Bloom, B. S. (Ed.) (1985). *Developing talent in young people.* New York: Ballantine.

Bloom, B. S. (1964). *Stability and change in human characteristics.* New York: John Wiley.

Bloom, L., & Lahey, M. (1978). *Language development and language disorders* New York: John Wiley.

Bobath, K., & Bobath, B. (1972). Cerebral palsy. In P. Pearson & C. Williams (Eds.). *Physical therapy services in the developmental disabilities.* Springfield, IL: Charles C. Thomas.

Bobath, B., & Bobath, K. (1975). *Motor development in the different types of cerebral palsy* London: William Heineman.

Bogdan, R. (1986). The sociology of special education. In R. J. Morns & B. Blatt (Eds.), *Special education: Research and trends.* Elmsford: Pergamon Press.

Bottorf, L., & DePape, D. (1982). Initiating communication systems for severely speech impaired persons. *Topics in Language Disorders, 2*, 55–71.

Bowman, B. (1986). Birthday thoughts. *Young Children, 41*(2), 3–8.

Boyer, E. L. (1983). *High school: A report on secondary education in America.* New York: Harper & Row.

Brackett, D., & Henniges, M. (1976). Communicative interactions of preschool hearing impaired children in the integrated setting. *The Volta Review, 778*, 276–290.

Bradshaw, J., & Lawton, D. (1978). Tracing the causes of stress in families with handicapped children. *British Journal of Social Work, 8*, 181–192.

Bredekamp, S. (1987). *Developmentally appropriate practice in early childhood programs serving children from birth through age 8.* Expanded Edition. Washington, DC: National Association for the Education of Young Children.

Breslau, N. (1982). Siblings of disabled children: Birth order and spacing effects. *Journal of Abnormal Child Psychology, 10*, 85–96.

Bricker, D. (1978). A rationale for the integration of

handicapped and nonhandicapped preschool children. In M. Guralnick (Ed.), *Early intervention and the integration of handicapped and non-handicapped children* (pp. 3–26). Baltimore: University Park Press.

Bricker, D., & Bricker, W. (1971). *Toddler research and intervention project report—year II.* (IMRID Behavioral Science Monograph No. 20). Nashville: Institute on Mental Retardation and Intellectual Development.

Bricker, D., & Bricker, W. (1972). *Toddler research and intervention project report—year II.* (IMRID Behavioral Science Monograph No. 20). Nashville: Institute on Mental Retardation and Intellectual Development.

Bricker, D., & Casuso, V. (1979). Family involvement: A critical component of early intervention. *Exceptional Children, 46,* 108–116.

Bricker, D., & Dow, M. (1980). Early intervention and the young severely handicapped child. *Journal of the Association for the Severely Handicapped, 5*(12), 130–142.

Bricker, D., & Sandall, S. (1979). Mainstreaming in preschool programs: How and why to do it. *Education Unlimited, 1,* 25–29.

Bricker, W. (1976). Service of research. In M. A. Thomas (Ed.), *Hey, don't forget about me! Education's investment in the severely, profoundly, and multiply handicapped child* (pp. 162–179). Reston, VA: Council for Exceptional Children.

Bricker, W., & Bricker, D. (1976). The infant, toddler, and preschool research and intervention project. In T. D. Tjossem (Ed.), *Intervention strategies for high risk infants and young children*. Baltimore: University Park Press.

Bricker, W., Macke, P., Levin, J., & Campbell, P. (1981). The modifiability of intelligent behavior. *Journal of Special Education, 15,* 145–163.

Briggs, B. A., & Walters, C. M. (1985). Single-father families: Implications for early childhood educators. *Young Children, 40*(3), 23–27.

Bromwich, R. (1984). *Working with parents and infants*. Baltimore: University Park Press.

Bronfenbrenner, U. (1974). Is early intervention effective? *A report on longitudinal evaluations of preschool programs* (Vol. 2). Washington, DC: Department of Health, Education, and Welfare.

Bronson, W. C. (1975). Developments in behavior with age-mates during the second year of life. In M. Lewis & L. A. Rosenblum (Eds.), *Friendship*

and peer relations (Vol. 4). New York: John Wiley.

Brookover, W. B., & Lezotte, L. W. (1979). *Changes in school characteristics coincident with changes in students' achievement*. East Lansing, MI: Institute for Research on Teaching.

Browder, D. M., & Shapiro, E. S. (1985). Applications of self-management to individuals with severe handicaps: A review. *Journal of the Association for Persons with Severe Handicaps, 10*(4), 200–208.

Brown, B. (1985). Head Start: How research changed public policy. *Young Children, 40,* 9–13.

Brown, J. D. (1972). Storytelling and the blind child. *The New Outlook for the Blind,* December, 356–360.

Brown, L., Branston, M., Hamre-Nietupski, S., Pumpian, I., Cecto, N., & Gruenwald, L. (1979). A strategy for developing chronological age appropriate and functional curricular content for severely handicapped adolescents and young adults. *AAESPH Review, 4,* 407–424.

Brown, L., Nietupski, J., & Hamre-Nietupski, S. (1976). The criterion of ultimate functioning and public school service for severely handicapped students. In M. A. Thomas (Ed.), *Hey, don't forget about me! Education's investment in the severely, profoundly, and multiply handicapped child*. Reston, VA: Council for Exceptional Children.

Brown, M., & Precious, N. (1970). *The integrated day in the primary school*. New York: Agathon Press.

Bruner, J. S. (1966). *Toward a theory of instruction*. Cambridge, MA: Harvard University Press.

Budolf, M., & Gottlieb, J. (1976). Special class EMR children mainstreamed: A study of an aptitude (learning potential) X treatment interaction. *American Journal of Mental Deficiency, 81,* 1–11.

Burstein, N. D. (1986). The effects of classroom organization on mainstreamed children. *Exceptional Children, 52,* 425–434.

Bryan, T., Pearl, R., Donahue, M., Bryan, J., & Pflaum, S. (1983). The Chicago Institute for the Study of Learning Disabilities, *Exceptional Education Quarterly, 4,* 1–23.

Caldwell, B. M. (1973). The importance of beginning early. In J. B. Jordan & R. F. Dailey (Eds.), *Not all little wagons are red: The exceptional child's early years*. Arlington, VA: Council for

Exceptional Children.

Caldwell, B. M. (1977). Aggression and hostility in young children. *Young Children, 32*, 4–13.

Callahan, C. M. (1986). The special needs of gifted girls. In J. R. Whitmore (Ed.), *Intellectual giftedness in young children: Recognition and development*. New York: Haworth Press.

Campbell, P. (1987). The integrated programming team: An approach for coordinating professionals of various disciplines in programs for students with severe and multiple handicaps. *Journal of the Association for Persons with Severe Handicaps, 12*, 107–116.

Campbell, P., Bricker, W., & Esposito, L. (1980). Technology in the education of the severely handicapped. In B. Wilcox & R. York (Eds.), *Quality education for the severely handicapped*, pp. 223–246. Washington, DC: U.S. Department of Education.

Campbell, P., McInerny, W., & Middleton, M. (1982). *A manual of augmented sensory feedback devices for training severely handicapped students*. Akron, OH: Children's Hospital Medical Center of Akron.

Cantrell, R., & Cantrell, M. (1976). Preventive mainstreaming: Impact of a supportive services program on pupils. *Exceptional Children*, April.

Cargill, F. R. (Ed.). (1987, December). *BRL Memorandum, VII*, Springfield, IL: Braille Revival League.

Carnegie Commission on Excellence (1985). A nation at risk. New York: Carnegie Corporation.

Cartledge, G., & Milburn, J. F. (1980). *Teaching social skills to children*. New York: Pergamon Press.

Cartwright, C. (1981). Effective programs for parents of young handicapped children. *Topics in Early Childhood Special Education, 1*, 91–28.

Cartwright, G. P., Cartwright, C. A., & Ward, M. E. (1985). *Educating special learners* (2nd ed.). Belmont, CA: Wadsworth.

Cass, R., & Kaplan, P. (1979, December). Middle ear disease and learning problems: A school system's approach to early detection. *Journal of School Health*, 557–560.

Cassidy, D. J., Myers, B. K. Benion, P. E. (1987). Early childhood planning: a developmental perspective. *Childhood Education, 64*, 2–8.

Casto, G., & Mastropieri, M. A. (1986). The efficacy of early intervention programs: A meta-analysis. *Exceptional Children, 52*, 417–424.

Casto, G., White, K., & Taylor, C. (1983). An early intervention research institute: Studies of the efficacy and cost effectiveness of early intervention at Utah State. *Journal of the Division for Early Childhood, 1*, 5–17.

Chinitz, S. P. (1981). A sibling group for brothers and sisters of handicapped children. *Children Today, 21*–23.

Chinn, P. C., Winn, J., & Walters, R. H. (1978). *Two-way talking with parents of special children: A process of positive communication*. St. Louis: C. V. Mosby.

Chomsky, N. (1965). *Aspects of the theory of syntax*. Cambridge, MA: MIT Press.

Church, J. F. (1987). An intergenerational approach to high quality child day care. *CAEYC Review: The Journal of the Cleveland Association for the Education of Young Children*, Spring, 36–40.

Cicerelli, V. G., Evans, J. W., & Schiller, J. S. (1969). *The impact of Head Start of children's cognitive and affective development: Preliminary report*. Washington, DC: Office of Economic Opportunity.

Clark, B. (1986). Early development of cognitive abilities and giftedness. In J. R. Whitmore (Ed.), *Intellectual giftedness in young children: Recognition and development* (pp. 5–15). New York: Haworth Press.

Clements, D. H. (1987). Computers and young children: A review of research. *Young Children, 43*, 34–44.

Clements, S. D. (1966). Minimal brain dysfunction in children. *NINDB Monograph* 3, Public Health Service Publication No. 1415. Washington, DC: U. S. Department of Health, Education, and Welfare.

Clunies-Ross, G. G. (1979). Accelerating the development of Down's syndrome infants and young children. *Journal of Special Education, 13*, 169–177.

Cohen, J. (1984). Exchange visits: A preschool awareness program. *Teaching Exceptional Children, 16*, 23–25.

Cohen, M. A., Gross, P. J., & Haring, N. G. (1976). In N. G. Haring & L. Brown (Eds.), *Teaching the severely handicapped* (Vol. 1, pp. 35–110). New York: Grune & Stratton.

Cohen, S. (1977). *Accepting individual differences.*

Allen, TX: Developmental Learning Materials.

Cohen, S., Semmes, M., & Guralnick, M. (1979). Public Law 94–142 and the education of preschool handicapped children. *Exceptional Children, 45,* 279–284.

Cohen, U., Beer, J., Kidera, E., & Golden, W. (1979). *Mainstreaming the handicapped: A design guide.* Milwaukee: University of Wisconsin, Center of Architecture and Urban Planning Research.

Coleman, J. M., & Fults, B. A. (1982). Self-concept and the gifted classroom: The role of social comparison. *Gifted Child Quarterly, 26,* 116–120.

Coleman, J. M., & Fultz, B. A. (1985). Special-class placement, level of intelligence, and the self-concepts of gifted children: A social comparison perspective. *RASP 6,* 7–12.

Cone, J. D., Delawyer, D. D., & Wolfe, V. V. (1985). Assessing parent participation: The parent/family involvement index. *Exceptional Children, 51,* 417–424.

Cook, R. E., & Armbruster, V. B. (1983). *Adapting early childhood curricula.* St. Louis: C. V. Mosby.

Cooke, T. P., & Apolloni, T. (1976). The development of positive social-emotional behaviors: A study of training and generalization effects. *The Journal of Applied Behavior Analysis, 9,* 65–78.

Cooke, T. P., Ruskus, J. A., Peck, C. A., & Apolloni, T. (1981). Handicapped preschool children in the mainstream; background, outcomes, and clinical suggestions. *Topics in Early Childhood Special Education, 1*(1), 73–83.

Cooper, J. O., Heron, T. E., & Heward, W. L. (1987). *Applied behavior analysis.* Columbus, OH: Charles E. Merrill.

Cress, P., Spellman, C. R., & Benson, H. (1984). Vision care for the preschool child with handicaps. *Topics in Early Childhood Special Education, 3,* 41–51.

Cruickshank, W. M., Bentzen, F., Ratzeburg, F., & Tannhauser, M. (1961). *A teaching methodology for brain-injured and hyperactive children.* Syracuse, NY: Syracuse University Press.

Culhane, B. R., & Mothersell, L. L. (1981). Suggestions for the regular classroom teacher. In M. E. Bishop (Eds.), *Mainstreaming: Practical ideas for educating hearing-impaired students for secondary and post-secondary teachers and administrators.* Washington, DC: A. G. Bell.

Curry, R. G. (1975). Using LEA to teach blind children to read. *The Reading Teacher, 29*(3), 272–279.

Darling, R. B., & Darling, J. (1982). *Children who are different: Meeting the challenge of birth defects in society.* St. Louis. C. V. Mosby.

Day, B., & Drake, K. N. (1986). Developments in experimental programs: The key to quality education and care of young children. *Educational Leadership, 44*(3), 24–27.

Dean, M. (1982). *A closer look at low vision aids.* (handbook). Hartford: Connecticut State Board of Education and Services for the Blind.

Deberry, J., Ristau, S., & Galland, H. (1984). Parent involvement programs: Local level status and influences. *Journal of the Division for Early Childhood, 8*(2), 173–185.

Degler, L. S., & Risko, V. J. (1979). Teaching reading to mainstreamed sensory impaired children. *Reading Teacher, 32,* 921–925.

Delisle, J. R. (1984). *Gifted children speak out.* New York: Walker.

DeLoach, C., & Greer, B. G. (1981). *Adjustment to severe physical disability: A metamorphosis.* New York: McGraw-Hill.

Deno, E. (1970). Special education as developmental capital. *Exceptional Children, 37,* 229–237.

Dettre, J. H. (1983). Bridges to academic success in young at-risk children. *Topics in Early Childhood Special Education, 3*(3), 57–64.

Deutsch, M. (1965). The role of social class in language development and cognition. *American Journal of Orthopsychiatry, 35,* 78–88.

Devoney, C., Guralnick, M., & Rubin, H. (1974). Integrating handicapped and nonhandicapped preschool children: Effects on social play. *Childhood Education, 50,* 360–364.

DeWeerd, J. (1977). Introduction. In J. B. Jordan, A. H. Havden, M. B. Karnes & M. M. Wood (Eds.) *Early childhood education for exceptional children: A handbook of ideas and exemplary practices.* Reston, VA: Council for Exceptional Children.

Dickstein, C. (1976). Mobility for the blind child. *The Exceptional Parent, 6.* April, 25–27.

Dittman, L. L. (1986). Finding the best care for your infant or toddler. *Young Children, 41,* 43–46.

Donlon, E. T. (1976). Visual disorders. In W. Cruickshank (Ed.), *Cerebral palsy: A de-*

velopmental disability (pp. 288–313). Syracuse, NY: Syracuse University Press.

Doremus, V. P. (1986). *Forcing works for flowers, but not for children. Education and Leadership, 44*(3), 32–35.

Drash, P. W., Raver, S. A., & Murrin, M. R. (1987). Total habilitation as a major goal of intervention in mental retardation. *Mental Retardation, 25,* 67–69.

Dubose, R. F. (1979). Working with sensorily impaired children. Part II: Hearing impairments. In S. G. Garwood (Ed.), *Educating young handicapped children: A developmental approach* (pp. 361–398). Germantown, MD: Aspen.

Dunlop, K., Stoneman, Z., & Cantrell M. (1980). Social interaction of exceptional and other children in a mainstreamed preschool classroom. *Exceptional Children, 47,* 132–141.

Dunn, L. M. (1968). Special education for the mildly retarded—Is much of it justified? *Exceptional Children, 35,* 5–24.

Eckstein, C., Reilly, K., Sicnolf, J., & Wilkinson, S. (1981). *Visually impaired students in the regular classroom: A resource book.* Columbus, OH: Ohio Resource Center for Low Incidence and Severely Handicapped.

Edgar, W., McNulty, B., Gaetz, J., & Maddox, M. (1984). Education placement of graduates of preschool programs for handicapped children. *Topics in Early Childhood Special Education, 4*(3), 19–29.

Edmonds, R. (1979). Effective schools for the urban poor. *Educational Leadership, 37,* 15–24.

Eheart, B. K., & Leavitt, R. L. (1985). Supporting toddler play. *Young Children, 40*(30), 18–22.

Ehrlich, V. Z. (1986). Recognizing superior cognitive abilities in disadvantaged, minority, and other diverse populations. In J. R. Whitmore (Ed.), *Intellectual giftedness in young children: Recognition and development* (pp. 55–70). New York: Haworth Press.

Eisenson, J. (1972). *Aphasia in children.* New York: Harper & Row.

Elder, J. O., & Magrab, P. R. (Eds.). (1980). *Coordinating services to handicapped children: A handbook for integrating collaboration.* Baltimore: Paul S. Brookes.

Elkind, D. (1981). *The Hurried Child.* New York: Addison-Wesley.

Elkind, D. (1986). Formal education and early child-

hood education: An essential difference. *Phi Delta Kappan, 67,* 631–636.

Engleman, S. (1966). *Preventing failure in the primary grades.* Chicago: Science Research Associates, Inc.

Ensher, G. L., & Clark, D. A. (1986). *Newborns at risk: Medical care and psychoeducational intervention.* Rockville, MD: Aspen.

Erickson, E. (1963). *Childhood and society* (2nd ed.). New York: W. W. Norton.

Evans, E. D. (1975). *Contemporary influences on early childhood education* (2nd ed.). New York: Holt, Rinehart & Winston.

Ezold, E. E., & Boss, M. S. (1978, April). You want to do what? Reflections on our integraton program. *The Volta Review,* 155–159.

Family Child Learning Center (1987). *Special Needs Report, 1:* Tallmadge, OH: Author.

Faught, K. K., Balleweg, B. J., Crow, R. E., & Van Den Pol, R. A. (1983). An analysis of social behaviors among handicapped and nonhandicapped preschool children. *Education and Training of the Mentally Retarded, 18,* 210–214.

Federal Register. (1977, August) (163); 20 U.S.C. 140 (1), (15).

Featherstone, H. (1980). *A difference in the family.* New York: Basic Books.

Feeney, S., & Chun, R. (1985). Effective teachers of young children. *Young Children, 41,* 47–52.

Ferrell, K. A. (1985). *Reach out and teach: Meeting the training needs of parents of visually and multiply handicapped young children: Parent handbook.* New York: American Foundation for the Blind.

Feuerstein, R. (1979). *The dynamic assessment of retarded performers.* Baltimore: University Park Press.

Fewell, R. R., & Vadasy, P. F. (1987). Measurement issues in studies of efficacy. *Topics in Early Childhood Special Education, 7,* 85–96.

Finnie, N. R. (1975). *Handling the young cerebral palsied child at home.* New York: E. P. Dutton.

Fiscella, J., Barnett, L. A. (1985). A child by any other name . . . A comparison of the play behaviors of gifted and non-gifted children. *Gifted Child Quarterly, 29,* 61–66.

Fletcher, J. (1983). Ethics and trends in applied human genetics. *Birth Defects, 15,* 341–354.

Ford, A., Brown, L., Pumpian, I., Baumgart, D.,

Nisbet, J., Schroeder, J., & Loomis, R. (1984). Strategies for developing individualized recreation and leisure programs for severely handicapped individuals. In N. Certo, N. Haring & R. York (Eds.), *Public school integration of severely handicapped students: Rational issues and progressive alternatives*. Baltimore: Paul H. Brookes.

Foster, M., Berger, M., & McLean, M. (1981). Rethinking a good idea: A reassessment of parent involvement. *Topics in Early Childhood Special Education, 1*(3), 55–65.

Fraiberg, S. (1974). Intervention in infancy: A program for blind infants. In B. Z. Friedlander, G. M. Sterrit & G. E. Kirk (Eds.), *Exceptional infant* (Vol. 3, pp. 40–62). New York: Brunner/Mazel.

Fraiberg, S. (1977). *Insights from the blind: Comparative studies of blind and sighted infants*. New York: Basic Books.

Fraiberg, S., & Fletcher, D. (1985). Facilitating children's adjustment to orthotic and prosthetic appliances. *Teaching Exceptional Children, 17*(3), 228–130.

Fraiberg, S., Smith, M., & Adelson, E. (1969). An education program for blind infants. *Journal of Special Education, 3,* 121–139.

Fredericks, H. D., Baldwin, V., Grove, D., Moore, W., Riggs, C., & Lyons, B. (1978). Integrating the moderately and severely handicapped preschool child into a normal day care setting. In M. J. Guralnick (Ed.), *Early intervention and the Integration of Handicapped and Nonhandicapped Children*. Baltimore: University Park Press.

Furman, R. A., & Katan, A. (Eds.). (1969). *The therapeutic nursery school: A contribution to the study and treatment of emotional disturbances in young children*. New York: International Universities Press.

Gabel, H., & Kotsch, L. S. (1981). Extended families and young handicapped children. *Topics in Early Childhood Special Education, 1*(3), 29–35.

Gallagaher, J. J. (1985). Peer acceptance of highly gifted children in elementary school. *Elementary School Journal, 58,* 465–470.

Gallagher, J. J., Beckman, P., & Cross, A. H. (1983). Families of handicapped children: Sources of stress and its amelioration. *Exceptional Children, 50,* 10–17.

Gallagher, J. J., & Bradley, R. H. (1971). Early identification of developmental difficulties. In I. J.

Gordon (Ed.), *Early childhood education: The seventy-first yearbook of the National Society for the Study of Education* (Part IV, pp. 68–69). Chicago: University of Chicago Press.

Gallagher, J. J., Scharfman, W., & Bristol, M. M. (1984). The division of responsibilities in families with preschool handicapped and nonhandicapped children. *Journal of the Division for Early Childhood, 8,* 3–11.

Galloway, J. E., & George, J. (1986). Junior kindergarten. *Educational Leadership, 44*(3), 68–69.

Gans, K. D. (1987). Willingness of regular and special educators to teach students with handicaps. *Exceptional Children, 54,* 41–45.

Gargiulo, R. M. (1985). *Working with parents of exceptional children: A guide for professionals*. Boston: Houghton Mifflin.

Garland, C., Stone, N. W., Swanson, J., & Woodruff, G. (Eds.) (1981). *Early intervention for children with special needs and their families: Findings and recommendations*. Prepared by INTERACT: The National Committee for Services to Very Young Children with Special Needs and Their Families. Seattle: University of Washington, Western States Technical Assistance Resource (WESTAR).

Garner, J. B. (1986). The young handicapped child: Philosophical issues and pragmatic actions. In C. S. McLoughlin & D. F. Gullo (Eds.), *Young children in context: Impact of self, family and society on development*. Springfield, IL: Charles C. Thomas.

Gearhart, B. R., & Weishahn, M. W. (1976). *The handicapped child in the regular classroom*. St. Louis: C. V. Mosby.

Gearhart, B. R., & Litton, F. W. (1975). *The trainable retarded: A foundations approach*. St. Louis: C. V. Mosby.

Gersten, R., & White, W. A. T. (1986). Castles in the sand: Response to Schweinhart and Weikart. *Education Leadership, 44*(3), 19–20.

Gickling, E. E., & Thompson, V. P. (1985). A personal view of curriculum-based assessment. *Exceptional Children, 52,* 205–218.

Gilhool, T. K., & Stutman, E. A. (1978). Integration of handicapped students. In *Developing criteria for the evaluation of the least restrictive environment provision* (pp. 191–227). Washington, DC: Bureau of Education for the Handicapped.

Ginsburg, H., & Opper, S. (1969). *Piaget's theory of*

intellectual development: An introduction. Englewood Cliffs, NJ: Prentice-Hall.

Glasser, W. (1969). *Schools without failure.* New York: Harper & Row.

Glazer, J. (1985). Kindergarten and early education issues and problems. *Childhood Education, 62.*

Glenn, S., & Cunningham, C. (1985). Nursery rhymes and early language acquisition by mentally handicapped children. *Exceptional Children, 51*(1), 72–74.

Globus, M. (1982). The current scope of antenatal diagnosis. *Hospital Practice,* April, 179–186.

Gold, M. J., Grant, C. A., & Rivlin, H. N. (Eds.). (1977). *In praise of diversity: A resource book for multicultural education.* Washington, DC: Teacher Corps and Association of Teacher Educators.

Gold, M. W. (1980). *Did I say that?* Champaign, IL: Research Press.

Goldstein, H. (1986). Promoting communication skills in the Classroom. Paper presented at the Second Annual Early Childhood Conference on Children with Special Needs. Louisville, KY: October 20.

Goodlad, J. I. (1984). *A place called school: Prospects for the future.* New York: McGraw-Hill.

Goodman, H., Gottlieb, J., & Harrison, R. H. (1972). Social acceptance of EMRs integrated into a nongraded elementary school. *American Journal of Mental Deficiency, 76,* 412–417.

Gottwald, S. R., Goldback, P., & Isack, A. H. (1985). Stuttering: Prevention and detection. *Young Children, 4*(1), 9–14.

Gould, S. J. (1981). *The mismeasure of man.* New York: W. W. Norton.

Grant, C. J. (1982). The classroom behavior of children labeled autistic. In P. Knoblock (Ed.), *Teaching and mainstreaming autistic children* (pp. 275–288). Denver: Love.

Gray, S. W., & Klaus, R. A. (1970). The early training project: A seventh year report. *Child Development, 41,* 909–924.

Greenman, J. T., & Fuqua, R. W. (Eds.). (1984). *Making day care better: Training, evaluation and the process of change.* New York: Teachers College Press.

Gresham, F. M. (1982). Misguided mainstreaming: The case for social skills training with handicapped children. *Exceptional Children, 48,* 422–433.

Griffith, P. L. (1985). Mode-switching and mode-finding in a hearing child of deaf parents. *Sign Language Studies, 48,* 196–222.

Griffith, P. L., Johnson, H. A., & Dastoli, S. L. (1985). If teaching is conversation, can conversation be taught? Discourse abilities in hearing impaired children. In D. N. Ripick & F. M. Spirelli (Eds.), *School discourse problems* (pp. 149–777). San Diego, CA: College-Hill Press.

Grossman, F. K. (1972). Brothers and sisters of retarded children. *Psychology Today, 5,* 82–84.

Grossman, H. (Ed.). (1983). *Classification in mental retardation.* Washington, DC: AAMD.

Gullo, D., Bersani, C., Clements, D., & Bayless, K. (1985). A comparative study of "all-day," "alternate-day", and "half-day" kindergarten schedules: Effects on achievement and classroom social behaviors. *Journal of Research in Childhood Education, 1,* 87–94.

Guralnick, M. J. (1978). Integrated preschools as educational and therapeutic environments: Concepts, design, and analysis. In M. J. Guralnick (Ed.), *Early intervention and the integration of handicapped and nonhandicapped children* (pp. 115–145). Baltimore: University Park Press.

Guralnick, M. J. (1976). The value of integrating handicapped and nonhandicapped preschool children. *American Journal of Orthopsychiatry, 46*(2), 236–245.

Guralnick, M. J. (1980). Social interactions among preschool children. *Exceptional Children, 46,* 248–253.

Guralnick, M. J. (1981a). Peer influences on the development of communicative competence. In P. S. Strain (Ed.), *The utilization of classroom peers as behavior change agents* (pp. 31–67). New York: Plenum.

Guralnick, M. J. (1981b). The social behavior of preschool children at different development levels: Effects of group composition. *Journal of Experimental Child Psychology, 31,* 115–130.

Guralnick, M. J. (1982). Mainstreaming young handicapped children: A public policy and ecological systems analysis. In B. Spoek (Ed.), *Handbook of research in early childhood education* (pp. 456–500). New York: Free Press.

Guralnick, M. J., & Paul-Brown, D. (1977). The nature of verbal interactions among handicapped and nonhandicapped preschool children. *Child Development, 48,* 254–260.

Guralnick, M. J., & Groom, J. M. (1988). Peer interactions in mainstreamed and specialized classrooms: A comparative analysis. *Exceptional
Children, 54*, 415–425.

Haberman, M. (1985). Can common sense effectively guide the behavior of beginning teachers?
Journal of Teacher Education, 36, 32–41.

Hadary, D. (1976). Interaction and creation through
laboratory science and art for special children.
Science and Children, 13, 31–33.

Hagen, M. (1981). "Burnout"—Teachers and parents. *Views, 1*, 4–6.

Halle, J. W., & Sindelar, P. T. (1982). Behavioral
observation methodologies for early childhood
education. *Topics in Early Childhood Special Education, 2*(1), 43–54.

Hammill, D. D., Goodman, L., & Wiederholt, J. L.
(1974). Visual-motor processes: Can we train
them? *Reading Teacher, 27*, 469–478.

Hanline, M. F. (1985). Integrating disabled children.
Young Children, January, 45–48.

Hannah, M. E., & Midlarsky, E. (1985). Siblings of
the handicapped: A literature review for school
psychologists. *School Psychology Review, 14*,
510–520.

Hanson, M. J. (1981). A model for early intervention with culturally diverse single and multiparent
families. *Topics in Early Childhood Special Education, 1*(3), 37–44.

Hanson, M. J. (1985). An analysis of the effects of
early intervention services for infants and toddlers with moderate and severe handicaps. *Topics
in Early Childhood Special Education, 5*(2), 36–
51.

Hanson, M. J., & Harris, S. R. (1986). *Teaching the
young child with motor delays: A guide for parents and professionals*. Austin, TX: Pro-Ed.

Hart, V. (1981). *Mainstreaming children with special needs*. White Plains: Longman, (pp. 74–75;
160–161).

Hasenstab, M. S. (1982). Nursery-level programming. In M. S. Hasenstab & J. S. Horner (eds.),
*Comprehensive intervention with hearing-im-
paired infants and preschool children*. Rockville,
MD: Aspen.

Hasenstab, M. S., & Horner, J. S. (1982). *Comprehensive intervention with hearing-impaired infants and preschool children*. Rockville, MD:
Aspen.

Hatcher, B. (ed.). (1987). *Learning opportunities

beyond the school*. Wheaton, MD: Association
for Childhood Education International.

Havighurst, R. J. (1972). *Developmental tasks and
education* (3rd ed.). New York: David McKay.

Hayden, A. H. (1977, June). The implication of infant intervention research. In *Proceedings of the
Conference on Early Intervention with Infants
and Young Children* (pp. 30–38). Milwaukee, WI:
University of Wisconsin.

Hayden, A. H., & Dmitriev, V. (1975). The multi-
disciplinary preschool program for Down's syndrome children at the University of Washington
Model Preschool Center. In B. Z. Friedlander,
G. M. Sterritt & G. E. Kirk (Eds.), *Exceptional
infant—Assessment and intervention* (Vol. 3).
New York: Brunner/Mazel.

Hayden, A. H., & Edgar, E. B. (1977). Identifica-
tion, screening, and assessment. In J. B. Jordan,
A. H. Hayden, M. B. Karnes & M. M. Wood
(Eds.), *Early childhood education for exceptional
children*. Reston, VA: Council for Exceptional
Children.

Hayden, A. H., & Haring, N. G. (1976). Early inter-
vention for high risk infants and young children:
Programs for Down's syndrome children. In T. D.
Tjossem (Ed.), *Intervention Strategies for High
Risk Infants and Young Children*. Baltimore: Uni-
versity Park Press.

Hayden, A. H., & Haring, N. G. (1977). The acceleration and maintenance of developmental gains in
Down's syndrome school-age children. In P. Mit-
tler (Ed.), *Research to practice in mental retardation care and intervention* (Vol. 6). Baltimore:
University Park Press.

Hayden, A. H., Morris, K., & Bailey, D. (1977).
*Final report: Effectiveness of early education for
handicapped children*. Washington, DC: Bureau
of Education for the Handicapped.

Hazen, N., Black, B., & Fleming-Johnson, F.
(1984). Social acceptance: Strategies children use
and how teachers can help children learn them.
Young Children, 39(6), 26–36.

Head Start, Economic Opportunity, and Commission Partnership Act of 1974 (P.L. 93–644).

Heber, R., & Garber, H. (1975). The Milwaukee
project: A study of the use of family intervention
to prevent cultural-familial mental retardation. In
B. Z. Friedlander, G. M. Sterritt & G. E. Kirk
(Eds.), *Exceptional infant: Assessment and intervention*. New York: Brunner/Mazel.

Hendrick, J. (1986). *Total learning: Curriculum for

the young child (2nd ed.). Columbus, OH: Charles E. Merrill.

Hensley, G. (1973). Special education: No longer handicapped. *Compact, 7,* 3–5.

Hershey, M. (1981). The least restrictive environment for gifted and talented students. *Roeper Review, 4,* 27–28.

Hildebrand, V. (1981). *Introduction to early childhood education* (3rd ed.). New York: Macmillan.

Hobbs, N. (1974). *The futures of children.* San Francisco: Jossey-Bass.

Hobbs, N. (1975). *Issues in the classification of children* (Vols 1 & 2). San Francisco: Jossey-Bass.

Hobbs, N. (1980). An ecologically oriented service-based system for classification of handicapped children. In E. Salzmeyer, J. Antrobus & J. Gliak (Eds.), *The ecosystem of the "risk" child.* New York: Academic Press.

Hobbs, N., Egerton, J., & Matheny, M. (1975). Classifying children: A summary of the final report of the project on classification of exceptional children. *Children Today,* July/August.

Hohmann, M., Banet, B., & Weikart, D. P. (1979). *Young children in action: A manual for preschool educators.* Ypsilanti, MI: High/Scope Press.

Hollinger, C., & Kosek, S. (1985). Early identification of the gifted and talented. *Gifted Child Quarterly, 29*(4), 168–171.

Hollingworth, L. S. (1942). Children above 180 IQ Stanford-Binet. Yonkers-on-Hudson, NY: World Book.

Honig, A. S. (1978). *Parent involvement and the development of children with special needs.* New York: Teachers College Press.

Honig, A. S. (1985a). High quality infant/toddler care: Issues and dilemmas. *Young Children, 41,* 40–66.

Honig, A. S. (1985b). Compliance, control, and discipline. *Young Children, 40*(3), 41–46.

Honig, A. S., (1986). Stress and coping in children (Part 2). *Young Children, 41,* 47–59.

Honig, A. S. (1987). The shy child. *Young Children, 42,* 62–63.

Horne, M. D. (1984). *Attitudes toward handicapped students.* Hillsdale, NJ: Lawrence Erlbaum Associates.

Howes, C., & Olenick, M. (1984). Family and child care influences on toddlers' compliance. New Orleans, LA: Paper presented at the Annual Meeting of the American Education Research Association.

Hunt, J. M. (1961). *Intelligence and experience.* New York: Ronald Press.

Hunt, P., Goetz, L., & Anderson, J. (1986). The quality of IEP objectives associated with placement of integrated and segregated school sites. *Journal of the Association for Persons with Severe Handicaps, 11*(2), 125–130.

Hutinger, P. L. (1981). Transition practices for handicapped young children: What the experts say. *Journal of the Division of Early Childhood, 4,* 8–14.

Hutt, C. (1976). Exploration and play in children. In J. S. Bruner, A. Jolly & K. Sylva (Eds.), *Play: Its role in development and education.* New York: Basic Books.

Hymes, J. L., Jr. (1974). *Teaching the child under six.* Columbus, OH: Charles E. Merrill.

Isaacs, S. (1929; 1933). *The nursery years: The mind of the child from birth to six years.* London: Routledge & Kegan Paul.

Isaacs, S. (1933). *Social development in young children.* London: Routledge & Kegan Paul.

Ispa, J. (1981). Social interactions among teachers, handicapped children, and nonhandicapped children in a mainstreamed preschool. *Journal of Applied Developmental Psychology 1,* 231–250.

Ispa, J., & Matz, R. (1978). Integrating handicapped and nonhandicapped preschool children within a cognitively oriented program. In M. J. Guralnick (Ed.), *Early intervention and the integration of handicapped and nonhandicapped children.* Baltimore: University Park Press.

Jacobs, J. C. (1971). Effectiveness of teacher and parent indentification of gifted children as a function of school level. *Psychology in the Schools, 8*(20), 140–142.

James, P., & James, C. (1980). The benefits of art for mainstreamed hearing-impaired children. *The Volta Review,* February–March, 103–108.

James, S. L. (1982). Language disorders in autistic children. In P. Knoblock (Ed.), *Teaching and mainstreaming autistic children* (pp. 155–175). Denver: Love.

Janos, P. M., Marwood, K. A., & Robinson, N. M. (1985). Friendship patterns in highly intelligent children. *Roeper Review, 8*(1), 46–49.

Jencks, C., Smith, M., Achland, H., Bane, M., Cohen, D., Gintis, H., Heyns, B., & Michelson, S.

(1972). *Inequality: An assessment of the effect of family and schooling in America.* New York: Basic Books.

Jenkins, J. R., Speltz, M. L., & Odom, S. L. (1985). Integrating preschoolers: Effects on child development and social interaction. *Exceptional Children, 52*(1), 7–17.

Jenkins, R. C. W. (1979). *A resource guide to preschool and primary programs for the gifted and talented.* Mansfield, CT: Creative Learning Press.

Johnson, D., & Johnson, R. (1975). *Learning together and alone: Cooperation, competition, and individualization.* Englewood Cliffs, NJ: Prentice-Hall.

Johnson, D. & Johnson, R. (1984). Classroom learning structure and attitudes toward handicapped students in mainstream settings: A theoretical model and research evidence. In R. Jones (Ed.), *Attitude and attitude change in special education* (pp. 118–142). Reston, VA: Council for Exceptional Children.

Johnson, R., & Johnson, D. (1981). Building friendships between handicapped and nonhandicapped students: Effects of cooperative individualistic instruction. *American Education Research Journal, 18,* 415–423.

Johnson, R., Johnson, D., & Rynders, J. (1981). Effects of cooperative, competitive, and individualistic experience on self-esteem of handicapped and nonhandicapped students. *Journal of Psychology, 108,* 31–34.

Joint Statement of the Division of Early Childhood of the Council for Exceptional Children and INTERACT—The National Committee for Young Children with Special Needs and Their Families, submitted to the Subcommittee for the Handicapped of the U.S. Senate, March, 1986.

Jones, S. N., & Meisels, S. J. (1987). Training family day care providers to work with special needs children. *Topics in Early Childhood Special Education, 7,* 1–12.

Kaiser, M. (1981). The Technical Assistant Project (TAP) for handicapped children in day care. In N. Klein, C. Ellison, M. Kaiser & M. Stoiber (Eds.), *Integrating handicapped children into day care: One community's approach.* Cleveland, OH: TAP.

Kamii, C., & DeVries, R. (1978). *Physical knowledge in preschool education: Implications of Piaget's theory.* Englewood Cliffs, NJ: Prentice-Hall.

Kamii, C., & Radin, N. A. (1970). A framework for preschool curriculum based on Piagetian concepts. In I. J. Atyhey & O. D. Rubaduau (Eds.), *Education implications of Piaget's theory* (pp. 89–100). Waltham, MA: Ginn-Blaisdill.

Karnes, M. B. (1973). Evaluation and implications of research with young handicapped and low-income children. In J. C. Stanley (Ed.), *Compensatory Education for Children Ages Two to Eight.* Baltimore: Johns Hopkins University Press.

Karnes, M. B. (1977). Exemplary early education programs for handicapped children: Characteristics in common. *Educational Horizons, 56*(1).

Karnes, M. B., & Johnson, L. J. (1986). Identification and assessment of gifted/talented handicapped and nonhandicapped children in early childhood. In J. R. Whitmore (Ed.), *Intellectual giftedness in young children: Recognition and development* (pp. 35–54). New York: Haworth Press.

Karnes, M. B., & Lee, R. C. (1978). *Early childhood: What research and experience say to the teacher of exceptional children.* Reston, VA: Council for Exceptional Children.

Karnes, M. B., Linnemeyer, S. A., & Shwedel, A. M. (1982, April). A survey of federally funded model programs for handicapped infants: Implications for research and practice. *Journal of the Division for Early Childhood.*

Karnes, M. B., Shwedel, A. M., & Linnemeyer, S. A. (1981). *Survey of programs for the gifted at the preschool level.* Unpublished manuscript. Urbana: University of Illinois, Institute for Child Behavior and Development.

Karnes, M. B., Steinberg, D., Brown, J. G., & Schwedel, A. M. (1982). *RAPHYT talent assessment preschool programming.* Mimeograph. Urbana: University of Illinois, Institute for Child Behavior and Development.

Kastein, S., Spaulding, I., & Scharf, B. (1980). *Raising the young blind child: A guide for parents and educators.* New York: Human Sciences Press.

Katz, L. G. (1984). The professional early childhood teacher. *Young Children, 39*(5), 3–10.

Kaufman, B. A. (1980). Early childhood education and special education: A study in conflict. *Volta Review, 82,* 15–24.

Kaufman, J. M. (1977). *Children's behavior disorders.* Columbus, OH: Charles E. Merrill.

Kaufman, M. J., Gottlieb, J., Agard, J. S., & Kukic, M. B. (1975). Mainstreaming toward an explanation of the construct. *Exceptional Children, 7*(3), 1–12.

Kelly, K. R., & Colangelo, N. (1984). Academic and social self-concepts of gifted, general, and special students. *Exceptional Children, 50*(6), 551–554.

Kendall, E. F. (1983). *Diversity in the classroom: A multicultural approach to the education of young children.* New York: Teachers College Press.

Kennedy, M. (1978). Findings from the follow through planned variation study. *Educational Researchers, 1,* 3–11.

Keogh, B. K., & Becker, L. D. (1973). Early detection of learning problems: Questions, cautions, and guidelines. *Exceptional Children, 40,* 5–11.

Keogh, B. K., & Daley, S. E. (1983). Early identification: One component of comprehensive services for at-risk children. *Topics in Early Childhood Special Education, 3*(3), 7–16.

Keogh, B. K., & Levitt, M. L. (1976). Special education in the mainstream: A confrontation of limitations. *Focus on Exceptional Children, 8* 1–11.

Keogh, B. K., Wilcoxen, A. G., & Berheinmer, C. (1983). Prevention services for risk children: Evidence for policy and practice. In D. C. Farrah & J. D. McKinney (Eds.), *The concepts of risk in intellectual and psychosocial development.* New York: Academic Press.

Kirk, S. A. (1958). *Early education of the mentally retarded: An experimental study.* Urbana: University of Illinois Press.

Kirk, W. D. (1966). A tentative screening procedure for selecting bright and slow children in kindergarten. *Exceptional Children, 33,* 235–241.

Kirk, S. A. & Gallagher, J. J. (1987). *Educating exceptional children* (5th ed.). Boston: Houghton Mifflin.

Kitano, M. (1982). Young gifted children: Strategies for preschool teachers. *Young Children, 38,* 14–24.

Kitano, M. (1986). Evaluating program options for young gifted children. In J. R. Whitmore (ed.), *Intellectual giftedness in young children: Recognition and development* (pp. 89–101). New York: Haworth Press.

Klein, J. W. (1975, July). Mainstreaming the preschooler. *Young Children,* 316–326.

Klein, N. K. (1981). Disabled children need day care, too. *Education Unlimited,* February, 50–53.

Klein, N. K., Pasch, M., & Frew, T. W. (1979). *Curriculum analysis and design for retarded learners.* Columbus, OH: Charles E. Merrill.

Klein, N. K. & Sheehan, R. (1987). Staff development: A key issue in meeting the needs of young handicapped children in day care settings. *Topics in Early Childhood Special Education, 7,* 13–27.

Knoblock, P. (1982). Models of mainstreamed programs. In P. Knoblock (Ed.), *Teaching and mainstreaming autic children* (pp. 15–30). Denver: Love.

Kolstoe, O. P. (1976). *Teaching educable mentally retarded children* (2nd ed.). New York: Holt, Rinehart & Winston.

Kopp, C. B. (1982). Antecedents of self-regulation: A developmental perspective. *Developmental Psychology, 18,* 199–214.

Krantz, P., & Risley, T. R. (1977). Behavior ecology in the classroom. In K. D. O'Leary & S. O'Leary (Eds.), *The successful use of behavior modification.* New York: Pergamon Press.

Krogh, S. L., & Kunzweiller, C. (1982). Mainstreaming will fail unless there is a change in professional attitude and instructional structure. *Education, 102*(3), 284–288.

Langley, M. B. (1979). Working with young physically impaired children: Part A—The nature of physical handicaps. In S. G. Garwood (Ed.), *Educating young handicapped children: A developmental approach.* (pp. 73–108). Germantown, MD: Aspen

Lavatelli, C. S. (1968). A Piaget-derived model for compensatory preschool education. In J. L. Frost (ed.), *Early childhood education rediscovered* (pp. 530–544). New York: Holt, Rinehart & Winston.

Lazar, I., & Darlington, R. (1979). *Summary report: Lasting effects after preschool.* (DHEW Publication No. OHDS 80–30179) Washington, DC: U. S. Government Printing Office.

Lazar, I., Darlington, R., Murray, H., Royce, J., & Snipper, A. (1982). Lasting effects of early education. Monographs of the Society for Research in Child Development, 47 (1–2 serial no. 194).

Lazerson, M. (1972). The historical antecedents of early childhood education. In I. G. Gordon (ed.),

Early childhood education: The seventy-first yearbook of the national society for the study of education (Part II), 33–54. Chicago: University of Chicago Press.

Lehman, E. B., & Erdwins, C. J. (1981). The social and emotional adjustment of young, intellectually gifted children. *Gifted Child Quarterly, 25*(3), 134–137.

Leigh, J. E. (1983). Early labeling of children: Concerns and alternatives. *Topics in Early Childhood Special Education, 3,* 1–6.

Leigh, J. E., & Riley, N. (1982). Learning disabilities in the early years: Characteristics, assessment, and intervention. *Topics in Learning and Learning Disabilities, 2*(3), 1–15.

Leinhardt, G. (1980). Transition rooms: Promoting maturation or reducing education? *Journal of Educational Psychology, 75,* 55–61.

Leonard, A. J., & Cansler, D. P. (1980). Serving gifted/handicapped preschoolers and their families: A demonstration project. *Rooper Review, 2,* 39–41.

Lerner, J. W. (1985). *Learning disabilities: Theories, diagnosis, and teaching strategies* (4th ed.). Boston: Houghton Mifflin.

Lerner, J., Mardell-Czudnowski, C., & Goldenberg, D. (1987). *Special education for the early childhood years* (2nd ed.). Englewood Cliffs, NJ: Prentice Hall.

Levine, M. H., & McColum, J. A. (1983). Peer play and toys: Key factors in mainstreaming infants. *Young Children, 38*(5), 22–26.

Lewis, M., Young, G., Brooks, J., & Michaelson, L. (1975). The beginning of friendship. In M. Lewis & L. A. Rosenblum (Eds.), *Friendship and peer relations* (Vol. 4). New York: John Wiley and Sons.

Libbey, S. S., & Pronovost, W. (1980). Communication practices of mainstreamed hearing-impaired adolescents. *The Volta Review,* May.

Lidz, C. (1983). Dynamic assessment and the preschool child. *Journal of Psychoeducational Assessment, 1*(1), 59–72.

Linder, T., & Chitwood, D. (1984). The needs of fathers of young handicapped children. *Journal of the Division for Early Childhood, 8*(2), 133–139.

Lobato, D. (1985). Siblings of handicapped children: A review. *Journal of Autism and Developmental Disorders, 15,* 345–350.

Love, H. D. & Walthall, J. E. (1977). *A handbook of medical, educational, and psychological information for teachers of physically handicapped children.* Springfield, IL: Charles C. Thomas.

MacMillan, D. L. (1982). *Mental retardation in school and society* (2nd ed.). Boston: Little, Brown.

MacMillan, D. L., & Borthwick, S. (1986). The new educable mentally retarded population: Can they be mainstreamed? *Mental Retardation, 18,* 155–158.

Madden, N., & Slavin, R. (1983). Mainstreaming students with mild handicaps: Academic and social outcomes. *Review of Educational Research, 53,* 519–569.

Maker, J. (1977). *Providing programs for the gifted handicapped.* Reston, VA: Council for Exceptional Children.

Mallory, B. L. (1981). The impact of public policies on families with young handicapped children. *Topics in Early Childhood Special Education, 1,* 77–86.

Maloney, P. L. (1981). *Practical guidance for parents of the visually handicapped preschoolers.* Springfield, IL: Charles C. Thomas.

Marion, M. (1981). *Guidance of young children.* St. Louis: C. V. Mosby.

Markowitz, J. (1984). Participation of fathers in early childhood special education programs: An exploratory study. *Journal for the Division for Early Childhood Education, 8,* 119–131.

Marland, S. (1972). *Education of the gifted and talented.* (Report to the Congress of the United States by the U.S. Commissioner of Education). Washington, DC: U.S. Government Printing Office.

Meichenbaum, D. H. (1977) *Cognitive–behavior modification: An integrative approach.* New York: Plenum.

Meichenbaum, D. H., & Goodman, J. (1971). Training impulsive children to talk to themselves: A means of developing self-control. *Journal of Abnormal Psychology, 77,* 115–126.

Moroney, R. M. (1981). Public social policy: Impact on families with handicapped children. In J. L. Paul (Ed.), *Understanding and working with parents of children with special needs.* New York: Holt, Rinehart, & Winston.

Mauser, A. J. (1981). Programming strategies for pupils with disabilities who are not gifted. *Rehabilitation Literature, 42,* 27–275.

Maxwell, M. L., & Palotta, R. F. (Eds.) (1979). *Parent education source book*. Cleveland, OH: Positive Education Program.

McCormick, L. (1986). Communication disorders. In N. G. Haring, & L. McCormick (Eds.), *Exceptional children and youth: An introduction to special education* (4th ed.) (pp. 201–231). Columbus, OH: Charles E. Merrill.

McCormick, L., & Kawate, J. (1982). Kindergarten survival skills: New directions in preschool special education. *Education and Training of the Mentally Retarded, 17,* 247–252.

McCormick, L., & Noonan, M. J. (1984). A responsive curriculum for severely handicapped preschoolers. *Topics in Early Childhood Special Education, 4,* 79–86.

McCoy, K. M., & Prehm, H. J. (1987). *Teaching mainstreamed students: Methods and techniques*. Denver: Love.

McEvoy, M. A., Nordquist, V. M., & Cunningham, J. L. (1984). Regular and special education teachers' judgments about mentally retarded children in integrated settings. *Journal of Mental Deficiency, 89,* 167–173.

McGlothlin, J. E. (1981). The school consultation committee: An approach to implementing a teacher consultant model. *Behavioral Disorders, 6,* 101–107.

McKey, R. H., Condelli, L., Ganson, H., Barrett, B., McConkee, C., & Plantz, M. (1985). *The impact of Head Start on children, families, and communities*. (Final report of the Head Start Evaluation, Synthesis, and Utilization Project.) Washington, DC: CSR, Inc.

Meisels, S. J. (1977). *Programming for atypical infants and their families: Guidelines for program evaluation*. Monograph No. 5 of the Nationally Organized Collaborative Project to Provide Comprehensive Services for Atypical Infants and Their Families. New York: United Cerebral Palsy Association.

Meisels, S. J. (1979). *First steps in mainstreaming: Some questions and answers*. Boston: Massachusetts Department of Mental Health, Media Resource Center.

Meisels, S. J. (1985a). Prediction, prevention, and developmental screening in the EPSDT program. In H. Stevenson & A. Siegel (Eds.), *Child development and social policy* (Vol. 1). Chicago: University of Chicago Press.

Meisels, S. J. (1985b). *Developmental screening in early childhood: A guide*. Washington, DC: National Association for the Education of Young Children.

Meisels, S. J. (1986). Testing four- and five-year-olds: Response to Salzer and to Shepard and Smith. *Educational Leadership, 44*(3), 90–92.

Mercer, C. D. (1983). *Students with learning disabilities* (2nd ed.). Columbus, OH: Charles E. Merrill.

Mercer, C. D. (1986). Learning disabilities. In N. G. Haring & L. McCormick (Eds.), *Exceptional children and youth: An introduction to special education* (4th ed., pp. 119–159). Columbus, OH: Charles E. Merrill.

Mercer, J. R. (1973). *Labeling the mentally retarded: Clinical and social system perspectives on mental retardation*. Berkeley, CA: University of California Press.

Merton, R. (1967). *Social structure and social theory*. New York: Free Press.

Meyer, D. J., & Vadasy, P. F. (1986). *Grandparent workshops: How to organize workshops for grandparents of children with handicaps*. Seattle. University of Washington Press.

Meyer, D. J., Vadasy, P. F., & Fewell, R. R. (1985). *Sibshops*. Seattle: University of Washington Press.

Meyer, D. J., Vadasy, P. F., Fewell, R. R., & Schell, G. C. (1985). *A handbook for the fathers program: How to organize a program for fathers and their handicapped children*. Seattle: University of Washington Press.

Meyer, L. (1983). Long-term academic effects of the Direct Instruction Project follow through. *Elementary School Journal, 84,* 380–394.

Meyers, C. E., & Blacher, J. (1987). Parents' perceptions of schooling for severely handicapped children: Home and family variables. *Exceptional Children, 53*(5), 441–449.

Miller, B. (1988). Personal communication.

Moncada, G. A. (1987). The facially disfigured child. *Topics in Early Childhood Special Education, 6,* 101–114.

Montessori, M. (1912). *The Montessori method*. New York: F. A. Stokes.

Montessori, M. (1949). *The absorbent mind*. Madras, India: Thesophical Publishing House.

Morado, C. (1986). Prekindergarten programs for 4-

year-olds: Some key issues. *Young Children, 41*(5), 61–63.

Morgan, D., & York, M. E., (1983). *Families of children with special needs: Early intervention techniques for the practitioner.* Rockville, MD: Aspen.

Mosteller, F., & Moynihan, D. P. (1972). On equality of educational opportunity: Papers deriving from the Harvard University Faculty Seminar on the Coleman Report. New York: Random House.

Mowder, B. A., & Widerstrom, A. H. (1986). Philosophical differences between early childhood education and special education: Issues for school psychologists. *Psychology in the Schools, 23,* 171–174.

Moyer, J., Egertson, H., & Isenberg, J. (1987). The child-centered kindergarten. *Childhood Education, 63,* 235–242.

Mueller, E., & Brenner, J. (1977). The origins of social skills and interaction among playgroup toddlers. *Child Development, 48,* 854–861.

Muir, K. A., Milan, M. A., Branston-McLean, M. E., & Berger, M. (1982). Advocacy training for parents of handicapped children: A staff responsibility. *Young Children, 1,* 41–46.

Murray, J. N. (1984). Handicapped children and their effect on the family. In J. N. Murray & C. S. Mcloughlin (Eds.), *Childhood disorders; preschool and elementary years.* Springfield, IL: Charles C. Thomas.

Musselwhite, C. R. (1986). *Adaptive Play for special needs children: Strategies to enhance communication and learning.* San Diego: College Hill Press.

Myklebust, H. (1964). Learning disorders: Psychoneurological disturbances in childhood. *Rehabilitation Literature, 25,* 354–360.

Naremore, R. C. (1979). Influences of hearing impairment on early language development. *Annals of Otology, Rhinology and Laryngology, 88,* 54–63.

National Society for the Prevention of Blindness. (1966). *N.S.P.B. fact book: Estimated statistics on blindness and visual problems.* New York: Author.

Neisworth, J. T., Willoughby-Herb, S. J., Bagnato, S. J., Cartwright, C. A., & Laub, K. W. (1980). *Individualized education for preschool exceptional children.* Rockville, MD: Aspen.

Nietupski, J., & Hamre-Nietupski, S. (1979).

Teaching auxiliary communication skills to severely handicapped students, *AAESPH Review, 4,* 107–124.

Nirje, B. (1976). The normalization principle. In R. B. Kirgel & A. Shearer (Eds.), *Changing patterns in residential services for the mentally retarded* (rev. ed.). Washington, DC: President's Committee on Mental Retardation.

Nix, G. W. (Ed.). (1976). *Mainstreaming education for hearing impaired children and youth.* New York: Gruene and Stratton.

Noonan, M. J., & Kilgo, J. L. (1987). Transition services for early age individuals with severe mental retardation. In R. N. Ianacone & R. A. Stodden (Eds), *Transition issues and directions* (pp. 1-24). Reston, VA: Council for Exceptional Children.

Nordyke, N. S. (1982). Providing services for young, handicapped children through local, interagency collaboration. *Topics in Early Childhood Special Education, 2*(1), 63–72.

Northcott, W. H. (1970). Candidate for integration: A hearing impaired child in a regular nursery school. *Young Children, 25,* 367–380.

Northcott, W. H. (Ed.). (1972). Curriculum guide—hearing-impaired children birth to three years and their parents. Washington, DC: Alexander Graham Bell Association for the Deaf.

Northcott, W. H. (Ed.). (1973). *The hearing-impaired child in a regular classroom: Preschool, elementary, and secondary years.* Washington, DC: Alexander Graham Bell Association for the Deaf.

Northern, J. L., & Downs, M. P. (1974). *Hearing in children.* Baltimore: Williams and Wilkins.

Odom, S. L., Deklyen, M., & Jenkins, J. R. (1984). Integrating handicapped and nonhandicapped preschoolers: Development impact on nonhandicapped children. *Exceptional Children, 51*(1), 41–48.

Odom, S. L., & Speltz, M. L. (1983). Program variations in preschools for handicapped and non-handicapped children: Mainstreamed vs. integrated special education. *Analysis and Intervention in Developmental Disabilities, 3,* 89–103.

Odom, S. L., & Strain, P. (1984). Peer-mediated approaches to increasing children's social interactions: A review. *American Journal of Orthopsychiatry, 54,* 544–557.

Oelwein, P. L., Fewell, R. R., & Pruess, J. B.

(1985). The efficacy of intervention at outreach sites of the program for children with Down's syndrome and other developmental delays. *Topics in Early Childhood Special Education, 5*(2), 78–87.

Olson, M. R. (1983). A study of the exploratory behavior of legally blind and sighted preschoolers. *Exceptional Children, 50*(2), 130–138.

Orlansky, M. D. (1977). *Mainstreaming the visually impaired child*. Austin, TX: Learning Concepts.

Orthner, D. K., Brown, T., & Ferguson, D. (1976). Single-parent fatherhood: An emerging family lifestyle. *The Family Coordinator, 25,* 429–437.

O'Shea H. (1960). Friendships and the intellectually gifted child. *Exceptional Children, 26,* 327–335.

Owens, R. (1984). The social and communication bases of language. In *Language development: An introduction* (pp. 117–156). Columbus: Charles E. Merrill.

Parent's Guide to Day Care, A. (1980). U. S. Department of Health and Human Services. Publication No. (OHDS) 80–30254. Order from the Superintendent of Documents, U. S. Government Printing Office, Washington, DC, 20402.

Parker, R. M., & Hansen, C. E. (1981). *Rehabilitation counseling*. Boston: Allyn & Bacon.

Paulus, P. (1984). Acceleration: More than grade skipping. *Roeper Review, 7*(2), 98–100.

Peck, C., Apolloni, T., Cooke, T., & Raver, S. (1978). Teaching retarded preschoolers to imitate the free play behavior of nonretarded classmates: Trained and generalized effects. *Journal of Special Education, 12,* 195–207.

Peterson, C., Peterson, J., and Scriven, G. (1977). Peer imitation by nonhandicapped and handicapped preschoolers. *Exceptional Children, 43,* 223–224.

Peterson, N. L. (1987). *Early intervention for handicapped and at-risk children: An introduction to early childhood special education*. Denver: Love.

Phillips, D., & Whitebook, M. (1986). Who are child care workers? The search for answers. *Young Children, 41*(4), 14–20.

Phillips, P. P. (1975). *Speech and hearing problems in the classroom*. Lincoln, NE: Cliff Notes.

Piaget, J. (1952). *The origins of intelligence in children*. New York: W. W. Norton.

Piaget, J. (1967). *Six psychological studies*. New York: Random House.

Pollard, A., Hall, H., & Keeran, C. (1979). Community service planning. In P. R. Magrab & J. O. Elder (Eds.), *Planning for services to handicapped persons: Community, education, health*. Baltimore, MD: Paul S. Brookes.

Polloway, E. A. (1987). Transition services for early age individuals with mild mental retardation. In R. N. Ianacone & R. A. Stodden (Eds.), *Transition issues and directions* (pp. 11–24). Reston, VA: The Council for Exceptional Children, The Division on Mental Retardation.

Poplin, M. S. (1984). Summary rationalizations, apologies, and farewell: What we don't know about the learning disabled. *Learning Disabilities Quarterly, 7,* 130–134.

Powell, B. F. (1981). Educational interpreting and the mainstreamed hearing-impaired child. In V. J. Froehlinger (Ed.), *Today's hearing-impaired child: Into the mainstream of education*. Washington, DC: Alexander Graham Bell Association for the Deaf.

Powell, T. H. (Ed.) (1986) *Sibling information network newsletter*. Storrs: The University of Connecticut, 4.

Powell, T. H., & Lindeman, D. V. (1983). Developing a social-interaction teaching program for young handicapped children. *Exceptional Children, 50*(1), 72–75.

Powell, T. H., & Ogle, P. A. (1985). Brothers and sisters—A special part of exceptional families. Baltimore: Paul H. Brookes.

President's Committee on Mental Retardation (1968). *Mental retardation: Century of decision*. Washington, DC: U.S. Government Printing Office.

Ramey, C. T., & Campbell, F. A. (1984). Preventive education for high risk children: Cognitive consequences of the Carolina Abecedarian Project. *American Journal of Mental Deficiency, 88,* 515–523.

Ramey, C. T., & Haskins, R. (1981). The causes and treatment of school failure: Insights from the Carolina Abecedarian Project. In M. Begab, H. C. Haywood, & H. L. Garber (Eds.), *Psychosocial influences in retarded performance: Strategies for improving competence* (Vol. 2), pp. 89–112. Baltimore: University Park Press.

Ramsey, M. E., & Bayless, K. M. (1980). *Kindergarten: Programs and Practices* St. Louis: C. V. Mosby.

Reinert, H. R. (1976). *Children in conflict*. St. Louis: C. V. Mosby.

Renzaglia, A. M., & Bates, P. (1983). Socially appropriate behavior. In M. E. Snell (Ed.), *Systematic instruction of the moderately and severely handicapped* (2nd ed.). Columbus, OH: Charles E. Merrill.

Renzulli, J. S. (1978). What makes giftedness: Reexamining a definition. *Phi Delta Kappan. 60*, 180–184.

Reynolds, L. Egan, R., & Lerner, J. (1983). The efficacy of early intervention on preacademic deficits: Review of the literature. *Topics in Early Childhood Special Education, 3*, 47–76.

Reynolds, M. C. (1978). Basic issues in restructuring teacher education. *Journal of Teacher Education, 29*(6).

Reynolds, M. C., & Lakin, K. C. (1987). Noncategorical special education: Models for research and practice. In M. C. Wang, M. C. Reynolds & H. J. Walberg (Eds.), *Handbook of special education: Research and practice*. Elmsford: Pergamon Press.

Reynolds, M. C., Wang, M. C., & Walberg, H. J. (1987). The necessary restructuring of special and regular education. *Exceptional Children, 53*, 391–398.

Riekehof, L. L. (1978). *The Joy of Signing*. Springfield, MO: Gospel Publishing House.

Roedell, W. C. (1986). Socioemotional vulnerabilities of young gifted children. In J. R. Whitmore (Ed.), *Intellectual giftedness in young children: Recognition and development*. New York: Haworth Press.

Roedell, W. C., Jackson, N. E., & Robinson, H. B. (1980). *Gifted young children*. New York: Teachers College Press.

Roehler, L, & Duffy, G. (1981). Classroom teaching is more than opportunity to learn. *Journal of Teacher Education, 32*, 7–13.

Rogers, D. L., & Ross, D. D. (1986). Encouraging positive social interaction among young children *Topics in Early Childhood Special Education, 2*(1), 21–32.

Rogers, V. (Ed.). (1970). *Teaching in the British Primary School*. New York: Macmillan.

Rogers-Warren, A. K. (1982). Behavioral ecology in classrooms for young handicapped children. *Topics in Early Childhood Special Education, 2*, 21–32.

Rogers-Warren, A. K. & Warren, S. G. (1984). The social basis of language and communication in severely handicapped preschoolers. *Topics in Early Childhood Special Education, 4*, 57–72.

Rogow, S. M. (1984). The uses of social routines to facilitate communication in visually impaired and multihandicapped children. *Topics in Early Childhood Special Education, 3*(4), 64–70.

Roopnarine, J. L., & Johnson, J. E. (Eds.) (1987). *Educational models for young children*. Columbus, OH: Charles E. Merrill.

Rosenthal, R., & Jacobsen, L. (1968). *Pygmalion in the classroom*. New York: Holt, Rinehart & Winston.

Rosentraub, M. S., & Harlow, K. S. (1983). Child care needs and policy issues: Implications from Texas surveys. *Social Work*, September/October, 354–358.

Ross, D. D. (1982). Selecting materials for mainstreamed preschoolers. *Topics in Early Childhood Special Education, 2*(1), 33–42.

Ross, M. (1978). Mainstreaming: Some social considerations. *The Volta Review*, January, 21–30.

Rudolph, M., & Cohen, D. H. (1984). *Kindergarten and early schooling* (2nd ed.). Englewood Cliffs, NJ: Prentice-Hall.

Safford, P. L. (1978). *Teaching young children with special needs*. St. Louis: C. V. Mosby.

Safford, P. L. (1983). Conceptions of special education: A quest for definition. In B. F. Nel, G. S. Jackson & D. S. Rajah (Eds.), *The changing world of education* (pp. 133–154). Durban, South Africa: Butterworths.

Safford, P. L., & Arbitman, D. C. (1975). *Developmental intervention with young physically handicapped children*. Springfield, IL: Charles C. Thomas.

Safford, P. L., Harvey, J. A., Krutilla, J. O., Safford, J. T., & Thompson, R. N. (1988). *Children and families served through an early intervention program—1972–1985: A follow-up of Project HEED*. Kent, OH: Cricket Press.

Safford, P. L., & Rosen, L. A. (1981). Mainstreaming: Application of a philosophical perspective in an integrated kindergarten program. *Topics in Early Childhood Special Education, 1*, 1–10.

Safran, J. S., & Safran, S. P. (1987). Teachers' judgments of problem behaviors. *Exceptional Children, 54*, 240–245.

Salend, S., & Johns, J. (1983). A tale of two teachers: Teacher commitment to mainstreaming. *Teaching Exceptional Children, 15,* 82–85.

Salvia, J., & Ysseldyke, J. E. (1981). *Assessment in special and remedial education* (2nd ed.). Boston: Houghton Mifflin.

Salzer, R. (1986). Why not assume they're all gifted rather than handicapped? *Educational Leadership, 44*(3), 74–77.

Sapon-Shevin, M. (1983). Teaching children about differences: Resources for teaching. *Young Children, 38*(2), 24–31.

Sattler, J. M. (1988). *Assessment of children's intelligence and special abilities* (3rd ed.). Boston: Allyn & Bacon.

Scarr, S. (1984). *Mother Care/Other Care.* New York: Basic Books.

Shell, G. (1981). The young handicapped child: A family perspective. *Topics in Early Childhood Special Education, 1*(3), 21–27.

Schoggen, P. (1975). An ecological study of children with physical disabilities in school and at home. In R. A. Weinbert & F. H. Wood (Eds.), *Observation of pupils and teachers in Mainstream and special education settings: Alternative strategies,* University of Minnesota, Minnesota Leadership Training Institute/Special Education.

Schultz, J. B., & Turnbull, A. P. (1983). Mainstreaming handicapped students: A guide for classroom teachers (2nd ed.) Boston: Allyn & Bacon.

Schweinhart, L. J., & Weikart, D. P. (1980). *Young children grow up: The effects of the Perry preschool program on youths through age 15.* Monographs of the High Scope Education Research Foundation. Ypsilanti, MI: High/Scope Press.

Schweinhart, L. J., & Weikart, D. P. (1986a). What do we know so far? A review of the Head Start Synthesis Project. *Young Children, 41*(2), 49–55.

Schweinhart, L. J., & Weikart, D. P. (1986b). Early childhood development programs: A public investment opportunity. *Educational Leadership, 44,* 4–12.

Scott, E. P. (1982). *Your visually impaired student: A guide for teachers.* Baltimore: University Park Press.

Seefeldt, C. (1980). *Teaching young children.* Englewood Cliffs, NJ: Prentice-Hall.

Seibert, J. M., Hogan, A. E., & Mundy, P. C., (1987). Assessing social and communication skills in infancy. *Topics in Early Childhood Special Education, 7,* 38–48.

Seligman, M. E. P. (1976). *Learned helplessness and depression in animals and man.* Morrison, NJ: General Learning Press.

Sendak, M. (1987, May 17). Where the wild things began. *The New York Times Book Review,* p. 1.

Serbin, L. A., O'Leary, K. D., Kent, R. N., & Tonick, I. J. (1973). A comparison of teacher responses to the preacademic and problem behavior of boys and girls. *Child Development, 44,* 796–804.

Shapiro, E., & Biber, B. (1972). The education of young children: A developmental interaction approach. *Teachers College Record, 74*(1), 55–79.

Shearer, M. S., & Shearer, D. E. (1977). Parent involvement. In J. Jordan, A. Hayden, M. Karnes & M. Ward (Eds.), *Early childhood education for exceptional children.* Reston, VA: Council for Exceptional Children.

Shephard, L. A., & Smith, M. L. (1986). Synthesis of research on school readiness and kindergarten retention. *Educational Leadership, 44*(3), 78–86.

Shores, R. E., Hester, D., & Strain, P. S. (1976). The effects of amount and type of teacher-child interaction on child-child interaction during free play. *Psychology in the Schools, 13,* 7–175.

Silberman, C. (1970). *Crisis in the classroom: The remaking of American education.* New York: Random House.

Silin, J. G. (1985). Authority as knowledge: A problem of professionalism. *Young Children, 40*(3), 41–46.

Silverman, L. K. (1986). What happens to the gifted girl? In C. J. Maker (Ed.), *Critical issues in gifted education.* Rockville, MD: Aspen.

Simner, M. (1983, April 11–14). Will raising the school entrance age reduce the risk of school failure? Paper presented at the annual meeting of the American Educational Research Association, Montreal, Canada.

Simon, E. P., & Gillman, A. E. (1979). Mainstreaming visually handicapped preschoolers. *Exceptional Children, 45,* 463–464.

Simpson, R. L. (1980). Modifying the attitude of regular class students toward the handicapped. *Focus on Exceptional Children, 13*(3).

Sisk, D., (1979). *Creative teaching of the gifted.* New York: McGraw-Hill.

Skeels, H. (1966). Adult status of children with contrasting early life experiences. *Monographs of the Society for Research in Child Development, 31.*

Skeels, H., & Dye, H. (1939). A study of the effects of differential stimulation on mentally retarded children. *Proceedings and Addresses of the 63rd Annual Session of the American Association on Mental Deficiency. 44,* 114–130.

Slavin, R., Madden, N., & Leavey, M. (1984). Effects of cooperative learning and individualized instruction on mainstreamed students. *Exceptional Children, 50,* 434–443.

Smith, C., & Greenberg, M. (1981). Step-by-step integration of handicapped preschool children in a day care center for nonhandicapped children. *Journal of the Division for Early Childhood, 2,* 96–101.

Snell, M. (Ed.). (1983). Systematic instruction of persons with severe handicaps (2nd ed.). Columbus, OH: Charles E. Merrill.

Snell, M. E. & Grigg, N. D. (1987). Instructional assessment and curriculum development. In M. E. Snell (Ed.), *Systematic instruction of persons with severe handicaps* (3rd ed.). Columbus, OH: Charles E. Merrill.

Snell, M. E., & Renzaglia, A. M. (1986). Moderate, severe, and profound handicaps. Columbus, OH: Charles E. Merrill.

Snyder, L. (1984). Communicative competence in children with delayed language development. In R. L. Schiefelbush & J. Picker (Eds.), *The acquisition of communicative competence.* Baltimore: University Park Press.

Snyder, L., Apolloni, T., & Cooke, T. P. (1977). Integrated settings at the early childhood level: The role of nonretarded peers. *Exceptional Children, 43,* 262–266.

Soderman, A. K. (1985). Dealing with difficult young children. *Young Children, 40*(5), 15–20.

Spodek, B. (1982). The kindergarten: Retrospective and contemporary view. In L. Katz (Ed.), *Current topics in early childhood education* (Vol. 4, pp. 173–191). Norwood, NJ: Ablex.

Spodek, B. (1985). *Teaching in the Early Years* (3rd ed.). Englewood Cliffs, NJ: Prentice-Hall.

Spodek, B. (1986). Early childhood education's past as prologue: Roots of contemporary concerns. *Young Children, 40*(5), 3–7.

Spodek, B., Saracho, O. N., & Lee R. (1984). *Mainstreaming young children.* Belmont, CA: Wadsworth.

Sprinthall, R. C., & Sprinthall, N. A. (1974). *Educational psychology: A developmental approach.* Reading, MA: Addison-Wesley.

Stainback, W., & Stainback, S. (1984). A rationale for the merger of special and regular education. *Exceptional Children, 51,* 102–111.

Stainback, S., & Stainback, W. (1985). *Integration of students with severe handicaps.* Reston, VA: Council for Exceptional Children.

Stainback, W., Stainback, S., Courtnage, L., & Jaben, T. (1985). Facilitating mainstreaming by modifying the mainstream. *Exceptional Children, 52*(2), 144–152.

Statement to the Subcommittee for the Handicapped of the U.S. Senate, March 1986.

Stauffer, D. T. (1983). A spina bifida student? You may have to catheterize! *DPH Journal 7*(1), 14–21.

Stedman, D. J. (1977). Early childhood intervention programs. In D. J. Stedman & B. M. Caldwell (Eds.), *Infant education: A guide for helping handicapped children in the first three years.* New York: Walker.

Steinfels, M. O. (1973). *Who's minding the children? The History and politics of day care in America.* New York: Simon & Schuster.

Stephens, T. M. (1977). Teaching learning and behavioral disordered students in least restrictive environments. *Behavioral Disorders, 2,* 146–151.

Sternat, S., Messina, R., Nietupski, J., Lyon, S., & Brown, L. (1977). Occupational and physical therapy services for severely handicapped students: Toward a naturalized public school service delivery mode. In E. Sontag, N. Certo & J. Smith (Eds.), *Educational Programming for the Severely Handicapped:* Reston, VA. Council for Exceptional Children.

Stock, J. R., Wnek, L. L., Newborg, J. A., Schenck, E. A., Gabel, J. R., Spurgen, M. S., and Ray, H. W. (1976). *Evaluations of handicapped children's early education program (HCEEP): Final report.* (Contract No. OE-0-74-0402). Columbus, OH: Battelle Center for Improved Education, (ERIC Document Reproduction Service No. 125 065)

Strain, P. S., (1982). *Social development of exceptional children.* Rockville, MD: Aspen.

Strain, P. S. (1986). Obtaining robust and lasting effects with early intervention. Paper presented at the Second National Early Childhood Conference on Children with Special Needs,

Louisville, KY, October 21.

Strain, P. S. (1987). Comprehensive evaluation of intervention for young autistic children. *Topics in Early Childhood Special Education, 7,* 97–110.

Strain, P. S. (1988). The evaluation of early intervention research: Separating the winners from the losers. *Journal of the Division for Early Childhood, 12,* 82–190.

Strain, P. S., & Fox, J. E. (1981). Peers as behavior change agents for withdrawn classmates. In A. E. Kazdin & B. Lahey (Eds.) *Advances in clinical child psychology.* New York: Plenum.

Strain, P. S., & Kerr, M. M. (1981). Modifying children's social withdrawal: Issues in assessment and clinical intervention. In M. Hersen, R. Eisler & P. Miller (Eds.) *Progress in behavior modification,* Vol. 2. New York: Academic Press.

Strain, P. S., Kerr, M. M., & Ragland, E. (1981). The use of peer social initiations in the treatment of social withdrawal. In P. Strain (Ed.), *The utilization of classroom peers as behavior change agents.* New York: Plenum.

Strain, P. S., McConnell, S., & Cordisco, L. (1983). Special educators as single-subject researchers. *Exceptional Education Quarterly, 4,* 40–51.

Strain, P. S., & Shores, R. E. (1983). A reply to "Misguided mainstreaming." *Exceptional Children, 50*(3), 271–273.

Strain, P. S., & Weigerink, R. (1976). The effects of sociodramatic activities on social interaction among behaviorally disordered preschool children. *Journal of Special Education, 10,* 71–73.

Strauss, A. A., & Lehtinen, L. E. (1947). *Psychopathology and education of the brain–injured child, Vol. 2. Progress in theory and clinic.* New York: Grune & Stratton.

Stremel-Campbell, K., & Rowland, C. (1987). Prelinguistic communication intervention: Birth-to-2. *Topics in Early Childhood Special Education, 7,* 49–58.

Stuckles, E. R., & Castle, W. W. (1981). The law and its implications for mainstreaming. In M. E. Bishop (Ed.), *Mainstreaming: Practical ideas for educating hearing-impaired students for secondary and postsecondary teachers and administrators.* Washington, DC: A. G. Bell.

Sutaria, S. (1985). *Introduction to learning disabilities.* Springfield, IL: Charles C. Thomas.

Swassing, R. (1985). *Teaching gifted children and adolescents.* Columbus, OH: Charles E. Merrill.

Swieringa, M. (1972). *See it my way.* Grand Rapids, MI: The Institute for the Development of Creative Child Care.

Talbot, M. E. (1964). *Edouard Seguin: A study of an educational approach to the treatment of mentally defective children.* New York: Teachers College, Columbia University.

Tawney, J. W. (1981). A cautious view of mainstreaming in early education. *Topics in Early Childhood Special Education, 1,* 25–36.

Taylor, S. J., Biklen, D., & Searl, S. J. (1986). *Preparing for life: A manual for parents on least restrictive environment.* Boston: The Federation for Children with Special Needs.

Technical Assistance Program (TAP). *We're more alike than different.* Cleveland, OH: Society for Crippled Children of Cuyahoga County, Inc.

Terman, L. M., & Odom, M. (1959). *Genetic studies of genius, the gifted group at mid-life: Thirty-five years' follow-up of the superior child* (Vol. 5). Stanford, CA: Stanford University Press.

Thomas, A., Chess, S., & Birch, H. G. (1968). *Temperament and behavior disorders in children.* New York: New York University Press.

Thomas, A., Chess, S., & Korn, S. J. (1982). The reality of difficult temperament. *Merrill-Palmer Quarterly, 28*(1), 1–20.

Thomas, D. (1985). The determinants of teachers' attitudes to integrating the intellectually handicapped. *British Journal of Education Psychology, 55,* 251–263.

Thomas, S. B. (1987). *Health related legal issues in education.* Topeka, KS: National Organization on Legal Problems of Education.

Tjossem, T. (Ed.). (1976). *Intervention strategies for high risk infants and young children.* Baltimore: University Park Press.

Torrance, E. (1983). Preschool creativity. In K. Paget & B. Bracken (Eds.), *Psychoeducational assessment of preschool children* (pp. 509–520). New York: Grune & Stratton.

Truan, M. B. (1984). Starting right: Selecting the optimum placement for visually impaired children. *Topics in Early Childhood Special Education, 3*(4), 71–77.

Tucker, J. A. (1985). Curriculum-based assessment: An introduction. *Exceptional Children, 52,* 199–204.

Tucker, J., Stevens, L. J., & Ysseldyke, J. E. (1983). Learning disabilities: The experts speak out. *Journal of Learning Disabilities, 16*, 6–14.

Turnbull, A. P. (1982). Preschool mainstreaming: A policy and implementation analysis. *Educational Evaluation and Policy Analysis 4*(3), 281–291.

Turnbull, A. P., & Schulz, J. B. (1979). *Mainstreaming handicapped students: A guide for the classroom teacher.* Boston: Allyn & Bacon.

Turnbull, A. P., & Turnbull, H. R. (1978). *Parents speak out: Views from the other side of the two-way mirror.* Columbus, OH: Charles E. Merrill.

Turnbull, A. P., & Turnbull, H. R. (1986). *Families and professionals: Creating an exceptional partnership.* (Columbus, OH: Charles E. Merrill.

Turnbull, A. P., Winton, P. J., Blacher, J., & Salkind, N. (1982). Mainstreaming in the kindergarten classroom: Perspectives of parents of handicapped and nonhandicapped children. *Journal of the Division for Early Childhood, 6*, 14–20.

Turnbull, H. R., & Turnbull, A. P. (1985). *Parents speak out: Then and now* (2nd ed.). Columbus, OH: Charles E. Merrill.

Turner, R., & Rogers, A. M. (1981). Project KIDS: Infant education for the handicapped in an urban public school system. *Journal of the Division for Early Childhood, 2*, 40–51.

Uphoff, J. K., & Gilmore, J. (1986). Pupil age at school entrance—How many are ready for success? *Young Children, 41*(2), 11–16.

U.S. Department of Health, Education, and Welfare (1978). Office of Human Development Services, Administration for Children, Youth, and Families. The status of handicapped children in Head Start programs: Fifth annual report of the U.S. Department of Health, Education, and Welfare to the Congress of the United States on services provided to handicapped children in Head Start. Washington, DC.

Vacca, R., & Vacca, J. (1986). *Content area reading.* Boston: Little, Brown.

Vacca, R., Vacca, J., & Gove, M. (1987). *Reading and learning to read.* Boston: Little, Brown.

Vadasy, P. F., Fewell, R. R., & Meyer, D. J. (1986). Grandparents of children with special needs: Insights into their experiences and concerns. *Journal of the Division for Early Childhood, 10*, 36–44.

Van Bourgondien, M. E. (1987). Children's responses to retarded peers as a function of social behaviors, labeling, and age. *Exceptional Children, 53*(5), 432–439.

Vandell, D. L., Wilson, K. S., & Buchanan, N. R. (1980). Peer interaction in the first year of life: An examination of its structure, content and sensitivity to change. *Child Development, 51*, 481–488.

Vanderheiden, G. C., & Grilley, K. (1978). *Nonvocal communication techniques and aids for the severely physically handicapped.* Baltimore, MD: University Park Press.

Van Riper, C. (1972). Speech correction: Principles and methods. Englewood Cliffs, NJ: Prentice-Hall.

Vincent, L., Brown, L., & Getz-Sheftel, M. (1981). Integrating handicapped and typical children during the preschool years. The definition of best educational practice. *Topics in Early Childhood Special Education, 1*(1), 17–23.

Vincent, L. J., Salisbury, C., Walter, G., Brown, P., Gruenwald, L. J., & Powers, M. (1980). Criteria of the next environment. In W. Sailor, B. Wilcox & L. Brown (Eds.), *Methods of instruction for severely handicapped students.* Baltimore: Paul H. Brookes.

Vygotsky, L. S. (1962). *Thought and language.* Cambridge, MA: MIT.

Voeltz, L. (1980). Children's attitude toward handicapped peers. *American Journal of Mental Deficiency, 84*, 455–464.

Walker, J. A., & Hallau, M. G. (1981). Why the "H" in ECEH? Considerations in training teachers of young handicapped children. *Journal of the Division for Early Childhood, 2*, 61–66.

Walker, H. M. McConnell, S. Walker, J., Clarke, J. Y., Todis, B., Cohen, G., & Rankin, R. (1983). Initial analysis of the ACCEPTS curriculum: Efficacy of instructional and behavior management procedures for improving the social adjustment of handicapped children. *Analysis and Intervention in Developmental Disabilities, 3*, 105–127.

Wallis, L. (1984). Selective early school entrance: Predicting school success. *Journal for the Education of the Gifted, 7*(2), 89–97.

Walter, G., & Vincent, L. (1982). The handicapped child in the regular classroom. *Journal of the Division for Early Childhood, 6*, 84–95.

Wang, M., & Birch, J. (1984). Effective special education in regular classes. *Exceptional Children, 50*, 391–399.

Weber, E. (1969). *The kindergarten: Its encounter*

with educational thought. New York: Teachers College Press.

Weber, E. (1971). *The English infant school and informal education*. Englewood Cliffs, NJ: Prentice-Hall.

Weber, E. (1984). *Ideas influencing early childhood education: A theoretical analysis*. New York: Teacher College Press.

Weikart, D., Rogers, L., Adcock, C., & McClelland, D. (1970). *The cognitively oriented curriculum: A framework for preschool teachers*. Washington, DC: National Association for the Education of Young Children.

Welsh, M., & Odum, C. (1981). Parent involvement in the education of the handicapped child: A review of the literature. *Journal of the Division for Early Childhood, 3,* 15–25.

White, B. P., & Phair, M. A. (1986). "It'll be a challenge!" Managing emotional stress in teaching disabled children. *Young Children, 41*(2), 44–48.

White, K., Mastropieri, M., & Casto, G. (1984). An analysis of special education early childhood projects approved by the Joint Dissemination Review Panel. *Journal of the Division for Early Childhood, 9*(1), 11–26.

White, N. A. (1981). The role of the regular classroom teacher. In V. J. Froehlinger (Ed.), *Today's hearing-impaired child: Into the mainstream of education* (pp. 108–127). Washington, DC: Alexander Graham Bell Association for the Deaf.

White, R. W. (1959). Motivation reconsidered: The concept of competence. *Psychological Review, 66,* 297–334.

Whitebook, M. (1986). The teacher shortage: A professional precipice. *Young Children, 41*(3), 10–11.

Whitmore, J. R. (1980). *Giftedness, conflict, and underachievement*. Boston: Allyn & Bacon.

Whitmore, J. R. (ed.) (1985). *Intellectual giftedness in young children: Recognition and development*. New York: Haworth Press.

Whitmore, J. R. (1986). Preventing severe underachievement and developing achievement motivation. In J. R. Whitmore (Ed.), *Intellectual giftedness in young children: Recognition and development*. New York: Haworth Press.

Widerstrom, A. H. (1986). Education of young handicapped children: What can early childhood education contribute? *Childhood Education, 63*(2), 78–83.

Wiegerink R., & Pelosi, J. W. (eds.) (1979). *Developmental disabilities: The DD movement*. Baltimore: Paul H. Brookes.

Wikler, L., Haack, J., & Intagliata, J. (1984). Bearing the burden alone? Helping divorced mothers of children with disabilities. In *Families with Handicapped Members: The Family Therapy Collection*. Rockville, MD: Aspen.

Wilcox, B., & Bellamy, G. T. (1982). *Design of high school programs for severely handicapped students*. Baltimore: Paul H. Brookes.

Wilcox, M. J., & Campbell, P. H. (1986). Family-infant programming: A prevention intervention approach. Paper presented at the Annual Convention of the American Speech-Language-Hearing Association, Detroit, MI, November.

Willert, M. K., & Kamii, C. (1985). Reading in kindergarten: Direct vs. indirect teaching. *Young Children, 40*(4), 3–9.

Winton, P. J., & Turnbull, A. P. (1981). Parent involvement as viewed by parents of preschool handicapped children. *Topics in Early Childhood Special Education, 1,* 11–19.

Winton, P. J., Turnbull, A. P., & Blacher, J. (1984). *Selecting a preschool: A guide for parents of handicapped children*. Baltimore: University Park Press.

Wolery, M. (1987). Program evaluation at the local level: Recommendations for improving services. *Topics in Early Childhood Special Education, 7,* 11–123.

Wolfensberger, W. (1969). The origin and nature of our institutional models. In R. Kugel & W. Wolfensberger (Eds.), *Changing patterns in residential services for the mentally retarded* (pp. 59–177). Washington, DC: President's Committee on Mental Retardation.

Wolfensberger, W. (1972). *The principle of normalization in human services*. Toronto: National Institute of Mental Retardation.

Wolfensberger, W. (1980). A brief overview of the principle of normalization. In R. J. Flynn & K. E. Nitsch (Eds.), *Normalization, social integration, and community services*. Baltimore: University Park Press.

Wolfensberger, W., & Glenn, L. (1973). *PASS: A method for the quantitative evaluation of human services: Field manual*. Toronto: Canadian Association for the Mentally Retarded, National Institute on Mental Retardation.

Wynne, S., Ulfelder, L., & Dakof, G. (1975). *Mainstreaming and early childhood for handicapped children: Review and implications of research.* Washington, DC: U.S. Office of Education, Division of Innovation and Development, Bureau of Education for the Handicapped.

York, J., Nietupski, J., & Hamre-Nietupski, S. A. (1985). A decision-making process for using microswitches. *Journal of the Association for Persons with Severe Handicaps JASH 10*(4), 214–223.

Ysseldyke, J., & Algozzine, B. (1982). *Critical Issues in special and remedial education.* Boston: Houghton Mifflin.

Ysseldyke, J. E., Algozzine, B., Richey, L., & Graden, J. (1982). Declaring students eligible for learning disability services: Why bother with the data. *Learning Disability Quarterly, 5* 37–44.

Ysseldyke, J. E., & Salvia, J. (1974). Diagonistic-prescriptive teaching: Two models. *Exceptional Children, 41,* 181–185.

Zentall, S. S. (1983). Effects of psychotropic drugs on the behavior of preacademic children: A review. *Topics in Early Childhood Special Education, 3*(3), 29–39.

Zigler, E. F. (1970). The environmental mystique: Training the intellect vs. development of the child. *Childhood Education, 46*(8).

Zigler, E. F., & Muenchow, S. (1979). How to influence social policy affecting children and families. *American Psychologist, 39,* 415–420.

Zigler, E., & Seitz, V. (1980). Early childhood intervention programs: A reanalysis. *School Psychology Review, 9*(4).

Zigler, E., & Valentine, J. (Eds.). (1979). *Project headstart: A legacy of the war of poverty.* New York: Free Press.

Zinkus, P., & Gottlieb, M. (1980). Patterns of perceptual and academic deficits related to early chronic otitis media. *Pediatrics, 66,* 246–253.

Index